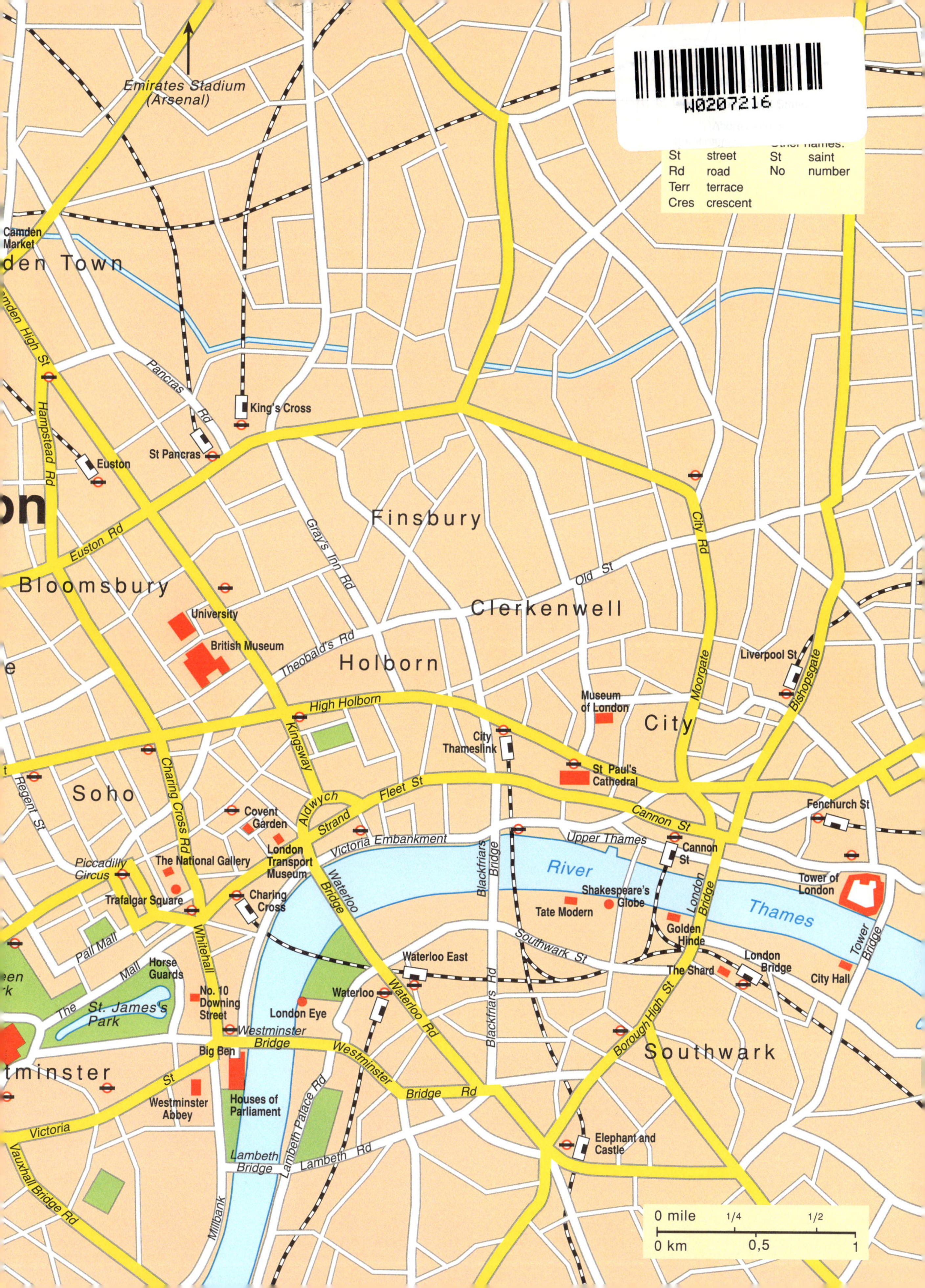

Emirates Stadium
(Arsenal)
St street
Rd road
Terr terrace
Cres crescent
Other names:
St saint
No number
Camden Market
den Town
nden High St
Pancras Rd
King's Cross
Hampstead Rd
Euston
St Pancras
on
Euston Rd
Finsbury
Gray's Inn Rd
City Rd
Old St
Bloomsbury
University
Clerkenwell
British Museum
Theobald's Rd
Holborn
Moorgate
Liverpool St
Bishopsgate
Museum of London
High Holborn
City
City Thameslink
Kingsway
Charing Cross Rd
St Paul's Cathedral
Regent St
Soho
Fleet St
Aldwych
Covent Garden
Strand
Cannon St
Fenchurch St
Victoria Embankment
Upper Thames
Cannon St
London Transport Museum
Piccadilly Circus
The National Gallery
Blackfriars Bridge
River
Tower of London
Waterloo Bridge
Trafalgar Square
Charing Cross
Shakespeare's Globe
London Bridge
Thames
Tate Modern
Golden Hinde
Whitehall
Pall Mall
Southwark St
Waterloo East
London Bridge
Tower Bridge
Horse Guards
The Shard
City Hall
Mall
No. 10 Downing Street
Waterloo
Waterloo Rd
The St. James's Park
London Eye
Blackfriars Rd
Borough High St
Westminster Bridge
Big Ben
Westminster Bridge Rd
Southwark
tminster
St
Westminster Abbey
Houses of Parliament
Lambeth Palace Rd
Victoria
Elephant and Castle
Lambeth Bridge
Lambeth Rd
Vauxhall Bridge Rd
Millbank
0 mile
1/4
1/2
0 km
0,5
1

westermann

NOTTING HILL GATE

Textbook 6

Erarbeitet von:
Hanna Hoof (Schacht-Audorf), Theresa Künzel-Giller (Pforzheim), Gabriele Linke (Marburg), Cedric Lütgert (Marburg), Sascha Mohr (Wiesbaden), Maike Pegler (Sarstedt/Gödringen)

sowie Denise Arrandale (Neumünster), Michael Biermann (Hamburg), Hannelore Debus (Mörfelden-Walldorf), Phil Mothershaw-Rogalla (Volkmarsen-Külte), Susanne Quandt (Bremen), Semra Siyli (Hamburg)

Fachliche Beratung:
Angela Berkenkamp (Wetzlar), Imke del Federico (Kerpen), Prof. Dr. David Gerlach (Wuppertal), Dr. Matthias Munsch (Frankfurt am Main), Jun.-Prof. Dr. Julia Reckermann (Münster), Anke Riemer (Hamburg), Kathleen Unterspann (Halstenbek)

Story „Kora and the New Zealand dragons“
von Amy Frances Koerner

Notting Hill Gate 6
Textbook

Zusatzmaterialien zu Notting Hill Gate 6

Für Lehrkräfte:
- Textbook für Lehrkräfte 6 (ISBN 978-3-14-128285-6)
- Materialien für Lehrkräfte 6 (ISBN 978-3-14-128295-5)
- Lernerfolgskontrollen 6 (ISBN 978-3-14-128321-1)
- CD für Lehrkräfte 6 (ISBN 978-3-14-128305-1)
- DVD für Lehrkräfte 6 (ISBN 978-3-14-128315-0)
- Online-Diagnose zu Notting Hill Gate 6 www.onlinediagnose.de

Für Schülerinnen und Schüler:
- Workbook 6 (inkl. Audios) (ISBN 978-3-14-128211-5)
- Interaktive Übungen 6 (WEB-14-128221)
- Arbeitsbuch Inklusion 6 (inkl. Audios) (ISBN 978-3-14-128231-3)
- Klassenarbeitstrainer 6 (ISBN 978-3-14-128247-4)
- Grammatiktrainer 6 (ISBN 978-3-14-128387-7)
- Wortschatztrainer 6 (ISBN 978-3-14-128241-2)

Das digitale Schulbuch und digitale Unterrichtsmaterialien für Schülerinnen und Schüler und für Lehrkräfte finden Sie in der BiBox – dem digitalen Unterrichtssystem passend zum Lehrwerk. Mehr Informationen über aktuelle Lizenzen finden Sie auf www.bibox.schule.

www.westermann.de/nhg

DIGITAL+

Alle digitalen Ergänzungen zum Buch erkennen Sie an an dem Symbol **DIGITAL+**. Dazu zählen Audiotracks, Videoclips, Arbeitsblätter zur Medienbildung, zusätzliche Übungen zu den Practise-Seiten und Zusatzmaterialien zum Buch. Gehen Sie auf **www.westermann.de/webcode** und geben Sie den Webcode **WES-128201-001** ein. Sie können auch den QR-Code scannen.

Druck A[1] / Jahr 2023
Alle Drucke der Serie A sind im Unterricht parallel verwendbar.

Redaktion: Lisa Fast, Dr. Katja Nandorf
Vokabelanhang: Doris Bos
Illustrationen: Mario Ellert, Bremen
Umschlaggestaltung: LIO Design GmbH, Braunschweig
Layout: LIO Design GmbH, Braunschweig
Druck und Bindung: Westermann Druck GmbH, Georg-Westermann-Allee 66, 38104 Braunschweig

ISBN 978-3-14-**128201**-6

So arbeitest du mit dem Buch

Im Buch findest du folgende Verweise:

1 audio	Hier gibt es einen Audiotrack, den du auch online abrufen kannst.
2 video	Hier gibt es einen Videoclip, den du auch online abrufen kannst.
3 workbook	Hier siehst du, auf welcher Seite im Workbook es weitere Übungen gibt.
4 wordbank	In den Wordbanks findest du Wörter nach Wortfeldern geordnet.
5 skill	Auf den Skills-Seiten findest du Tipps und Strategien fürs Lernen.
6 grammar	Zu dieser Aufgabe gibt es Erklärungen und Beispiele im Grammatik-Teil.
7 media worksheet	Dieser Hinweis kennzeichnet Aufgaben, in denen du Medienkompetenz aufbaust und trainierst. Zu diesen Aufgaben gibt es Arbeitsblätter, die du über den Webcode oder den QR-Code auf Seite 2 abrufen kannst.
DIGITAL+	Dieser Hinweis zeigt, dass es zusätzliches Material auf der Webseite gibt.

In den Units gibt es verschiedene Arten von Aufgaben:

8 CHOOSE YOUR LEVEL	Bei diesen Aufgaben gibt es drei unterschiedliche Schwierigkeitsgrade: I **leicht** II **mittel** III **schwierig**
9 GET TOGETHER Partner A: I Go to page 128. II Go to page 131. III Go to page 134. Partner B: I Go to page 137. II Go to page 140. III Go to page 143.	Hier arbeitest du mit einem Partner oder einer Partnerin zusammen. Entscheidet, wer Partner A und wer Partner B ist und wählt jeweils einen Schwierigkeitsgrad. Geht dann zur entsprechenden Seite und bearbeitet die Aufgabe.
10 CHOOSE YOUR TASK	Hier gibt es drei Aufgaben, von denen du dir eine aussuchen kannst. Du kannst mit einem Partner oder einer Partnerin oder in einer Gruppe arbeiten.
TARGET TASK	In der Target Task (Zielaufgabe) wendest du an, was du gelernt hast. Du erarbeitest ein kleines Produkt, das du in der Klasse vorstellen und in deinem Portfolio aufbewahren kannst.

Unit 1 – Holidays 7

Part A: Holiday fun 8
Part B: Sightseeing in London 18
Story: A dragon-taming emergency 28
Challenge: Message in a bottle 30

Unit 2 – Celebrations 31

Part A: Festivals and traditions 32
Part B: Let's celebrate! 42
Story: Looking for the dragon 52
Challenge: The Clarke family blog 54

Unit 3 – Living together 55

Part A: Getting along 56
Part B: Take care! 66
Story: In the dragon's cave 76
Challenge: Don't 78

Unit 4 – The future 79

Part A: My dreams 80
Part B: Stories 90
Story: The Clan-Howlus dragon 100
Challenge: Time capsules 102

Unit 5 – Out and about 103

Part A: A trip to the museum 104
Part B: A play 114
Story: Taming the dragon 124
Saving the day 126
Challenge: Sherlock Holmes – a world-famous detective 127

Get together 128

Projects 146

Project 1: A country profile: the UK 146
Project 2: A country profile: the USA 148

Skills 150

1. Wortschatzarbeit 150
2. Hören 151
3. Mit anderen sprechen 152
4. Schreiben 153
5. Lesen 154
6. Sprachmittlung 155
7. Videoclips verstehen 156
8. Im Internet recherchieren 157
9. Präsentationen halten 158
10. Eine Szene vorspielen 159

Wordbanks ... 160

Holidays ... 160
Getting around ... 162
Celebrations ... 163
Rules ... 164
Talking about conflicts ... 165
Wildlife ... 166
Jobs ... 167
Talking about the future ... 167
Describing people ... 168
Good style ... 169

Classroom phrases ... 170

Glossary ... 172

Grammar ... 174

1. Die einfache Vergangenheit: bejahte Aussagen ... 174
2. Die einfache Vergangenheit: verneinte Aussagen ... 175
3. Die einfache Vergangenheit: Fragen ... 176
4. Die Steigerung von Adjektiven ... 177
5. Die einfache Gegenwart: Aussagen *(revision)* ... 178
6. Die einfache Gegenwart: Fragen *(revision)* ... 179
7. Die Verlaufsform der Gegenwart: Aussagen *(revision)* ... 180
8. Die Verlaufsform der Gegenwart: Fragen *(revision)* ... 181
9. Mengenangaben ... 182
10. Die Modalverben *must* und *mustn't* ... 183
11. Die Modalverben *can*, *be allowed to* und *may* ... 184
12. Wortstellung im Aussagesatz *(revision)* ... 185
13. Das Futur mit *will*: Aussagen ... 186
14. Das Futur mit *will*: Fragen ... 187
15. Adverbien der Art und Weise ... 188
16. Verbindung von Sätzen mit *linking words* ... 189
17. Das Perfekt: Aussagen ... 190
18. Das Perfekt: Fragen ... 191
19. Das Futur mit *going to*: Aussagen ... 192
20. Das Futur mit *going to*: Fragen ... 193

Words ... 194

Nach Vokabeln suchen ... 194
Die richtige Aussprache / *The English alphabet* / *English sounds* ... 195
Bekannte Wörter ... 196
Wortlisten nach Units ... 197
Dictionary ... 221
Numbers ... 244
Names ... 245
Irregular verbs ... 247

Ausführliches Inhaltsverzeichnis ... 250

Bild- und Textquellen ... 256

Ein ausführliches Inhaltsverzeichnis befindet sich auf den Seiten 250 bis 255.

Welcome back to Notting Hill!

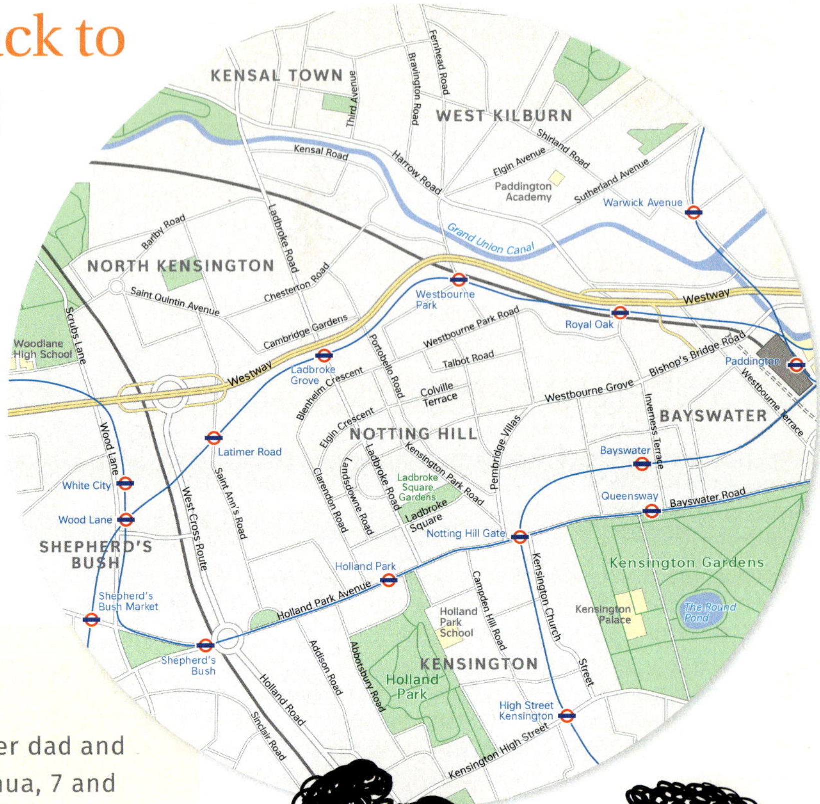

Ava Kogan

- 12 years old
- lives with her mum, her dad and her two brothers (Joshua, 7 and Noah, 13)
- has a dog, Ollie
- likes skateboarding
- goes to the book club at school
- her grandmother Edyta lives in Poland

Lily and Harry Norris

- 12 years old (twins)
- live with their mums, Olivia and Sarah
- have two rabbits, Double and Trouble
- like playing board games
- Lily: goes to the science club and the book club at school
- Harry: plays the guitar in the school band

Tarek Adil

- 13 years old
- lives with his dad
- has an uncle, Sami
- likes cooking and playing football
- goes to the cooking club at school

1

1. Look at the pictures. Where are the people?
2. What are the people doing?
3. Which of the places do you like best? Why?

Holidays

Part A Holiday fun

- Du erfährst etwas über die Ferienaktivitäten verschiedener Kinder.
- Du lernst, über Vergangenes zu sprechen.
- Du schreibst einen Blogeintrag zum Thema Ferien.

Part B Sightseeing in London

- Du lernst Sehenswürdigkeiten in London kennen.
- Du übst Wegbeschreibungen.
- Du planst einen Tag in London und erstellst eine Seite für einen Reiseführer.

Holiday activities

1a

Look at these holiday photos. Talk about them in class.

1

2

3

4

1b audio 1/1

Listen to the statements and read along. Then match them to the pictures.

A Hi, I'm Sarah. In the holidays I stayed at home. One day my parents took me to an adventure park. It was a lot of fun!

B My name is George. I went abroad in the holidays. I went to the USA by plane with my brother, my dad and my grandpa. We hiked every day in the Rocky Mountains. It was fantastic! The views from the mountaintops were spectacular.

C Salut! That's French for 'hello'. I learnt some French on my holiday in France. I just loved Paris! We went on a sightseeing tour by bus. There was so much to see!

D Hi guys, I'm David and I spent my holidays at the seaside. The weather was fantastic for outdoor activities: I went swimming, played beach volleyball and collected seashells. I made lots of new friends, too.

1c wordbank: holidays p. 160, workbook p. 4 / 1-2

What do you like doing in the holidays?

You can say:

I like going to the beach.

I like visiting …

…

staying at home · going on holiday · visiting my relatives / friends · going sightseeing · going on a day trip · playing video games · doing sports · going swimming · ...

The children's holidays

2a

Read the text messages. Where are Tarek and Ava?

4friends

Ava Hi guys! How are you all? I'm still at my grandma's in Poland. Last week I went riding. I had a very lazy horse. At first it didn't want to go anywhere. It just stood there and ate grass. But it was fun. 5:10pm

Tarek I arrived at Green Farm in Wales on Friday. It's great here! 5:13pm

Lily What did you say before you left? "Farms are sooo boring!" When did you change your mind? 5:14pm

Tarek I didn't say that, Lily! Yesterday I milked a cow for the first time in my life and I liked it. Actually, I was really good at it! Later we had fresh milkshakes. Yummy! 5:15pm

4friends

Lily Haha, that sounds like fun! Did your dad take a picture? 5:15pm

Tarek

5:16pm

Tarek No, he didn't. He didn't have time. He milked his own cow. 5:16pm

Harry Aren't you afraid of cows, Tarek? That's what I thought, anyway. 5:17pm

Tarek No, I'm not. And it was not all farm stuff I did. I also went cycling two days ago. And now it's dinner time for the chickens. Talk to you later! Video chat at 7pm? 5:18pm

2b CHOOSE YOUR LEVEL skill: reading p. 154

I Read again. Complete the sentences and write them down.

1 ??? went riding.
2 Ava had a very lazy ???.
3 ??? arrived in Wales on Friday.
4 ??? and ??? milked cows.

II Read again. Match the questions and answers and write them in your exercise book.

1 What did Ava do last week?
2 What did Ava's horse eat?
3 When did Tarek arrive at the farm?
4 What did Tarek do?

A It ate grass.
B He milked a cow and went cycling.
C She went riding.
D He arrived on Friday.

III Read again. Complete the sentences and write at least two more sentences about Ava and Tarek's holidays.

1 Ava went ...
2 Ava's horse ...
3 Tarek arrived ...
4 Tarek milked ...

2c

What about you? What do you think about holidays on a farm? Talk to a partner.

GRAMMAR HELP

the simple past: positive statements p. 174

Wenn du über etwas sprechen willst, das in der Vergangenheit liegt und abgeschlossen ist, verwendest du die einfache Vergangenheit *(simple past)*. Die Formen *was* und *were* zur Grundform *be* kennst du schon. Sieh dir die Beispielsätze an. Kennst du die Grundformen der Verben? Was fällt dir auf?

I stayed at home in the holidays. He liked his holiday in the mountains. She loved Paris. We visited our grandmother two days ago. They arrived at the farm on Friday.	I went abroad in the holidays. You made a lot of new friends. Tarek went cycling two days ago. She had a lazy horse. They took me to an adventure park.

Auf den Seiten 174-175 findest du weitere Erklärungen zu Aussagesätzen im *simple past* – auch zu verneinten Aussagesätzen. Eine Übersicht der unregelmäßigen Formen des *simple past* gibt es auf den Seiten 247-249.

Uncle Sami's holidays

3a

grammar: simple past p. 174-175

What did Uncle Sami do in the holidays? What did he not do? Write sentences.

+ go to Italy · stay in a hotel at the seaside · visit Rome · go to a famous museum · eat delicious Italian food · take photos at the beach

You can write:

Uncle Sami went to Italy.

He …

- go to France · visit his family in Egypt · milk a cow · drive a car · do sports · work

You can write:

Uncle Sami didn't go to France.

He …

3b

grammar: simple past p. 174-175, wordbank: holidays p. 160, workbook p. 5/3-4

What about you? What did you do in the holidays? What didn't you do? Write two or more positive and two or more negative sentences.

How to say the letters -ed

4a

audio 1/3

Listen to the words and repeat them.

worked · stayed · visited · loved · hiked · started · wanted · arrived · looked · liked · collected · played

4b

Make lists in your exercise book and listen again. Write the words in your lists.

/-t/	/-d/	/-ɪd/
worked	*stayed*	*visited*
…	…	…

4c

audio 1/4, workbook p. 6/5

Listen and check your lists.

A video chat

5a audio 1/5

Listen to the video chat and read along. What are the friends talking about?

It's 7pm. The friends are on a video chat.

Harry: Hi guys – nice to see you all!
Tarek: Hey Harry, how are you?
Ava: Awww, great to see you guys!
Harry: I am fine, thanks.
Lily: Hi everybody! Tarek, did the chickens like their dinner?
Tarek: Yes, they did – they loved it! What did you two do last week?
Harry: We renovated Lily's new room. She moved her stuff last weekend.
Tarek: What did you do with Double and Trouble? Did they move to Lily's room, too?
Harry: No, they didn't. We decided to share them between us. One week they live with Lily and the next week they live with me.
Ava: Good idea. Did you do anything else?
Lily: Yes, we did. We cycled a lot and we had a picnic in the garden.

Harry: And we went to the Museum of London.
Tarek: Were you in London all the time?
Harry: No, we weren't. We visited our grandparents in Bristol for a couple of days.
Ava: Was it good?
Lily: Yes, it was OK. When are you guys back in London? I could show you all my new room.
Ava: Great idea! What about next Saturday?
Lily: Sounds good!
Tarek: See you next Saturday then!
Harry: Bye!

5b skill: reading p. 154

Read again. What did the children do in the holidays?

5c CHOOSE YOUR LEVEL

I Copy the text and fill in the gaps.

Tarek gave the chickens their dinner and they ??? it. Lily has got a new ???. She moved her stuff ??? weekend. Harry and Lily did not stay in ??? all the time. They also ??? their grandparents in Bristol.

II Correct the sentences.

1 The chickens hated their dinner.
2 Lily moved into a new house.
3 The rabbits only live in Lily's room.
4 Harry and Lily didn't go to a museum.
5 The children want to meet next Sunday.

III What did Harry and Lily do in the holidays? Write five or more sentences.

5d grammar: simple past questions p. 176, workbook p. 6/6-7

Ask and answer questions with a partner.

You can ask:

Did Harry and Lily cycle a lot?
…

You can answer:

Yes, they did.
No, they didn't. They …

Back in Notting Hill

6a

Tarek took some pictures on his holiday in Wales. What can you see in the pictures? Talk about them in class.

6b audio 1/6

Listen and read along. What is Tarek talking about?

Ava: Lily, your new room looks amazing! You have so much space now.

Harry: And so do I. No more socks everywhere ... Tarek, how were the last days of your holiday in Wales?

Tarek: After our week on the farm, my dad and I went to Cardiff for a couple of days. It was great. We went to Cardiff Castle and the Welsh Folk Museum.

Lily: What was that like?

Tarek: The Welsh Folk Museum is an open-air museum. There is a roundhouse, for example, that shows how people lived two thousand years ago. Look, I've got a picture. There's also an old school, a hotel, old shops and lots of old farmhouses ...

Ava: And how did you like the castle? What did you do there?

Tarek: We went on a tour of the castle. At first I thought it would be boring, but the guide was really cool. Did you know that the Romans first built a fort there? Later the Normans came and built the castle.

Lily: Thank you for the history lesson, Tarek. Did you learn any words in Welsh?

Tarek: Yes, I did. But I found Welsh really difficult. For example, Wales is "Cymru" in Welsh. And "Good morning" is "Bore da". But there are also harder words, like "Shwmae" – that's "Hello".

Harry: Wow! That sounds really difficult to me.

6c skill: reading, p. 154

Read the text again. Find information about the things in the pictures. Take notes and compare them with a partner.

6d CHOOSE YOUR LEVEL workbook p. 8/8

Make a word web about Tarek's holidays.

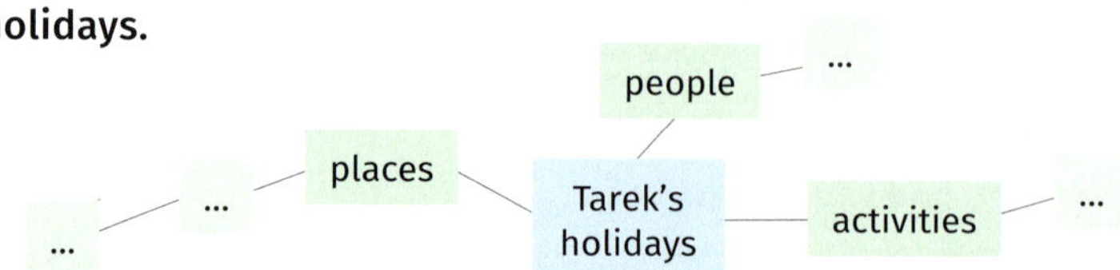

II **Tarek sent some pictures from Cardiff to Uncle Sami.**
Read the text again and write the messages that Tarek sent with the pictures.

III **Read the text again.**
Then write about Tarek's holiday in Wales. What did he do?

You can write:
Tarek and his dad went to Wales for the holidays. First they stayed at … Then they …

Catching up with Ellen

7a

Look at the pictures. What did Lily's friend Ellen do in the holidays?

7b

audio 1/8, skill: listening p. 151

Listen to Lily and Ellen on the phone. What are they talking about?

7c

workbook p. 8/9-10

Read the questions. Then listen again, take notes and answer the questions.

1 Where did Ellen spend her holiday?
2 Who was with her?
3 What did Nick do a lot?
4 Where did Ellen take lots of photos?
5 What did she buy at the market?
6 What happened at the airport?
7 When do the two girls plan to meet in London?

How was your last holiday?

8

grammar: simple past questions p. 176, wordbank: holidays p. 160, workbook p. 9/11-12

Walk around the classroom and ask and answer questions.

You can ask:
What did you do on your last holiday?
Where did you go on holiday?
Did you stay at home?

You can answer:
I went … / I stayed at home. / I didn't …
I went to …
No, I didn't. I visited …

Blog posts about the holidays

9a

Look at the pictures. What did the people do in the holidays?

9b skill: reading p. 154

Read the blog posts. Who wrote them? Where did they spend their holidays?

1

Hello there! I hope you all enjoyed your holidays. I stayed at home this year. My mum and dad went to work every day and I looked after my two brothers. We had a lot of fun together. We often went to the park near our house. Some of our friends were at home as well so we could meet them there and play football. One day we went to the swimming pool, and one rainy day we went to the cinema. **Philipp, 15**

 *Roddy on 23rd August at 11:24am said:*

I stayed at home as well and I think holidays at home are brilliant! Thanks for writing about yours!

2

Hi everyone! I hope you all had a great holiday. I had a really good time – I went to a summer camp in Cumbria. It was my first holiday without my parents and it was so cool! The summer camp was in Ravenglass, a small town by the seaside. I stayed at the camp for two weeks and met lots of new friends. We did activities like playing games, doing sports and cooking. We also went on long walks along the beach.
I hope I can go back to Camp Cumbria next summer! **Daniel, 13**

 *Querx on 2nd August at 8:02pm said:*

Could you post the name and address of the camp? I'd really like to check it out.

3

Hey! Did you all enjoy your holidays? I went on holiday with my mum, dad and my little sister to the Peak District. We stayed in different B&Bs. I thought the holiday would be really boring, but actually it was great. The weather was amazing. It was sunny every day and it was pretty warm as well! We walked a long way every day — about 12 miles up and down the hills. But one day we rented bikes and cycled. My dad had a really good travel app for the Peak District on his phone. We only got lost a few times because the signal was bad. One day we walked through Derby which is a city in Derbyshire. It is famous for Bakewell tarts so we tried some. They tasted delicious!
Melek, 12

 *James on 9th September at 2:18pm said:*

My parents want to go hiking in the Peak District next year. I really didn't want to go with them, but your holiday sounds pretty good. I might change my mind now!

9c CHOOSE YOUR LEVEL

I Read the first blog post again. Then copy the text and fill in the gaps.

Philipp ??? at home for the holidays this year. His parents ??? to work every day and he looked after his two ???. He and his brothers ??? went to the park near their house to ??? football with their friends. One rainy day they went to the ???.

II Read the second blog post again and answer the questions.

1 Where did Daniel go for the holiday?
2 How long was he there?
3 What did he do there?
4 Did he like his holiday? Why / Why not?

III Read the third blog post again and write about Melek's holiday.

You can write:

Melek went to the Peak District with her mum, her dad and … She …

Our summer holidays

10a video 1, skill: watching a video clip p. 156, media worksheet 1

Watch the video clip. Where did the children go on holiday? Take notes.

10b skill: mediation p. 155, workbook p. 10/13

Read the questions. Then watch the video clip again and take notes. Answer the questions in German.

1 Wen hat der Junge gefragt?
2 Was war seine erste Frage?
3 Was hat er danach gefragt?
4 Wo liegt Grimsby?
5 Was hat Lewis gemacht?
6 Wo liegen Devon und Dorset?

Holidays

11 CHOOSE YOUR TASK skill: writing p. 153, wordbank: holidays p. 160, workbook p. 10/14

A **Write a poem with eleven words about (your) holidays.**
B **Choose a melody you know and write a song about holidays.**
C **Write a diary entry about your or someone else's holidays. You could write as Tarek or Ava, for example. Think about something nice or funny or horrible or …**

A

Holidays
free time
really long drive
hotel by the sea
happiness

B (melody: the ABC song)

We went on a holiday,
but it wasn't nice, I say.
The beds were …
and the food was …,
…

Mum said later
"Oh my dear,
let's just stay at home
next year."

C

12 July
Today was a great day!
Dad and I arrived at …
…

What did they do?

12 CHOOSE YOUR LEVEL grammar: simple past p. 174

I Copy the text into your exercise book and fill in the gaps with the verbs from the box.

had · thought · went · didn't stay · liked · visited

In the holidays, Ava's grandparents ??? to Bristol.
They ??? ??? in a hotel but in a B&B.
On their last day they ??? an art museum.
Afterwards they ??? dinner in a small restaurant.
Ava's grandma ??? the food very much, but her grandfather ??? it wasn't very nice.

II Copy the text into your exercise book and fill in the gaps with the past form of the verbs from the box.

renovate · visit · play · not ask · have · give · be

Double and Trouble: "During the summer holidays we ??? a busy time. Lily and Harry sometimes ??? us and ??? with us. They ??? us our food as well – one day even strange purple carrots! The children ??? also really busy: they ??? a new room, just for us! Unfortunately, they ??? us about our favourite colour. Now everything is purple!"

III What did Ollie do on his dream holiday? Use the past form of the verbs in the box and write a short text.

go · stay · visit · love · not like · eat · swim

You can write:

On his dream holiday, Ollie went abroad.
He ...

What is it like?

13a

Copy the sentences and fill in the gaps with adjectives from the box.

yummy · interesting · small · lazy · new

1 Ava's ??? horse just stood there.
2 Tarek and his dad made some ??? milkshakes.
3 Lily moved into her ??? room.
4 Ellen went sightseeing in a ??? town.
5 Uncle Sami visited lots of ??? places.

13b

Are the sentences more interesting with or without adjectives? Why?

DIGITAL+ practise more 2

My holiday post TARGET TASK

14 workbook p. 11/15, wordbank: holidays p. 160, skill: writing p. 153, media worksheet 2

Your task is to write a blog post about holidays.
Before you start, look at these steps:

STEP 1

Think about what you would like to write about: a real holiday, a dream holiday, the summer holidays, a cool event in the holidays, your day at the swimming pool, …

STEP 2

Make a word web to organize your ideas.
Choose information that makes your holidays sound interesting.

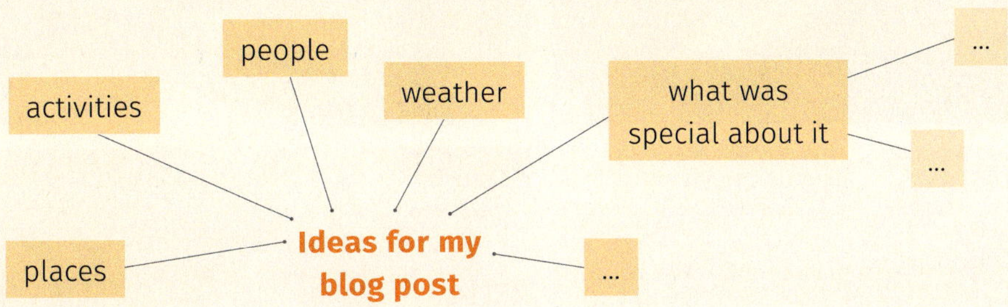

STEP 3

If you like, you can add one or more photos.
Be careful not to show people's faces – especially not on the Internet.

STEP 4

Write your post.

Tips for a good writing style:

- Add adjectives that make your sentences fun and interesting.
- Be polite. Respect other cultures and opinions.
- A good title makes your post look interesting.

You can write:

Hi, I'm … / Hi my name is …
I want to tell you about … because …
A funny thing / An unusual event that happened was …
I really liked …
It was fantastic / fun / great / brilliant to …
I recommend … because …

STEP 5

Present your post in a gallery walk.
You can also publish your post on your class website.

STEP 6

If you like, you can comment on your classmates' posts.
Remember to be polite!

Sights of London

1a workbook p. 12/1

What comes to mind when you think about London? Talk to your classmates.

1b audio 1/11

Listen to the sounds and match them to the photos.

A

B

C

D

E

F

G

H

1c skill: reading p. 154

Read these info texts. Which photo from page 18 goes with which text?

1 The London Eye is one of the tallest ferris wheels in Europe, and it is one of the most popular tourist attractions in the United Kingdom. When the weather is good, you can see all of London from the top. Until a few years ago, the wheel was the highest viewing point in London, but now the Shard is even higher.

2 Buckingham Palace is where the British king or queen lives and works. It is in the heart of London and there are 775 rooms. Although this place is very big, Windsor Castle (another home of the royal family, about 22 miles from London) is even bigger.

3 Big Ben is the name of the famous bell inside the Elizabeth Tower – a very tall clock tower at the Houses of Parliament near the River Thames. It is one of the world's most famous tourist attractions, but only people who live in the UK can go on a tour of it. There is no lift inside the tower. You have to climb 334 stairs to get to the top.

4 20 Fenchurch Street is a very tall skyscraper in London. Some people say that it is one of the ugliest buildings in the UK. At the top of the building there is a garden – the Sky Garden – with cafés and restaurants. From here you have a great view of another famous skyscraper: the Shard. 20 Fenchurch Street is not as tall as the Shard, but you can have one of the best views of London from there.

5 The Natural History Museum is a great place to go – and entry to the museum is free. You can discover the history of life on earth there. The museum is most famous for its huge dinosaur exhibition. There are lots of skeletons, and you can even see a moving model of a T-Rex, one of the largest dinosaurs that ever existed.

6 London Zoo is one of the oldest zoos in the world. It opened to the public in 1874. Today, you can see more than 19,000 animals and 673 different species there.

1d workbook p. 12/2

Read the texts again and answer the questions.

1 What is the London Eye?
2 How many rooms are there in Buckingham Palace?
3 What is the name of the bell inside the Elizabeth Tower?
4 Who can go on a tour of the Elizabeth Tower?
5 What is at the top of 20 Fenchurch Street?
6 Where can you see skeletons?
7 When did London Zoo open?

1e CHOOSE YOUR LEVEL wordbank: holidays p. 160

I Which two sights would you like to see and why?

You can write:

I would like to see … because …

II Which sights do you find interesting and why? Write about three or more of them.

III Which of the sights are more interesting for children? Which are more interesting for adults? Why do you think so?

You can write:

I think the London Eye is more interesting for … because …

GRAMMAR HELP the comparison of adjectives p. 177

Wenn du Personen oder Dinge näher beschreiben möchtest, verwendest du Adjektive. Möchtest du Personen oder Dinge vergleichen, kannst du Adjektive steigern. Sieh dir die Beispiele an. Was fällt dir auf?
Tipp: Achte auf die Silbenanzahl der Adjektive.

Tower Bridge is tall, the Elizabeth Tower is taller, but the London Eye is the tallest.	I think 20 Fenchurch Street is interesting, the Shard is more interesting, but the London Eye is the most interesting.
London Zoo is old, Buckingham Palace is older, but the Palace of Westminster is the oldest.	London Zoo is popular, the Natural History Museum is more popular, but Buckingham Palace is the most popular with tourists.

Es gibt auch unregelmäßige Formen, z. B. good – better – the best und bad – worse – the worst.
Auf Seite 177 findest du weitere Erklärungen zur Steigerung von Adjektiven.

Different people

2 grammar: comparison of adjectives p. 177, wordbank: describing people p. 168

Look at the friends and write six or more comparisons.

old · long · short · tall · young · small

You can write:

Noah is older than …
Lily's hair is … than …
Ollie's legs are the …

Good, better, the best

3a grammar: comparison of adjectives p. 177

Copy the adjectives into your exercise book.
Add the comparative and superlative forms. Pay attention to the spelling.

big · beautiful · bad · funny · interesting · famous · useful · easy · good · clever

3b grammar: comparison of adjectives p. 177, workbook p. 12/3

Use adjectives from 3a and write three or more comparisons with "than" and three or more comparisons with "as … as".

You can write:

I think … is better than …
Double is as … as Trouble.
…

DIGITAL+ practise more 3

Planning a day in London

4a
wordbank: getting around p. 162

Look at the map. What can you see?

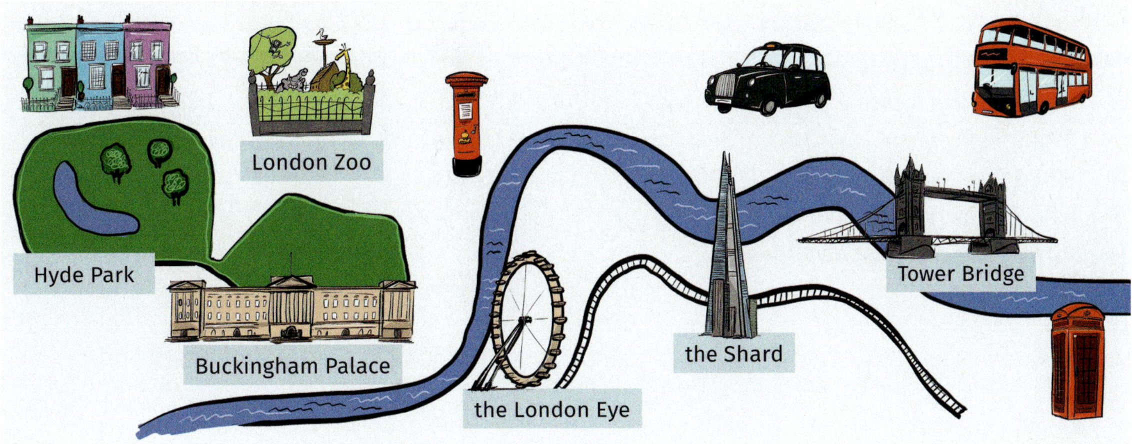

4b
video 2, skill: watching a video clip p. 156, workbook p. 13/4, media worksheet 1

Watch the video clip about London. What do you find interesting?

4c
audio 1/12, skill: listening p. 151

Ellen and her brother Nick from Brighton are visiting Harry and Lily.
Listen to the children. Which of the sights on the map in 4a are they talking about?

4d CHOOSE YOUR LEVEL

I Listen again.
What does Ellen want to do?

You can say:

Ellen wants to …

II Listen again. What does Harry say about museums in London?

You can say:

Harry says that …

III Listen again. Which sights do the children not want to visit today? Why?

You can say:

They don't want to … because …

Tube timetable

5 workbook p. 14/5, media worksheet 7

Look at the timetable on Lily's mobile phone and find out …

1 … what lines the children take.
2 … how long the journey to Westminster Station takes.
3 … when the next train leaves.
4 … where they have to change lines.
5 … how much a Day Travelcard for children is.

10:11

Notting Hill Gate Station
→ Westminster Station

10:18 **Notting Hill Gate**
(platform 3)
Central Line towards Epping
Departs in 6min 7sec

10:24 **Bond Street**
walk 88m (1min)

10:25 **Bond Street**
(platform 1)
Jubilee Line towards Stratford

10:28 **Westminster Station**

Day Travelcard children £6.90

Finding your way

6a audio 1/14, skill: listening p. 151

Look at the map. Listen and follow the directions. Where does the family want to go?

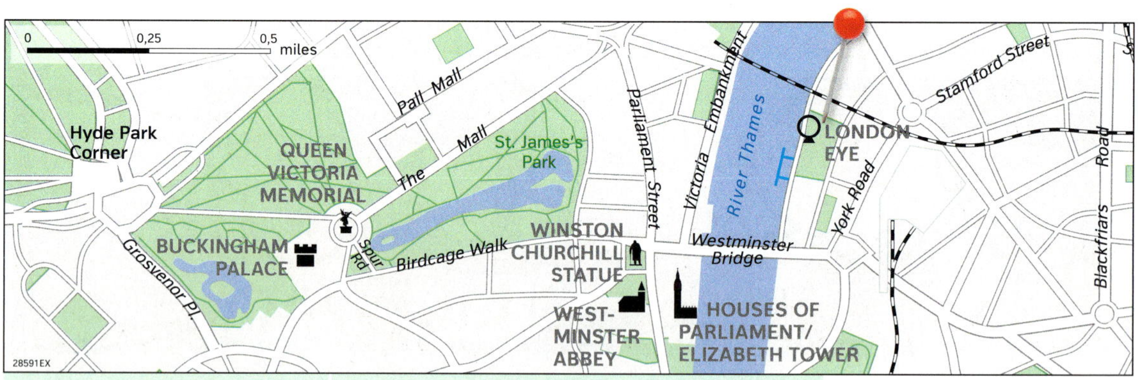

- go straight on
- turn left (onto)
- turn right (onto)
- walk past
- walk on until you get to …
- on your left
- on your right
- cross the road / street / river

6b wordbank: getting around p. 162, workbook p. 14/6-7

Give directions to a partner. Guide him or her through your classroom or your school.

Giving directions

7 GET TOGETHER

Get together with a partner. Listen to each other and follow the directions.

Partner A

I Go to page 128.
II Go to page 131.
III Go to page 134.

Partner B

I Go to page 137.
II Go to page 140.
III Go to page 143.

The London Eye

8a

Read Ellen's text to her mum. What does she say about the view from the top of the London Eye?

8b

wordbank: getting around p. 162, skill: writing p. 153

Choose another sight in London and write a text message about it.

Ellen Hi Mum, London is great!
But it's really expensive. 😉 We're in a London Eye capsule. The London Eye is not as high as the i360 in Brighton, but the view is a lot more interesting. Less water. We can see the Tower of London and Tower Bridge – that's where we're going tomorrow. Talk to you later.
Ellen and Nick xxx
12:43pm

LAND & LEUTE 1 video 3, workbook p. 15/8

Der Tower of London

Der *Tower of London* diente den britischen Königen und Königinnen unter anderem als Wohnort, Waffenkammer, Werkstatt, Lager, Museum, Archiv, Gefängnis, Münzprägestätte, Zoo und Hinrichtungsstätte.

Die Wachleute im Londoner Tower, die eine sehr spezielle Uniform tragen, werden auch *Beefeaters* genannt, weil sie früher besonders reichhaltige Fleischrationen bekamen.
Zu ihren Pflichten gehört es unter anderem, sich um die Raben *(ravens)* zu kümmern.
Im Londoner Tower leben stets mindestens sechs Raben. Einer Legende nach wird England untergehen, wenn die Raben den *Tower of London* verlassen.

Sieh dir den Videoclip an. Was erfährst du noch über die Raben im Londoner Tower?

So much more to see and do

9a

audio 1/16, skill: listening p. 151

Listen to Harry and Lily and their mum Sarah. What are Sarah's favourite sights in London?

9b

Listen again. What are the children's plans for the afternoon?

9c

Read these texts from a travel guide for kids. Which sight would you like to see?

Covent Garden

Covent Garden Market was a fruit and flower market for hundreds of years. Today it is one of London's most popular shopping neighbourhoods with many outdoor cafés. You can buy great clothes there. Covent Garden is also famous for street entertainment. Watch acrobats or listen to one of the many musicians. Just round the corner, the London Transport Museum is also worth a visit.

Platform 9¾

Platform 9¾ is a must for every Harry Potter fan. It is a popular attraction at King's Cross Station. It's a funny number for a platform, right? Well, it's actually not a platform. It comes from the Harry Potter books. It looks like the entrance to the platform that the students of Hogwarts use to get to their magical school. The Harry Potter books are so famous that people decided to build it at King's Cross. Lots of people take photos with it. And the best thing about it is that it's free to visit!

Madame Tussauds

What about time travelling through the history of London in one of the famous black London taxis or taking a selfie with Queen Elizabeth II, the Beatles, James Bond, ...? At Madame Tussauds you can travel through London's past and present or visit the royal family in their living room. More than 150 wax statues are waiting for you!

Online tickets are £27.50 for children and £30.50 for adults. If you are planning to visit other attractions, too, check out the different combination tickets. Opening times are from 10am to 4pm every day, and you can walk there from Baker Street, the nearest underground station.

9d CHOOSE YOUR LEVEL skill: reading p. 154, workbook p. 15/9-10

I Read text 1 again and answer the questions.

1 What was Covent Garden Market for hundreds of years?
2 What is Covent Garden famous for?
3 What can you do there?

II Read texts 1 and 2 again and answer the questions.

1 What is Covent Garden famous for?
2 Why is there an entrance to a platform 9¾ at King's Cross Station?
3 How much is it to take a picture at the entrance to platform 9¾?

III Read all three texts again and answer the questions.

1 What can you do at Covent Garden?
2 Why is the entrance to platform 9¾ a tourist attraction?
3 What can you see and do at Madame Tussauds?

Tower Bridge

10 skill: mediation p. 155, workbook p. 16/11

A German family needs help with this flyer. Look at the flyer and answer their questions in German.

1 Worum geht es denn hier?
2 Was steht da über den Fußboden?
3 Wovor darf man keine Angst haben?
4 Wie viel kostet der Eintritt für Kinder?
5 Wie viel kostet der Eintritt für Erwachsene?
6 Kann man das auch nachts machen?
7 Mit welcher U-Bahn-Linie kommt man dahin?

DON'T MISS THIS GREAT EXPERIENCE!

THE TOWER BRIDGE GLASS FLOOR WALKWAY

Did you know that you can walk on a glass floor high up inside Tower Bridge? Through the floor, you have a fantastic view of London below. The glass floor walkway is 42 metres above the River Thames and 33.5 metres above the road. We hope you're not afraid of heights! Entry is £10.60 for adults and £5.30 for children. The Bridge is open to visitors every day from 9.30am to 6pm. Our address is Tower Bridge Road, London, SE1 2UP. The nearest Tube station is Tower Hill. You can take the District and Circle Lines to get here.

London

11 CHOOSE YOUR TASK

A **Create a word search with London words for a partner.**
B **Choose a place or a building in London and write a fact file about it.**
C **Prepare a London quiz for a partner.**

B

The London Transport Museum
What to see / do there:
London's transport history / go on tours
How to get there: on the underground
How old: opened in 1980
Entry: free for children under 17
Opening times: every day 10:00 - 18:00

Places

12a audio 1/17

Listen to the CD and repeat the names.

Tower Bridge · the London Eye · Sky Garden · Big Ben · Buckingham Palace · London Zoo · the Natural History Museum · Wembley Stadium · the Houses of Parliament · the Shard · Covent Garden · the Tower of London · Platform 9¾ · Madame Tussauds · the London Transport Museum

12b

Match the parts to make phrases. Sometimes there is more than one possibilty.

1 a fantastic view
2 a perfect museum
3 Don't
4 worth
5 the entry is

A a visit
B free
C for children
D of the city
E miss ...

12c workbook p. 17/12

Use the phrases from 12b to write sentences about the sights in 12a.

You can write:
From Tower Bridge you have a fantastic view of the city.

Tourist attractions

13 CHOOSE YOUR LEVEL workbook p. 17/13-15

I Match the sentence parts. Write the sentences about sights in London in your exercise book.

1 More than 19,000 animals
2 The blue whale skeleton in the Natural
3 The London Eye is one of the most
4 You have to climb 334 steps to get

A to the top of the Elizabeth Tower.
B live in London Zoo.
C History Museum is 25.5 metres long.
D expensive tourist attractions in London.

II Unscramble the texts about Buckingham Palace and Wembley Stadium. Copy one of the texts into your exercise book.

Buckingham Palace is one of the many homes of the British royal family. Wembley Stadium is the largest stadium in the UK. Queen Victoria was the first queen who really lived here. She moved in in 1837. The England national football team plays matches here, but there are also other sports events and concerts. There are 775 rooms, 78 of which are bathrooms. During the summer visitors can go on a tour of some of the rooms. You can go on 90-minute tours of the stadium, and there is something for the whole family to enjoy. More than 50,000 people visit the palace each year.

III Write about the London Eye. You can use the words from the box for help.

ferris wheel · the tallest · near · capsule · in · the River Thames · the most expensive · ...

DIGITAL+ practise more 4

A day out in London TARGET TASK

14 workbook p. 19/16, wordbank: holidays p. 160, getting around p. 162, searching the Internet p. 157, media worksheet 4

Your task is to create one page for a travel guide for different days out in London. Before you start, look at these steps.

STEP 1

Get together in groups. Choose a theme for a perfect day out in London. You could plan ...

- ... a day for free
- ... a day for fans of the royal family
- ... a day for people who love animals and nature
- ... a day for families
- ...

Decide which group works on which theme.

STEP 2

Collect information. You can go to www.westermann.de/webcode and enter the webcode WES-128201-001 or use a search engine on the Internet for your research.

STEP 3

In your group, create a draft of your page with texts and pictures.

STEP 4

Give each other feedback and edit your drafts.

STEP 5

Create your page.

STEP 6

Put all your pages together in a travel guide for someone who speaks English but no German.

A ... day in London

Why not start ... ?
Don't miss ...
Then travel to ...
It's only a short journey on the ... line .
Enjoy the ...
... is always worth a visit, too.
In the afternoon ...
Take a walk along ... or have a ...
You could also visit ... .
In the evening you could ...

Check out

Kannst du verstehen, was jemand über seine Ferien berichtet? Workbook, p. 20
Kannst du von Ereignissen in der Vergangenheit erzählen? Workbook, p. 20
Kannst du jemandem Fragen über die vergangenen Ferien stellen? Workbook, p. 20
Kannst du Sehenswürdigkeiten in London beschreiben? Workbook, p. 21
Kannst du Personen oder Dinge vergleichen? Workbook, p. 21
Kannst du jemandem eine Wegbeschreibung geben? Workbook, p. 21

A dragon-taming emergency

"I hate washing up!" said Kora. She picked up another pot and started to dry it.
"Me too!" her dad replied.
"Can we watch a film tonight, Dad?" Kora asked.
"I'd like to …"
"PING!"
"Oh! That's my dragon tamer's watch!"
Kora dried her hands and opened the message on her watch.

NAME KORA
AGE 15
CITY NELSON, SOUTH ISLAND, NEW ZEALAND
ID NUMBER 26149
EYE COLOUR BROWN
HAIR COLOUR BROWN
SPECIALITY NEW ZEALAND DRAGONS, YOUNG DRAGONS

DRAGON TAMER'S ID

"Dad, I have to go! It's an emergency!"
"Be safe!" he said. "Good luck!"
She gave her dad a hug and ran out of the kitchen.
"Where are you going, Kora?" her little brother asked.

"On a dragon-taming mission, Ari!" she replied. "It's an emergency! Bye!"
Kora picked up her dragon tamer's ID card and her dragon-taming kit. Then she ran outside to wait for her driver William.

"PING!" There was another message on her watch. It was a map of New Zealand. It showed her where to look for the dragon – near Mount Taranaki, a volcano on the North Island.

dragon tamer = *Drachenzähmer/in;* dragon taming = *Drachenzähmen;* emergency = *Notfall;* give a hug = *umarmen;* watch = *Armbanduhr*

Just at that moment, William arrived in a big camper van. They always used the camper van for undercover missions, and Kora hated it. The helicopter was so much cooler!
"Hi, William!" Kora shouted. She jumped into the camper van.

"We need to take the ferry to the North Island! Someone saw the dragon there, near Mount Taranaki."
"OK," William replied. "Let's go!"

On the way, Kora looked at photos of the dragon. Then she looked at the map again. Mount Taranaki. She knew that name …
Suddenly, she remembered why.
"William, guess what?" she said.
"What, Kora?"
"I tamed a dragon near Mount Taranaki last year! Her name is Shirook, and we became friends. Maybe she can help!"

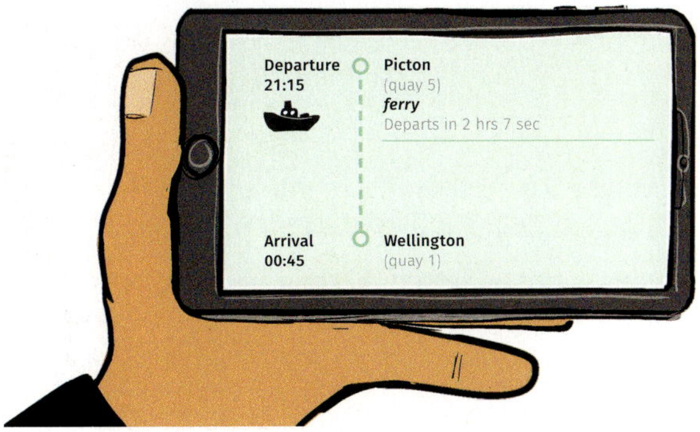

"Good idea!" William replied. "Hey, Kora, can you check the ferry times, please?"
"No problem!" Kora replied.
She opened the ferry app on her phone.
"Um, William? There's only one more ferry today … at quarter past nine this evening. We need to get that ferry. We can't wait until tomorrow. Quick, drive faster! "

arrival = *Ankunft;* become friends = *sich anfreunden;* camper van = *Wohnwagen;* departure = *Abfahrt;* ferry = *Fähre;* shout = *rufen;* quay = *Kai*

Message in a bottle

A woman sent a message in a bottle when she was just ten years old and received a reply more than twenty years later.

Zoe went to Germany for a holiday with her family when she was a schoolgirl. When they were on the ferry, her father had the idea that she should send a message in a bottle. So she threw a bottle with a letter in it into the sea near Hull in East Yorkshire.

She never got a reply at the time and soon forgot about it. Twenty years later Zoe's parents received a letter from the Netherlands. It was addressed to Zoe.

When Zoe opened it, she found a copy of her message in the bottle from more than twenty years ago. There was also a note from Piet from the Netherlands, who had found the message when he was walking his dog near Rotterdam.

Zoe was a bit emotional when she got the letter and saw her handwriting as a child. She contacted Piet in the Netherlands and he wrote her an email saying: "I know you are no longer a little girl, but you asked me to write to you, and I have. I am keeping your little letter on my piano."

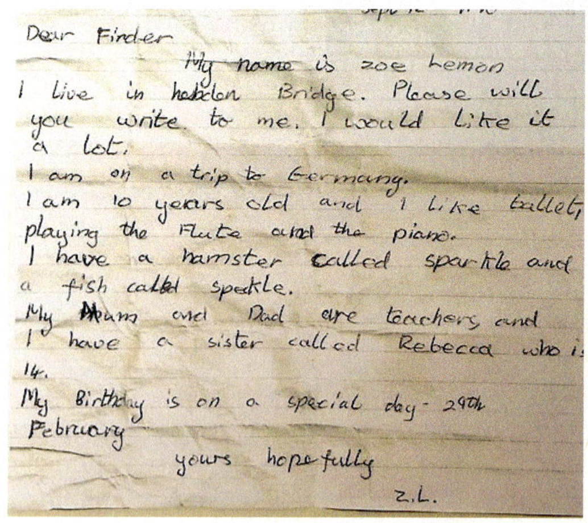

Dear Finder

My name is zoe lemon

I live in hebden Bridge. Please will you write to me. I would like it a lot.

I am on a trip to Germany.

I am 10 years old and I like ballet, playing the Flute and the piano.

I have a hamster called sparkle and a fish called speckle.

My Mum and Dad are teachers and I have a sister called Rebecca who i 14.

My Birthday is on a special day - 29th February

yours hopefully

Z.L.

Maybe Zoe will one day tell her son to send a message in a bottle – when he is older and can write a letter. Perhaps someone will answer his letter, too?

A friend wants to know what the article is about. Summarize it in German for him or her. Would you send a message in a bottle? What would you write? Write your message in a bottle.

2

1 Look at the picture. What can you see?
2 What festivals or holidays do you celebrate?
3 Which of them is your favourite festival or holiday?

Celebrations

Part A Festivals and traditions

- Du erfährst etwas über Feste und Feiertage in verschiedenen Kulturen.
- Du sprichst über Neujahr und Halloween.
- Du gestaltest ein Poster zu einem Fest oder Feiertag.

Part B Let's celebrate!

- Du erfährst etwas über *Bonfire Night*.
- Du übst, über Pläne für die nähere Zukunft zu sprechen.
- In einer Kleingruppe sammelst du Ideen für ein Klassenfest und diskutierst darüber.

Festivals

1a workbook p. 22/1

What festivals do you know?
What do you know about them?

1

2

1b

Look at the pictures and talk about them.
What are the people doing?
What do you think they are celebrating?

You can say:

I can see …
There is … / There are …
The people are …
I think the people are celebrating …

3

4

5

1c skill: reading p. 154

Read the texts on the following page. Match them to the pictures.
What is new to you? What do you find interesting? Talk about it.

A Like many other festivals, **Easter** is a religious festival. Christians celebrate it in spring. In my family, we always have an Easter egg hunt on Easter Sunday. My little brother still believes that the Easter bunny hides the eggs. We sometimes also go to a traditional Easter egg roll.

B **Eid** is at the end of the four weeks of Ramadan. During Ramadan, Muslims don't eat or drink during daylight hours but only after sunset. There are a lot of different traditions all over the world for Eid. In my family, we usually go to the mosque for a special prayer. In the evening we celebrate with our relatives. There's always lots of food.

C **Diwali**, the festival of lights, is one of the most popular festivals in Hinduism. Diwali stands for the victory of light over darkness or good over evil. It is a five-day festival with music, dancing, a lot of decorations and of course, light! Here you can see me and my sister. We're lighting candles for the celebration.

D **Chinese New Year**, or spring festival, is the main Chinese festival of the year. It doesn't take place on the same day every year because the date depends on the moon. Many Chinese people clean their houses before the festival.
The festival lasts fifteen days and it ends with the Lantern Festival. There are parades with people in dragon costumes and dancers. There are also lots of fireworks. We always watch the parade in Trafalgar Square.

E **Hanukkah** is the Jewish festival of lights. For eight days in winter, each night Jewish people light another candle on a special candle holder, the Hanukkah menorah. In my family, we always eat a lot during Hanukkah. All our relatives come to visit and there's music and we play games. In the picture, my father and I are playing with a dreidel. That's a typical Hanukkah game.

1d CHOOSE YOUR LEVEL

I Match the sentence parts and write down the sentences.

1 Easter is a
2 Christians celebrate
3 There are a lot of different traditions
4 During Ramadan, Muslims do not

A eat before sunset.
B all over the world for Eid.
C Easter in spring.
D religious festival.

II Correct the sentences and write them down.

1 Christians celebrate Easter in summer.
2 Eid is at the beginning of Ramadan.
3 Diwali stands for the victory of darkness.
4 You should not clean your house before Chinese New Year.
5 Hanukkah lasts nine days.

III What do festivals have in common? Think about food, decorations, …

You can write:
When people celebrate, they often …

1e wordbank: celebrations p. 163, workbook p. 22/2-3

What is your favourite festival? Why? Talk to a partner.

You can say:
My favourite festival is … because …

GRAMMAR HELP the simple present: statements (R) p. 178

Die Zeitform *simple present* kennst du schon. Du benutzt sie zum Beispiel, wenn jemand etwas regelmäßig tut, wenn etwas regelmäßig stattfindet oder wenn etwas über längere Zeit oder allgemein gültig ist.

Sieh dir die Beispielsätze an. Erinnerst du dich? Worauf musst du beim *simple present* besonders achten?

Diwali stands for the victory of light over darkness.

Christians celebrate Easter in spring.

The Chinese New Year doesn't take place on the same day every year.

During Ramadan, Muslims don't eat during daylight hours.

Auf den Seiten 178-179 sind die wichtigsten Punkte zum *simple present* zusammengefasst.

Christmas with my family

2 grammar: simple present statements p. 178

Use the correct form of the verb and write the sentences in your exercise book.

1 We usually (not celebrate) Christmas at our house.
2 We (meet) all our relatives at my grandma's house in Hamburg and (go) to church together.
3 Sometimes, even my uncle from Berlin and my aunt from Munich (come) to Hamburg.
4 My grandmother always (give) everyone lots of presents.
5 My father usually (get) socks.
6 He never (like) them.
7 But he (not say) anything.

Celebrations

3a

Copy the sentences and complete them with nouns from the box.

1 I invite my cousin to my party. I send him an ???.
2 My parents decorate the house. The house is full of ???.
3 My grandmother celebrates her birthday. It's a big ???.
4 Our teacher informs us about the class party. She gives us a lot of ???.

decorations · celebration · information · invitation

3b skill: working with words p. 150

Which verbs and nouns from 3a go together? Underline them in your exercise book.

You can write:

I invite my cousin to my party.
I send him an invitation.

3c workbook p. 23/4

Can you find the nouns for these verbs? Check in your dictionary.

collect · present · introduce

Happy New Year – all over the world

4a

Look at the pictures of New Year's traditions. What can you see?

4b audio 1/22, skill: listening p. 151

Listen to the people. Which of these countries are they talking about? Take notes.

India · Spain · France · China · Italy · Scotland

4c CHOOSE YOUR LEVEL workbook p. 23/5-6

I Read the sentences, then listen again and fill in the correct information from the box.

twelve grapes · guest · calendars · 15 days · good luck

1 The celebration of Chinese New Year is ??? long.
2 In India, there are many New Year celebrations because of the different ???.
3 First footing means that the first ??? in the new year brings ??? into the house.
4 People in Spain eat ??? at midnight.

II Read the sentences, then listen again and fill in the correct information.

1 The Chinese New Year is not on a ??? date. It changes every ???.
2 In India, different regions ??? New Year's Eve on different ???.
3 The Scottish ??? for New Year's Eve is "Hogmanay".
4 People in ??? believe that eating twelve grapes at twelve o'clock brings good luck for the ??? year.

III Read the questions. Then listen again and write the answers in your exercise book.

1 What do the Chinese do for good luck for the next year?
2 How does Farida celebrate New Year's Eve?
3 What presents does the first guest of the year usually bring in Scotland?
4 How many grapes do people in Spain eat at midnight?

What about you?

5 grammar: simple present questions p. 179, wordbank: celebrations p. 163, workbook p. 24/7-9

How do you celebrate the New Year? Walk, stop and talk.

You can ask:
What do you eat / drink on New Year's Eve?
Do you have any special traditions?
...

Halloween

6a

What do you know about Halloween?
Talk about it in class.
You can look at the pictures for inspiration.

6b

Read the article.
Who brought Halloween to the USA?

A VERY SHORT HISTORY OF HALLOWEEN

Did you know that Halloween is one of the world's oldest holidays? All over the world people celebrate Halloween on 31 October. But what is so special about this day?

It probably all began with a Celtic festival about 2,000 years ago. The Celts lived in the area that is now Ireland, the United Kingdom and northern France. They built bonfires and came together on the evening of 31 October because they believed that the ghosts of the dead came back that night. Some of the Celts wore scary costumes, others offered food to the ghosts so they would go back to the world of the dead. That is probably where the trick-or-treating of today comes from.

From the year 43 to about the year 410 the Romans ruled over large parts of Britain. Two of their important festivals mixed with this Celtic festival. The first was a day in late October when the Romans thought of their dead. The second was a day to honour the Roman goddess of fruit and trees. Her symbol is often an apple – maybe that is where the tradition of apple bobbing comes from.

In the 8th and 9th century, Christians began to celebrate All Hallows' Day on 1 November to honour all Christian saints. The evening before this day is All Hallows' Eve. That is where the name Halloween comes from.

In the 20th century, Catholics from Ireland brought Halloween to the USA where it became a popular festival. Irish people also brought the tradition of carving jack-o'-lanterns with them.

Today, Halloween is a very popular festival all over the world. Children, especially, like to dress up in scary costumes and go trick-or-treating – although the sweets are probably more important to them than scaring away ghosts.

6c skill: talking with people p. 152

Read the article again. What was new to you? What did you find surprising? Talk to a partner.

You can say:

It was new to me that …
I found it surprising that …
I didn't know that …
…

6d CHOOSE YOUR LEVEL skill: reading p. 154, workbook p. 25/10-12

I What did the Celts do on 31 October? Take notes.

You can write:

The Celts
– built …
…

II What happened when? Make a timeline.

Celtic festival …
2000 years ago → 43 to 410

III Make a Halloween quiz for your classmates.

When do people celebrate Halloween?

Why did the Celts wear costumes?

LAND & LEUTE 2 video 4

Viele Kulturen – viele Feste

Im Vereinigten Königreich gibt es viele verschiedene Kulturen und Nationalitäten. Allein in London werden über 300 Sprachen gesprochen, und neben dem Christentum sind auch der Islam, der Buddhismus, der Hinduismus, das Judentum und der Sikhismus sehr verbreitet.
Durch diese Vielfalt gibt es über das Jahr verteilt viele verschiedene Feste, die nicht nur von den Anhängern einer Religion oder Kultur gefeiert werden, sondern von vielen Menschen in der Bevölkerung. Feste wie *Diwali*, das *Holi Festival*, aber auch der *St Patrick's Day* werden im Vereinigten Königreich gefeiert.

Manchmal fallen sogar Feste wie *Diwali* und *Bonfire Night* auf das gleiche Datum und werden zusammen gefeiert.

Welche Feste sind typisch für die Gegend, in der du wohnst?

Halloween today – opinions

7a

Do you celebrate Halloween? If yes, what do you do on Halloween?

7b

Read the statements about Halloween. Who likes Halloween? Who does not?

Jessica, 14
"Halloween is only about spending money. You have to buy costumes, decorations, sweets, ... It's so commercial. I don't think that's cool!"

Tom, 13
"For my family, 31 October is still the Christian holiday of All Hallows' Eve. I think Halloween is stupid. Dressing up in scary costumes is for little children, and I don't like going to people's houses and asking them for sweets. I don't like Halloween!"

Liam, 12
"I love Halloween! It's fun to dress up in scary costumes and go around the neighbourhood to collect sweets. You say: "Trick or treat". That means that you ask people to give you sweets or you play funny tricks on them. My favourite costume is the mummy. You just have to wrap yourself in toilet paper and that's it!"

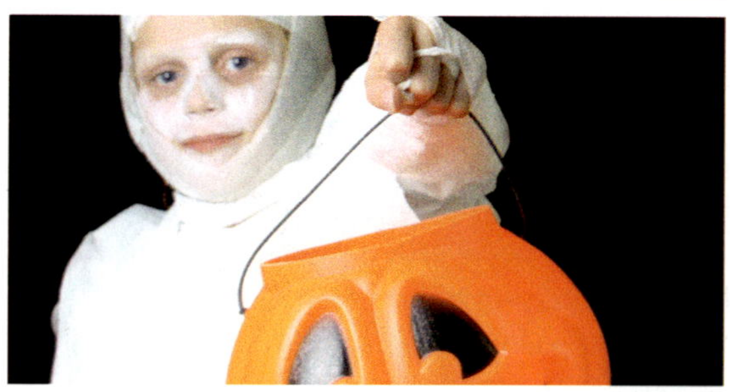

Christopher, 14
"Halloween is great! Why? Because you can be a really scary character, eat lots of sweets and do all kinds of fun games like apple bobbing or you can carve jack-o'-lanterns out of pumpkins. My cousin John lives in the USA. Halloween is huge there! One day I want to go to New York and watch the Halloween parade!"

7c skill: reading p. 154

What do the people in 7b like or not like about Halloween? Make a list.

You can write:

pro	con
sweets, …	*commercial, …*

7d skill: writing p. 153, workbook p. 27/13-14

What do you think about Halloween? Write a short text. You can use your list from 7c and add your own ideas.

You can write:

I think Halloween is … because …

Party time

8 CHOOSE YOUR TASK A: skill: presentations p. 158, B: performing a scene p. 159, C: wordbank: celebrations p. 163

A **Design a Halloween costume and present your idea to the class. Make notes first to help you with your presentation.**

B **Work with a partner. Write a dialogue: one person wants to go to a Halloween party, the other one does not. Act out your dialogue.**

C **Go to www.westermann.de/webcode and enter the webcode WES-128201-001 to find information about New Year's traditions from all over the world. What is your favourite tradition? Why?**

Halloween decorations

9 CHOOSE YOUR LEVEL skill: mediation p. 155

I **Tell someone who does not understand English how to make Halloween stress balls in German.**

Halloween stress balls

Don't worry, these stress balls are really easy to make. Use orange or white balloons to make pumpkin or ghost stress balls. Fill them with rice or sand. Take a felt-tip and draw a scary face on the balloons.

II **Tell someone who does not understand English how to make mummy glass jars in German.**

Mummy glass jars

These mummy glass jars are sooo easy and also fun to make! You don't need much material. Take a glass jar and wrap it with some toilet paper and put some tape around it. Put a pair of googly eyes onto the glass jar and then a little LED candle inside it.

III **Tell someone who does not understand English how to make ghost garlands in German.**

Ghost garland

You can make your own decorations with these scary ghost garlands. You need paper, a pencil, a pair of scissors and a ruler. Fold the paper into 7cm sections, then draw a ghost on the top piece and cut it out. Make sure that you don't cut the sections apart. Repeat with more paper if you want to make a longer garland.

Celebrations during the year

10 CHOOSE YOUR LEVEL grammar: simple present p. 178, workbook p. 28/15

I Match the sentence parts.

1 At Easter people often
2 Eid is the celebration
3 During Hanukkah people light
4 During Diwali people celebrate

A at the end of Ramadan.
B the victory of light over darkness.
C give each other chocolate eggs.
D a new candle every evening.

II Unscramble the sentences.

1 spring. – never – Christmas – in – is
2 people – their relatives – Jewish – often – visit – during Hanukkah.
3 different cultures – from – often – Chinese New Year – People – together. – celebrate
4 celebrate – Some people – traditional egg roll. – Easter – with a – in the UK
5 New Year's Day – of – first – year. – day – the – the – is

III Copy the sentences and complete them.

1 At Christmas people usually ???.
2 People in the UK often ??? at Easter.
3 Hanukkah is ???.
4 In India, many people ???.
5 On Halloween children often ???.
6 ??? during Ramadan.

Categories

11a names p. 244

Read the words in the box and sort them into categories: religions / religious groups, festivals / holidays, countries, days and months.

India · Hinduism · Christians · Ireland · Halloween · Sunday · Easter · October · China

You can write:

religion / religious groups	*festivals / holidays*	*countries*	*days*	*months*
Hinduism	...	*India*	...	...
...	...	...	...	...

11b workbook p. 28/16

Find more examples for each category.
Then look at the spelling: what do the words have in common?

DIGITAL+ practise more 6

A festival poster TARGET TASK

12 workbook p. 29/17, wordbank: celebrations p. 163

Your task is to present a festival or a holiday on a poster.
Before you start, look at these steps:

STEP 1
In class, write a list of festivals or holidays.

STEP 2
Decide which festival or holiday you would like to present. Get together in groups.

STEP 3
In your group collect information and do some research about the festival or holiday.
Think about:

- When do people celebrate?
- Where do people celebrate?
- What is the history or background?
- Are there different traditions in different parts of the world?
- What do people usually eat?
- Are there special activities, decorations, ...?
- ...

New Year's Eve

When?
People celebrate New Year's Eve on 31 December.

Where?
People all over the world celebrate New Year's Eve.

What is the background of the festival?

STEP 4
Plan your poster and make a draft.

STEP 5
Create the poster.

STEP 6
Put up your posters in class and do a gallery walk to present them.
You can use your posters to create a festival calendar for your classroom.

A Bonfire Night flyer

1a

Do you know any festivals where bonfires play a role? Talk about them in class.

1b workbook p.30/1

Look at the flyer. What is it about?

1c

Work with a partner. Look at the flyer again. Ask and answer questions about it. Take turns.

You can ask:

When is Bonfire Night? How much does it cost? What can families / children do? What …?

Bonfire Night plans

2a audio 1/32

Listen to Lily and Harry and their mums and read along. What are they talking about?

Lily: It's Bonfire Night on Saturday. The fireworks in Brighton were always so cool! So what are we doing this year? We are not staying at home, are we?
Harry: Look. I found this flyer in a shop yesterday. There is a big party here in Notting Hill we could go to. It looks pretty cool. They are having live music, a funfair and food stalls – just like in Brighton. But I'm sure it's much bigger and the fireworks are even more spectacular!
Lily: That sounds great.
Sarah: May I have a look at the flyer, please? Hmm, it's quite expensive. It costs five pounds for kids and even more for adults. I'm not paying that much money to stand out in the cold.
Olivia: And I don't really like big parties like that. Usually they're full of people and you always have to queue for the food, for the toilets, for everything! And it's so loud.
Sarah: Phew, I also don't think that the party is a good idea. What are your friends doing for Bonfire Night? Maybe they can give you some ideas.
Harry: Tarek told me that he and his dad are thinking about going to the big fireworks show at Alexandra Palace again. They went last year and he said it was really good. Maybe we can go with them?
Lily: I don't know what Ava and her family are planning right now. Let's talk to Ava and Tarek tomorrow. But I really want to celebrate Bonfire Night because …
Harry: … it gives you an excuse to eat lots of toffee apples.
Lily: Yeah! Toffee apples are the best thing about Bonfire Night.

2b CHOOSE YOUR LEVEL skill: reading p. 154

I Match the sentence parts and write down the sentences.

1 Lily says that the fireworks
2 Harry found a flyer for
3 Sarah is not paying that much money

A a big Bonfire Night party in Notting Hill.
B to stand out in the cold.
C in Brighton were always so cool.

II True or false? Correct the false statements and write them down.

1 Bonfire Night is on Sunday.
2 Olivia loves big parties.
3 Sarah thinks that going to the party is a great idea.
4 Tarek and his dad are thinking about celebrating at home.

III Answer the questions.

1 What does Lily say about Bonfire Night in Brighton?
2 Why does Olivia not like big parties?
3 What does Sarah say about the party in Notting Hill?
4 Who is thinking about going to Alexandra Palace?
5 Why do Lily and Harry want to talk to their friends the next day?

2c workbook p. 30/2-4

Would you like to go to a Bonfire Night party? Say why or why not.

GRAMMAR HELP the present progressive: statements (R) p. 180

Die Zeitform *present progressive* kennst du bereits. Vergleiche die Sätze im *present progressive*. Für welche Situationen kannst du es verwenden?

I'm watching a film right now.
Lily is doing her homework at the moment.
Tarek and his dad are having dinner at the moment.

We're watching the fireworks next weekend.
What are you doing tomorrow?
We're having a party next Saturday.

Ab Seite 180 findest du weitere Informationen zur Bildung und Verwendung des *present progressive*.

What is Tarek planning for next week?

3 grammar: present progressive p. 180, workbook p. 31/5

Write down Tarek's plans for next week.

Monday afternoon: play hockey
Tuesday: watch football match with dad
Wednesday: ~~meet Uncle Sami~~
Thursday: do science experiments (school lab)
Friday afternoon: ~~play football~~, go to cinema
Saturday: help dad clean the house
Sunday: meet friends (park)

You can write:
Next Monday afternoon Tarek is playing …
Next Wednesday Tarek is not …

My plans

4 grammar: present progressive p. 180

What are you doing next week? Write about your plans.

You can write:
Next Tuesday I'm …
Next weekend I'm …
…

Sound check

5a audio 1/35

Listen to the words and repeat them.

celebrate · remember · bonfire · expensive · yesterday · fireworks · chocolate · fantastic · spectacular · popular · Internet · November

5b

Where is the stress? On the first or on the second syllable? Make two lists.

first syllable	*second syllable*
celebrate	*remember*
…	…

5c audio 1/36

Listen and check your lists.

DIGITAL+ practise more 7

ACTIVATE PRACTISE DEVELOP PRACTISE APPLY

A special Bonfire Night

6a audio 1/37

Listen and read along. What is the friends' plan?

Lily: Bonfire Night is almost here. So, what are your plans for Saturday, Ava?
Ava: We don't know yet. Last year we celebrated at home. It was OK, but I think it's more fun with more people.
Noah: Yes, definitely. We had a few sparklers and lots of great snacks and made s'mores on the bonfire, but it was a bit boring. And there wasn't any music.
Tarek: S'mores! Yummy! The fireworks at Alexandra Palace last year were really spectacular! But I had to queue forever to get some popcorn. We're not going this year. My dad says it is too expensive.
Harry: Maybe we could have our own Bonfire Night party? We could ask our mums if we can do it at our place. Everybody brings something to eat or to drink, and we can play games like apple bobbing …
Lily: Haha Harry, isn't that for children …? But … it could be fun, too. Our own party … sounds good to me!
Ava: Brilliant idea! Let's do it! I can make toffee apples. I found a recipe online last year. How many do we need?
Lily: Lots! I love toffee apples. Any more ideas?
Tarek: We have to make sure we have some hot drinks, too. I can bring hot apple juice and hot chocolate. How much wood do we need for the fire? And where do we get it?
Ava: Noah and I can bring the wood. I'm sure our dad can help us. Let me just text him.
Harry: Why don't we cook some jacket potatoes in the fire?
Lily: Oh man, it's going to be the best Bonfire Night party ever! Let's make a list.

6b CHOOSE YOUR LEVEL skill: reading p. 154, workbook p. 32/6-8

I Ava is writing a text message to her dad. Copy the text into your exercise book. Fill in the gaps with the words from the box.

drink · talking · bring · place · Bonfire Night · wood

Hi Dad. I'm with Harry, Lily and Noah and we're ??? about our plans for ???. We'd love to have our own party at Harry and Lily's ??? this year. We would all ??? something to eat and to ???. But we need your help with the ??? for the fire. Could you do that? Pleeeeeease?

II Harry is writing a text message to his mum. Unscramble the sentences and write the text message in your exercise book.

1 our own Bonfire Night party – Hi Sarah, – at our place? – could we maybe have
2 the wood – could bring – Ava's dad – for the fire.
3 something to eat – would bring – Everybody – or to drink.
4 Love you, Harry. – please? – Say yes,

III Lily is writing a text message to Ellen in Brighton. Write her text message in your exercise book.

You can write:
Hi Ellen, we're planning … First … Then …
What are you doing on Bonfire Night?
Love, Lily

A Bonfire Night recipe

7a

Look at the recipe. What is it for?

You need: 8 apples
400 g sugar
1 tbsp lemon juice
100 ml water

Step 1
Place the apples in a large bowl, then cover with boiling water. Dry the apples and remove the stalks.

Step 2
Push a wooden skewer into each apple.

Step 3
Put the apples on a sheet of baking paper. Put the sugar and the water into a pot. Cook for 5 minutes until the sugar melts, then add the lemon juice and boil a little longer. You can test the toffee by putting a little into a bowl of cold water. It should get hard instantly.

Step 4
Put each apple in the pot with the hot toffee and cover the apple with toffee, then place it on the baking paper. Leave the toffee to cool before you eat your delicious toffee apples!

7b CHOOSE YOUR LEVEL skill: reading p. 154

I Read the recipe again and look at the pictures. Write these steps in the right order in your exercise book.

A Put each apple in the hot toffee.
B Dry the apples and remove the stalks.
C Let the apples cool before you eat them.
D Push wooden skewers into the apples.

II Read the recipe again and look at the pictures. Write these steps in the right order in your exercise book.

A Put each apple in the hot toffee.
B Dry the apples and remove the stalks.
C Let the apples cool before you eat them.
D Push wooden skewers into the apples.
E Prepare the toffee.
F Cover the apples with boiling water.

III Read the recipe again and answer the questions.

1 How many toffee apples do you get?
2 Where do you place the apples first?
3 What do you do with the stalks?
4 What do you do with the skewers?
5 How long do you have to cook the sugar and the water?
6 When do you add the lemon juice?
7 How can you test if the toffee is ready?

Bonfire Night safety tips

8a skill: watching a video clip p. 156, nedia worksheet 1

Look at this picture from a video clip.
What do you think the video clip is about?

8b video 5, skill: mediation, p. 155, workbook 34/9-11

One of your friends found the video and does not understand it.
Watch the video clip and answer his or her questions in German.

1 Worum geht es in dem Video?
2 Was wird über Lagerfeuer gesagt?
3 Was soll man bei Wunderkerzen beachten?
4 Was wird über Feuerwerkskörper gesagt?

LAND & LEUTE 3 video 6

Bonfire Night

Am 5. November feiern die Menschen in Großbritannien *Bonfire Night* – auch *Guy Fawkes Night* genannt – mit großen Freudenfeuern *(bonfires)* und Feuerwerk. Dieses Fest geht auf ein Ereignis aus dem Jahr 1605 zurück, die sogenannte Pulververschwörung *(Gunpowder Plot)*. Eine Gruppe von katholischen Verschwörern, zu denen Guy Fawkes gehörte, wollte den protestantischen König James I und die Mitglieder des Parlaments durch eine Explosion mit Schießpulver, das sie in den Kellergewölben der *Houses of Parliament* versteckt hatten, töten.
Dieser Plan schlug fehl. Die Männer wurden gefangen genommen und verurteilt. Der König und die Mitglieder des Parlaments blieben unverletzt, und das feiert man seitdem an diesem Tag.
Lange gehörte das Herstellen einer Art Strohpuppe, die Guy Fawkes darstellen sollte, dazu: Kinder bastelten eine solche Puppe und sammelten Geld *(„a penny for the Guy“)*. Die Strohpuppe wurde dann im Feuer mit verbrannt. Auf diese fragwürdige Tradition wird heute meistens verzichtet. Mittlerweile bemühen sich viele Menschen auch, ihre *Bonfire Night* möglichst umweltverträglich zu gestalten. Sie verzichten auf privates Feuerwerk, achten darauf, dass sie nichts verbrennen, das schädliche Gase produziert und versuchen, möglichst wenig Abfall zu produzieren.

Welche Feiertage, die auf ein geschichtliches Ereignis zurückgehen, kennst du noch?

Asking Mum

9a audio 1/38, skill: listening p. 151

Listen to Harry and his mum. What is Sarah's first reaction to the children's plan?

9b workbook p. 35/12

Listen again. What does Sarah think about fireworks? What is her suggestion?

Remember, remember …

10a audio 1/40, skill: listening p. 151

There is an old rhyme about Guy Fawkes and the Gunpowder Plot that many people in the UK know. Listen to the rhyme and read along.

10b skill: working with words p. 150

Look up the words you do not know.

10c

Read the rhyme aloud.

10d

Learn it by heart.

Remember, remember
The fifth of November,
Gunpowder, treason and plot.
I see no reason
Why gunpowder treason
Should ever be forgot.

Bonfire Night

11 CHOOSE YOUR TASK A+B: wordbank: celebrations p. 163

A Make an acrostic about a Bonfire Night party.
B Noah talks about the party plan with his parents. Write the dialogue.
C Go to www.westermann.de/webcode and enter the webcode WES-128201-001 to find out more about the history of Bonfire Night. Tell your class about it.

A

B alloons
O range pumpkins
N oisy
F ireworks
I …
R …
E …

The Bonfire Night party

12a skill: reading p. 154

Read Ava's text message to her mum. How is the party?

Ava Hi Mum, we are having a good time. Noah and Tarek are roasting marshmallows on the bonfire. Earlier we grilled sausages and cooked jacket potatoes in the fire. So good! Lily is eating one of my toffee apples, they are really yummy. Later we are watching the fireworks live stream from Alexandra Palace and lighting more sparklers. See u. Love, Ava Saturday 9:17pm

12b grammar: present progressive p. 180, workbook p. 35/13-14

Look at the picture and describe it. What is everyone doing?

A calendar of world festivals

13 GET TOGETHER

Get together with a partner.
Read and talk about different festivals.

Partner A	Partner B
I Go to page 128.	I Go to page 137.
II Go to page 131.	II Go to page 140.
III Go to page 134.	III Go to page 143.

Talking about ideas

14 CHOOSE YOUR LEVEL workbook p.36/15

I Unscramble the sentences and write them down.

1 any ideas – for games? – Have you got
2 dress up – in scary costumes. – We should
3 We could – with a few pumpkins. – decorate the room
4 we need – some biscuits. – I think
5 food – What about – from different countries?

II Unscramble the sentences and write them down.

1 we need – I think – for dancing. – some music
2 should – We – a costume contest. – have
3 toffee apples – How many – need? – do we
4 party games? – some – Why don't – we play
5 a special – What – playlist? – about
6 think – I don't – any decorations. – we need

III A classmate needs help for the discussion. Help him or her. Write down the sentences in English.

1 Ich denke, wir brauchen ein paar Dekorationen.
2 Wir sollten Essen aus verschiedenen Ländern mitbringen.
3 Wir könnten Spiele wie *Apfelfischen* spielen.
4 Lasst uns eine Playlist mit Lieblingsliedern zusammenstellen.
5 Wie ist es mit Getränken?
6 Ich glaube nicht, dass wir Kostüme brauchen.
7 Das klingt gut.

A party checklist

15 grammar: quantifiers p.182, workbook p.36/16

Tarek is planning a party at his house.
Write down what he is thinking. Complete the sentences with *some* or *any*.

First I need ??? cool music. Do I have ??? good music for dancing? I need to check that. I should get ??? fun games, too. Harry and Lily love playing games. And I need ??? balloons to decorate the room. I definitely need ??? sweets and crisps. But I should get ??? healthy snacks, too. What about drinks? We've always got water, but we haven't got ??? lemonade or orange juice.

DIGITAL+ practise more 8

Our class party TARGET TASK

16 workbook p. 37/17, wordbank: celebrations p. 163, skill: presentations p. 158

Your task is to make plans for a class party.
Before you start, look at these steps:

STEP 1

In class, talk about how you want to organize your party.

- What kind of party would you like to have? An autumn party? A Halloween party? A ... party?
- How much time do you have for your party? One lesson? Two lessons? An afternoon? A whole day?
- Where do you want to celebrate? In your classroom? Somewhere else?
- When do you want to celebrate your class party?

STEP 2

Get together in small groups and collect ideas for the party on a placemat.

You can say:

I think we need ...
We could / should ...
Let's ...
What about ...?
Why don't we ...?
That's a great idea.
That sounds good.
I don't know.
I think ... is better.

STEP 3

Discuss in your group and write down your top three ideas for each category.
Present them to the rest of the class.

STEP 4

Choose the best ideas and decide who brings or does what. Then have a great party!

Check out

Kannst du ein Telefongespräch über Pläne für ein Fest verstehen?	Workbook, p. 38
Kannst du kurze Texte zu Feiertagen und Festen verstehen?	Workbook, p. 38
Kannst du erzählen, was du üblicherweise an einem Feiertag oder Fest machst?	Workbook, p. 38
Kannst du Bastelanleitungen auf Deutsch wiedergeben?	Workbook, p. 39
Kannst du einen Flyer zu einer Veranstaltung verstehen?	Workbook, p. 39
Kannst du darüber schreiben, was jemand für die nähere Zukunft plant?	Workbook, p. 39

Looking for the dragon

"Well done, William!" said Kora. "We're on the ferry!" "Thank goodness!" William replied. Kora picked up her phone and sent a text message to Blaze.

Kora was tired. It was time to go to bed. She brushed her teeth and climbed up the little ladder at the back of the campervan. Her bed was at the top.
"Boo!"
"Aah!" Kora screamed.

"What …? Ari! You scared me! What are you doing here?"
"I wanted to come with you," Ari said. "I know lots about dragons. And look – I've got my dragon book with me. The one from the Natural History Museum. I can help!"
"Oh Ari," said Kora. "Dad is probably really worried! We need to call him."

So they called their dad. He was angry, but happy that Ari was safe.

"Let's go to sleep, Ari," said Kora after the phone call. "Tomorrow we have to find and tame a dragon!"

angry = *wütend;* emergency mission = *Notfalleinsatz;* ferry = *Fähre;* go to sleep = *schlafen gehen;* scare = *erschrecken;* scream = *schreien*

DIGITAL+ You can listen to Kora's phone call to her dad: audio 3/18

The next day

When they woke up, they were at Mount Taranaki. After breakfast, Kora showed Ari the photos of the dragon. Then they went to find Shirook.
"OK, Ari," Kora said. "The dragon we need to tame is possibly VERY dangerous. So stay close to me, OK?"
Ari nodded. "OK, Kora."
They walked towards the huge volcano.
"Do you remember any Skkaddraa?" Kora asked Ari. "You know – the dragon language?"
"Yes, of course! I remember everything you told me!" Ari said.
"Good! Let's call Shirook, then."
"Shirook!" they shouted. "Wahhraah bes taa? Where are you?"
They shouted and shouted, but they couldn't find Shirook anywhere.
Then, finally, Kora saw her, high in the sky. "Here she comes, Ari," she said.
"Get ready to meet a dragon!"
Shirook landed on the ground near Kora and Ari. Kora looked at Shirook and then, very slowly, she bowed. Next, she gave Shirook a kiwi fruit – Shirook's favourite food.
"Hello Kora," said Shirook. Then she looked at Ari. "Who is this?"
"That's Ari, my little brother," Kora said.
"Hi," Ari whispered.
"Hi, little brother," Shirook replied.
"Shirook, we need to find a dragon – an unknown kind of dragon," Kora began.
"I know. I saw this dragon," Shirook said. "Yesterday. At the top of the volcano. I can take you."
The huge dragon lay down and Kora and Ari climbed up onto her back.
Soon they were up in the air, but they couldn't see the dragon anywhere. Just lots of snow.
Suddenly, Ari shouted, "Look! Look!" He pointed towards a cave below them.
He moved over a bit – and started to slide off Shirook's back.
"Kora, help!" he shouted, as he started to fall …

bow = *sich verbeugen;* dangerous = *gefährlich;* nod = *nicken;* slide off = *heruntergleiten;* volcano = *Vulkan;* whisper = *flüstern*

The Clarke family blog

Christopher and his cousin John from New York are writing messages on the family blog.

John *(November 1)*: Hi everyone! What's up? How was your Halloween? As I am 16 now, I was allowed to go to the Halloween parade here in New York alone with my friends for the first time. It was cool! Shortly before 7pm we met in Mick's backyard – you know, my friend and neighbor – and went to 6th Avenue to wait for the parade. There were thousands of people in all kinds of costumes, lots of bands and dancers and also some giant puppets. I took a picture of my favorite one ... The parade was just awesome, I'm definitely going again next year!

Christopher *(November 1)*: Oh wow, that looks fantastic! We celebrated Halloween here in London, too, but we don't have any parades. Instead, my friends and I had a Halloween party. We all dressed up and played some Halloween games. My favourite was apple bobbing. Have you ever tried it? It's really hard! Then we went trick-or-treating – we didn't play any tricks though, we just got a lot of sweets – we had a whole bag full of sweets by the end of the evening! But now I'm really looking forward to Bonfire Night!

John *(November 1)*: Wow! A whole bag full of candy! But what's Bonfire Night? What are you doing for it?

Christopher *(November 1)*: Bonfire Night is on 5th November every year and people light bonfires and fireworks. This year, we're meeting all our family and friends at the park to watch the fireworks. There's also a funfair at the park. We normally eat food from one of the food stalls and this year, my mum is making toffee apples, too. They're delicious! I'm so excited!

John *(November 1)*: That really sounds fun! We don't celebrate that here in the US, but we have another big festival in the fall: Thanksgiving. It's always on the fourth Thursday in November and the whole family gets together to celebrate. We usually have a traditional Thanksgiving dinner with a turkey, mashed potatoes, corn and pumpkin pie. I posted a picture from Thanksgiving last year for you to look at.

Christopher *(November 1)*: Thanks for the nice picture! I'm getting hungry just by looking at it. What a shame we don't have another festival in autumn.

What do you find interesting? What is new to you?

3

1 What can you see in the picture?
2 What do you think the problem is? Collect ideas.
3 What do you think: what are the people saying?

Living together

Part A Getting along

- Du sprichst über Regeln im Alltag.
- Du erfährst etwas über Schulregeln an einer britischen Schule.
- Du präsentierst ein Rollenspiel, in dem es um die Lösung eines Konflikts geht.

Part B Take care!

- Du sprichst über Ausflugsziele in der Natur.
- Du erfährst etwas über die Tierwelt Großbritanniens.
- Du entwickelst Ideen für kleine Umweltprojekte.

School rules

1a

Work with a partner. What are the rules at your school? Make notes and talk about them with a partner.

You can write:

We can …
We can't …
We have to …
We don't have to …
…

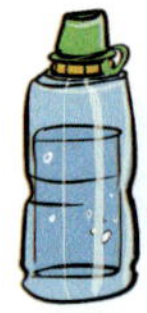
drink during lessons

eat in the classrooms

use mobile phones at school

wear school uniform

…

1b wordbank: rules p. 164

Read the Holland Park School rules. Which rules are the same at your school? Which rules are different? Talk about the rules in class.

SCHOOL RULES

1. Be polite and show respect for other students and the teachers.
2. School starts at 8:40am. Students who are late must first report to the headteacher's office.
3. Students must not run in the school building.
4. Students must wear the correct school uniform.
5. Eat and drink at break and at lunchtime in the cafeteria. Eating is not allowed in the classrooms.
6. Students are not allowed to use mobile phones at school.
7. Students are not allowed to wear make-up or piercings.
8. Students are not allowed to wear hats or caps on school grounds.
9. Do not enter a room without knocking first.
10. Students must not bring dangerous things with them.

1c CHOOSE YOUR LEVEL skill: reading p. 154, workbook p. 40/1

I Look at the pictures. Which rules are the students breaking?

You can write:

1. The girl in picture one is breaking rule number …
2. The boy in picture …
3. …

II Read the school rules again and answer the questions.

1 When do the students have to be at school?
2 What do the students have to do if they are late?
3 What do the students have to wear?
4 Where can the students eat at lunchtime?
5 What are the students not allowed to use at school?

III Read the school rules again and answer the questions.

1 Robin is sitting in his maths lesson and he is really hungry. What is he not allowed to do?
2 Kerem was bored in science class and listened to some music on his phone. Why is he in trouble now?
3 Adam is late. He arrives at school at 9am. What does he have to do?
4 Sharon got a bad mark in a test and shouted at a teacher. Which rule did she break?
5 Nasaar has got cool new jeans. Why can't she wear them to school?

Your opinion

2

Which of the Holland Park School rules do you find important / not important? Why? Talk about them in class.

You can say:

In my opinion … because …
…

GRAMMAR HELP the modal verbs must and mustn't p. 183

Die Wörter *must* und *must not (= mustn't)* benutzt du z. B., wenn du über Regeln sprechen willst.
Sieh dir die Beispielsätze an. Wie würdest du die Sätze auf Deutsch formulieren? Was fällt dir auf?

Harry must wear the correct school uniform.
Students must always be on time for school.
Ava mustn't listen to music when she does her homework.
Students must not talk during tests.

Auf den Seiten 183-184 findest du weitere Beispiele dafür, wie du darüber sprechen kannst, was jemand tun muss oder nicht tun darf.

Rules

3
grammar: modal verbs p. 183

Complete the school rules with must or mustn't.

1 You ??? sleep in class.
2 You ??? arrive late to school.
3 You ??? bring your books to school every day.
4 You ??? play football in class.
5 You ??? forget your homework.
6 You ??? eat in the classroom.
7 You ??? listen to the teacher.
8 You ??? use your mobile phone in class.
9 You ??? do your homework.

Rules at our school

4
grammar: modal verbs p. 183, wordbank: rules p. 164, workbook p. 40/2-4

Write six or more sentences about the rules at your school.

We can bring our mobile phones to school, We can bring our own lunch, We are allowed to wear cool clothes, We are allowed to ride our bikes to school, ...	but we	must ... have to ... can't ... must not ... are not allowed to ... don't have to ... ...

Silent letters

5a
audio 2/3

Listen to the words and repeat them.

talk · answer · listen · write · knife · Wednesday · knee · half · mustn't

5b

Copy the words. Then listen again and circle the letters you do not hear.

Dress code

6a workbook p. 42/5a

Look at the picture. What do you think the children are thinking or saying? Write down your ideas and share them in class.

6b audio 2/4, workbook p. 42/5b

Listen to Ava, Tarek and Lily. What are they talking about?

6c CHOOSE YOUR LEVEL skill: listening p. 151

I Listen again. Match the sentence parts. Then write down the sentences.

1 Lily is in trouble
2 Usually Tarek doesn't get into trouble
3 Ava doesn't like the dress code
4 Tarek was in trouble last week

A because he ran in the school building.
B because she wants to express her style.
C because he always wears the correct school uniform at school.
D because her skirt was too short.

II Listen again. Are the following statements true or false? Correct the false statements.

1 Lily is in trouble because she was late.
2 Tarek wants to choose his own shoes to wear to school.
3 Ava thinks it's good that everybody looks the same.
4 The students are allowed to wear jewellery.
5 Tarek wants long hair.
6 Tarek was in trouble because he was late for a lesson.

III Listen again and answer the questions.

1 Why did Lily get into trouble?
2 What does Lily think about the school uniform?
3 Why do the teachers think that school uniforms are a good idea?
4 What do the school rules say about jewellery?
5 What do the school rules say about hair?
6 What happened to Tarek last week?

LAND & LEUTE 4 video 7, workbook p. 42/6-7

Schuluniformen

In Großbritannien tragen die Schülerinnen und Schüler an fast allen Schulen Schuluniformen. Es gibt allerdings Ausnahmen. An einigen Schulen gibt es den *Casual Friday*, das heißt, dass man am Freitag etwas lässiger gekleidet sein darf. Manchmal gilt das allerdings nur für die älteren Schülerinnen und Schüler. Auch für Wohltätigkeitsprojekte gibt es uniformlose Tage: Man spendet etwas Geld für einen guten Zweck und darf dafür dann seine Privatkleidung tragen.

Sieh dir das Video an. Findest du, dass Schuluniformen eine gute Sache sind?

Talking about problems

7a

Talk about the pictures.
What can you see?
What do you think the problems are?

You can say:
Tarek's dad is …
Harry and Lily look …
I think …

7b

audio 2/5, skill: listening p. 151, workbook p. 43/8

Listen to the dialogues.
Which one goes with which picture?

7c

wordbank: describing people p. 168, workbook p. 43/9-10

How do you think the children and their parents feel?

angry · sad · tired · annoyed · worried · scared · happy · relaxed · …

Family problems

8 CHOOSE YOUR LEVEL skill: writing p. 153, wordbank: talking about conflicts p. 165, workbook p. 44/11

I Look at the picture.
What do you think Dad and Joshua are thinking or saying?
Write down your ideas.

stop watching TV · too much · too late · only five more minutes · not tired

II Look at the picture.
What do you think Mum and the children are thinking or saying?
Write a dialogue.

III Look at the picture.
What do you think Ava, Noah and Mum are saying?
Write a dialogue in which they find a solution to the problem.

Rules, rules, rules

9 CHOOSE YOUR TASK wordbank: rules p. 164, workbook p. 45/12

A Draw or make signs for rules at home or in a friendship that are important to you. Then tell your class about them.
B Write a list of rules for your dream school.
C Make a poster with rules for a pet. They can be silly or funny.

C

Rules for Ollie

1. Ollie may borrow Ava's skateboard, but he has to ask first.
2. Ollie mustn't sleep in Ava's bed.
3. Ollie is only allowed to eat spaghetti on Wednesdays.
4. Ollie must

Ava's diary

10a

What is a diary? Why do you think people write a diary? Share your ideas in class.

10b skill: reading p. 154

Read Ava's diary entry. How does she feel?

Wednesday 7th February

Why can't I do what I want? *Mum always knows better.*
I've got some cool new jeans, but Mum says I'm not allowed to wear them to Dad's birthday party. And I'm not allowed to wear make-up.
Everybody else can use their phone until ten. I can't. Mum says I must be in bed by half past nine. ***Rules, rules, rules!*** *That's all we have in this house!* ***I hate them!!!***
And I always have to be home by seven. Then there is homework! I'm not allowed to listen to music or check my phone while I'm doing it. And I have to finish it before I can go out or play with Ollie.
On Saturday we are having a family meeting to discuss when Noah and I have to be at home at the weekend. I hope Dad is on our side. Sometimes he's not as strict as Mum.

10c

Look at the words in the box. Which of these topics does Ava write about in her diary entry?

clothes · music · make-up · holidays · homework · pets · going out · friends · TV · phone · ...

10d CHOOSE YOUR LEVEL workbook p. 46/13

I Unscramble the sentences and write them down.

1 she can't do – Ava is angry – what she wants. – because
2 to her – wear her new jeans – Ava is not allowed to – dad's birthday party.
3 in bed – Ava - by half past nine. – must be
4 is not – stay out – until ten. – allowed to – Ava

II Are the sentences true or false? Correct the false sentences and write them down.

1 Ava is really happy because she can wear her cool new jeans to her dad's birthday party.
2 Ava is not allowed to wear make-up.
3 Ava can send text messages to her friends after ten o'clock in the evening.
4 Ava's parents say that she should listen to music while doing her homework.
5 Ava must finish her homework before she can play with Ollie.

III Write down all the rules for Ava you can find in her diary entry.

The family meeting

11a

The Kogans are having their family meeting. What do you think: what do Ava and Noah want?

11b audio 2/6, skill: reading p. 154

Listen to the dialogue and read along. Do Ava and Noah get what they want?

Dad: OK everyone, welcome to today's family meeting. Our first point is: when do Ava and Noah have to be home at the weekends?
Ava: Seven o'clock for me and eight o'clock for Noah is much too early. All my friends are allowed to stay out till eight and I can't. That's not fair! Harry and Lily can even ...
Noah: And Tim is allowed to stay out till nine on Friday and Saturday!
Mum: Don't interrupt your sister, please.
Ava: But he's right. Why do we have to be home so early? We're not babies anymore.
Mum: Your dad and I think that you're still too young to stay out so late. And last Saturday Noah wasn't even on time! I don't think we should change the rules.
Ava: That's stupid! I was always on time!
Dad: Ava!
Ava: Sorry.
Noah: What about trying something: Ava and I come home on time and stick to all our family rules for two weeks. If that works, I can stay out till nine and Ava till eight on Fridays and Saturdays.
Ava: Yes, please! I think that's a good idea.
Mum: Wait, wait, wait. Not so fast!
Dad: I think that's quite a good suggestion. What about trying it for a month?
Mum: Well, OK. I think I can live with that.
Noah and Ava: Yay!
Dad: OK then. Point two: Joshua's room ...

11c

Look at the rules for a family meeting. Did the Kogans stick to the rules? Say why / why not.

1. Listen to each other.
2. Be polite.
3. Do not interrupt each other.

Teenager rules

12 skill: mediation p. 155, workbook p. 46/14

A friend from England is at your house. He or she does not understand the sign on your older brother's door. Tell him or her what the sign says in English.

MEIN ZIMMER – MEINE REGELN!

- ***Frag erst***, *bevor du etwas aus meinem Zimmer nimmst!*
- *Kleine Geschwister dürfen das Zimmer* ***nur in Begleitung eines Erwachsenen*** *betreten.*
- *Bitte vor dem Betreten des Zimmers* ***klopfen****! (Am Wochenende die Tür* ***NICHT vor 10:00*** *öffnen!!!!)*

Dad, can I …?

13 grammar: modal verbs p. 183, workbook p. 46/15

Match the boy's questions to his dad's answers.

Dad, can I …?

Dad, may I …?

Yes, but …

… watch TV after ten?
… do my homework later?
… wear my cool new jeans?
… meet some friends at the park?

… not today. You can meet them on Saturday.
… not for Grandma's birthday.
… not a horror film.
… do it before you go out.

Asking questions

14 CHOOSE YOUR LEVEL grammar: simple present p. 178

I Copy the questions into your exercise book. Find the matching answers and write them down.

1 When do I have to be at home?
2 Am I allowed to watch TV until 10pm?
3 Can I play computer games now?
4 Why can't I wear make-up?

A Because we think that you are too young
B No, you can't. You have to do your homework first.
C At nine o'clock.
D No, you're not. That's too late.

II Write down the six questions. Answer three or more of them.

Do you have to
Are you allowed to

look after a pet?
stay up late at the weekend?
be at home before nine o'clock?
finish your homework before you meet friends?
watch TV for as long as you want?

III Read the answers. Then write a question for each answer and copy the answers.

1 No, I can't. My mum says I have to be home at six o'clock.
2 No, I'm not. My parents say I'm too young.
3 Yes, I do. I have to empty the dishwasher.
4 No, I don't. My dad does it.
5 Yes, I am. But I have to wear a helmet.
6 Yes, I can. But only on Fridays and Saturdays.

DIGITAL+ practise more 10

A family meeting TARGET TASK

15 workbook p. 47/16, wordbank: talking about conflicts p. 165, skill: performing a scene p. 159, media worksheet 5, 6

**Your task is to do a role play of a family meeting.
Before you start, look at the following steps:**

STEP 1

Work in groups of three or four.

STEP 2

**Plan your role play.
What is the reason for your family meeting?
Think about:**

- a conflict between the children in the family
- the family rules
- chores
- problems at school
- ...

The children all want their own smartphone.

**Who takes part in the family meeting?
What are their opinions?
Think of different arguments.**

Dad is against smartphones for children. Mum is not sure.

What could be a solution? Think about:

- a compromise
- a new family rule
- ...

Solution: only one hour per day, not too expensive, ...

STEP 3

**What could the family members say?
Make notes for each family member.**

Child 1:
Why can't we ...?
I think ...

Dad:
Oh no!
I don't think ...

Mum:
But couldn't we ...?
Maybe ...

STEP 4

Decide who is playing which role.

STEP 5

**First practise your role play, then present it.
You can present it as an audio recording or a video clip or you can act it out in class.**

Tips for a great day out

1a workbook p. 48/1

Look at the flyers. What can you see? Talk about the photos in class.

1b

Which place do you find most interesting? Why?

1

BRITISH WILDLIFE CENTRE

Discover Britain's wildlife!

Discover British wildlife at the British Wildlife Centre all year round!

From foxes, deer and red squirrels to fish and birds there is a whole world of wildlife waiting for you just 25 miles away from London!

Go to our website before your visit. There you can find a map, animal feeding times, and much more information.

Please note:

- You can book tickets online.
- Do not feed the animals.
- Parking is free.
- Open from 10am every day. Closed 25 December.

2

Welcome to Southwold Beach!

THE place for family fun

Please help us to keep the beach safe and beautiful. Here are our beach rules:

- No swimming in the sea when there are red flags.
- Swim between the blue flags.
- Parents must watch their children in the water at all times.
- Take your rubbish with you when you leave.
- Respect other beach visitors.
- No fires or barbecues allowed.
- No dogs on the beach from May to October.
- No glass bottles on the beach.
- No loud music.

Please make sure that you use enough sun cream!

3

HALDON FOREST

LOTS TO DISCOVER!

Haldon Forest Park is just 15 minutes from Exeter by car. With miles of paths for walkers, runners, cyclists and horse riders, there's something for everyone.

ACTIVITIES:

→ **Nordic walking** – 1 hour tours start from the information point at 10am, Wed–Sun.

→ **Horse riding** – Book a tour on our website before your visit.

→ You can **hire bikes** at the information point every day, from 10am to 6pm.

→ Hungry? You can get fresh sandwiches and cakes at our **Forest Café** daily from 9am to 6pm.

→ **Dogs** on a lead **are welcome**.

4

THE COUNTRYSIDE IS FOR EVERYONE
Beautiful forests and moors invite you to explore and enjoy the amazing countryside just 90 minutes from London by train.

There are some rules for your visit:
- Keep dogs on a lead.
- Don't touch the wild animals and don't feed them.
- Take your rubbish away with you.
- The weather might change suddenly, so make sure to bring appropriate clothes!
- No fires or barbecues allowed.
- Camping is allowed – but at campsites only.
- Close gates behind you.

Take nothing but photographs!
Leave nothing but footprints!

1c CHOOSE YOUR LEVEL skill: reading p. 154, workbook p. 48/2-3

I Read the first two flyers. Are the statements true or false?

1 You can see foxes at the Wildlife Centre.
2 The Wildlife Centre hasn't got a website.
3 You are allowed to feed the animals.
4 Visitors have to pay for parking at the Wildlife Centre.
5 You are not allowed to swim between the blue flags at Southwold Beach.
6 You mustn't take your dog to the beach between May and October.

II Read the first three flyers. Are the statements true or false? Correct the false statements and write them down.

1 There are no red squirrels at the Wildlife Centre.
2 You can find information about animal feeding times at the Wildlife Centre's website.
3 Parking at the Wildlife Centre costs £1.50.
4 Parents don't have to look after their children at Southwold Beach.
5 Bikes are not allowed in Haldon Forest.
6 At Haldon Forest you can buy fresh sandwiches at the Forest Café every day from 9am to 6pm.

III Read the flyers. Answer the questions.

1 What can you find on the Wildlife Centre's website?
2 When are dogs not allowed at Southwold beach?
3 What do you have to do if you want to try Nordic walking at Haldon Forest?
4 What do you have to do if you bring your dog to the New Forest?
5 What should you do if you see wild animals at the New Forest?
6 Where can you go camping at the New Forest?

Places in your area

2 workbook p. 48/4-5

Are there any places like the ones on the flyers in your area? Talk about them in class.

GRAMMAR HELP word order in statements (R) p. 185

Du hast schon gelernt, dass Subjekt, Verb und Objekt in englischen Aussagesätzen immer in einer bestimmten Reihenfolge stehen. Wie ist es mit Orts- und Zeitangaben? Sieh dir die Beispielsätze an. Was fällt dir auf?

You can discover British wildlife at the British Wildlife Centre all year round.
Visitors mustn't bring dogs to the beach between May and October.

Parents must watch their children in the water at all times.
You can get fresh sandwiches at our Forest Café from 9am to 6pm.

Auf Seite 185 findest du weitere Informationen zur Wortstellung in englischen Aussagesätzen.

Where and when?

3 grammar: word order in statements p. 185

Unscramble the sentences and write them down.

1 next weekend – to the zoo – Let's go – .
2 to the British Wildlife Centre – went – We – last Saturday – .
3 can go – next week – on a day out – to the New Forest – The students – .
4 at the gate – meeting – We're – at 10am – our tour guide – .
5 the tickets – buy – I – before we leave – have to – online – .
6 at campsites only – and October – are allowed to – You – go camping – between May – .

Park rules

4 grammar: modal verbs p. 183, workbook p. 50/6-7

Fill in the gaps with the words from the box and write down the rules.

mustn't · are allowed to · must

1 You ??? feed the animals.
It is not good for them.
2 You ??? take your dog with you but it ??? be on a lead.
3 No cars in the park! You ??? leave your car in the car park.
4 You ??? take all your rubbish with you.
5 You ??? stay on the paths.
6 You ??? have a barbecue.

How to say *oo*

5a audio 2/8

Listen and repeat.

food · good · door · afternoon · look · choose · cook · zoo · book · floor · foot

5b

Listen again.
Copy the table and make three lists.

/uː/	/ʊ/	/ɔː/
food	good	door
...	...	...

5c audio 2/9, workbook p. 51/8

Listen and check your lists.

DIGITAL+ practise more 11

ACTIVATE PRACTISE DEVELOP PRACTISE APPLY

A field trip

6a

Look at the text. What kind of text is it? A postcard? A text message? A letter? Explain your answer.

6b skill: reading p. 154

Read the text.
Who is Mr Patel writing to?
Why is he writing?

Holland Park School
Airlie Gardens, Campden Hill Rd
London W8 7AF

To: Year 8 parents

Dear parents,
I'm writing to inform you about our field trip to the British Wildlife Centre on 25th March.
The trip costs £15 for each student.
We are leaving by bus from the school's car park at 8am and are coming back at 6pm.
Please make sure that your child is wearing appropriate clothes (no school uniform, warm jacket, good shoes for walking).
All students must bring a packed lunch and something to drink (no glass bottles, please).
Please return the permission slip and pay the £15 by 15th March.
We cannot take any students without payment and written permission!
I am looking forward to an interesting and educational trip!

Yours sincerely,
R. Patel

6c CHOOSE YOUR LEVEL skill: reading p. 154

I Read again and match the sentence parts. Write down the sentences.

1 The year 8 students are
2 They are visiting
3 The bus leaves
4 They have to

A from the school's car park.
B wear appropriate clothes.
C the British Wildlife Centre.
D going on a field trip.

II Read again and complete the sentences.

1 The year 8 students are visiting the ??? on ???.
2 They are going there by ???.
3 The parents have to ??? that their children are wearing ???.
4 They have to bring ??? and ???.
5 ??? are not allowed.

III Read again and answer the questions. Write down full sentences.

1 Where and when are the year 8 students going on their field trip?
2 How long is the field trip?
3 What are appropriate clothes?
4 What do the students have to bring for the trip?
5 What do the parents have to do?

At the Wildlife Centre

7a

Look at the pictures. What do you think: what is the guide talking about?

7b audio 2/10

Now listen and read along. Who is Polly?

Katy: Welcome to the British Wildlife Centre! I'm Katy, your guide today. My job is to look after the animals here.
I'd like to tell you about animals in Britain and how you can protect them. Here at the centre we have over forty different species, for example foxes, squirrels and birds.
Today we are looking at our hedgehogs and bees, starting with the hedgehogs. This way, please.
This is our hedgehog Polly! We found her near a busy road and brought her to the Wildlife Centre. Cars are often a problem for hedgehogs, and it's also difficult for hedgehogs to find places to live and enough to eat. Especially in winter, they need a safe place where they can sleep. If you have a garden, you can leave areas with long grass and dry leaves for them. Or you can build a hedgehog house – you only need wood, a hammer and some nails.
Harry: That sounds fun!
Katy: You can also leave food outside for hedgehogs – cat or dog food is perfect! But you must not give them milk. They only drink water. But let's have a look at the bees now. OK, here we are. Here's a question for you: what do bees need?
Ava: Food!
Lily: Water!
Katy: Correct, they need food and water and also ... a place to live! These boxes here are our "bee hotels". There are over 20,000 bee species in the world. Only seven of them are honeybees. In the UK we have about 270 species. Only one of them produces honey.

Some bees live in trees, some build nests in the ground. Did you know that bees are very important for us? They help to pollinate the plants we need for food.
Unfortunately, they are in danger, too, for example because we destroy the places where they can live. We help by building homes for them and by growing lots of bee-friendly plants. At home you can make your own bee hotel for your garden.
Tarek: I don't have a garden, I live in a flat.
Katy: You can still grow bee-friendly plants in flower pots. That helps, too!
OK, so we've talked about how you can help bees and hedgehogs. And there's much more you can do. We've got some activity sheets with ideas for your own mini projects. You can take some home later.

7c skill: reading p. 154

Read again. Answer the questions.

1 What is Katy's job? What does she do?
2 How many different species are there at the Wildlife Centre?
3 What animals does Katy show the children?
4 What do hedgehogs need in winter?
5 Why shouldn't you give hedgehogs milk?
6 How many bee species are there in the world?
7 Why are bees important for us?
8 How can you help bees?

7d CHOOSE YOUR LEVEL workbook p. 52/9

I Read again. What do you learn about hedgehogs from the text? Take notes on:

- why they need help
- what they eat and drink
- how you can help them
- …

II Read again. What do you learn about bees from the text? Take notes on:

- what they need
- how many species there are in the world and in the UK
- why they are in danger
- how you can help them
- …

III Read again. What do you learn about bees and hedgehogs from the text? Take notes. Include information on what the dangers for the animals are and how you can help them.

7e skill: mediation p. 155

An English friend wants to know what the flyer says. Tell him or her in English.

You can say:
The flyer is about …
They need …
You can … or …
…

Die Igelstation braucht eure Hilfe!

Unsere Igelstation kümmert sich jedes Jahr um etwa 350 Igel, die bei uns abgegeben werden, und sucht noch Helferinnen und Helfer.
So könnt ihr helfen:

- Eine Igelstation zu führen kostet Geld, z. B. für Futter, Wasser, Tierarzt usw. Jede Spende ist daher sehr willkommen!
- Die Igel brauchen auch hilfsbereite Menschen, die sich um sie kümmern. Wenn ihr helfen wollt, die Igel zu füttern oder dafür zu sorgen, dass sie gut durch den Winter kommen, dann meldet euch bei p.schmidt@igelstation.de.

Am Samstag, dem 1. Oktober, bieten wir in unserer Igelstation eine Infoveranstaltung und Führung an. Wir freuen uns auf euren Besuch!

LAND & LEUTE 5 video 8

Tiere an der britischen Küste

Im Vereinigten Königreich bekommt man vor allem an der Küste viele Tiere zu sehen, die man dort vielleicht nicht unbedingt erwartet hätte – zum Beispiel Delfine, Schildkröten und Haie.

Bottlenose dolphins (Tümmler) werden regelmäßig im Moray Firth in Schottland, in Wales und in Cornwall gesichtet. Sie leben in kleinen Gruppen von bis zu 15 Tieren. Jedes Tier hat eine unverwechselbare Rückenflosse. Hobbybeobachter können oft einzelne Tiere wiedererkennen.

Harbour porpoises (gewöhnliche Schweinswale) tauchen vergleichsweise häufig an der Küste des Vereinigten Königreichs auf. Wenn man nah genug an sie herankommt, kann man ihr charakteristisches Schnaufen hören.

Leatherback turtles (Lederschildkröten) lassen sich seltener beobachten, aber zwischen Mai und September kann man sie manchmal an der Westküste entdecken. Diese Riesenschildkröten können dank einer Fettschicht auch in kälterem Wasser leben und legen weite Entfernungen zurück. Sie können bis zu 1200 Meter tief tauchen und ernähren sich hauptsächlich von Quallen. In den Gewässern des Vereinigten Königreichs gibt es sogar über 40 verschiedene Arten von Haien, unter anderem den *basking shark* (Riesenhai), den zweitgrößten Fisch der Welt.

Sieh dir den Videoclip an.
Was findest du überraschend?

Wildlife

8 CHOOSE YOUR TASK wordbank: wildlife p. 166, C: skill: searching the Internet p. 157, media worksheet 4, workbook p. 52/10-11

A **Do you know about a project for animals in your area? Find out more about it and tell your class.**

B **Make a flyer for a tour of the British Wildlife Centre with Katy.**

C **Find out more about animals in the sea around the UK. Choose one animal and tell your class about it in three to five sentences.**

Animals in Britain

9 GET TOGETHER

Get together with a partner.
Talk about animals in Britain.

Partner A	Partner B
I Go to page 129.	I Go to page 138.
II Go to page 132.	II Go to page 141.
III Go to page 135.	III Go to page 144.

A mini project

10a

Look at the pictures. What are the instructions for?

HOW TO MAKE YOUR OWN BIRD FEEDER

What you need:
- birdseed
  or nuts
  or dried fruit

- hard fat
- a coconut half or a yoghurt pot
- string

What to do:
1. Mix the food together in a bowl.

2. Put everything inside the coconut half or the yoghurt pot.

3. Hang your feeder where you can watch the birds while they enjoy their food.

10b

skill: mediation p. 155

Your little sister wants to make a bird feeder. Answer her questions in German.

1 Wieso sind da Bilder von einer Kokosnuss und einem Joghurtbecher?
2 Was brauche ich denn alles?
3 Was muss ich mischen?
4 Wo soll man die Futterstation hinhängen?

A Notting Hill environment project

11a

Look at the picture. Where are the children? What do you think they are doing?

11b

audio 2/11, skill: listening p. 151, workbook p. 53/12

Listen to the interview. What do Tarek and Lily tell the reporter about the children's project?

Garden arts and crafts

12 CHOOSE YOUR LEVEL skill: reading p. 154, workbook p. 54/13

I Read the sentences and copy them in the right order.

A To finish your hedgehog house, put some dry grass and leaves inside and cover it with earth.
B To make a hedgehog house, you need: wood, hammer, nails.
C Then put the house in a quiet place in your garden.
D First, build a small house out of the wood.

II Read the sentences and copy them in the right order.

A Find a good place to put your insect hotel and hang it up in a tree or on a wall.
B Build a box out of the wood.
C The box should be at least 10cm long.
D To make an insect hotel, you need: wood, hammer, nails, dry leaves, string.
E Fill your box with dry leaves and dry grass etc.

III Read the sentences and copy them in the right order.

A The next morning, you can take your ice decoration off the plate and hang it up in the garden or on your balcony.
B Then put the plate outside overnight (or in the freezer if it is not cold enough outside).
C Put water on the plate over the leaf or flower.
D To make ice decorations, you need plates, water, dry leaves and dry flowers.
E Put one leaf or one flower on a plate.

A spelling exercise

13a audio 2/12

Listen to the words and repeat them.

13b

Listen again and write down the words.

13c skill: working with words p. 150, workbook p. 54/14

How do you spell the words? What do you notice? Talk to a partner.

DIGITAL+ practise more 12

Our environment brochure TARGET TASK

14 workbook p. 55/15, wordbank: wildlife p. 166, skill: writing p. 153, media worksheet 3, 4

Your task is to create a page for an environment brochure with ideas for mini projects. Before you start, look at these steps:

STEP 1
In class, collect ideas for mini projects that help the environment.

STEP 2
Decide which project you would like to write about.
You can work alone, with a partner or in a group.

STEP 3
Collect information on your project.
You can use the information from your book, ask an expert, do research on the Internet, go to the library, …
Think about:
- why the project is good for the environment
- where you can do the project (do you have to ask anyone for permission?)
- what you need
- …

STEP 4
Create your page. You can add pictures or photos.

STEP 5
Put all your pages together in a brochure.
You can publish it on your school's website if you like.

Check out

Kannst du Schulregeln verstehen?	Workbook, p. 56
Kannst du deine Meinung zu Regeln formulieren?	Workbook, p. 56
Kannst du die Beschriftung eines deutschen Schildes auf Englisch wiedergeben?	Workbook, p. 56
Kannst du Flyer zu Ausflugszielen verstehen?	Workbook, p. 57
Kannst du einem Brief wichtige Informationen entnehmen?	Workbook, p. 57
Kannst du ein gehörtes Interview zusammenfassen?	Workbook, p. 57

In the dragon's cave

"Shirook, fly lower!" Kora shouted. "Ready, Ari? One, two, three!" She pulled REALLY hard.
"Ooof!" she said, as Ari landed on Shirook's back. "You're heavy, Ari!"
Ari started to cry. "I … was … so … scared!"

"It's OK, Ari," said Kora. "You're safe now."
Shirook landed near the cave. Kora and Ari got off her back, and Kora gave her brother a hug.
"Are you OK?" she asked.
Ari nodded.
"You have to be really quiet now, OK?
The dragon is probably close. You mustn't make any sudden movements. And you mustn't shout or talk too loudly, OK? Stay here and be quiet!"
"Yes, Kora," said Ari in a quiet voice.
Then Kora saw something near the cave.
"Ari, look," she whispered. "Dragon footprints!"
Ari came to look too. "Wow, they're really cool!" he said.

Kora went quietly into the cave. It was warm inside. And dark. She turned on the torch on her dragon tamer's watch and looked around. It was a huge cave and there were two paths – one on the left and one on the right.
She didn't know which way to go. So she opened the Detect-A-Dragon app on her watch. It quickly detected the dragon.
She took the path on the right. She walked really slowly and really softly.

fly lower = *tiefer fliegen;* pull = *ziehen;* sudden movements = *plötzliche Bewegungen;* turn on the torch = *die Taschenlampe anschalten*

Most dragons don't like sudden movements or loud noises. Maybe this dragon was the same …
Kora saw pieces of egg shell on the floor – big pieces! What a huge egg! Maybe the dragon had eggs for breakfast, she thought.
Suddenly, Kora heard a loud noise. HMMMM-BRRRRRR. HMMMM-BRRRRRR. Dragon snores!
She followed the sound and soon found the dragon. It was asleep. Smoke came out of its nose with each snore.

Really quietly, she put some chillies and kiwi fruit down on the ground in front of the dragon – a small dragon-taming present. Lots of New Zealand dragons love kiwi fruit, and all dragons love chillies! Then she sat down to wait for it to wake up.
Kora's heart beat really fast. To make her feel less scared, she made up a rhyme in her head:

Little dragon, big snores,
green body, big claws.
Long tail, no name,
attacking others, not tame!

DIGITAL+ You can listen to Kora's little rhyme: audio 3/19

Suddenly, there was a loud noise in the cave. RING-RING! RING-RING!
It was Kora's phone. She quickly got it out of her pocket. Blaze's face was on the screen – but this was NOT the time for a phone call! She quickly pressed the red button. Finally, everything was quiet. No more ringing. But also … no more dragon snores!

DIGITAL+ You can listen to Blaze's voicemail message: audio 3/20

She looked up from her phone … and saw two yellow eyes. The dragon was awake.
Kora didn't move. "Ma nominaadraa hes Kora," she said quietly. "Ent taa?"
But the dragon didn't tell Kora its name. It just looked at her. Then it moved its big tail.
SWOOOSH! It hit Kora hard.
She flew through the air. "Aah!"
She landed with a BUMP on the other side of the cave. Her arm hit the floor. CRACK! Everything went dark. Kora looked at her dragon tamer's watch. No torch. She tried to turn the watch on.
Nothing.
And then she heard something. Footsteps. Dragon footsteps.

attack = *angreifen*; beat = *schlagen*; claw = *Klaue*; footstep = *Schritt*; noise = *Geräusch*; shell = *Schale*; tail = *Schwanz*

Don't

DIGITAL+ video 9

Why do people say "don't" so much,
Whenever you try something new?
It's more fun doing than don'ting
So why don't people say "do"?

Don't slurp your spaghetti
Don't kiss your cat
Don't butter your fingers
Don't walk like that

Don't wash your books
Don't bubble your tea
Don't jump on your sister
Don't goggle at me

Don't climb up the curtains
Don't feed the chair
Don't sleep in the wardrobe
Don't cut off your hair

Don't draw on the pillow
Don't change all the clocks
Don't water the phone
Don't hide my socks

Don't cycle upstairs
Don't write on the eggs
Don't chew your pyjamas
Don't paint your legs

Oh, why do people say "don't" so much,
Whenever you try something new?
It's more fun doing than don'ting
So why don't people say "do"?

Richard Edwards

Listen to the poem and read along.
Do you like it? Say why or why not.
Find the ryhyming words and write them down.
Write your own "Don't" verse, learn it by heart and present your version of the poem.
You can also make a short video if you like.

4

1 What can you see in the picture? Collect words.
2 What do you think: what are the children's ideas about their futures?
3 What do you think: what is important to the children?

The future

Part A My dreams

- Du lernst, über die Zukunft und über Zukunftsträume zu sprechen.
- Du beschäftigst dich mit Berufswünschen.
- Du präsentierst deine Ideen über die Zukunft.

Part B Stories

- Du liest die Geschichte *Kate and Jonathan's adventure*.
- Du lernst, wie du eigene Texte lebendiger und interessanter machen kannst.
- Du schreibst eine eigene kurze Geschichte.

A time capsule project

1a workbook p.58/1

Look at the flyer. What is the project about?

1b

Read the flyer. What is a time capsule?

What will the future bring?
What are your dreams?

TAKE PART IN OUR SCIENCE MUSEUM TIME CAPSULE PROJECT!

????

What do you think: what will life be like in 20 years' time?
What will the world look like?
What are your dreams for the future?

The Science Museum is inviting children between 6 and 14 to take part in our project.

Write about, draw, paint, film, ... your ideas about the future. How will we live, work, eat, learn, travel, ...?

We will show your works at the museum until 10 December. Then we will choose 15 of them that will stay at the museum after the exhibition.

We will then put these 15 works in a time capsule and there will be a public opening of the capsule in 20 years.

Please hand in your work by 26 May either online or at the museum!

Ideas about the future

2a

Look at the picture. What is Lily doing?

2b audio 2/15

Listen and read along. What jobs do the children talk about?

Ava: Hi Lily, what are you doing?
Lily: Hi guys. I am working on a collage for this project.
Tarek: What project?
Lily: It's a project at the Science Museum about children's ideas about life in the future. You can hand in a drawing, a film, a poem, a story, whatever you like. There'll be an exhibition and they'll keep 15 works in a time capsule at the museum.
Ava: And what happens with the capsule?
Lily: In 20 years, there will be a public opening. You leave your email address with them and the museum will contact you and invite you to the opening.

Ava: Cool!
Harry: OK Lily, so where will you be in 20 years? Still in this room? Haha ...
Lily: Very funny, Harry. No, I won't. I'm sure I won't be here with you anymore. I'll live in a fancy flat in New York and I'll be a famous fashion designer. What about your plans, guys?
Ava: I want to be an engineer when I grow up. I'll invent lots of useful things to help people.
Harry: I won't have a regular job: I'll be a really famous singer and play the world's biggest stages. And don't worry guys – I'll still remember you and put you on the guest lists.
Ava: Go big or go home, right?
Harry: Exactly!
Lily: Phew – as if! You can sing, Harry – but it's loud rather than good to be honest! Tarek, where will you be in 20 years?
Tarek: I'll be a famous chef! I'll be the best chef in London and have my own restaurant!
Ava: Great – and we'll be your best customers!
Harry: Yes, and I'll bring my hungry band mates after all our concerts in London!
Lily: We'll see about that ... Guys, I have a great idea: why don't you all take part in the project, too? If we're lucky, all our works will stay in the museum, and then we'll all meet at the public opening. I'll even come from New York.
Ava: That's a cool idea, Lily! But I think we should write about technology and food and houses and so on, not just our jobs. To make it more interesting, you know?
Tarek: I'll draw some food from the future!
Harry: I'll record a song. Then I can include my guitar playing!
Ava: And I'll do something about technology in the future. Brilliant!

2c CHOOSE YOUR LEVEL skill: reading p. 154

I Match the sentence parts.

1 There is a project
2 Lily is making
3 The museum will put some of the children's works
4 Lily's dream for the future

A in a time capsule and keep them for 20 years.
B at the Science Museum.
C is to be a fashion designer.
D a collage for the project.

II Complete the sentences.

1 Lily is working on a ??? for a ???.
2 The project is about children's ??? about ???.
3 The museum will keep some of the children's works in a ??? for ??? years.
4 Lily's plan is to be a ??? and live in ???.
5 Ava wants to be an ??? in 20 years.
6 Harry won't have a ???.

III Write about the children's ideas about the jobs they want to have when they grow up.

You can write:
Ava wants to be an … when she grows up because …
Tarek's dream job is …

2d workbook p. 59/2-3

Would you like to take part in a time capsule project? Say why or why not.

GRAMMAR HELP the will-future: statements p. 186

Wenn du über die Zukunft sprechen möchtest, kannst du das *will-future* verwenden. Sieh dir die Beispielsätze an. Wie würdest du die Sätze auf Deutsch formulieren? Was fällt dir auf?

There will be an exhibition.
We'll be your best customers.
I will not live here with you anymore.
I won't have a regular job.

Ab Seite 186 findest du weitere Beispiele und Erklärungen zum *will-future*.

Future jobs

3

grammar: will-future statements p. 186

Match the sentences and write them down.

1 I enjoy cooking.
2 I love music.
3 I like fancy clothes.
4 I want to invent useful things.
5 I love board games.

A You'll be a fashion designer.
B You'll be a board game designer.
C You'll be an engineer.
D You'll be a chef.
E You'll be a famous singer.

When I grow up

4a

grammar: will-future statements p. 186

Look at the pictures and write about the children's ideas for their futures.

You can write:
George thinks that he will be married and …
He won't …
…

4b

grammar: will-future statements p. 186, workbook p. 60/4

What are your ideas about your future? Write three or more sentences.

You can write:
I think I will / I won't …

How to say *v* and *w*

5a

audio 2/17

Listen and repeat the words.

wait · will · visit · very · word · version · won't · vacuum

5b

Find five or more words with *v* or *w*. Write them down and practise saying them.

DIGITAL+ practise more 13

People at work

6a

What jobs do you know? Collect words in class.

6b

Look at the photos.
What do these people do in their jobs?

You can say:
A firefighter fights fires. A police officer …

- cut and colour people's hair
- take care of ill people
- repair bikes
- help people in trouble and arrest criminals
- fight fires and help people and animals
- design computer games
- take care of ill animals
- act on a stage or in films

1

firefighter

2

police officer

3

computer game designer

4

actor / actress

5

(bike) mechanic

6

nurse

7

hairdresser

8

vet

6c CHOOSE YOUR LEVEL wordbank: jobs p. 167

I **Choose a job and collect words and phrases about it.**

II **Choose a job and write three or more sentences about it.**

III **Choose one of the people from the pictures. Imagine you are him or her and write about your job.**

You can write:
I'm a … My job is to …
In my job I … I like my job because …

6d workbook p. 60/5-6

Which of the jobs would you like to do? Which wouldn't you like to do? Say why.

An interview

7a wordbank: jobs p. 167

**Look at the picture of Mehti doing his job.
What do you think his job is?**

7b audio 2/19, skill: listening p. 151

**Listen to the podcast.
How does Mehti earn his money?**

7c skill: mediation p. 155

Your grandmother is listening to the podcast with you and does not understand the concept of unboxing. Answer her questions in German.

1 Was macht der? Der packt Sachen aus? Warum?
2 Der packt da nur Dinge aus?
3 Wer guckt denn das?
4 Warum gucken die das denn?
5 Woher bekommt der denn die ganzen Sachen?
6 Bezahlen die Firmen für gute Bewertungen?
7 Womit verdient der denn dann sein Geld?
8 Muss man dafür eine Ausbildung machen?

A job quiz

8a wordbank: jobs p. 167

Who does what? Answer the questions.

1 Who helps you when you want to buy something in a shop?
2 Who washes and cuts your hair?
3 Who looks after you when you are in a hospital?
4 Who looks after your pet when it is ill?
5 Who designs games on the computer?

You can write:

That's a shop assistant.
That's …
…

8b grammar: simple present questions (R) p. 179

Write more questions for your classmates. Ask and answer questions in class.

You can ask:

Who bakes … ?
Who …?
…

You can answer:

A baker.
A / An …
…

Our dream jobs

9a video 10, skill: watching a video clip p. 156, media worksheet 1

Watch the video clip. What are these job words in German? Which words are similar? Which are different?

chef · photographer · baker · vet · zoologist · pilot · singer · racing driver · actress

9b CHOOSE YOUR LEVEL workbook p. 61/7-9

I Watch the clip again. Match the sentence parts and write down the sentences.

1 Lewis wants to be
2 Rosa would like to be
3 Eran's dream job is to be
4 George would love to be

A a photographer or a baker.
B a pilot.
C a chef.
D a vet or a zoologist.

II Watch the clip again and take notes. Then write about four or more of the children.

Lewis Rosa Eran George Joe Maria Zoe	wants to be a / an would like to be a / an	photographer or a baker. chef. ...

III Who wants to have which job? Why? Watch the clip again and take notes. Then write about the children.

Lewis · Rosa · Eran · George · Joe · Maria · Zoe

You can write:

Lewis wants to be a / an … because …
Rosa would like / love to be …
Eran's dream job is to be a / an …

Jobs

10 CHOOSE YOUR TASK A+B: wordbank: jobs p. 167, C: wordbank: Talking about the future p. 167, workbook p. 62/10

A **Make an ABC of job words.**
B **Write a short text about your dream job. Describe it and say why you would like to do it.**
C **Imagine you are an inventor in the future. What would you like to invent? Describe your invention in a short text and present it to the class.**

Joshua's questions

11a audio 2/20

Listen to Joshua and Ava. What are they talking about?

11b CHOOSE YOUR LEVEL skill: listening p. 151, workbook p. 63/11

I Listen again. Match Ava's answers to Joshua's questions.

1 What will you be when you grow up?
2 Will you invent really cool things?
3 Will you still need your skateboard?
4 Where will you work?

A Of course! I'll go to work on my skateboard.
B I don't know yet.
C I'll be an engineer.
D Yes, I will. I'll invent a lot of useful technology.

II Listen again. Answer the questions about Ava's and Joshua's ideas.

1 What will Ava be when she grows up?
2 Where will Ava live?
3 What will she invent?
4 How will Ava go to work?
5 Will Ava have children?
6 What pets will Joshua have?

III Listen again and take notes. Write about Ava and Joshua's ideas about their future.

You can write:

Ava will be a … She will …

…

Joshua has got lots of ideas about …

…

Tell me about your future

12a grammar: will-future questions p. 187

Write down four or more questions for an interview with a classmate.

You can write:

Will you be a film star / a hairdresser / … ?

Where will you live?

How many … will you have?

What …?

12b workbook p. 63/12-13

Work with a partner. Interview each other about your futures. Your answers can be funny.

You can answer:

Yes, I will. / No, I won't.

I will live on Mars.

I will have …

…

Lily's predictions

13a

Look at the pictures.
What are Lily's ideas about the future?

13b skill: reading p. 154

Read Lily's predictions. What does she think about school in the future?

In 20 years there won't be any more cars. People will fly solar-powered helicopters or ride their bikes.
At school the students won't have exercise books or pens and pencils anymore. They can read and write on their tablets and learn with VR glasses.
All our houses will be smart homes. The fridge will tell you when you need to go shopping and what you need to buy. You will be able to tell your kitchen what you would like for dinner and then the kitchen will cook it for you. TVs will be even bigger than today. Or maybe there won't be any TVs anymore and people will watch holograms in their living rooms.

13c workbook p. 64/14

Copy the table and sort the words from the box into categories.

no more cars · no exercise books · smart home · solar-powered helicopters · tablets · VR glasses · bikes · bigger TVs

travel	*learning*	*houses*
no more cars	*no books*	…
…	…	…

13d skill: talking with people p. 152

What do you think: Which of Lily's predictions will come true? Talk to a partner. Say why / why not.

In the future, there will be …

14a audio 2/22

Listen to the song.
Then listen again and sing along.

14b audio 2/23, workbook p. 64/15

Write your own verses for the song.

In the future, there will be a lot of robots,
lot of robots, lot of robots,
in the future, there will be a lot of robots.
Oh, the future will be wonderful!

In the future, there won't be a lot of plastic, …

In the future, I will have a flying car, …

The future

15 CHOOSE YOUR LEVEL grammar: will-future questions p. 187

I What do you think about the future?
Match the question parts and answer the questions.

1 Will robots do
2 Will we still have
3 Will people live
4 Will we all be

A vegetarians?
B on the moon?
C all our chores?
D cars?

II What do you think about the future?
Unscramble these questions and answer them.

1 be - all our homes - Will - smart homes?
2 still - Will - go to work - people - by car?
3 students - online lessons? - Will - only have
4 robots - our chores? - all - do - Will
5 live - Will - all people - in cities?

III What do you think about the future?
Unscramble these questions and answer them.

1 people - will - ? - live - where
2 how - ? - will - get - to work - people
3 in - what - will - their people - ? - do - free time
4 ? - will - what - look - shops - like
5 pay - how - we - ? - for - things - will
6 the - will - ? - we - in - eat - future - what

Odd one out

16 skill: working with words p. 150

Find the odd one out. Can you say why it is the odd one out?

1 car, bus, plane, bike
2 hairdresser, daughter, baker, photographer
3 computer, book, tablet, mobile phone
4 living room, library, science lab, cafeteria

Rhyming pairs

17a audio 2/24

Listen and repeat.

fight · worse · fill · more · earn · thing · fly · smart · nurse · will · string · learn · art · dry · door · might

17b

Find the rhyming pairs and write them down.

You can write:
fight – might
...

DIGITAL+ practise more 14

My ideas about the future TARGET TASK

18 workbook p. 65/16, wordbank: talking about the future p. 167, skill: presentations p. 158, media worksheet 3, 5, 6, 7

Your task is to present your ideas about the future.
Before you start, look at these steps:

STEP 1

What do you think?
What will the future be like?
Make notes.
You can think about:

- technology
- jobs
- food
- school
- houses
- travelling
- ...

STEP 2

Decide how you want to present your ideas.
You could:

- draw your ideas and label them
- make a collage or a poster
- write a text
- record your ideas
- film your ideas
- ...

In the future, there will be ...
There won't be any ...
Everybody will ...
I will ... in the future.
...

STEP 3

Plan your work. You can do a first draft if you like.

STEP 4

Create your poster, collage, text, ...

STEP 5

Present your work, for example in a gallery walk.

STEP 6

If you like, you can put all your work in a "class time capsule".

Kate and Jonathan's adventure – part one

1a

**Look at the pictures.
What do you think the story is about?**

1b workbook p. 66/1

Read the story. Where are Kate and Jonathan? What do they discover?

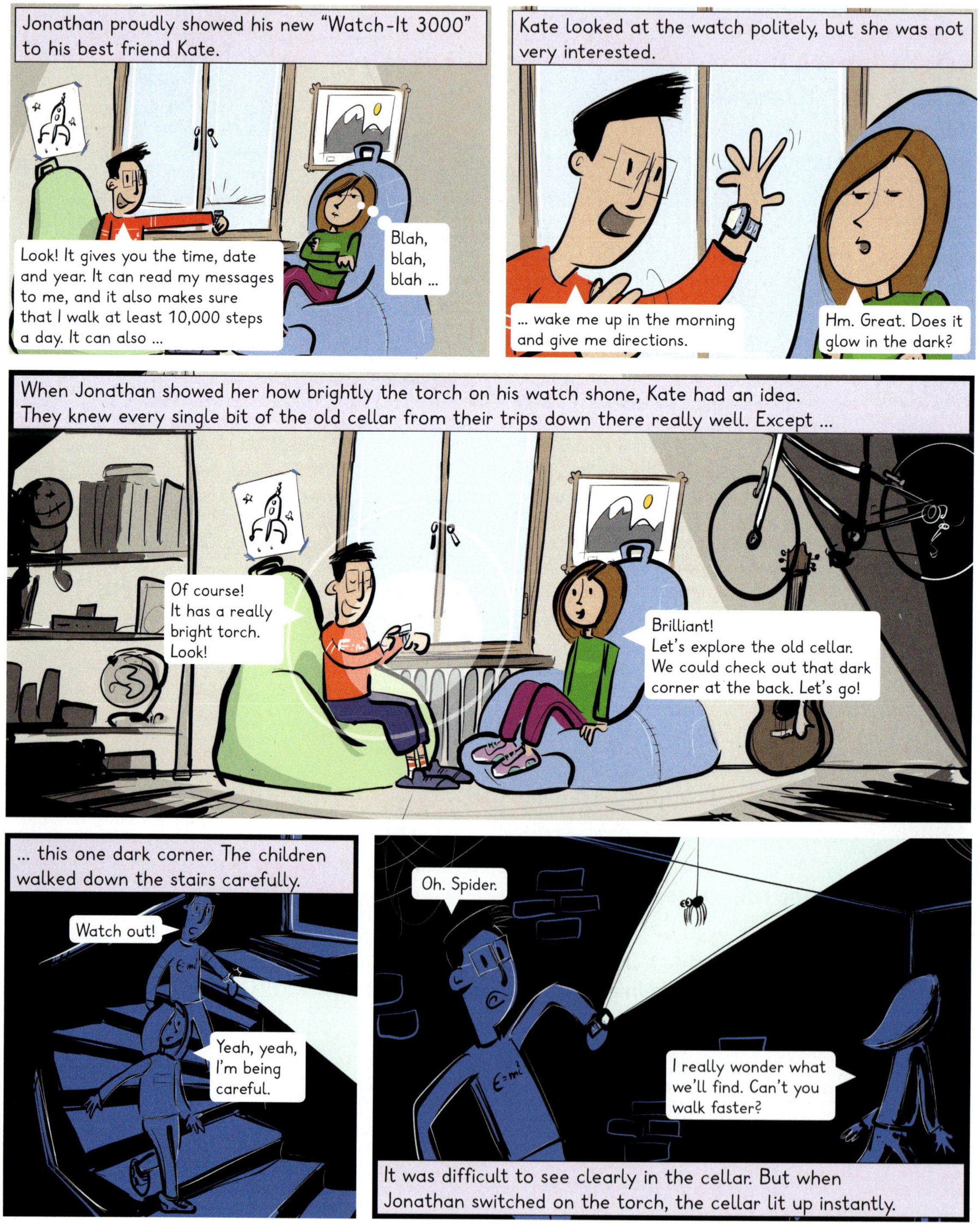

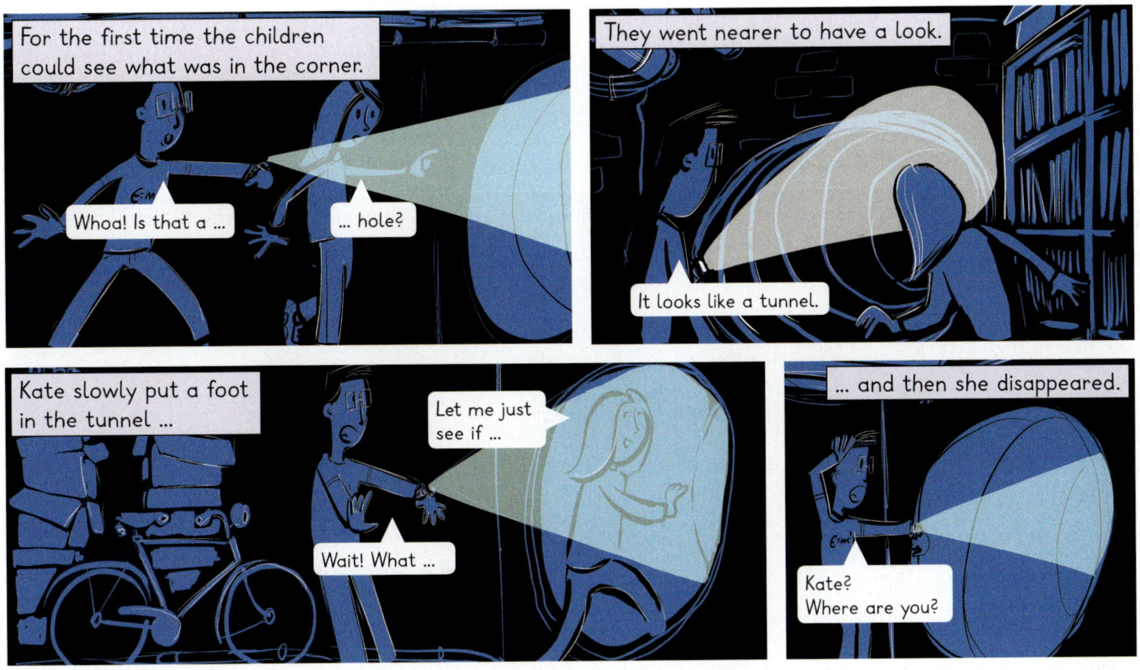

1c CHOOSE YOUR LEVEL skill: reading p. 154

I Read the story again. Complete the sentences and write them down.

1 Jonathan showed his new watch to his best ???.
2 Kate was not very ???.
3 Kate had an ???.
4 She wanted to explore ???.
5 They walked down the ???.
6 In the corner, they found a tunnel and Kate ???.

II Read the story again. Put the sentences in the right order and write them down.

A They went down there carefully.
B First, they could not see clearly in the cellar.
C At the end Kate put a foot in the tunnel and disappeared.
D Kate had the idea to explore the old cellar.
E Jonathan was really proud of his new watch.
F But then they saw a hole in the corner.

III Imagine you are Kate or Jonathan and write about what happened in the story in five or more sentences.

You can write:
First, I …

1d workbook p. 66/2-4

What do you think: what will happen next? Talk about your ideas.

You can say:
I imagine that Jonathan will go …
Maybe Kate will / won't …
…

GRAMMAR HELP adverbs of manner p.188

Du kennst bereits Adjektive zum Beschreiben von Personen, Tieren oder Sachen. Wenn du beschreiben willst, wie jemand etwas tut oder wie etwas geschieht, benutzt du ein Adverb der Art und Weise *(adverb of manner).* Vergleiche die Sätze und Wörter. Was fällt dir auf? Achte auf die Bildung der *adverbs of manner.*

The bright torch lit up the cellar.
Jonathan was very careful.

The light shone brightly.
He walked down the stairs carefully.

Einige *adverbs of manner* haben unregelmäßige Formen. Auf Seite 188 findest du mehr Informationen dazu.

What is it like?

2a grammar: adverbs of manner p.188

Make adverbs from the adjectives in the box.

careful · slow · loud · fast · happy · sad · beautiful · good · hard

You can write:
careful – carefully
loud – …

2b grammar: adverbs of manner p.188

Read the sentences and add an adverb. You can use your adverbs from 2a. There is more than one solution for each sentence.

1 The man is driving.
2 An old man is walking.
3 The dog is running.
4 The girl is singing.
5 The boys are playing.
6 The woman is working.
7 The girls are laughing.

2c grammar: adverbs of manner p.188

Write down three or more sentences with adverbs. They can be funny or silly.

You can write:
The spider is dancing happily. …

Proud or proudly?

3 grammar: adverbs of manner p.188, workbook p.68/5-6a

Choose the correct word to complete the sentences and write them down.

1 Jonathan proud / proudly presented his new watch.
2 Kate looked at Jonathan's watch polite / politely.
3 The kids walked down the stairs careful / carefully.
4 The light was bright / brightly.
5 The kids could see clear / clearly what was in the dark / darkly corner.
6 Kate slowly / slow put a foot in the tunnel.

DIGITAL+ practise more 15

Kate and Jonathan's adventure – part two

4a audio 2/26, skill: listening p. 151

Listen to the next part of the story. What do Kate and Jonathan find out about the slide inside the tunnel?

4b CHOOSE YOUR LEVEL

I Listen again. Complete the sentences and and write them in your exercise book.

1 Jonathan goes
- A up a hill.
- B down a huge slide.
- C down the river on a boat.

2 When Jonathan comes out of the tunnel
- A he sees Kate.
- B he is very wet.
- C he hasn't got his watch anymore.

3 Kate finds it all
- A really boring.
- B really scary.
- C really exciting.

4 In the end the children find out that they are
- A in another country.
- B in another time.
- C in another town.

II Listen again. Then put the sentences in the right order and copy them into your exercise book. Complete the last sentence.

A When he comes out of the tunnel he sees Kate.
B Jonathan looks at his watch.
C Jonathan follows Kate into the tunnel.
D He goes down a slide.
E In the end the children realize that they are in the ...

III Listen again and write the answers to the questions in your exercise book.

1 Why does Jonathan go into the tunnel?
2 Why does Kate want to go back to the house?
3 Why does Jonathan tell Kate to look at his watch?
4 What year is it?
5 What is special about the slide?

4c workbook p. 68/6b-7

What do you think: how do Kate and Jonathan feel during their adventure?

excited · scared · happy · bored · terrible · sick · surprised · worried · good · bad

You can say:
I think ... feels excited and a bit ... at first.
When they realize ..., they ...

Kate and Jonathan's adventure – part three

5a

**Look at the pictures.
What do you think: how will the story end?**

5b skill: reading p. 154

**Read part three of the story.
What happens to Kate and Jonathan?**

1 The children were quiet for a moment. Then they freaked out. When they were calm again, they sat down to think. Their first idea was to walk back into the tunnel and just go back in time. That did not work. There was something like a wall inside the tunnel. Then they tried to change the year on Jonathan's watch but the watch simply changed it back to 2128. In the end they realized that they needed help. They walked towards Kate's house – or rather towards what used to be Kate's house. There it really became clear to them – in the place of her old red house stood something completely different. "Oh dear. We really ARE in the future." Jonathan said. They decided to hide in the bushes and find out who lived in the house now.

2 At first nothing happened, but then the door opened and a girl came out. "She looks nice," Jonathan said. "Let's go and ask her if she can help us," Kate said. "Wait, maybe …," Jonathan started to say, but Kate was already walking towards the girl. When the girl saw Kate, she looked at her and asked, "Who are you? And what are you doing here?" "Hi," Kate said as friendly as she could. "I'm Kate. And over there is Jonathan." Jonathan came out of the bush. "This might sound really strange, but we, … we're from the past. From like a hundred years ago." The girl looked at them silently. Then she smiled. "Kate! I can't believe that you're really here! I'm Georgia. I got a letter from you. I found it and this strange thing in a corner at the back of the old cellar when we moved in. Wait, let me go get it." She ran towards the house.

3 A few minutes later, Georgia was back. She showed them the letter and a small object. "That's my grandfather's old compass," Kate said. "He gave it to me for my last birthday. But how …?"
„I found the compass and this note from you on a small piece of paper in the old cellar," Georgia said. "It explains everything. It says that you can only travel here if you are the owner of the compass or with the owner of the compass. The compass will also get you back to your time." "Oh, thank God! We can go back home," Jonathan said.

4 "Let's not go right now," Kate said. "Couldn't you tell us all about the future first, Georgia?" "Sure," Georgia replied. The children sat down and Georgia told Kate and Jonathan about solar-powered transport, smart homes and virtual teachers. The future sounded like a pretty good place, Kate and Jonathan thought. They told Georgia about the old house that used to stand on the hill, about their school and how they travelled there by bus every morning.

5 When it began to get dark, Kate and Jonathan said that they should go back. They could go back through the tunnel without any problems while they were holding the compass. A few seconds later they were back in Kate's old cellar. "OK," Jonathan said. "That was brilliant! Now we have to write that letter to Georgia and hide it together with the compass in the cellar, so that Georgia can find it in the future?" "Yes," Kate said. "And obviously it worked or we wouldn't be here. One day we should visit Georgia again. Maybe she would like to come back with us for a visit."

5c

Match the headings to the paragraphs. There are two more than you need.

Georgia's family

The robot

A letter from the past

What now?

Going home

Life in the future – what is it like?

Meeting Georgia

5d CHOOSE YOUR LEVEL workbook p. 70/8

I What happens in the first paragraph? Write about it in three sentences.

You can write:

Jonathan and Kate try to …

They … Then they decide …

II What happens in the first and second paragraphs? Write about it in no more than five sentences.

You can write:

Kate and Jonathan …

They meet … She …

III What happens in part three of the story? Write about it in no more than seven sentences.

Your opinion

6

Do you like the story? Say why or why not.

You can say:

I like / don't like the story because …

In my opinion, the story is …

The characters are …

…

The story

7 skill: mediation p. 155

Your mother asks you what you are doing in your English lessons. Tell her about the story *Kate and Jonathan's adventure* in German. Think about what happens at the beginning, in the middle and at the end.

Good style

8a wordbank: good style p. 169

Compare the two texts. Which words make the second text more interesting? Write them down.

Jonathan showed his "Watch-It 3000" to his friend Kate. Kate looked at the watch. She was not interested. Kate thought Jonathan's watch was boring. She wanted to do something exciting. "Let's go to the cellar," she said.

Jonathan proudly showed his new "Watch-It 3000" to his best friend Kate. Kate looked at the watch politely, but she was not very interested. Kate thought Jonathan's watch was terribly boring and wanted to do something exciting. "Let's go to the old cellar," she said.

8b

Explain why these words make the second text more interesting.

8c workbook p. 70/9

Look at the boxes. Find more words for each category.

people:
happy · friendly · angry · clever · ...

weather:
sunny · cold · rainy · ...

buildings:
old · red · tall · small · new · ...

actions:
quickly · carefully · slowly · ...

situations:
dangerous · funny · exciting · ...

Time travelling

9 CHOOSE YOUR TASK B: skill: writing p. 153, C: skill: performing a scene p. 159, workbook p. 70/10, media worksheet 5, 6

A **Design a time machine. Explain how it works.**
B **Write Kate's letter to Georgia.**
C **Work with a partner. Look at page 90 again and act out the first part of the story. You can record your role play if you like.**

B
Dear Georgia,
...
We're really looking forward to seeing you again in the future.
Love, Kate

Past, present or future?

10a video 11, skill: watching a video clip p. 156

Watch the video clip. How many of the children would like to travel to the future?

10b workbook p. 71/11

Watch again. What time does Archie want to travel to? Why?

10c skill: talking with people p. 152

Work with a partner. What time would you like to travel to? Interview each other.

You can ask:

What time would you like to ...?
Who would you like to meet?
What would you take with you?
What would you do there?
...

You can answer:

I would like to ...
I would ...
...

Travelling in time

11 GET TOGETHER PARTNER A: audio 2/28, PARTNER B: audio 2/29

Get together with a partner.
Listen to Hiroto and Sarah's adventures and talk about them with a partner.

Partner A	Partner B
I Go to page 129.	I Go to page 138.
II Go to page 132.	II Go to page 141.
III Go to page 135.	III Go to page 144.

LAND & LEUTE 6 video 12, workbook p. 71/12-14

Science-Fiction

Bücher und Filme, die moderne Technologien wie zum Beispiel die Raumfahrt oder Roboter, Begegnungen mit Außerirdischen, oder Maschinen mit hoher künstlicher Intelligenz zum Thema haben, nennt man *science fiction* – manchmal benutzt man auch Abkürzungen wie *sci-fi* oder *SF*.
Die ältesten Bücher dieser Art sind über 200 Jahre alt. Berühmte Autoren sind Jules Verne und H. G. Wells. H. G. Wells beschrieb schon 1895 in seinem Roman *The time machine* eine Zeitreise in die Zukunft mithilfe einer Zeitmaschine.

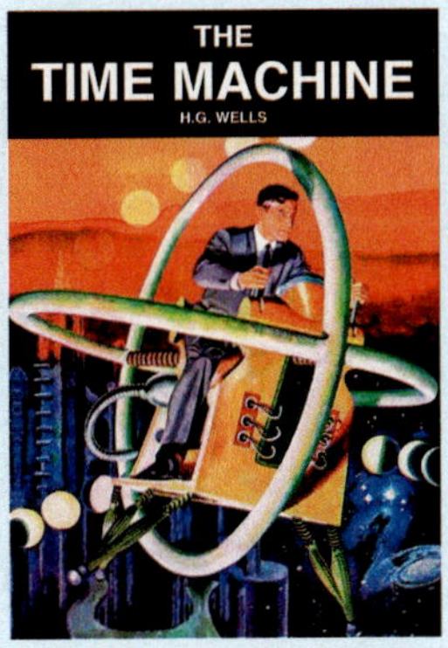

Vor allem seit den 1960er Jahren sind auch Filme zu dem Thema sehr beliebt. Besonders bekannt sind die drei Filme *Back to the future 1, 2* und *3* des Regisseurs Steven Spielberg.
In den Filmen reist ein Jugendlicher mit einem zur Zeitmaschine umgebauten Auto durch die Zeit.

Welche Science-Fiction-Filme, -Comics oder -Bücher kennst du?

Linking words

12 grammar: linking words p. 189

Make one sentence out of two by using linking words from the box. Write down the sentences.

so that · because · but · and · before · when

1 Jacob travelled back in time. He wanted to learn about life in the past.
2 Olivia tried to take a picture of the dinosaur. Her camera did not work.
3 In the year 2070 people don't travel by car. They don't travel by bus.
4 Mia was surprised. She found out that she was in the year 2812.
5 She could not travel back in time. She found the time machine.
6 Dan built a time machine. He could visit Albert Einstein.

Improve your text

13 CHOOSE YOUR LEVEL grammar: linking words p. 189, workbook p. 72/15

I Read the beginning of this story. Choose one word from the brackets and write the text in your exercise book. You can add more sentences and write an ending to the story.

It was a ??? (sunny / rainy) Monday morning. Buzz woke up ??? (really / very) early. He was ??? (very / terribly) excited. Today was his ??? (big / special) day ??? (and / so) he couldn't wait to get up.

II Read the beginning of this story. Then use words from the box to improve it and write the text in your exercise book. You can add more sentences and write an ending to the story.

It was a ??? Monday morning. Buzz woke up ??? early. He was ??? excited. Today was his ??? day so he couldn't wait to get up. He ??? got out of bed and walked into the kitchen. He took his ??? laptop and opened his mailbox.

stormy · special · really · very · terribly · new · sunny · big · slowly · quickly · rainy

III Read the beginning of this story. Then use words from one of the boxes to improve it and write the text in your exercise book. You can add more sentences and write an ending to the story.

It was a ??? Monday morning ??? Buzz woke up ??? early. He was ??? excited ??? today was his ??? day ??? he couldn't wait to get up. He ??? got out of bed and walked into the kitchen. He took his ??? laptop ??? opened his mailbox. He was ??? nervous ??? he expected a ??? letter. ???, he heard ??? noises that came from the ??? street.

stormy · special · really · very · terribly · carefully · loud · new · dark · big · slowly · quickly · rainy · suddenly

but · because · and · so · before · when · so that

DIGITAL+ practise more 16

My story TARGET TASK

14 workbook p. 73/16, wordbank: good style p. 169, skill: writing p. 153, media worksheet 3

Your task is to write a short story about a time travelling adventure.
Before you start, look at these steps:

STEP 1

Collect ideas. Is your story about ...

- ... somebody travelling to the future?
- ... somebody travelling to the past?
- ... somebody from the future travelling back in time?
- ...?

STEP 2

Plan your story.

- Organize your ideas.
- Your story needs a beginning, a middle and an ending.

who	*where*	*when*	*what*
my friend	*moon*	*2750*	*big house* *meet aliens* *...*

STEP 3

Write your story.

- You can write your story on a computer.
- Think of a title.
- Think of a good first sentence.
- Use adjectives, adverbs and linking words to make your story more interesting to read.

STEP 4

Check it.

- Is the English OK?
- Is your story interesting enough?
- Ask a classmate for feedback.
- Edit your text if necessary.

STEP 5

Present your story.

- Have a reading session in class.

STEP 6

Publish your stories.

- You can put all your stories together and make a (digital) class story book.

Check out

Kannst du einen Flyer über ein Projekt verstehen? Workbook, p. 74
Kannst du darüber sprechen, wie sich Personen die Zukunft vorstellen? Workbook, p. 74
Kannst du verstehen, was Leute über ihren Beruf sagen? Workbook, p. 74
Kannst du darüber schreiben, wie jemand etwas tut? Workbook, p. 75
Kannst du darüber schreiben, wie sich jemand fühlt? Workbook, p. 75
Kennst du Möglichkeiten, eine Geschichte interessanter zu machen? Workbook, p. 75

The Clan-Howlus dragon

DIGITAL+ If you want to know what happened outside the cave, you can listen to Ari and Shirook talking: audio 2/21

The dragon footsteps came closer. Kora started to RUN! Even dragon tamers need to run away sometimes. She ran back through the cave. It was so dark. She kept one hand on the warm cave wall. It helped her to find her way. She heard the dragon behind her. It wasn't far away …
Finally, she reached the entrance to the cave. She quickly got a box out of her dragon-taming kit and put it down on the ground. It was a box of marbles – a present for the dragon. Most dragons love presents. And they all have a favourite colour. In the box there were marbles of every colour. Kora hoped the dragon would like some of them!

She went to join Ari and Shirook. Suddenly, the dragon stomped out of the cave – and fell over the box of marbles! It landed with a BUMP in the snow. "Oh no!" Ari whispered to Kora. "Look at those flames – and all that smoke!" The dragon looked very angry. Ari hid behind Shirook.
"Keep quiet, Ari," Kora whispered. "OK, Kora!" Ari said quietly. "But guess what? … I know what kind of dragon it is!" "You do?" she whispered. "Tell me …"
Ari showed Kora a page in his dragon book. "It's a Clan-Howlus dragon.

The book says they don't exist today. They went extinct 200 years ago. But look at their footprints … they're the same as the ones near the cave!"
Kora read the text. "But if Clan-Howlus dragons went extinct 200 years ago … what is this dragon doing here?" she said.
"I don't know … but I think it's a young Clan-Howlus dragon," said Ari. "It's not very big!"
Suddenly, Kora remembered something. "You're right!" she said. "I saw pieces of its egg in the cave!"
"Maybe the egg was 200 years old!" Ari said. "But then … why did it crack open now? There was no mum or dad dragon to keep it warm."

Kora thought for a moment. "I don't know," she replied. "But it was warm in the cave …"
Suddenly, Shirook turned to Kora and Ari. "I must talk to the dragon," she said. "Stay here."
Shirook walked slowly towards the angry Clan-Howlus dragon. "Maa nominaadraa hes Shirook," she said. "Ent taa?"
The other dragon looked at her. Then it opened its mouth and breathed out huge red flames. Shirook jumped back, then breathed flames and lots of smoke back at the Clan-Howlus dragon.
"Shirook, stop," Kora said. "I don't want you to get hurt!"

breathe flames = *Feuer speien*; cave = *Höhle*; crack open = *aufbrechen*; entrance = *Eingang*; go extinct = *aussterben*; marble = *Murmel*

Suddenly, Ari started to laugh. He pointed at the Clan-Howlus dragon. "It looks so funny!" he said. "Look!" He laughed and laughed.
"Shhh, Ari," whispered Kora. "Stop it!"
But Ari couldn't stop. And then Kora remembered something: Most dragons love to laugh, too. What would the Clan-Howlus dragon find funny?
She picked up two marbles, held them up to her eyes and made a funny face. Ari laughed but the dragon did not.
Next, she got three sandwiches out of her dragon-taming kit – and juggled with them!
Again, Ari laughed but the dragon didn't.

Then she found three oranges and a banana in her dragon-taming kit. She made a smiley fruit face in the snow. The dragon still didn't laugh. Finally, Ari stopped laughing and picked up the banana. He started to eat it. "What are you doing?" whispered Kora.
"I'm hungry!" he said.

"Hey Kora, let's do a funny dance. Come on!" So they started to dance. Suddenly, Kora slipped and fell down with a BUMP.
Then she saw the banana skin.
"Ari!" she said. "That's NOT funny!"
But then Kora heard a strange noise. She looked up.
"Ari!" she said. "The dragon is laughing! Finally!"

Suddenly, the ground shook.

"What was that?" asked Ari.
"I don't know," Kora replied. "But I don't think it was good. Wait … The ground is shaking. And it was warm in the cave. And … we're standing on a volcano … OH NO!"
"What?" asked Ari.
"The volcano is going to erupt!" she shouted. "We have to get away and warn people! NOW!"

erupt = *ausbrechen;* fall down = *hinfallen;* get away = *flüchten;* juggle = *jonglieren;* shake = *beben;* slip = *ausrutschen;* volcano = *Vulkan*

Time capsules

Everyday objects can tell you a lot about their time. Putting such objects into a time capsule can be a message to your future self or to future generations. Creating a personal time capsule is quite popular today, but the idea of creating time capsules and sending them through time or even space is not new.

Here are a few fun facts about time capsules:

Did you know that ...

... there are at least 10,000 time capsules around the world right now? Experts also think that more than 80% of all time capsules are lost and no one will ever open them.

... buildings sometimes have a special stone in them with objects from the year of construction, for example a newspaper or a coin? Sometimes people find these objects hundreds of years later.

... the oldest time capsule in the USA is from the year 1795? People found it in a public building in Boston in December 2014 during repairs. There was a public opening of the capsule in January 2015 and you can watch videos about it online. In the box there were newspapers, coins and some other objects from more than 200 years ago.

... there is a famous time capsule at Oglethorpe University in Atlanta, USA? The time capsule from 1940 is actually a special room full of objects like books, voice recordings, children's toys, a toaster and lots of other things. The opening will take place on 28 May 8113.

... in 1977 a kind of time capsule – a golden record with pictures, sounds and greetings from the Earth – started its journey through time and space on board the Voyager spacecraft? The spacecraft is still travelling through space – and should aliens ever find it, they can listen to human voices, whale songs and other interesting sounds from planet Earth.

... in 2018 German astronaut Alexander Gerst took a time capsule on board the ISS (International Space Station) and the time capsule travelled around the Earth a few thousand times? In the time capsule there are texts from children about their hopes and dreams for the future. The time capsule is now back on Earth and the opening will take place in 2068.

What would you put in a time capsule for future generations? Why? Write about your ideas.

5

1 Look at the picture. What can you see?
2 Where are the people?
3 What do you think the people are thinking or saying?

Out and about

Part A A trip to the museum

- Du beschäftigst dich mit interessanten Museen in London.
- Du übst, Dinge zu beschreiben.
- Du beschreibst Objekte für eine Ausstellung.

Part B A play

- Du unterhältst dich über Ferienaktivitäten.
- Du lernst die Geschichte *The Canterville Ghost* kennen.
- Du spielst mit einer Gruppe eine kurze Szene aus einem Theaterstück vor.

A place to visit

1 workbook p. 76/1

**Make a list of museums and other interesting places you can visit.
What do you know about them? Tell a partner about the places on your list.**

science museum · old castle · zoo · ...

learn about · see · ...

Museums in London

2a skill: reading p. 154, workbook p. 76/2

Read the flyer. What museums is it about?

DISCOVER LONDON'S MUSEUMS

THE BRITISH MUSEUM

Have you ever wondered how to read Egyptian hieroglyphs? At the British Museum you can learn how to write your name in ancient hieroglyphs. Or have a look at the mummy of a cat that is more than 4,000 years old.

THE VICTORIA AND ALBERT MUSEUM

Do you think your trainers are a piece of art? So does the V&A. From 3,000 year old Egyptian shoes to modern trainers, they have collected more than 2,000 pairs of shoes.
But there's a lot more to discover in the fashion collection from hats and glasses to theatre and musical costumes.

THE SHERLOCK HOLMES MUSEUM

Do you like detective stories? At the Sherlock Holmes Museum you can step right into the house of the most famous detective of them all. Have a look at his pipe collection, his desk, his microscope or his violin. Walk through this 19th century house and take a picture with Sherlock Holmes himself or his friend and assistant Dr Watson.

2b

Which of the three museums would you like to visit? Say why.

You can say:
I'd like to visit ... because ...

Let's do something different!

3a audio 3/1

Listen and read along. What is the children's plan?

The children are at Harry and Lily's place.

Harry: I've just looked at my weather app – rain for the rest of the day. Any ideas what we could do?

Lily: Wait, let me see ... Ah, I've found it. Look at this flyer for museums in London. They have put together lots of interesting information on museums.

Ava: Museums? Is there anything more boring we could do? Haven't you been to enough museums on school trips?

Lily: No, no, no, wait. Look. There's a shoe collection at the V&A. Have you ever seen a shoe that's 3,000 years old?

Ava: No, I haven't yet. I'm not sure I want to. It's probably really smelly.

Lily: Well, we can always stay at home but why not try something different?

Harry: Wow, the British Museum looks really good. I've never been there.

Lily: There are real mummies! Have you ever seen a mummy?

Tarek: Yes, I have, actually.

Ava: Here's something else – the Sherlock Holmes Museum at 221B Baker Street. You can even take pictures with him. Look!

Harry: Oh! We've read a story about him at school. He was a clever detective, who solved lots of cases with his assistant Dr Watson.

Tarek: Wow, I like it. Look at the pictures. There's his collection of pipes.

Lily: And his violin.

Harry: Let's go there. I want to see what the real home of Sherlock Holmes looks like.

Lily: Harry, you know he's just a character from Sir Arthur Conan Doyle's books, don't you? He didn't really live in that house.

Harry: Erm ... of course I do.

3b CHOOSE YOUR LEVEL skill: reading p. 154

I Match the sentence parts.

1 Lily suggests
2 At first Ava says that
3 A shoe that is 3,000 years old
4 Harry has never been

A to the British Museum.
B is probably really smelly.
C a trip to a museum.
D museums are boring.

II Correct the sentences and write them down.

1 Harry has just looked at his fitness app.
2 You can see a shoe that is 3,000 years old at the Sherlock Holmes Museum.
3 There are no mummies at the British Museum.
4 Sherlock Holmes was a police officer.

III Answer the questions.

1 What is the weather like?
2 What is Lily's idea for the afternoon?
3 What does Ava think about Lily's idea?
4 What can you see at the British Museum?
5 Where is the Sherlock Holmes Museum?
6 Who was Sherlock Holmes?

3c workbook p. 77/3

Tell your class what you know about Sherlock Holmes and Dr Watson.

GRAMMAR HELP the present perfect: statements p. 190

Das *present perfect* verwendest du, wenn du über etwas sprechen möchtest, das irgendwann in der Vergangenheit begonnen hat und immer noch andauert oder in der Vergangenheit passiert ist und Einfluss auf die Gegenwart hat. Sieh dir die Beispiele an. Was fällt dir an den Verbformen auf?

I have just looked at my weather app.
Lily has found a flyer.
They have collected 2,000 pairs of shoes so far.
We have read a story about Sherlock Holmes.

I have not been to the British Museum yet.
Lily has not seen a real mummy yet.
They haven't bought the tickets yet.
We haven't watched the new Sherlock Holmes film yet.

Ab Seite 190 findest du eine ausführlichere Erklärung und weitere Beispiele – auch zur Bildung von Fragen. Die Liste der unregelmäßigen Verben ab Seite 246 kennst du schon – dort findest du auch die *past participles*, die du für das *present perfect* brauchst.

What have they done?

4 grammar: present perfect statements p. 190, workbook p. 77/4-5

Copy the sentences and fill in the gaps with the correct forms.

1. Ava has ??? (be) to a lot of museums.
2. Noah has ??? (watch) a lot of Sherlock Holmes films.
3. Lily has ??? (find) a flyer about museums in London.
4. Joshua has ??? (not read) any Sherlock Holmes stories yet.
5. Tarek has already ??? (see) a real mummy.
6. Harry has ??? (read) detective stories at school.
7. Ava has ??? (never see) a shoe that is 3,000 years old.
8. Ava has ??? (find) information about the British Museum.

Been there, done that

5 grammar: present perfect statements p. 190, irregular verbs p. 247

Paul is on holiday in London.
Look at his list.
What has he already done?
What hasn't he done yet?
Write about his list.

You can write:

Paul hasn't visited the Science Museum yet.
He has already watched a musical.
…

- visit the Science Museum
- ✓ watch a musical
- look at platform 9¾
- ✓ buy tickets for Madame Tussauds
- walk around Holland Park
- find a souvenir for Grandma
- ✓ book a table at an Indian restaurant
- listen to street music at Covent Garden
- ✓ call Mum
- …

At the Sherlock Holmes Museum

6a audio 3/2

Listen and read along.
Do the children like the museum?

Lily: OK, here are your tickets. Let's start.
Harry: Great, thanks Lily.
Tarek: This really looks like someone's home.
Ava: Yes, it does. There's so much stuff here. Have you ever seen so many pipes? And look at the microscope over there.
Tarek: Oh yes, I've read about that. Sherlock Holmes used a microscope to solve his cases. He looked at blood and fingerprints and that was quite new in the 19th century.
Lily: There's also some chemistry equipment. It looks as if he's left it right in the middle of an experiment. Huh, who's that?
Tarek: Oh, that's Dr Watson, Sherlock Holmes's friend. They've put wax models of characters from the books all over the house.
Ava: That's a cool idea! Look, there's Sherlock Holmes, too. They've put that funny hat on his head.
Harry: Oh, and here's his bedroom. It looks so real, it's hard to believe that Sherlock Holmes didn't actually live here.

Ava: Yes, look, they've left a newspaper on his desk.
Lily: And a book next to his bed.
Harry: They've also put his violin next to his desk.
Tarek: I wonder what's up there? Oh wow! Guys, come up here. This is really funny. I've found Sherlock Holmes's toilet!

6b CHOOSE YOUR LEVEL skill: reading p. 154

I Make a list of what you can see at the museum.

You can write:
- *pipe collection*
- *microscope*
- *…*

II Write about four things the children talk about.

You can write:
Sherlock Holmes used a microscope to …
He had a …
… and he played the …

III Write a short text about the Sherlock Holmes Museum and what you can see there.

You can write:
The Sherlock Holmes Museum is at …
You can see … there. There is … and …

6c workbook p. 78/6

Work in groups of four. Practise reading the dialogue. Present it to the class.

Museums in London

7a

Look at the photos and talk about them.

1

2

3

4

7b workbook p. 78/7

Read the descriptions of the museums and look at the photos. Match the photos to the texts.

A At the Science Museum you can see and even touch objects from different fields of science and technology – clocks, telescopes, telephones, planes or this Apollo 10 space capsule.

B The Horniman Museum has many different collections – for example of instruments or paintings. There is also an aquarium, but the most famous object in the museum is an overstuffed walrus.

C At the London Transport Museum you can find every type of vehicle that has ever driven on London's streets. There is a playzone for small children where they can ride mini vehicles – from the famous red buses to Thames sightseeing boats.

D At the Museum of London you can learn about the history of London. There are a lot of things from London's past, for example Roman coins from 2,000 years ago. People still find old coins in London today, especially in or near the River Thames.

LAND & LEUTE 7 video 13, workbook p. 79/8-9

Museen in London

In London gibt es über 200 unterschiedliche Museen – vom *Arsenal Football Club Museum* bis zum *Wimbledon Windmill Museum*. Drei der beliebtesten Museen finden sich in unmittelbarer Nachbarschaft zueinander in Kensington: Das *Science Museum*, das *Natural History Museum* und das *Victoria and Albert Museum* (*V&A*).

Im *Science Museum* kannst du die wichtigsten technischen Entwicklungen der letzten 300 Jahre sehen, anfassen und zum Teil auch ausprobieren. Gleich nebenan, im *Natural History Museum*, steht ein lebensgroßes Modell eines T-Rex.
Im *V&A* gibt es eine fantastische Sammlung der Mode der letzten Jahrhunderte.

Gibt es bei dir in der Nähe ähnliche Angebote?

Announcements

8 audio 3/4, skill: mediation p. 155

Listen to the announcements and answer the questions in German.

1 Wann schließt das Museum?
2 Warum ist die Ausstellung über Ägypten heute nicht geöffnet?
3 Was ist im Museum verboten?
4 Wonach wird in der 4. Ansage gefragt?
5 Welche Kleidung trägt das Mädchen, das verloren gegangen ist?
6 Wie heißen die Gemälde von Picasso?

A museum of everyday objects

9a audio 3/5, skill: listening p. 151

Listen to Harry, Lily, Ava and Tarek after their visit to the Sherlock Holmes Museum. What is Lily's idea?

9b CHOOSE YOUR LEVEL workbook p. 79/10

I Listen again. Which three of these objects do the children talk about?

guitar

socks

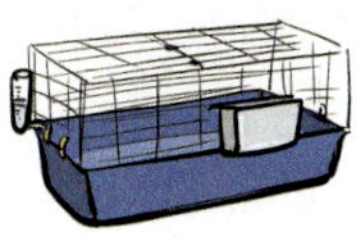
rabbit cage

football shirt

hockey stick

II Listen again and take notes. What objects do the children talk about?

III Listen again and take notes on the objects the children talk about. What makes them special?

Museums

10 CHOOSE YOUR TASK C: skill: searching the Internet p. 157, media worksheet 4

A Write quiz cards with questions and answers for your classmates.
B Create a flyer for a museum. It can be a real museum or a dream museum, it can be in London, in your town, in …
C Find out about an unusual museum in the UK. Tell your class about it.

A *You can see a collection of pipes and a violin here. Which museum is it?*
1 *The Sherlock Holmes Museum*
2 *The British Museum*
3 *The Museum of London*

Have you ever …?

11a audio 3/6

Listen to the song and sing along.

Have you ever been to Paris?
Have you ever been to Rome?
Have you ever been to London?
No, I've just been here at home.

Have you ever met a stunt man?
Have you ever met the Queen?
Have you ever met a T-Rex?
No, I've just seen them on screen.

Have you ever eaten snails?
Have you ever eaten snake?
Have you ever eaten frogs' legs?
No, I've just had too much cake.

Have you ever done a back flip?
Have you ever done things wrong?
Have you ever done a marathon?
No, I've just done a song and the last line got too long.

11b grammar: present perfect questions p. 191, irregular verbs p. 246

Ask and answer questions in class. You can ask questions from the song or make up your own.

You can ask:	You can answer:
Have you ever been to Paris?	*Yes, I have.*
Have you ever been to …?	*No, I haven't.*

11c CHOOSE YOUR LEVEL grammar: present perfect questions p. 191, workbook p. 80/11-13

Write down three or more questions.
Then get together with a partner and ask and answer questions.

Have you ever	been to	a mummy?
	seen	a science museum?
	touched	Sherlock Holmes's bedroom?
	walked through	a dinosaur's egg?
	looked at	the British Museum?
	…	…

II Write down four or more questions. Then get together with a partner and ask and answer questions.

be to · see · eat · play · watch · touch · …

the violin · a bat · Scotland · a Sherlock Holmes film · …

III Use the words from the box and write down five or more questions. Then get together with a partner and ask and answer questions.

go · find · listen to · travel · be · …

An exhibition of everyday things

12a

Read the texts and match them to the pictures.

1

2

3

4

A This beautiful vase is Grandma Edyta's masterpiece. You can see two painted roses – Edyta's favourite flowers – on the vase. She sculpted the vase in a workshop in 2022. It is 40cm tall and weighs 2.3kg.

B Lily designed this lamp when she still lived in Brighton. She used aluminium, plastic and her creativity. The modern and functional design makes it special. It is 38cm tall and weighs 1.3kg.

C These pink trainers with white stripes on their sides play an important role in Mrs Kogan's life. She wore these trainers when she ran her first marathon in 2013. Mrs Kogan is a great athlete now and has run many marathons since 2019. The trainers are size six and weigh 280g.

D This is Harry's first guitar. It is a wooden guitar for children. Harry played his first tunes on this instrument when he was five years old. Everybody could hear that there was a lot of musical talent in Harry. The guitar is green. It is 62cm long and weighs 510g.

12b

skill: talking with people p. 152

Have you got a special object or a collection of special things? Talk about it in a small group.

You can say:

I have a collection of …

… is special to me because …

…

The great opening

13a grammar: present perfect statements p. 190

The friends are almost ready to open their museum. Write about what they have done so far.

tidy room · clean old tables · collect everyday objects · ask parents for special things · put objects on display · write a brochure · ...

You can write:

They have tidied the room.

...

13b

**Look at the picture.
What has Lily forgotten to do?**

Describing objects

14 CHOOSE YOUR LEVEL grammar: simple past p. 174, workbook p. 82/14-15

I Copy the text and fill in the gaps with words from the box.

cycle · small · first · old · blue · a lot · ...

This ??? children's bike was Gina's ??? bike. It is now ten years ??? and much too ??? for her. Gina liked her bike ???. She used it to ??? up and down the street.

II Look at the picture and write a short text about Julie's masterpiece.

You can write:

Julie painted this picture in ...

It shows a ...

In the back you can see ...

The painting was a present for ...

...

III Look at the picture and write about Tony's favourite soft toy.

DIGITAL+ practise more 18

Our exhibition of everyday objects TARGET TASK

15 workbook p. 83/16, skill: writing p. 153, media worksheet 3

Your task is to write a short text about an everyday object.
Before you start, look at the following steps:

STEP 1

Imagine your class wants to create an exhibition of everyday objects.
Decide what you would like to show.
Think about:

- things you can find at school
- things you have at home
- things you have created
- special or unusual things
- ...

STEP 2

Write your text. Think about:

- How can you describe your object?
- How old is your object?
- What do (or did) you do with it?
- Where is it from?
- Why is it special?
- ...

STEP 3

Display your texts in class.

STEP 4

You can put all your texts together in an exhibition catalogue.
If you like, you can organize a real exhibition in your classroom or have a digital exhibition.

What's on in the holidays?

1a

Read about the holiday activities at the Notting Hill youth club. Match the pictures to the workshops.

1  2  3  4 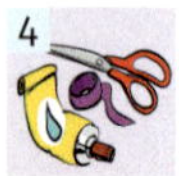

1b workbook p.84/1

**Read the notes again.
Which workshop would you choose?
Say why.**

** NOTTING HILL YOUTH CLUB * HOLIDAY PROGRAMME **

For further information on all courses visit ***www.chasgcfv.co.uk***

CLIMBING UP!
Three days filled with action at the Bassett's Farm Rocks

DRAMA, BABY!
In this one-week drama workshop we're going to write our own version of "The Canterville Ghost" and perform it

KICK IT!
A two-week football practice course with professional coaches

IS IT RUBBISH OR IS IT ART?
Don't throw it away! We're going to use your old stuff to create beautiful new things in our two-day upcycling workshop

The children's plans

2a audio 3/10

Listen and read along. What are the children talking about?

Ava: Have you already got plans for the summer holidays?
Lily: Oh yes, I have. I'm going to join an upcycling workshop at the youth club. I'm really looking forward to creating new things out of old stuff.
Ava: That sounds good. Where do you get the old stuff?
Lily: Oh, we all have to bring something we don't want or don't need anymore. I'm going to create a new lamp for my room. What are you going to do, Ava?
Ava: We are going to visit my grandmother in Poland for the first two weeks. I don't know what I'm going to do in the last weeks yet. What about you, Tarek? Are you going to do another cooking workshop?

Tarek: No, I'm not. I thought about the hockey camp, but then I looked at the noticeboard at the youth club. Now I'm going to do a drama workshop there.
Harry: Really? How cool! Are you going to be on stage in a real theatre?

Tarek: Oh yes! There's going to be a performance at the end of the workshop! Why don't you join the workshop, too, Harry?
Harry: I don't know ... Is there going to be music? I'm better at singing than at acting.
Tarek: We're going to create a new version of "The Canterville Ghost". On the website it also says that we need people for lighting, sound, props, costumes, ...
Harry: I'm definitely not acting!
Tarek: It's going to be great anyway!
Lily: And Ava and I are going to come and watch your performance! You have to save tickets for us.

2b CHOOSE YOUR LEVEL skill: reading p. 154, workbook p. 84/2

I Who is going to do what in the summer holidays?

Lily is		visit her grandmother.
Ava is	going to	do a drama workshop.
Harry and Tarek are		join an upcycling workshop.

II Match the sentence parts.

1 Lily is going to
2 Lily wants to create
3 At first Tarek wanted to go to
4 Tarek and Harry are going to
5 Harry does not want to

A act in the play.
B join an upcycling workshop.
C do a drama workshop at the youth club.
D the hockey camp.
E a new lamp.

III Unscramble the sentences.

1 is going to – in the summer holidays. – join – Lily – an upcycling workshop
2 old stuff. – means – new things – create – Upcycling – out of – that you
3 has already got – for the first two weeks – plans – Ava – of the holidays.
4 what – in the last weeks. – She – she is going to do – does not know
5 Harry and Tarek – a drama workshop – are going to – at the youth club. – join

Your plans

3 skill: talking with people p. 152

What are your classmates' plans for the summer holidays? Walk around the classroom and ask each other questions.

visit ... · play computer games · stay at home · meet friends · go to ... · go camping · spend time with ... · ...

You can ask:
Have you already got any plans for the summer holidays? What are your plans?

You can answer:
Yes, I have. I'm going to visit ...
...

GRAMMAR HELP the going to-future: statements p. 192

Wenn du über Pläne für die Zukunft sprechen möchtest, kannst du das *going to-future* verwenden. Sieh dir die Beispiele an. Was fällt dir auf?

I am going to do a drama workshop.
Ava is going to go to Poland.
The children are going to act in a play.

I am not going to do a cooking workshop.
She is not going to go to Scotland.
They are not going to act in a musical.

Auf Seite 192 findest du weitere Erklärungen und Beispiele zum *going to-future*. Wie man Fragen und Kurzantworten im *going to-future* formuliert, kannst du auf Seite 193 nachschlagen.

Next weekend

4 grammar: going to-future statements p. 192, workbook p. 85/3

Write down what the people are going to do next weekend.

1 Ben: not go to London / go to Paris
2 Israh and Melike: not play football / go on a bike tour
3 Jacob: not get up early / sleep till ten
4 Poppy: not work / read a lot
5 Pablo and his friends: not watch a film / go to the swimming pool

You can write:

Ben is not going to go to London. He is …
Israh and Melike are not …
…

Lots of questions

5 grammar: going to-future questions p. 193, workbook p. 85/4

Unscramble the questions and answer them in your exercise book.

1 Is – join – an upcycling workshop? – going to – Lily
2 go – going to – When – to Poland? – Ava and her family – are
3 in a play? – act – is going to – Who
4 is – on stage? – Why – Harry – not going to – be
5 do – the holidays? – you - going to – in – What – are
6 you – Are – visit – going to – your uncle?

Ollie's holidays

6 grammar: going to-future questions p. 193, workbook p. 85/5

Work with a partner. Think of an activity that Ollie is going to do in the next holidays. Your partner has to guess the activity. Only five questions are allowed. Take turns.

You can ask:

Is Ollie going to sleep a lot?
Is he going to …?

You can answer:

No, he isn't.
Yes, he is!

DIGITAL+ practise more 19

Try something new, Harry!

7a

Look at the picture.
What do you think Tarek is telling Harry?

7b audio 3/13

Listen to Harry and Tarek.
What is the ghost's problem in the story?

7c CHOOSE YOUR LEVEL skill: listening p. 151, workbook p. 86/6-8

I Listen again and match the sentence parts.

1 The Canterville ghost lives
2 One day a family moves
3 The ghost tries
4 No one in the family is

A to scare them away.
B afraid of the ghost.
C in an old house.
D into the old house.

II What happens in the story?
Copy the sentences in the right order into your exercise book.

The ghost is not happy with the family living in his house.
But it just does not work – no one in the family is afraid of ghosts.
One day a family moves into the old house.
He tries to scare them so that they move out again.
In a very old house in the country lives a ghost – the Canterville ghost.

III What do you think: how does the story end? Write down your ideas in a few sentences.

An email to Gus

8 workbook p. 87/9

Copy Harry's email to the workshop leader and fill in the gaps with words from the box.

To: Gus@thenhgyouth.co.uk
Subject: Drama workshop

Dear Gus,
I am Tarek Adil's ???, Harry. Tarek told me about the drama ??? in the summer ???.
The deadline to sign up was ???, but I would really ??? to take part in the workshop.
Can I still ????
Thank you for your ???.
Yours sincerely,
Harry Norris

workshop · like · holidays · yesterday · friend · help · join

Get creative

9 CHOOSE YOUR TASK A+B: wordbank: holidays p. 160, C: skill: searching the Internet p. 157, media worksheet 4, 5

A **Create a flyer for a workshop you would like to do in your summer holidays.**

B **Record a podcast about summer activities. Talk about your favourite activities and give tips. Present it to the class!**

C **Do you know any ghosts from films or books? Collect information on one or more of them and present your findings.**

Choose a workshop

10 GET TOGETHER

**Get together with a partner.
Decide on a workshop.**

Partner A	Partner B
I Go to page 130.	I Go to page 139.
II Go to page 133.	II Go to page 142.
III Go to page 136.	III Go to page 145.

LAND & LEUTE 8 video 14

Theater für Kinder

In London gibt es viele Theater-Angebote, auch speziell für Kinder und Jugendliche. Das Theater *The Unicorn* zum Beispiel bietet Theaterstücke für Kinder in jedem Alter an. Selbst Babys haben hier die Möglichkeit, erste Erfahrungen mit Theater zu machen. Besonders Märchen von den Gebrüdern Grimm oder fantastische Geschichten, wie die von Gullivers Reisen, werden dort gezeigt.
Im *Polka Theatre* in Wimbledon kann man nicht nur Aufführungen anschauen, hier gibt es auch Workshops, an denen die ganze Familie teilnehmen kann.
Sogar im berühmten *Globe Theatre*, wo hauptsächlich Stücke von William Shakespeare aufgeführt werden, gibt es besondere Veranstaltungen und Angebote für Kinder.
Zur Weihnachtszeit ist es eine englische Tradition, sich eine *pantomime* anzuschauen. Das hat nichts mit der Pantomime zu tun, wie wir sie aus dem Deutschen kennen, sondern ist eine Mischung aus Theater, Musical, Märchen und Comedy. Alle im Publikum sind aufgefordert, aktiv mitzumachen und die Lieder mitzusingen, bei Zaubertricks zu assistieren, den Bösewicht auszubuhen und dem Helden zu helfen, indem sie ihn laut vor Gefahren warnen.

Sieh dir das Video an. Welches Theater in London würdest du gerne besuchen?

At the workshop

11 skill: reading p. 154, workbook p. 87/10-13

Read the story. What are the children's ideas for their own version of the story?

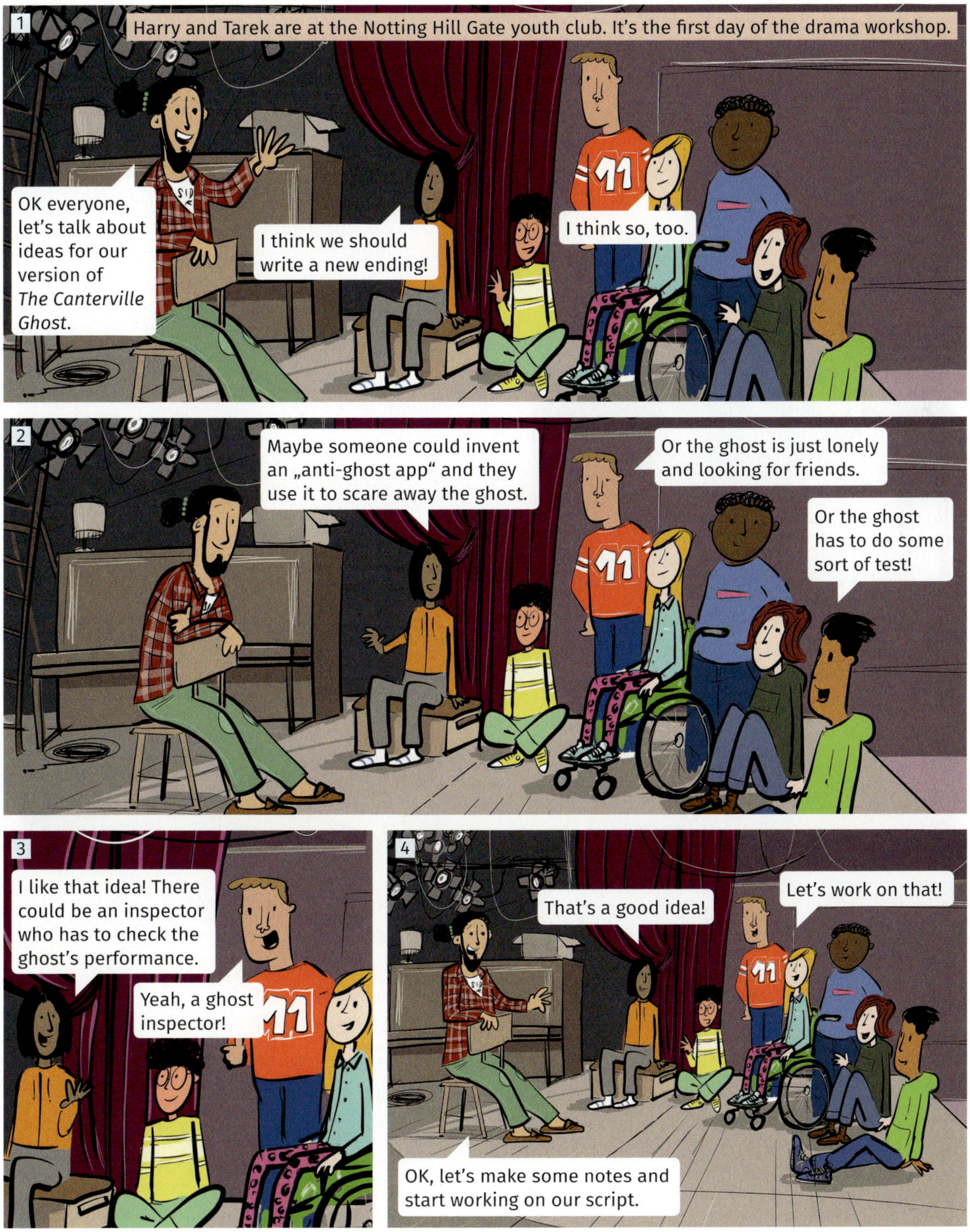

The Canterville Ghost

12a audio 3/15

Listen to the performance at the youth club and read along.
Who is your favourite character in the play? Say why.

SCENE 1: In front of the house

The Otis family arrives at Canterville House.
Mrs Otis: This is our new home.
The twins: Ohhh! Is there a ghost here?
Mr Otis: No. There are no ghosts here! Ghosts don't exist.
Sir Simon: What? I don't exist? What rubbish! I'll show these people what a scary ghost I am.

SCENE 2: In the twins' bedroom

Sir Simon: *(rattles his chains)* Aahhh! I am the ghost of Sir Simon de Canterville. This is my house. Go away and never come back. Aaaah!
David: *(in a sleepy voice)* What's all this noise? We want to sleep!
Jack: *(bored)* Go away, Mr Ghost. We're tired.
Sir Simon: *(disappointed)* Right, I'll have to be even scarier tomorrow.

SCENE 3: In Mr and Mrs Otis' bedroom

(sound) CLANG, CLANG, CLANG
Sir Simon: *(nervous)* For 300 years I have lived in this house. Everyone was afraid of me. *(loud)* Wake up! I am the ghost of Canterville House!
Mrs Otis: Excuse me, Mr Ghost, please stop making all that noise.
Mr Otis: We can't sleep.
Sir Simon: *(angry, frustrated)* It's impossible to live in the same house as this family!

SCENE 4: On the stairs

(sound) CLONK, CLONK, CLONK
Sir Simon: I'm going to frighten everybody in this family. First the twins, then Mrs Otis. And of course Mr Otis ... I must practise my terrible laughter. Haaa. Haaaa. Haaa.
Mr Otis: What's all this about?
David: Go away!
Jack: And let us get back to sleep.
Sir Simon: Haaaa! My terrible laughter will frighten you away and ... *(stumbles and falls down the stairs)* CRASH!
Otis family: Hahaha!

SCENE 5: In the living room

Sir Simon: These people are not afraid of me. I'm not a good ghost.
(enter Mr and Mrs Otis)
Mrs Otis: Oh you poor thing. Why are you crying?
Sir Simon: I'm sad. I can't stay here if you're not afraid of me. The ghost inspector will find out and I will have to leave.
Mr Otis: Don't worry. We'll help you so that you can stay here. Where are the twins?

SCENE 6: Somewhere in the house

The ghost inspector has arrived.

Sir Simon: *(rattles his chains)* BOO!

David and Jack: *(run away)* Aaaah!

Sir Simon: *(shows his terrible laughter)* Haaa. Haaaa. Haaa.

Mrs and Mrs Otis: Help!

Ghost inspector: Well done, Sir Simon. Very scary. You may stay at Canterville House. Goodbye.

David: Is he gone?

Sir Simon: Yes, I think he's gone.

The family and Sir Simon: Yipppeeeee!

12b CHOOSE YOUR LEVEL skill: reading p. 154

I Read the script again and answer the questions.

1 What does Mr Otis say about ghosts?
2 Who are David and Jack?
3 Who is Sir Simon?
4 What is Sir Simon's full name?

II Read the script again and answer the questions.

1 What is Mr Otis's opinion about ghosts?
2 What is Sir Simon's reaction?
3 What does Sir Simon do in the twins' bedroom?
4 How do the twins react?
5 How long has Sir Simon lived in the house?
6 How do Mr and Mrs Otis react to the ghost?

III Read the script again and answer the questions.

1 What takes place in scene 1?
2 What do the members of the family do when Sir Simon tries to scare them?
3 Why is Sir Simon crying in scene 5?
4 Why does the ghost inspector come?
5 How does the Otis family help Sir Simon?
6 What do you think will happen after scene 6?

12c skill: performing a scene p. 159, workbook p. 90/14-15

Work in groups. Choose one scene from the script and do a dramatic reading.

Ghostly questions

13 skill: mediation p. 155

A German ghost has questions about Sir Simon. Look at the script again and answer them in German.

1 Wie versucht Sir Simon, die Familie zu erschrecken?
2 Warum kommt da ein Inspektor?
3 Wie geht das dann aus?

Drama words

14

Unscramble these words and write them down.

1 rloe 2 seagt 3 sence 4 atcor 5 stprci 6 cemsuto 7 pecnefromra

Improve your performance

15 CHOOSE YOUR LEVEL workbook p. 90/16

I Match the German and the English sentences. Write them down.

1 Sprich laut und deutlich.
2 Überlege, wie dein Charakter sich fühlt.
3 Lerne deinen Text auswendig.
4 Übe mit deiner Gruppe.

A Learn your lines by heart.
B Practise in your group.
C Speak loudly and clearly.
D Think about how your character feels.

II Match the sentence parts. Write down the sentences.

1 You should
2 Try to imagine how
3 Make sure you pronounce
4 Costumes and props can help

A everything correctly.
B you perform.
C speak loudly and clearly.
D your character is feeling in the situation.

III Unscramble the tips and write them down.

1 loudly and clearly – you – Make sure – speak – enough.
2 performance. – costumes – props – Use – and – for your
3 character's – you – express – can – feelings. – Think about – how – your
4 your – matches – Make sure – text. – that – your – body language
5 feedback – somebody – to give you – your performance. – Ask – on

Words and moods

16a

Work with a partner. Say each sentence in different ways: sad, angry, excited, bored, happy, scared, worried or tired. Your partner has to guess the mood.

1 Ohhh! Is there a ghost here?
2 What? I don't exist?
3 I'll have to be even scarier tomorrow.
4 What's all this about?
5 Go away!
6 Yes, I think he's gone.

16b

Find more sentences and say them in different ways.

DIGITAL+ practise more 20

Our play TARGET TASK

17 workbook p. 91/17, skill: performing a scene p. 159, media worksheet 5, 6

Your task is to perform *The Canterville Ghost*.
Before you start, look at these steps:

STEP 1
Work in small groups.
In class, decide which group performs which scene from the script on page 120.

STEP 2
Decide who plays which role.

STEP 3
What do you need? Make a list of props and costumes.
Who can bring what?

STEP 4
Practise your scene.
You can learn your text by heart or work with cue cards.

STEP 5
Present your scene. You can record or film it if you like or you can invite your parents or another class to a public performance.

Check out

1. Kannst du darüber schreiben, was jemand schon oder noch nicht gemacht hat? Workbook, p. 92
2. Kannst du den Inhalt kurzer Durchsagen auf Deutsch wiedergeben? Workbook, p. 92
3. Kannst du Gegenstände beschreiben? Workbook, p. 92
4. Kannst du Workshopankündigungen verstehen? Workbook, p. 93
5. Kannst du darüber sprechen, was jemand in seinen Ferien vorhat? Workbook, p. 93
6. Kannst du eine Rolle in einer kurzen Theaterszene spielen? Workbook, p. 93

Taming the dragon

"We need to go, but we can't leave the Clan-Howlus dragon here!" Kora said to Ari.
"I HAVE to tame it – and fast!"
She looked at Ari's dragon book again. "That's it!" she said. "It likes orange things!"
Kora picked up the oranges and took off her scarf. She looked in her dragon-taming kit for other orange things. "Yes!" she said. "My sunglasses!" She put the oranges, the scarf and the sunglasses down in front of the dragon.
Then she said to it, in Skkaddraa, "For you. We must leave. Please come with us. It's dangerous here." "I think it likes them!" said Ari. But the dragon still looked angry. Suddenly, it got up and walked to Kora's dragon-taming kit. It put its nose inside and sniffed.
"What is it doing?" Ari whispered.
"I have no idea!" Kora replied. "Kora!" said Shirook. "Kiwi fruit! It smells them. In your bag."
"Of course! Thanks, Shirook!" said Kora.
She walked very, very slowly towards the angry dragon. She got the kiwi fruit out of her dragon-taming kit. Then she put them on the ground between the Clan-Howlus dragon and Shirook. She kept one kiwi fruit in her hand for later. "Please, Shirook," she said. "You love kiwi fruit, too. Will you eat some together? The dragon needs to trust you."
She turned to Ari. "Sharing food is important to dragons. If they share the kiwi fruit, it means they trust each other."

The Clan-Howlus dragon sniffed the kiwi fruit. So did Shirook. Then the two dragons looked at each other. For a REALLY long time. Finally, they both started to eat.
"Yes!" said Kora. "They trust each other!"
The ground shook again. They needed to go – and soon!

Kora walked slowly towards the Clan-Howlus dragon. She held out the last kiwi fruit, and the dragon ate it from her hand. Then it put its head down on the ground. Kora stroked its head.

"That's it!" Kora said. "The dragon is tame! Come on, we need to go. NOW!"
"Can you ride Shirook?
Then I can go with the young one."
"Me? Ride a dragon? Yes, I guess I can," Ari said.
"If it's OK for Shirook." he quickly added.
Shirook smiled "Of course it is.
Come on, little brother."

shake = *beben*; smell = *riechen*; sniff = *riechen an*; stroke = *streicheln*; tame = *zähmen*; trust = *vertrauen*; turn to = *sich wenden an*

Kora climbed onto the Clan-Howlus dragon's back and Ari got onto Shirook's back. They quickly flew away from the volcano. Kora soon saw William and their camper van. "William!" she shouted. "The volcano is going to erupt! Get away now! We'll meet you in the forest later."

Kora, Ari and the two dragons flew to all the towns and villages nearby. "Get away now! Leave your houses!" they shouted. "The volcano is going to erupt!" Then they flew to the forest. "Kora! Ari! Are you OK?" William said when he saw them.

"We're fine thanks, William. We need to say goodbye to the dragons, then we can go home." Kora walked over to Shirook. "Will you look after the Clan-Howlus dragon?" she asked. "It needs a family. And it trusts you now. I think it was lonely and sad. That's why it attacked other dragons."
"I will take the dragon with me, Kora," said Shirook. "I will teach it to be a good dragon."
"Thank you," said Kora.

back = *Rücken*; erupt = *ausbrechen*; guess = *vermuten*; save = *retten*; the young one = *das Junge*; village nearby = *Dorf in der Nähe*

Saving the day

"Kora! Kora!" said Ari. "Can we take some photos of the Clan-Howlus dragon? I want to send them to the Natural History Museum, for their Dragons of New Zealand exhibition."
"Great idea, Ari!" said Kora.
So they took lots of photos of the dragon. Then it was time to say goodbye. Kora and Ari bowed slowly in front of the dragons. Then Shirook and the Clan-Howlus dragon flew up into the air.
"Fly safely!" said Kora. "Goodbye!" shouted Ari. Kora, Ari and William got into the camper van. It was time to go home. Kora was really tired. She and Ari both fell asleep straight away!

Later that night

"Kora! Ari! Wake up!" said William. "You're home!" Kora looked out the window.
"Dad!" she shouted. "Come on, Ari!"
They jumped out of the camper van and ran to their dad.
"There you are! I'm so glad you're home and safe!" their dad said. He gave them both a big hug.
"I saw the news! The volcano erupted just now. You saved the day!"
They went into the house, and their dad made them all some hot chocolate.

Then Kora and Ari told him about their dragon-taming mission.
"Ari was really helpful, Dad," she said.
She gave Ari a big hug. "One day, you will be a FANTASTIC dragon tamer! But please never follow me secretly again."
"Oh no, I won't," Ari said. "I'll just ask."
"Yes, but you ask ME, please," their father said. "And I'm not sure how to handle two dragon-taming kids ..."

Finally, tired but happy, Kora sent an email to Blaze. She told him all about the volcano and the Clan-Howlus dragon.
And she asked him to never again call her during a mission ...

air = *Luft*; bow = *sich verbeugen*; fall asleep = *einschlafen*; handle = *bewältigen*; mission = *Einsatz*; news = *Nachrichten*; secretly = *heimlich*

Sherlock Holmes – a world-famous detective

One of the most famous detectives in the world is Sherlock Holmes, a character from Sir Arthur Conan Doyle's detective stories.

Sir Arthur Conan Doyle was born in Edinburgh in 1859. After school, he studied medicine and worked as a doctor. He loved writing stories in his free time.

Doyle wrote science fiction and historical stories, but he is most famous for his detective stories with Sherlock Holmes and his friend Dr Watson. He published his first detective story in 1887 and started to work as a full-time author only four years later. In his lifetime he wrote another three novels and 56 short stories with Sherlock Holmes. He published his last story in 1927, three years before he died in 1930.

All of Doyle's Sherlock Holmes stories take place in the late 1800s or early 1900s. Holmes's methods to solve crimes are new and unusual for his time: he works analytically and pays attention to small details like fingerprints or very small objects with the help of a magnifying glass. A real person was the inspiration for the character of the clever detective: one of Doyle's teachers at medical school always paid attention to really small details when he was looking after patients.

Even though the Sherlock Holmes stories are much older than 100 years now, they are still very popular today. There are books especially for children, and there are lots of Sherlock Holmes films, TV series, musicals and plays.
Many other authors have used the original stories as inspiration for their own Sherlock Holmes stories. Some of them take place in the present or even in the future – and in some stories, Sherlock Holmes is a woman.

For those who want to find out more about the world of Sherlock Holmes, there is a small museum on Baker Street 221B in London, the home of Sherlock Holmes and Dr Watson in Doyle's stories.

Write about a Sherlock Holmes film, series, musical or book that you know or find out about one and write about it.

Giving directions

7 UNIT 1, p. 23 PARTNER A, wordbank: getting around p. 162

**Look at the map. You are at Tower Bridge, your partner is at the London Eye.
Ask for directions and guide each other to one or more sights. You start, then take turns.**

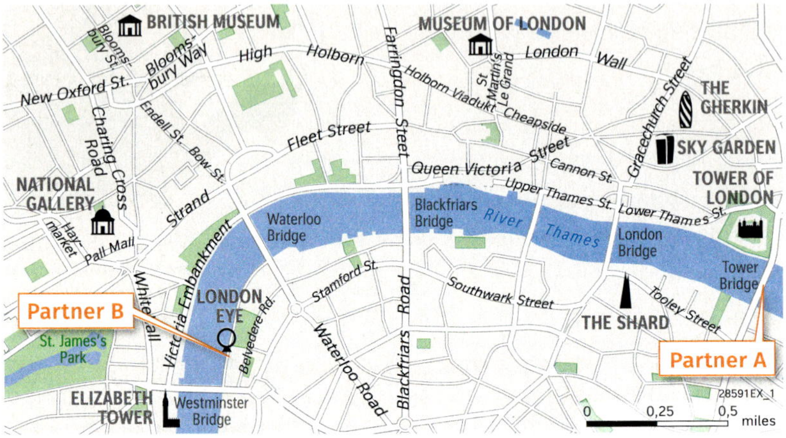

You can ask:

Excuse me, where is …, please?

You can answer:

Yes, sure.
Go straight on. On your left there is …
Then turn left. On your right there is …
Turn right. Cross the road and then …

A calendar of world festivals

11 UNIT 2, p. 49 PARTNER A, wordbank: celebrations p. 163

**Copy the table.
Then ask and answer questions with your partner and make notes in the table.**

What?	When?	What do people do?	Other information
Christmas	*25 December*		*Christian festival, birth of Jesus Christ, Father Christmas, …*
Halloween			*very old festival, …*
Easter	*spring*		*Christian festival, Easter bunny, …*
Diwali		*light candles, …*	*Hindu festival, festival of light, light wins over dark*
Eid	*always different*	*eat a lot, …*	*Muslim festival, end of fast, …*

You can ask:

When is Halloween?
What do people do on …?

You can answer:

Christmas is on 25 December.
People …

Animals in Britain

9a UNIT 3, p. 72 PARTNER A, skill: reading p. 154

Read the text about red and grey squirrels in the UK. Take notes on:

1 Where do grey squirrels come from?
2 How long have they lived in the UK?
3 Why are they a problem?

Squirrels in the UK

There are two kinds of squirrel in the United Kingdom – red squirrels and grey squirrels.
Red squirrels have lived in the UK for 10,000 years.
Grey squirrels came from North America and have lived in the UK for the last 200 years.
Since the grey squirrels arrived, red squirrels have been in danger. Grey squirrels carry a virus – squirrelpox. They themselves are immune to the virus, but they can infect red squirrels. Some people say that in ten years' time there won't be any red squirrels left in the UK.

9b UNIT 3, p. 72 PARTNER A

Use your notes and tell your partner two or more things about squirrels in the UK.

Travelling in time

11a UNIT 4, p. 97 PARTNER A, audio 2/28, skill: listening p. 151

Listen to Hiroto talking about his time travelling adventure. Take notes on:

1 Where he lives.
2 What year he lives in.
3 What time he travelled to.
4 What he saw.

11b UNIT 4, p. 97 PARTNER A

Now find out about Sarah. Ask your partner questions.

1 Where does Sarah live?
2 What year does she live in?
3 What year did she travel to?
4 What did she see there?

11c UNIT 4, p. 97 PARTNER A

Use your notes and answer your partner's questions about Hiroto.

Choose a workshop

10a UNIT 5, p. 118 PARTNER A, skill: performing a scene p. 159

You want to do a summer holiday workshop with a partner. You would like to join the drama workshop, but your partner would like to do a singing workshop. Can you find a workshop that both of you like? Look at the boxes and do a role play. You start.

1 Versuche, deinen Partner / deine Partnerin zum Mitmachen beim Theaterworkshop zu gewinnen.
You can say:
Let's join the drama workshop!

2 Partner B antwortet.

3 Sage, warum du den Theaterworkshop für eine gute Idee hältst.
You can say:
It will be so much fun! There will be a real performance at the end.

4 Partner B möchte lieber etwas anderes machen.

5 Erkläre, dass in dem Stück bestimmt auch gesungen werden kann.
You can say:
I'm sure there will be some singing in the drama workshop as well.

6 Partner B antwortet.

7 Du findest den Vorschlag deines Partners / deiner Partnerin gut.
You can say:
That's a good idea. Let's look again.

8 Partner B macht einen weiteren Vorschlag.

9 Du findest, dass das ein guter Kompromiss ist.
You can say:
That sounds good. And I like singing, too.

10 Partner B reagiert.

11 Du bist ebenfalls froh, dass ihr eine Lösung gefunden habt.
You can say:
I'm happy that we found a solution!

10b UNIT 5, p. 118 PARTNER A, media worksheet 5, 6

You can record your role play if you like.

Giving directions

7a UNIT 1, p. 23 PARTNER A, wordbank: getting around p. 162

Look at the map. You are at Tower Bridge, your partner is at the London Eye. Ask for directions and guide each other to one or more sights. You start, then take turns.

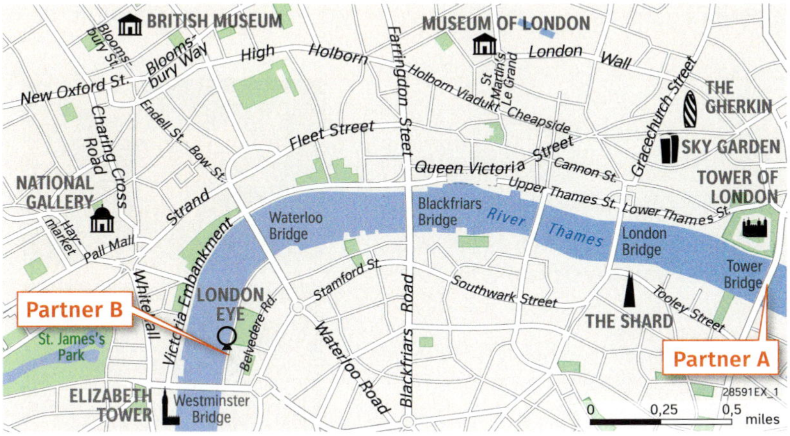

↑ go straight on
↰ turn left
↱ turn right
walk past
carry on until you get to ...
on your left
on your right
cross the road

You can ask:

Excuse me, could you tell me the way to ..., please?

...

You can answer:

Yes, sure.

Go straight on. Then ...

...

A calendar of world festivals

11a UNIT 2, p. 49 PARTNER A, wordbank: celebrations p. 163

Copy the table.
Then ask and answer questions with your partner and make notes in the table.

What?	When?	What do people do?	Other information
Christmas	*25 December*		*Christian festival, birth of Jesus Christ, Father Christmas, ...*
Halloween			*very old festival, ...*
Easter	*spring*		*Christian festival, Easter bunny, ...*
Diwali		*light candles, ...*	*Hindu festival, festival of light, light wins over dark*
Eid	*always different*	*eat a lot, ...*	*Muslim festival, end of fast, ...*

You can ask:

What do people do on ...?

...

You can answer:

People ...

...

Animals in Britain

9a UNIT 3, p. 72 PARTNER A, skill: reading p. 154

Read the text about red and grey squirrels in the UK. Take notes on:

1 Where do grey squirrels come from?
2 How long have they lived in the UK?
3 Why are they a problem?
4 How many red squirrels are there in the UK?

Squirrels in the UK
There are two kinds of squirrel in the United Kingdom – red squirrels and grey squirrels. Red squirrels have lived in the UK for 10,000 years. Grey squirrels came from North America and have lived in the UK for the last 200 years. Since they arrived, red squirrels have been in danger. Grey squirrels carry a virus – squirrelpox. They themselves are immune to the virus, but they can infect red squirrels. Red squirrels are not immune to the virus and die. Today there are only about 140,000 red squirrels but 2.5 million grey squirrels in the UK. Some people say that in ten years' time there won't be any red squirrels left in the UK.

9b UNIT 3, p. 72 PARTNER A

Use your notes and tell your partner three or more things about squirrels in the UK.

Travelling in time

11a UNIT 4, p. 97 PARTNER A, audio 2/28, skill: listening p. 151

**Listen to Hiroto talking about his time travelling adventure.
Take notes on:**

1 Where he lives.
2 What year he lives in.
3 What time he travelled to.
4 What he saw.
5 How he liked time travelling.

11b UNIT 4, p. 97 PARTNER A

**Now find out about Sarah.
Ask your partner questions about:**

1 Where she lives.
2 What year she lives in.
3 What time she travelled to.
4 What she saw.
5 How she liked time travelling.

11c UNIT 4, p. 97 PARTNER A

Use your notes and answer your partner's questions about Hiroto.

Choose a workshop

10a UNIT 5, p. 118 PARTNER A, skill: performing a scene p. 159

You want to do a summer holiday workshop with a partner. You would like to join the drama workshop, but your partner would like to do a singing workshop. Can you find a workshop that both of you like? Look at the boxes and do a role play. You start.

1 Versuche, deinen Partner / deine Partnerin zum Mitmachen beim Theaterworkshop zu gewinnen.
You can say:
Let's ...

2 Partner B antwortet.

3 Sage, warum du den Theaterworkshop für eine gute Idee hältst.
You can say:
It will be ...

4 Partner B möchte lieber etwas anderes machen.

5 Erkläre, dass in dem Stück bestimmt auch gesungen werden kann.
You can say:
I'm sure there will be some ...

6 Partner B antwortet.

7 Du findest den Vorschlag deines Partners / deiner Partnerin gut.
You can say:
That's .... Let's look again.

8 Partner B macht einen weiteren Vorschlag.

9 Du findest, dass das ein guter Kompromiss ist.
You can say:
That ...

10 Partner B reagiert.

11 Du bist ebenfalls froh, dass ihr eine Lösung gefunden habt.
You can say:
So am I.

10b UNIT 5, p. 118 PARTNER A, media worksheet 5, 6

You can record your role play if you like.

Giving directions

7a UNIT 1, p. 23 PARTNER A, wordbank: getting around p. 162

Look at the map.
You are at Tower Bridge, your partner is at the London Eye.
Ask for directions and guide each other to one or more sights.
You start, then take turns.

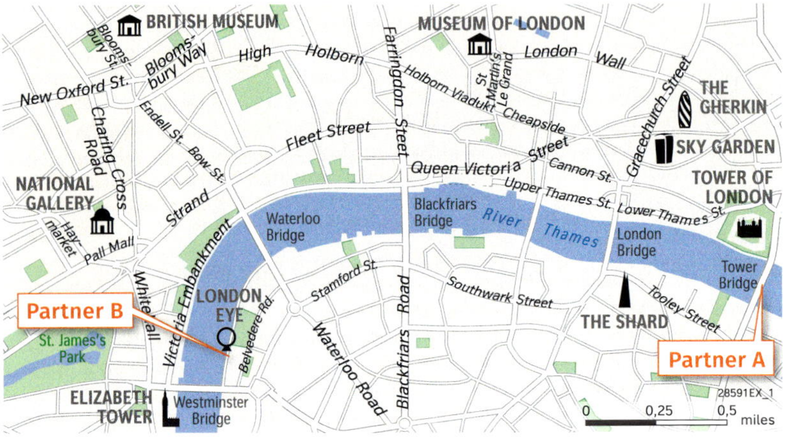

- ↑ go straight on
- ↰ turn left
- ↱ turn right
- walk past
- carry on until you get to …
- on your left
- on your right
- cross the road

A calendar of world festivals

11a UNIT 2, p. 49 PARTNER A, wordbank: celebrations p. 163

Copy the table.
Then ask and answer questions with your partner and make notes in the table.

What?	When?	What do people do?	Other information
Christmas	*25 December*		*Christian festival, birth of Jesus Christ, Father Christmas, …*
Halloween			*very old festival, …*
Easter	*spring*		
Diwali		*light candles, …*	*Hindu festival, festival of light, light wins over dark*
Eid	*always different*	*eat a lot, …*	

You can ask:

What do people do on …?

Have you got other information about Easter?

…

Animals in Britain

9a UNIT 3, p. 72 PARTNER A, skill: reading p. 154

Read the text about red and grey squirrels in the UK. Take notes on:

1 Where do grey squirrels come from?
2 How long have they lived in the UK?
3 What do red and grey squirrels eat?
4 Why are grey squirrels a problem?
5 How many red squirrels are there in the UK?

Squirrels in the UK

There are two kinds of squirrel in the United Kingdom – red squirrels and grey squirrels. Red squirrels have lived in the UK for 10,000 years. Grey squirrels came from North America and have lived in the UK for the last 200 years. Since their arrival, red squirrels have been in danger. Grey squirrels carry a virus – squirrelpox. They themselves are immune to the virus, but they can infect red squirrels. Red squirrels are not immune to the virus and die. Red and grey squirrels also eat the same food, but the grey ones are a bit more flexible with their food and so they can find more to eat. Today there are only about 140,000 red squirrels but 2.5 million grey squirrels in the UK. Some people say that in ten years' time there won't be any red squirrels left in the UK.

9b UNIT 3, p. 72 PARTNER A

Use your notes and tell your partner four or more things about squirrels in the UK.

Travelling in time

11a UNIT 4, p. 97 PARTNER A, audio 2/28, skill: listening p. 151

Listen to Hiroto talking about his time travelling adventure. Take notes on:

1 Where he lives.
2 What year he lives in.
3 What year he travelled to.
4 What he saw.
5 How he liked time travelling.
6 How he came back to his own time.

11b UNIT 4, p. 97 PARTNER A

Now find out about Sarah. Ask your partner questions about:

1 Where she lives.
2 What year she lives in.
3 What year she travelled to.
4 What she saw.
5 How she liked time travelling.
6 How she came back to her own time.

11c UNIT 4, p. 97 PARTNER A

Use your notes and answer your partner's questions about Hiroto.

Choose a workshop

10a UNIT 5, p. 118 PARTNER A, skill: performing a scene p. 159

**You want to do a summer holiday workshop with a partner.
You would like to join the drama workshop, but your partner would like to do a singing workshop. Can you find a workshop that both of you like?
Look at the boxes and do a role play. You start.**

1 Versuche, deinen Partner / deine Partnerin zum Mitmachen beim Theaterworkshop zu gewinnen.
You can say:
Let's ...

2 Partner B antwortet.

3 Sage, warum du den Theaterworkshop für eine gute Idee hältst.

4 Partner B möchte lieber etwas anderes machen.

5 Erkläre, dass in dem Stück bestimmt auch gesungen werden kann.
You can say:
I'm sure there will be ...

6 Partner B antwortet.

7 Du findest den Vorschlag deines Partners / deiner Partnerin gut.

8 Partner B macht einen weiteren Vorschlag.

9 Du findest, dass das ein guter Kompromiss ist.

10 Partner B reagiert.

11 Du bist ebenfalls froh, dass ihr eine Lösung gefunden habt.
You can say:
So am I.

10b UNIT 5, p. 118 PARTNER A, media worksheet 5, 6

You can record your role play if you like.

Giving directions

7 UNIT 1, p. 23 PARTNER B, wordbank: getting around p. 162

Look at the map. You are at the London Eye, your partner is at Tower Bridge. Ask for directions and guide each other to one or more sights. Your partner starts, then take turns.

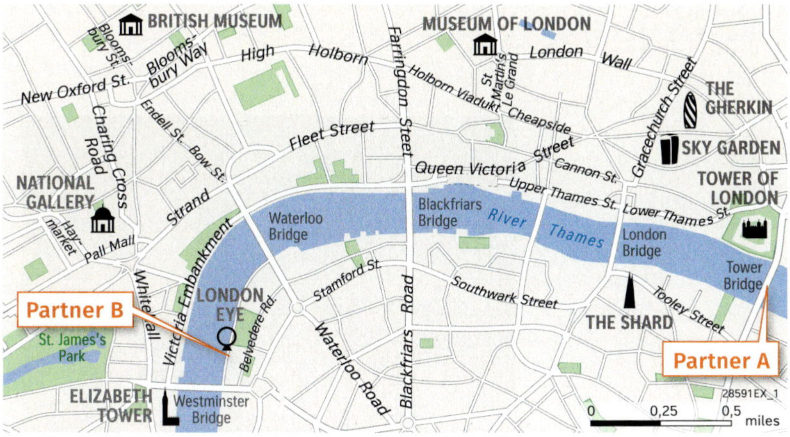

You can answer:

Yes, sure.
Go straight on. On your left there is …
Then turn left. On your right there is …
Turn right. Cross the road and then …

You can ask:

Excuse me, where is the …, please?

A calendar of world festivals

11a UNIT 2, p. 49 PARTNER B, wordbank: celebrations p. 163

Copy the table.
Then ask and answer questions with your partner and make notes in the table.

What?	When?	What do people do?	Other information
Christmas		*go to church, put up tree, decorate, give presents, …*	*Christian festival, birth of Jesus Christ, Father Christmas, …*
Halloween	*31 October*	*wear costumes, go trick-or-treating, …*	*very old festival, …*
Easter		*hide easter eggs, go to church, …*	*Christian festival, Easter bunny, …*
Diwali	*in October or November*		*Hindu festival, festival of light, light wins over dark*
Eid			*Muslim festival, end of fast, …*

You can ask:

When is Christmas?
What do people do on …?

You can answer:

Halloween is on 31 October.
People …

Animals in Britain

9a UNIT 3, p. 72 PARTNER B, skill: reading p. 154

Read the text about foxes in London. Take notes on:

1 When did foxes first appear in London?
2 How many foxes are there in London?
3 At what time of the day do you often see foxes in London?

Foxes in London
The first foxes appeared in London in the 1920s. Some people say that between 5,000 and 10,000 foxes live there today.
Foxes quickly realized that they could find a lot to eat in the city and that they could live in the many parks and gardens in London. It is not unusual to see a fox right in the middle of London, especially at night.

9b UNIT 3, p. 72 PARTNER B

Use your notes and tell your partner two or more things about city foxes in the UK.

Travelling in time

11a UNIT 4, p. 97 PARTNER B, audio 2/29, skill: listening p. 151

Listen to Sarah talking about her time travelling adventure. Take notes on:

1 Where she lives.
2 What year she lives in.
3 What time she travelled to.
4 What she saw.

11b UNIT 4, p. 97 PARTNER B

Use your notes and answer your partner's questions about Sarah.

11c UNIT 4, p. 97 PARTNER B

Now find out about Hiroto. Ask your partner questions.

1 Where does Hiroto live?
2 What year does he live in?
3 What year did he travel to?
4 What did he see there?

Choose a workshop

10a UNIT 5, p. 118 PARTNER B, skill: performing a scene p. 159

You want to do a summer holiday workshop with a partner. You would like to do a singing workshop, but your partner would like to join the drama workshop. Can you find a workshop that both of you like? Look at the boxes and do a role play. Your partner starts.

1 Partner A beginnt.

2 Drücke aus, dass du nicht so überzeugt bist.
You can say:
Really? The drama workshop?

3 Partner A antwortet.

4 Erkläre deinem Partner / deiner Partnerin, warum du lieber beim Gesangsworkshop mitmachen möchtest.
You can say:
But I'm not very good at acting. I'm much better at singing. I would like to do the singing workshop instead.

5 Partner A reagiert.

6 Versuche, einen Kompromiss zu finden.
You can say:
Maybe we can find a workshop that we both like?

7 Partner A antwortet.

8 Schlage den Musicalworkshop vor.
You can say:
There's a musical workshop. That's singing AND acting. What about that?

9 Partner A reagiert.

10 Du bist froh, dass ihr eine Lösung gefunden habt.
You can say:
I'm glad we found something we both like.

11 Partner A reagiert.

10b UNIT 5, p. 118 PARTNER B, media worksheet 5, 6

You can record your role play if you like.

Giving directions

7 UNIT 1, p. 23 PARTNER B, wordbank: getting around p. 162

Look at the map. You are at the London Eye, your partner is at Tower Bridge. Ask for directions and guide each other to one or more sights. Your partner starts, then take turns.

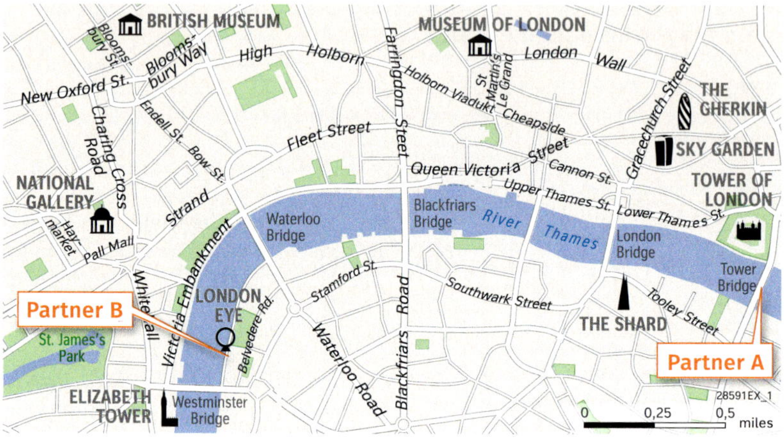

- ↑ go straight on
- ↰ turn left
- ↱ turn right
- walk past
- carry on until you get to ...
- ⇤ on your left
- ⇥ on your right
- cross the road

You can ask:

Excuse me, could you tell me the way to …, please?

…

You can answer:

Yes, sure.

Go straight on. Then …

…

A calendar of world festivals

11a UNIT 2, p. 49 PARTNER B, wordbank: celebrations p. 163

Copy the table.
Then ask and answer questions with your partner and make notes in the table.

What?	When?	What do people do?	Other information
Christmas		*go to church, put up tree, decorate, give presents, …*	*Christian festival, birth of Jesus Christ, Father Christmas, …*
Halloween	*31 October*	*wear costumes, go trick-or-treating, …*	*very old festival, …*
Easter		*hide eggs, go to Easter egg roll, …*	*Christian festival, Easter bunny, …*
Diwali	*in October or November*		*Hindu festival, festival of light, light wins over dark*
Eid			*Muslim festival, end of fast, …*

You can ask:

What do people do on …?

…

You can answer:

People …

…

Animals in Britain

9a UNIT 3, p. 72 PARTNER B, skill: reading p. 154

Read the text about foxes in London. Take notes on:

1 How many foxes are there in London?
2 What do they eat?
3 At what time do you often see foxes in London?
4 What is a danger for foxes in London?

Foxes in London
The first foxes appeared in London in the 1920s. Some people say that between 5,000 and 10,000 foxes live there today. Foxes quickly realized that they could find a lot to eat in the city. They often search for food in the rubbish from restaurants, for example, but they also catch small animals like mice. It is not unusual to see a fox right in the middle of London, especially at night. The only real problem for them is cars – crossing a street can be very dangerous for foxes in London.

9b UNIT 3, p. 72 PARTNER B

Use your notes and tell your partner three or more things about foxes in London.

Travelling in time

11a UNIT 4, p. 97 PARTNER B, audio 2/29, skill: listening p. 151

Listen to Sarah talking about her time travelling adventure. Take notes on:

1 Where she lives.
2 What year she lives in.
3 What time she travelled to.
4 What she saw.
5 How she liked time travelling.

11b UNIT 4, p. 97 PARTNER B

Use your notes and answer your partner's questions about Sarah.

11c UNIT 4, p. 97 PARTNER B

Now find out about Hiroto. Ask your partner questions about:

1 Where he lives.
2 What year he lives in.
3 What time he travelled to.
4 What he saw.
5 How he liked time travelling.

Choose a workshop

10a UNIT 5, p. 118 PARTNER B, skill: performing a scene p. 159

**You want to do a summer holiday workshop with a partner.
You would like to do a singing workshop, but your partner would like to join the drama workshop. Can you find a workshop that both of you like?
Look at the boxes and do a role play. Your partner starts.**

1 Partner A beginnt.

2 Drücke aus, dass du nicht so überzeugt bist.
You can say:
Really?

3 Partner A antwortet.

4 Erkläre deinem Partner / deiner Partnerin, warum du lieber beim Gesangsworkshop mitmachen möchtest.
You can say:
But I'm not very good at …

5 Partner A reagiert.

6 Versuche, einen Kompromiss zu finden.
You can say:
Isn't there …?

7 Partner A antwortet.

8 Schlage den Musicalworkshop vor.

9 Partner A reagiert.

10 Du bist froh, dass ihr eine Lösung gefunden habt.
You can say:
I'm glad we …

11 Partner A reagiert.

10b UNIT 5, p. 118 PARTNER B, media worksheet 5, 6

You can record your role play if you like.

Giving directions

7 UNIT 1, p. 23 PARTNER B, wordbank: getting around p. 162

Look at the map.
You are at the London Eye, your partner is at Tower Bridge.
Ask for directions and guide each other to one or more sights.
Your partner starts, then take turns.

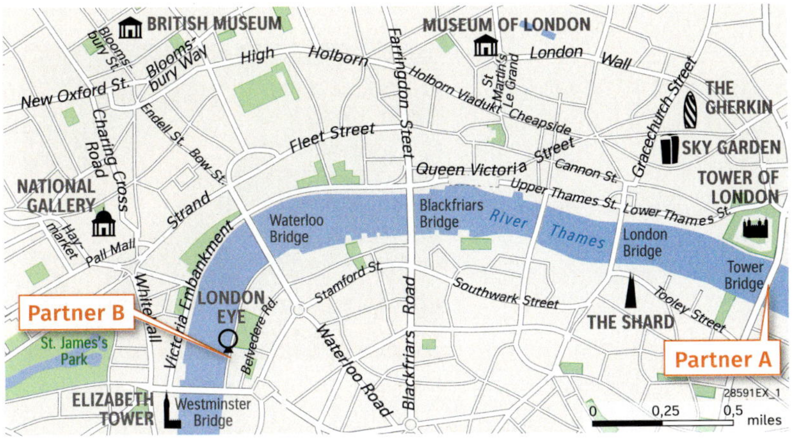

↑ go straight on
↰ turn left
↱ turn right
walk past
carry on until you get to ...
on your left
on your right
cross the road

A calendar of world festivals

11a UNIT 2, p. 49 PARTNER B, wordbank: celebrations p. 163

Copy the table.
Then ask and answer questions with your partner and make notes in the table.

What?	When?	What do people do?	Other information
Christmas		*go to church, put up tree, decorate, give presents, ...*	
Halloween	*31 October*	*wear costumes, go trick-or-treating, ...*	
Easter		*hide eggs, go to Easter egg roll, ...*	*Christian festival, Easter bunny, ...*
Diwali	*in October or November*		
Eid			*Muslim festival, end of Ramadan, ...*

You can ask:

What do people do on ...?
Have you got other information about Diwali?
...

Animals in Britain

9a UNIT 3, p. 72 PARTNER B, skill: reading p. 154

Read the text about foxes in London. Take notes on:

1 How many foxes are there in London?
2 When did the first foxes appear in London?
3 What do they eat?
4 What do they like about London?
5 At what time do you often see foxes in London?
6 What is a danger for foxes in London?

Foxes in London

Some people say that between 5,000 and 10,000 foxes live in London today. The first foxes appeared in the city in the 1920s when London grew into the surrounding areas. Foxes quickly realized that they could find a lot to eat in the city. They often search for food in the rubbish – from restaurants, for example – but they also catch small animals like mice.

They like the many parks and gardens in London and find lots of places where they can live. It is not unusual to see a fox right in the middle of London, especially at night. The only real problem for them is cars – crossing a street can be very dangerous for foxes in London.

9b UNIT 3, p. 72 PARTNER B

Use your notes and tell your partner four or more things about foxes in London.

Travelling in time

11a UNIT 4, p. 97 PARTNER B, audio 2/29, skill: listening p. 151

Listen to Sarah talking about her time travelling adventure. Take notes on:

1 Where she lives.
2 What year she lives in.
3 What year she travelled to.
4 What she saw.
5 How she liked time travelling.
6 How she came back to her own time.

11b UNIT 4, p. 97 PARTNER B

Use your notes and answer your partner's questions about Sarah.

11c UNIT 4, p. 97 PARTNER B

Now find out about Hiroto. Ask your partner questions about:

1 Where he lives.
2 What year he lives in.
3 What year he travelled to.
4 What he saw.
5 How he liked time travelling.
6 How he came back to his own time.

Choose a workshop

10a UNIT 5, p. 118 PARTNER B, skill: performing a scene p. 159

III You want to do a summer holiday workshop with a partner. You would like to do a singing workshop, but your partner would like to join the drama workshop. Can you find a workshop that both of you like? Look at the boxes and do a role play. Your partner starts.

1 Partner A beginnt.

2 Drücke aus, dass du nicht so überzeugt bist.
You can say:
Really?

3 Partner A antwortet.

4 Erkläre deinem Partner / deiner Partnerin, warum du lieber beim Gesangsworkshop mitmachen möchtest.

5 Partner A reagiert.

6 Versuche, einen Kompromiss zu finden.
You can say:
Isn't there ...?

7 Partner A antwortet.

8 Schlage den Musicalworkshop vor.

9 Partner A reagiert.

10 Du bist froh, dass ihr eine Lösung gefunden habt.
You can say:
I'm glad we ...

11 Partner A reagiert.

10b UNIT 5, p. 118 PARTNER B, media worksheet 5, 6

III You can record your role play if you like.

A country profile: the UK DIGITAL+

Introduction

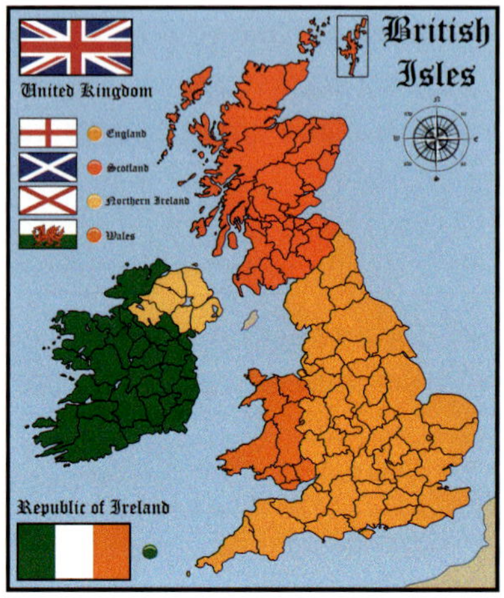

You have already learnt quite a lot about the UK – but why not take a closer look at the country and find out more about its four parts: England, Scotland, Wales and Northern Ireland? There are many questions you can ask, for example:

- What are the most famous sights for visitors in the different parts of the UK?
- What are good places to visit for nature lovers?
- What famous people (musicians, sportspeople, actors, actresses, authors, ...) come from the UK?
- What official languages are there in the UK?

Find answers to these and other interesting questions in a project about the UK!

Plan it

1 In class, collect ideas for topics. You could create profiles for each of the four parts of the country. Or you could start with general aspects you would like to look at. You can make notes in a word web. Here is an example:

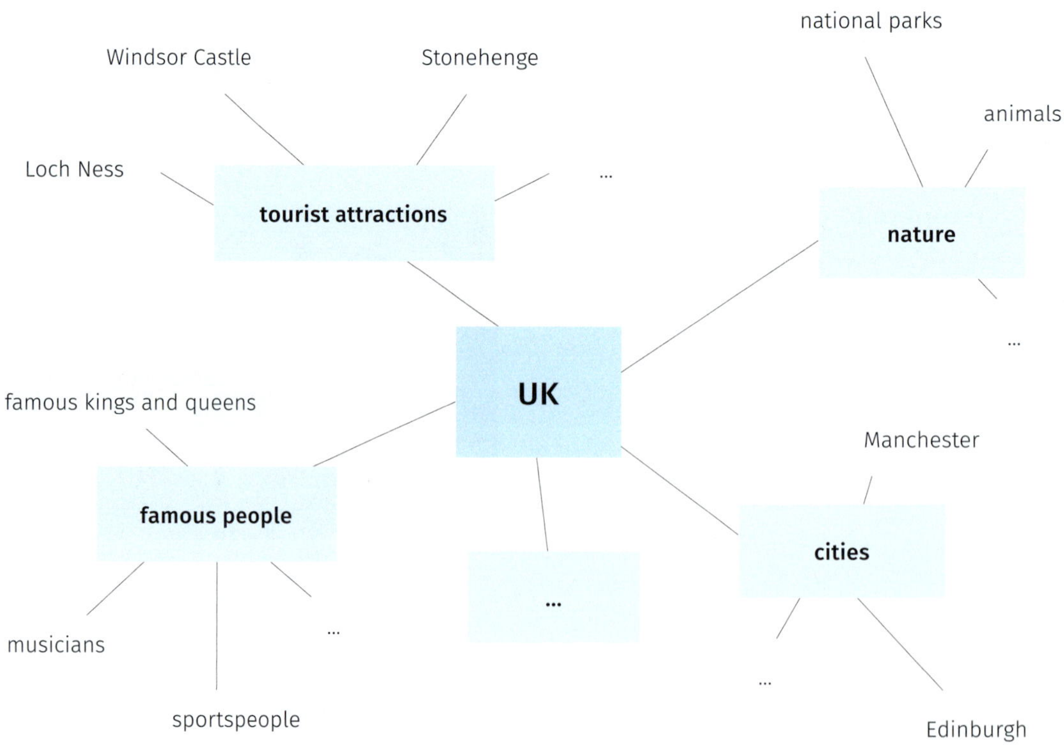

2 **Now collect ideas about what you could create. For example:**

- fact files
- posters
- pages for a computer presentation
- podcasts
- ...

Tip

You can make a class product, for example a brochure: every group creates one page and you put everything together in the end.

Wales

- capital: Cardiff
- population: about 3.1 million
- languages: English, Welsh
- ...

3 **Now get together in small groups and make a detailed plan. Write down:**

- what information you need
- how you can find information
- how you want to present your work
- what material you need for your project work (for example: computer, paper, glue, ...)
- who does what and when

Tip

When you as a group have a plan about what to do and how to present your work, you can ask your classmates from other groups for feedback on your plan.

Do it

video 31-34, skill: searching the Internet p. 157, media worksheet 3, 4, 7

And ... action! Do research, collect pictures, write texts, ... and create an interesting fact file, poster, computer presentation, ...

Check it

Check everything. Are there any spelling or grammar mistakes? Are the pictures big enough? Is everything easy to understand? If you want to give a presentation, practise it before you give it.

Present it

skill: presentations p. 158

Present your work. You can ask your classmates for feedback after the presentation.

A country profile: the USA DIGITAL+

Introduction

What comes to mind when you think of the USA? The USA is a huge country: it is the third largest country in the world with fifty individual states. There is a lot to discover – so why not take a first look and find out a bit more?

Plan it

1 In class, collect ideas for topics you would like to focus on. You can collect your ideas in a list, for example:

- Important cities: New York, San Francisco, Los Angeles, ...
- Nature: Rocky Mountains, ...
- Popular sports: American football, basketball, ...
- Important festivals: Thanksgiving, ...
- Language: differences between American English and British English, ...
- Music: ...
- ...

2 **Now collect ideas about what you could create. For example:**

- fact files
- posters
- pages for a computer presentation
- podcasts
- ...

Tip

You can make a class product, for example a brochure: every group creates one page and you put everything together in the end.

The United States of America
- capital: Washington D.C.
- population: about 330 million
- largest state: Alaska
- ...

3 **Now get together in small groups and make a detailed plan. Write down:**

- what information you need
- how you can get the information
- how you want to present your work
- what material you need for your project work (for example: computer, paper, glue, ...)
- who does what and when

Tip

When you as a group have a plan about what to do and how to present your work, you can ask your classmates from other groups for feedback on your plan.

Do it

video 35, skill: searching the Internet p. 157, media worksheet 3, 4, 7

And ... action! Do research, collect pictures, write texts, ... and create an interesting poster, fact file, ...

Check it

Check everything. Are there any spelling or grammar mistakes? Are the pictures big enough? Is everything easy to understand? If you are planning to give a presentation, practise it before you present it.

Present it

skill: presentations p. 158

Present your work. You can ask your classmates for feedback after the presentation.

1 WORKING WITH WORDS
Wortschatzarbeit

Wenn man eine Fremdsprache lernt, stößt man häufig auf unbekannte Wörter. Manchmal kann man sich die Bedeutung von Wörtern aus dem Zusammenhang erschließen. Manchmal muss man sie aber auch nachschlagen, und wichtige Wörter, die häufig vorkommen, sollte man sich merken.

1. Mit dem Wörterbuch in *Notting Hill Gate* arbeiten

- Du kannst die deutschen Übersetzungen für alle englischen Wörter aus deinem Englischbuch im *dictionary* ab Seite 220 nachschlagen.
- Sieh dabei gut hin: Die Wörter sind alphabetisch geordnet. Du musst nicht nur auf den ersten Buchstaben im Wort achten, sondern auch auf den zweiten oder sogar den dritten. Das Wort *back* steht zum Beispiel vor *banana*.
- Für manche Wörter gibt es mehrere Übersetzungen. Das Wort *work* beispielsweise ist einmal ein Nomen (Arbeit) und einmal ein Verb (arbeiten, funktionieren). Sieh genau hin, welche Übersetzung am besten passt.

2. So kannst du dir Wörter merken und sie notieren

- Außer dem alphabetisch sortierten *dictionary* gibt es in deinem Buch ab Seite 197 eine nach Kapiteln sortierte Wortliste, die auf Seite 194 erklärt wird.
- Die Wörter, die du lernen möchtest, kannst du dir immer wieder laut vorlesen, bis du sie dir eingeprägt hast. Es ist sinnvoll, ein Wort in einem Satzzusammenhang zu lernen, dann weißt du auch immer sofort, wie es verwendet wird.
- Wenn du gut durch Zuhören lernst, kannst du die Wörter und Beispielsätze auch aufnehmen und sie dir immer wieder anhören.
- Vielleicht hilft es dir aber auch, Wörter aufzuschreiben und zu sortieren. Du kannst zum Beispiel Wörter, die zu einem Begriff passen, in einem *word web* oder einer Liste sammeln, oder dir eigene *wordbanks* anlegen.
- Versuche, Gegensatzpaare zu finden, also Wörter wie *young – old, boy – girl, student – teacher, true – false, happy – unhappy* usw.
- Versuche, Wörter einer Wortfamile zu finden, zum Beispiel *invite – invitation, sing – singer, bake – baker, China – Chinese* usw.
- Übe Vokabeln immer nur fünf bis zehn Minuten am Stück, aber dafür regelmäßig.

Tipp: Übe auch die Aussprache

- Wenn du gern mit dem Computer lernst, kannst du die Vokabeln auch mit der Vokabeltrainer-App lernen. Hier kannst du dir auch die richtige Aussprache anhören.
- Wenn du auf www.westermann.de/webcode den Webcode von Seite 2 eingibst oder den QR-Code scannst, den du dort findest, findest du Videos, mit denen du Wortschatz zu bestimmten Wortfeldern üben kannst.

2 LISTENING Hören

Du kennst bestimmt schon einige Methoden, mit denen du Hörtexte besser verstehen kannst. Hier ist eine Übersicht über die wichtigsten:

1. Vor dem Hören

- Gibt es eine Höraufgabe im Buch? Dann lies sie dir genau durch. Was sollst du herausfinden?
- Wie lautet die Überschrift des Hörtextes? Welche Hinweise gibt sie dir?
- Gibt es Bilder? Was ist darauf zu sehen? Vielleicht kannst du vor dem Hören schon etwas über die Situation herausfinden.
- Überlege: Worum könnte es gehen? Was weißt du schon über das Thema?

2. Während des Hörens

- Höre dir den Hörtext einmal ganz an und verschaffe dir einen Überblick. Wer ist beteiligt? Was ist passiert? Vielleicht kannst du auch schon etwas heraushören, das du für die Bearbeitung der Aufgabe brauchst.
- Dabei musst du nicht jedes einzelne Wort verstehen. Versuche erst einmal herauszufinden, worum es ganz allgemein geht *(listening for gist).*
- Achte auch auf die Stimmen der Sprechenden, auf ihre Körpersprache, Gesichtsausdruck und Gesten. Auch Hintergrundgeräusche können dir helfen zu verstehen, worum es geht.
- Sieh dir noch einmal an, was du herausfinden sollst. Dann höre wieder zu. Achte diesmal auch auf Details *(listening for detail)* und mache dir Notizen. Notiere nur Stichwörter, keine ganzen Sätze.

3. Nach dem Hören

- Konntest du alles heraushören, was du für die Höraufgabe herausfinden solltest?
- Vergleiche deine Ergebnisse mit denen eines Partners oder einer Partnerin.
- Gibt es Stellen, an denen du gar nicht verstehst, worum es geht? Suche dir einen Partner oder eine Partnerin. Versucht zusammen, den Text zu verstehen.

Tipp: Nutze jede Gelegenheit, um Englisch zu hören (media worksheet 1)

- Alle Hörtexte zum Buch findest du, wenn du auf www.westermann.de/webcode den Webcode von Seite 2 eingibst oder den QR-Code scannst, den du dort findest.
- Wenn du englischsprachige Musik hörst, achte auf den Text. Was kannst du schon verstehen? Viele Liedtexte findest du im Internet und kannst sie beim Hören mitlesen.
- Sieh dir Filme, Serien oder Berichte zu Themen, die dich interessieren auf Englisch an. Auf DVDs oder bei Streaming-Diensten kannst du fast immer den englischen Ton und englische Untertitel einschalten.

3 TALKING WITH PEOPLE
Mit anderen sprechen

Im Englischunterricht arbeitest du oft mit einem Partner, einer Partnerin oder in einer Gruppe zusammen. Auch wenn es dir vielleicht komisch vorkommt, solltest du mit deinen Mitschülerinnen und Mitschülern Englisch sprechen. So übst du, dich immer besser auf Englisch zu verständigen.

1. Versuche, so viel wie möglich auf Englisch auszudrücken

- Wenn du über ein bestimmtes Thema sprechen willst, überlege dir vorher einige Ausdrücke, die du im Gespräch verwenden kannst. Die *wordbanks* ab Seite 160 können dir dabei helfen.
- Wenn du etwas nicht verstanden hast, bitte darum, dass es wiederholt wird:
  „Can you say that again, please?“ oder: *„Can you repeat that, please?“*
- Wenn dir ein Wort nicht einfällt, kannst du es umschreiben:
  „Excuse me, I need a ... erm ... it's a school thing. You can write with it.“

2. Präge dir Redewendungen und Sätze ein

- Es gibt eine Reihe von Redewendungen und Sätzen, die du im Englischunterricht häufig verwenden kannst.
- Wenn du Vorschläge machen möchtest:
  What about ...?
  Why don't we ...?
- Wenn du deine eigene Meinung ausdrücken möchtest:
  I think that's wrong. / I don't think he's right.
  In my opinion that's ...
  I agree. / I think that's right.
- Wenn du mit jemandem zusammenarbeitest:
  Let's do it like this.
  It's my / your turn.

3. Sprich so oft Englisch, wie du kannst

- Höre dir die Hörtexte aus deinem Englischbuch an und lies die Texte laut mit. Versuche, die Aussprache der Sprecherinnen und Sprecher nachzuahmen.
- Singe englischsprachige Lieder mit.
- Unterhalte dich auf Englisch mit jemandem, der ebenfalls Englisch sprechen kann.

Tipp: Nimm dich auf (media worksheet 5, 6)

- Lies einen Text aus dem Buch laut vor oder sprich Englisch und nimm dich auf. Dann kannst du dich selbst anhören und überprüfen, wie dein Englisch klingt.
- Wenn du mit einem Partner oder einer Partnerin zusammenarbeitest, könnt ihr Dialoge aufnehmen und gemeinsam prüfen, ob es noch etwas zu verbessern gibt.

4 WRITING Schreiben

Wenn du einen Text schreiben willst, gehst du am besten Schritt für Schritt vor.

1. Planen

- Überlege: Was für einen Text willst du schreiben – eine E-Mail, eine Textnachricht, eine Geschichte? An wen richtet sich der Text?
- Überlege dir eine Reihenfolge. Was schreibst du zuerst, was folgt darauf, was steht am Ende?
- Sammle Ideen und Wörter zum Thema deines Textes in einem *word web* oder einer Liste.

2. Schreiben

- Schreibe erst einmal in kurzen, einfachen Sätzen einen ersten Entwurf.
- Dann überarbeite deine Sätze. Sieh dir auch Texte zu deinem Thema im Buch an. Du kannst sie als Muster benutzen. Übernimm nützliche Satzanfänge und Ausdrücke und ersetze die Wörter, die nicht zum Thema passen oder dir nicht gefallen.
- Achte darauf, dass dein Text eine Einleitung, einen Mittelteil und einen Schluss hat.
- Beginne deine Sätze nicht immer mit dem gleichen Wort, damit dein Text abwechslungsreicher wird. Zum Beispiel:
  Georgia opened the compass. Georgia said: "Look, here it is."
  Georgia opened the compass. She said: "Look, here it is."
- Adjektive und Adverbien machen deinen Text interessanter.
  A man opened the door and looked at us.
  Suddenly a tall man opened the door and looked at us angrily.
- Verbinde Sätze mit *and, or, but, so* oder *because*. Zum Beispiel:
  They tried to find the dog. They did not find it. It hid in a bush.
  They tried to find the dog, but they did not find it because it hid in a bush.
- Überlege dir eine passende Überschrift zu deinem Text.

3. Überarbeiten

- Sieh dir deinen Text noch einmal genau an.
- Bist du bei der Grammatik unsicher? Schau im Grammatik-Teil ab Seite 174 nach.
- Falls nötig, schreibe eine zweite, verbesserte Version deines Textes.

Tipp: Benutze Textverarbeitungsprogramme (media worksheet 3)

- Wenn du deinen Text mithilfe eines Textverarbeitungsprogramms am Computer schreibst, kannst du zunächst Ideen und nützliche Wörter in einem Dokument sammeln und speichern. Du kannst deine Ideensammlung und deinen Text dann jederzeit bearbeiten, ändern und ergänzen.

5 READING Lesen

Es gibt viele Strategien, die dir helfen, einen englischen Text zu verstehen. Probiere doch einmal die folgenden Tipps beim Lesen aus:

1. Gibt es ein Bild? Was verrät es? Worum könnte es in der Geschichte gehen?
2. Was erfährst du aus der Überschrift?
3. Überfliege den Text erst einmal *(reading for gist)*. Versuche herauszufinden, worum es geht. Was passiert? Wer ist beteiligt? Dafür brauchst du nicht jedes Wort zu verstehen. Versuche, unbekannte Wörter aus dem Zusammenhang zu erschließen.
4. Lies den Text noch einmal gründlich *(reading for detail)*. Mit den wh-Fragen kannst du die wichtigsten Informationen herausbekommen:
   Who? Where? When? What?
   Mach dir Notizen. Auf Kopien kannst du auch wichtige Textstellen markieren.

The orienteering trip

Last summer a group of twenty boys went camping and orienteering in Scotland for two days. They had small tents and sleeping bags in their rucksacks. Every pair had a map, a compass, food and drink and warm pullovers and trousers. Jim and Kevin were partners. The two boys walked and walked and talked and laughed about lots of things. But they didn't look at their maps and they didn't look at their watches. It got dark and foggy. They looked for the others but couldn't find them, so they put up their tent, ate some chocolate and told ghost stories. Suddenly there were strange noises. And then a big dark thing came to their tent. It opened the tent and said, "Ah, it's you two! The others are all here, too. But they're still putting up their tents, so you're the winners. Congratulations!" It was the guide, John. Jim and Kevin were at the campsite!

5. Auf den *Practise-reading*-Seiten im Workbook kannst du weitere hilfreiche Lesestrategien ausprobieren.

Tipp: Suche dir englische Texte zu Themen, die dich interessieren

- Du kannst im Internet und in Büchereien nach interessanten Texten auf Englisch suchen.
- Am Ende jeder Unit in diesem Buch findest du ein Kapitel der Geschichte *Kora and the New Zealand dragons*.

6 MEDIATION
Sprachmittlung

Manchmal gibt es Situationen, in denen du jemandem helfen musst, der deine Sprache oder eine Fremdsprache nicht so gut kann wie du. Hier erfährst du, wie das funktioniert:

1. Gib den Sinn wieder

Es kommt nicht darauf an, dass du alles Wort für Wort übersetzt. Wichtiger ist es, den Sinn wiederzugeben. Es muss nur klar werden, worum es geht.

2. Fasse dich kurz

Bilde einfache, kurze Sätze. Unwichtige Einzelheiten kannst du weglassen.

48-hour theatre workshop with Gus
Do you like acting? Then come and join our special weekend acting workshop. We are going to stage a play in just 48 hours. Everybody is welcome!
Where: in the assembly hall
When: next Saturday and Sunday

Tipp: Habe keine Angst vor Fehlern!

- Wenn dir ein wichtiges Wort nicht einfällt, kannst du es umschreiben. Du weißt zum Beispiel nicht, was „Geschenk" auf Englisch heißt? Dann kannst du sagen: *„You give it to a friend. It's for a birthday."*
- Versuche, dich an Redewendungen aus dem Englischunterricht zu erinnern – zum Beispiel daran, dass du mit *„What about …?"* Vorschläge machen kannst.

7 WATCHING A VIDEO CLIP
Videoclips verstehen

Englischsprachige Videoclips anzuschauen macht nicht nur Spaß. Es ist auch eine tolle Möglichkeit, die Sprache noch besser zu lernen. Dabei solltest du einige Dinge beachten:

1. Bevor es losgeht
- Gibt es Bilder zu dem Videoclip in deinem Buch oder Workbook? Was ist zu sehen?
- Lies den Titel des Videoclips. Welche Hinweise gibt er auf den Inhalt?
- Worum könnte es gehen? Stelle Vermutungen an. Weißt du vielleicht schon etwas über das Thema?

2. Währenddessen
- Schaue dir den Videoclip in Ruhe an. Konzentriere dich dabei zunächst vor allem auf das, was du siehst.
  Who? Wer ist zu sehen? Um wen geht es?
  Where? Wo findet das Geschehen statt?
  When? Wann findet das Geschehen statt?
  What? Worum geht es? Was passiert?
- Was ist dein erster Eindruck? Mache dir Notizen. Es ist nicht schlimm, wenn du nicht alles verstehst. Achte auf die Stimmen, Körpersprache und Gesichtsausdrücke der Personen im Videoclip.
- Gibt es eine Aufgabe zu dem Videoclip in deinem Buch oder dem Workbook? Was sollst du herausfinden? Behalte die Frage im Kopf, während du ein zweites Mal zuschaust. Konzentriere dich stärker auf das, was du hörst. Kannst du jetzt schon mehr verstehen? Gibt es Wörter, die immer wieder vorkommen? Notiere sie dir.
- Versuche, gleich danach die Frage zu beantworten. Wenn nötig, schaue dir dann den Clip ein weiteres Mal an. Überprüfe dabei deine Antworten.

3. Hinterher
- Tausche dich mit deinen Mitschülerinnen und Mitschülern aus. Welche Eindrücke habt ihr bekommen? Was habt ihr herausgefunden?

Tipp: Schaue dir Videoclips und Filme auf Englisch an (media worksheet 1)
- Alle Videoclips zum Buch findest du, wenn du auf www.westermann.de/webcode den Webcode von Seite 2 eingibst oder den QR-Code scannst, den du dort findest.
- Sieh dir Filme, Serien oder Berichte zu Themen, die dich interessieren, auf Englisch an.
- Auf DVDs oder bei Streaming-Diensten kannst du fast immer den englischen Ton und englische Untertitel einschalten. Das kann eine große Hilfe sein. Nach und nach lernt man so besser zu verstehen, was auf Englisch gesagt wird.

8 SEARCHING THE INTERNET
Im Internet recherchieren

Hier erfährst du, wie du im Internet zu einem Thema recherchieren kannst.

1. Benutze eine Suchmaschine

- Gute Suchbegriffe erleichtern dir die Suche im Internet. Versuche, möglichst genau zu formulieren, wonach du suchst – und zwar auf Englisch.
- Gib die Suchbegriffe in eine Suchmaschine ein.
- Es kann sein, dass die Suchmaschine eine riesige Anzahl an Treffern anzeigt. Oft genügt es, sich die ersten 10 bis 20 Suchergebnisse anzuschauen.

2. Suche auf englischsprachigen Seiten

- Suche am besten gleich auf englischsprachigen Seiten – dann steht dir der nötige Wortschatz gleich zur Verfügung. Bei vielen Suchmaschinen kannst du Englisch als Sprache wählen.
- Es gibt Webseiten, auf denen du Informationen in einfacherem Englisch finden kannst. Dein Lehrer oder deine Lehrerin kann dir helfen, sie zu finden.

3. Halte nützliche Informationen fest

- Überfliege erst einmal die Seiten, die dir interessant erscheinen. Dafür brauchst du nicht jedes Wort zu verstehen.
- Wenn du interessante Webseiten gefunden hast, kannst du dir Notizen zu den Inhalten machen.
- Denke daran, dir auch das Datum der Recherche aufzuschreiben und die Quelle zu sichern. Die Quelle ist die URL. Das ist die Adresse der Webseite, die du einfach aus der obersten Zeile in deinem Browser kopieren und speichern kannst. So weißt du später noch, wo du die Informationen gefunden hast.
- Wenn du Textausschnitte für deine eigenen Texte unverändert aus dem Internet übernimmst, musst du zeigen, dass es Zitate sind. Setze sie in Anführungszeichen und gib das Datum, an dem du sie gefunden hast, und die Quelle an.

Tipp: Sei kritisch (media worksheet 4)

- Informationen, die du im Internet findest, sind nicht immer richtig.
- Sei deshalb kritisch und überprüfe die Informationen noch einmal auf anderen Seiten oder in einem Lexikon.
- Einige Webseiten sind vertrauenswürdiger als andere. Suche möglichst auf Seiten, von denen du weißt, dass du dich auf die Informationen verlassen kannst. Deine Lehrkraft kann dir sicher Tipps geben.

9 PRESENTATIONS
Präsentationen halten

Manchmal musst du vor der Klasse oder einer größeren Gruppe etwas vortragen oder präsentieren. Folgende Tipps können dir dabei helfen:

1. Bevor du etwas präsentierst

- Überlege: Was möchtest du zu deinem Thema sagen? Wie viel Zeit hast du für deinen Vortrag?
- Sammle deine Ideen und schreibe sie auf, zum Beispiel in einem *word web* oder in einer Liste.
- Gliedere deinen Vortrag: Überlege, in welcher Reihenfolge du deine Ideen vorstellen und wie du anfangen möchtest.
- Du kannst auch ein Poster mit Bildern oder Fotos anfertigen, um deine Präsentation interessanter zu gestalten. Wenn du Bilder oder Texte aus dem Internet oder aus einem Buch kopiert hast, dann vermerke immer, wo und wann du sie gefunden hast.
- Notiere Stichpunkte zu dem, was du sagen möchtest, auf Karteikarten.
- Übe deinen Vortrag vor dem Spiegel, vor Freunden oder vor deiner Familie.

2. Während du präsentierst

- Sprich langsam und deutlich.
- Sieh deine Zuhörerinnen und Zuhörer an, wenn du sprichst.
- Versuche, frei zu sprechen. Du kannst die wichtigsten Punkte von deinen Notizen oder deinem Poster ablesen.

Wichtig für ein gelungenes Poster

- ansprechende Überschrift
- interessante Informationen, aber nicht zu viel Text
- lesbare Schrift
- passende Bilder mit Bildunterschriften

Hello everyone. Today I'd like to tell you something about ...

In this picture you can see ...

This picture shows ...

Thank you for listening. Have you got any questions?

Tipp: Überprüfe deine Aussprache (media worksheet 5, 7)

- Du kannst deinen Vortrag zur Probe aufnehmen, zum Beispiel mit dem Handy. Prüfe dann, ob du flüssig, verständlich und langsam genug gesprochen hast.
- Wenn du dir bei der Aussprache eines Wortes nicht sicher bist, kannst du dir das Wort in einem Online-Wörterbuch anhören.

10 PERFORMING A SCENE
Eine Szene vorspielen

Auch Rollenspiele und Theaterstücke sind eine gute Methode, um dein Englisch zu trainieren. Hier findest du einige Tipps, wie du erfolgreich Szenen vorspielen kannst.

1. Rollenspiele

- In einer Gruppe könnt ihr das, was ihr sagen wollt, auf einzelne Kärtchen schreiben. Nummeriert sie und legt sie in der richtigen Reihenfolge hin.
- Mit der Methode *read – look up – speak* kannst du deine Rolle auswendig lernen: Du liest deinen Satz still, siehst dann auf und sprichst ihn.
- Halte beim Sprechen Augenkontakt zu deinem Gegenüber.
- Im Englischen drückt man sich oft sehr höflich aus. Achte daher auf eine höfliche Ausdrucksweise und verwende an passenden Stellen *thank you, please* und *excuse me*.
- Wechselt auch mal die Rollen und übt mit anderen Partnerinnen und Partnern. So lernt ihr, spontan zu reagieren.

2. Theaterstücke

- Bei Theaterstücken geht es noch mehr als bei Rollenspielen um das Schauspielern. Du solltest deinen Text gut auswendig lernen, damit du dich besser darauf konzentrieren kannst.
- Versetze dich in die Person hinein, die du darstellst. Überlege, in welcher Stimmung die Person ist.
- Denke beim Sprechen an den passenden Gesichtsausdruck (Mimik) und die passende Bewegung (Gestik).
- Bevor es losgeht, kannst du dich mit kleinen Übungen warm machen. Dein Lehrer oder deine Lehrerin kennt bestimmt einige.
- Mit Requisiten *(props)* und Kostümen fällt es leichter, richtig in eine Rolle hineinzuschlüpfen.
- Denke immer daran, nicht zu schnell und laut und deutlich zu sprechen, damit das Publikum dich gut verstehen kann.

3. Präsentieren

- Rollenspiele, kleine Szenen, Sketche und Theaterstücke sind gute Mittel, um auch anderen zu zeigen, wie viel Englisch ihr schon könnt. Bei einem Schulfest oder an einem Tag der offenen Tür könnt ihr Eltern, Mitschülerinnen und Mitschüler zu einer Vorführung einladen.

Tipp: Schaut euch selbst zu (media worksheet 5, 6)

- Ihr könnt euch auch aufnehmen und so gemeinsam überprüfen, ob es noch etwas zu verbessern gibt.

Holidays

DIGITAL+ video 15

You can travel by …

bike · boat · bus ·
car · ferry · plane · train

You can stay …

at home · at summer camp ·
on a farm · at your grandparents' house ·
at a hotel · at a B&B

You can visit …

a castle

a museum

a zoo

a city

the seaside / a beach

a market

a shopping centre

a church

Countries

Egypt · England · France ·
Germany · India · Ireland ·
Italy · the Netherlands ·
New Zealand · Poland ·
Scotland · Spain ·
the USA · Wales

Activities

go sightseeing · go horse riding ·
do sports · go on a day trip ·
go swimming · go cycling · play video games ·
take photos · have a picnic ·
go shopping · go hiking · go abroad ·
visit relatives · go to an adventure park ·
play beach volleyball

Places can be …

big ↔ small
good ↔ bad
boring ↔ interesting, fun
new ↔ old
quiet ↔ loud
ugly ↔ beautiful, nice

The weather can be …

fantastic · great · good · brilliant ·
perfect · OK · fine · bad · terrible ·
stormy · rainy · sunny ·
cold · warm · hot

What do you like doing in your holidays?

I like going sightseeing.

I like doing sports.

Talking about your last holidays

What did you do in the holidays?

Did you stay at home?

I ...

Yes, I did. / No, I didn't.

Where did you go?

I went abroad.
I went to Italy / France / ...

What did you do?

I went sightseeing.

I did a lot of sports.

I spent my holidays at the beach.

How was it?

It was great because the castle that we visited was very old.

I loved the food. It was very special and yummy.

We went to an adventure park. It was great fun.

Getting around

DIGITAL+ video 16

London sights

Buckingham Palace · Big Ben · the Palace of Westminster · the River Thames · Sky Garden · Hyde Park · the Natural History Museum · London Zoo · Elizabeth Tower · the Shard · Notting Hill · the London Eye · Westminster Abbey · Trafalgar Square · Wembley Stadium · Covent Garden · Platform 9¾ · the Houses of Parliament · the Tower of London · Madame Tussauds · the London Transport Museum

Where do you want to go?

I'd love to go on the London Eye and see Big Ben.

Great. We can also see Buckingham Palace!

Can we go to a museum, too?

Of course. Most museums in London are free.

Brilliant. What a great plan. Let's book our tickets.

We're going to ... tomorrow.

The view from ... is spectacular.

We're at ... now.

London is great / fantastic!

Travelling with the Tube

What time does the next train leave?

The next train leaves at 10.48.

What line do we have to take?

We have to take the Central Line to Bond Street.

Where do we have to change lines?

We change lines at Bond Street and take the Jubilee Line to Westminster Station.

Great. How much is a Day Travelcard?

A Day Travelcard costs £6.90.

Giving or following directions

Turn left!

Turn right!

Walk past ...

Go straight on!

Walk on until you get to ...

Cross the road!

On your left you can see ...

On your right there is ...

Excuse me! How do I get to ...?

Turn left here and then walk ...

Celebrations

DIGITAL+ video 17

Festivals and holidays around the world

Easter · New Year's Eve · Hanukkah · Christmas · Chinese New Year · Halloween · Diwali · Eid · Bonfire Night · Ramadan · Hogmanay · Lantern festival

Food and drink

Easter eggs · sweets · cake · pumpkin · toffee apples · chocolate · s'mores · crisps · sausages · jacket potato · marshmallows · biscuits · lemonade · hot apple juice · orange juice · water · hot chocolate

Religions and cultures

Christians celebrate Christmas and Easter.

Muslims celebrate Eid and Ramadan.

Diwali is a popular festival of Hinduism.

Jewish people celebrate Hanukkah.

Many people in the UK celebrate Bonfire Night.

Many people around the world celebrate Halloween and New Year's Eve.

Let's celebrate!

We have a meal / dinner / a party / ...

We eat snacks / food / ...

We meet relatives / friends / your family / ...

We have decorations / balloons / fireworks / a parade / a funfair / a bonfire / an Easter egg hunt / music / fun / ...

We play games / apple bobbing / with a dreidel / ...

We dress up in costumes / ...

We light candles / a bonfire / / ...

We go to a traditional Easter egg roll / ...

We dance / sing / ...

Traditions

People in Spain eat 12 grapes at midnight to bring luck for the **new year**.

Jewish people light a candle on the Hanukkah menorah for eight days during **Hanukkah**.

During **Ramadan**, families go to the mosque for a special prayer.

For the **Chinese New Year**, many people clean their houses.

People have bonfires and fireworks to celebrate **Bonfire Night** in the UK.

Hindus traditionally light candles for **Diwali**.

In Scotland, "first footing" is when the first man who enters the house in the **new year** brings small presents for good luck.

On **Easter Sunday**, many children look for Easter eggs. In the UK, there are often Easter egg rolls, in some regions Germany you can find bonfires.

Children dress up and knock on doors to ask for sweets at Halloween. This is called **trick-or-treating**.

Rules

You must … / You mustn't …

You must wear school uniform.

You must do your homework.

You must not run in school.

You mustn't eat in the classroom.

You must always listen to the teacher.

You must show respect and be quiet.

You mustn't listen to music in the classroom.

You mustn't use your mobile phone in class.

Following the rules

We can drink during lessons, but we can't eat in the classroom.

We are allowed to bring our mobile phones to school, but we aren't allowed to use them in class.

We have to wear school uniform, but we don't have to wear the jacket in class.

We must be on time and we must not wear make-up.

We may talk to our friends in the breaks, but we may not talk during class.

We have to bring our books into school, but we don't have to carry them around with us.

Asking for something

Can I watch TV now? – Yes, you can. / No, you can't.
Am I allowed to have some sweets? – Yes, you are. / No, you aren't.
May I go to the cinema with my friends? – Yes, you may. / No, you may not.

Talking about conflicts

Problems

You play on your computer too much.

You go to bed too late.

You watch too much TV.

You haven't tidied your room.

You stayed out too late with your friends at the party on Saturday.

Arguments

Can I go to the park to play football with my friends?

No, you have to do your homework before you go.

But it will be dark then!

Fine. You can go now, but you have to be home by 6pm and do you homework then!

Of course I will! Thank you very much!

Why don't we go to the party?

I'm tired, I would rather watch a film and stay at home.

Please let's go, I'm so bored!

Why don't you go alone? Then we can both do what we want!

Good idea!

Discussions

I want ... · I don't want ... · I would like to ... · That's not fair. · Why can't I ...? · Could we ...? · I can live with that. · You're still too young. · All my friends are allowed to ... · OK then. · I don't think we should change the rules. · What about trying ...? · That's a good suggestion. · Don't interrupt, please. · Sorry.

I feel ...

angry · annoyed · bad · bored · excited · frustrated · good · happy · relaxed · sad · scared · terrible · tired · worried

Wildlife

DIGITAL+ video 18

Nature

trees · flowers · plants · animals · forest · moors · mountain · beach · lake · grass · leaves · environment

Things to do in nature

horse riding · Nordic walking · cycling · watching animals · swimming · walking your dog · going for walks · searching for animals

Wild animals

squirrel · fox · hedgehog · snail · bee · insect · fish · bird

Where can we find wild animals?

at a national park / forest / zoo / garden / park · at the wildlife centre / beach · in the street

Protecting the environment

We need to protect the environment. People destroy the homes of many wild animals.

Bees pollinate plants and have their nests in trees. We can build a bee hotel and grow more flowers in the garden.

Good idea. We can also make a bird feeder to hang in the garden.

Sure. We can also leave parts of the garden with long grass for animals to live in.

Excellent. Let's make a list of what we need.

Perfect. Let's go.

Wild animals

squirrel

bird

turtle

dolphin

insects

bee

tortoise

hedgehog

fox

mouse

Leatherback turtle

Lives in …
Eats …
Is in danger because …
…

Jobs / Talking about the future

DIGITAL+ video 19, 20

Jobs

an engineer · a fashion designer · a chef · a singer · a firefighter · an actor / actress · a nurse · a boardgame designer · a computer game designer · a police officer · a mechanic · a vet · a hairdresser · a baker · a photographer · a zoologist · a pilot · a racing driver · an inventor · a rock star

Who does what?

A firefighter fights fires.

A photographer takes pictures with a camera.

A chef cooks food for people.

A pilot flies planes.

A police officer helps people in trouble.

A singer sings on a stage.

A hairdresser cuts people's hair.

When I grow up ...

I'll be a really famous singer. I'll play the world's biggest stages.

When I grow up, I'll be a famous fashion designer.

When I'm older, I want to be an engineer. I'll invent lots of useful things.

When I grow up, I'll be a chef and have my own restaurant.

Predictions: In the future, there will be ...

robots · solar-powered helicopters · no books · VR glasses in school · smart homes · bigger TVs · no more cars · flying cars · less plastic · people that live on the moon · tablets in class · fridges that tell you when to go shopping and what foods to buy · kitchens that cook for you · no more pens and paper

Making plans

In the summer holidays, I'm going to do a drama workshop!

I am going to practise acting.

There is going to be a performance at the end of the workshop.

Describing people

People can be ...

careful · slow · fast · beautiful · funny · good · bad · quiet · nice · young · old · strange · friendly · clever · stupid · famous · loud · short · tall

He is feeling excited.
He is jumping excitedly.

People can feel ...

happy · sad · worried · sick · terrible · bored · scared · surprised · calm · angry · excited

They are angry.
They are shouting angrily.

There are three children in the picture, a girl and two boys. The girl is blond and she has got long hair. She is wearing a green T-shirt, pink shorts and white trainers. She is looking at the boy on the right. She doesn't look very happy. The two boys are taller than the girl. The boy on the left has black hair. He is wearing a short green shirt, blue shorts and white trainers. The boy on the right has brown hair. He is wearing blue clothes.

Adjectives and adverbs

careful → carefully
slow → slowly
loud → loudly
fast → **fast**
happy → happ**ily**
good → **well**
beautiful → beautifully
calm → calmly

They did really well.

She is a careful person.
She rides her bike carefully.

Good style

Every text needs …

- a beginning
- a middle
- an ending

What else should your text have?

- an interesting title
- a good first sentence
- adjectives, adverbs and linking words to make it interesting

first / at the beginning → then → after that → finally / in the end

Plan your story

Who?	→	my friend John
Where?	→	the moon
When?	→	2062
What?	→	time travelling / meet aliens

Making texts more interesting

Michael showed his car to Laura.
↓
Michael proudly showed his new red car to his sister Laura.

Laura looked at the car. She was not interested.
↓
Laura looked politely at the car, but she was not that interested.

Linking words

and · or · but · because · so · so that · before · when

She has to go shopping **so that** she can eat.

She wanted to eat, **but** the food didn't taste good. The food didn't taste good **so** she didn't eat it.

They discuss what to do **when** it is raining outside.

He always brushes his teeth **before** he goes to bed.

In the break, students and teachers are outside **and** walk around **or** talk.

Noah has to go home **because** it is late.

Classroom phrases

Wenn man ankommt oder geht

Good morning.	Guten Morgen.
What's for homework?	Was haben wir als Hausaufgabe auf?
See you tomorrow.	Bis morgen.
Bye.	Tschüs.

Wenn es ein Problem gibt

Sorry I'm late.	Tut mir leid, dass ich zu spät bin.
Sorry, I haven't got my exercise book with me.	Tut mir leid, ich habe mein Heft nicht dabei.
Sorry, I haven't got my homework with me.	Tut mir leid, ich habe meine Hausaufgaben nicht dabei.
What's the matter?	Was ist los?
I'm fine.	Mir geht's gut.
I feel sick.	Mir ist schlecht.
I've got a headache.	Ich habe Kopfschmerzen.
Can I open the window, please?	Kann ich bitte das Fenster öffnen?
Can I go to the toilet, please?	Kann ich bitte zur Toilette gehen?

Wenn man Hilfe braucht

Can you help me, please?	Können Sie / Kannst du mir bitte helfen?
I've got a question.	Ich habe eine Frage.
I don't understand this.	Ich verstehe das hier nicht.
How can I do this exercise?	Wie kann ich diese Aufgabe machen?
What's ... in English / German?	Was heißt ... auf Englisch / Deutsch?
What does ... mean?	Was bedeutet ... ?
Is that correct?	Ist das richtig?
Can you write that on the board, please?	Können Sie das bitte an die Tafel schreiben?
Can you spell that, please?	Können Sie das bitte buchstabieren?
Can you say that again, please?	Können Sie / Kannst du das bitte noch einmal sagen?
Can we listen to the audio track again, please?	Können wir den Audiotrack bitte noch einmal hören?
Sorry, I don't know.	Tut mir leid, das weiß ich nicht.
What page, please?	Auf welcher Seite bitte?

Wenn man zusammen arbeitet oder spielt

Whose turn is it?	Wer ist dran?
Do you want to work with me?	Möchtest du mit mir arbeiten?
Let's check ...	Lass uns ... überprüfen.
Let's compare ...	Lass uns ... vergleichen.

Wenn man mit dem Computer arbeitet

What's your email address?	Wie ist deine E-Mail-Adresse?
You can click on this link.	Du kannst auf diesen Link klicken.
Can I print that out?	Kann ich das ausdrucken?
Can I download it?	Kann ich es herunterladen?
I saved it.	Ich habe es gespeichert.

Was die Lehrerin oder der Lehrer sagt

Open your books at page ...	Öffnet eure Bücher auf Seite ...
Turn to page ...	Blättert zu Seite ...
Look at line ...	Seht euch Zeile ... an.
Look at the next paragraph.	Seht euch den nächsten Absatz an.
Read the text on page ...	Lies / Lest den Text auf Seite ...
Work in pairs / in groups of four.	Arbeitet zu zweit / zu viert.
Sit in a circle.	Bildet einen Sitzkreis.
Listen to the audio track.	Hör dir / Hört euch den Audiotrack an.
Listen to audio track number ...	Hör dir / Hört euch Audiotrack Nummer ... an.
Write about ...	Schreibe / Schreibt über ...
Talk about ...	Sprich / Sprecht über ...
Ask questions about ...	Stelle / Stellt Fragen zu ...
Answer the question, please.	Beantworte / Beantwortet bitte die Frage.
Match the sentences.	Ordne / Ordnet die Sätze zu.
Who wants to read out the text?	Wer möchte den Text vorlesen?
Write down the answers.	Schreibt die Antworten auf.
Act out the dialogue.	Spielt den Dialog vor.
Change roles.	Tauscht die Rollen.
Make your own dialogue.	Entwirf / Entwerft selbst ein Gespräch.
Take a card.	Nimm / Nehmt eine Karte.
Come to the board, please.	Komm / Kommt bitte zur Tafel.
Do this exercise at home, please.	Mache / Macht diese Aufgabe bitte zu Hause.
Be quiet, please.	Sei / Seid bitte ruhig.
Sit down, please.	Setz dich bitte. / Setzt euch bitte.
Please speak up.	Sprich / Sprecht bitte lauter.
You can do better.	Das kannst du besser.
Try again.	Versuch es noch einmal.
That's it.	Das ist es. / Richtig!
Well done.	Gut gemacht.

Deutscher Begriff	Englischer Begriff	Beispiele	Grammatik-Kapitel
Adjektiv (Eigenschaftswort)	adjective /ˈædʒɪktɪv/	big, expensive, boring	4, 15
Adverb der Art und Weise (pl. Adverbien)	adverb of manner /ˈædvɜːb‿əv ˌmænə/	quickly, happily, well	15
Aussagesatz	statement /ˈsteɪtment/	I love spaghetti.	
bejaht	positive /ˈpɒzətɪv/	Tarek likes hockey.	1, 5a, 7a, 9, 12, 13a, 17a, 19a
verneint	negative /ˈnegətɪv/	Ava doesn't like carrots.	2, 5b, 7b, 9, 13b, 17b, 19b
einfache Gegenwart (Präsens)	simple present /ˌsɪmpl ˈpreznt/	Harry lives in Notting Hill.	5, 6
einfache Vergangenheit (Präteritum)	simple past /ˌsɪmpl ˈpɑːst/	It was a sunny day.	1, 2, 3, 10, 17
Entscheidungsfrage (Ja/Nein-Frage)	yes/no-question /jes ˈnəʊ ˌkwestʃn/	Are you from Notting Hill?	3a, 6a, 8a, 14a, 18a, 20a
Frage mit Fragewort	wh-question /ˌdʌblju: ˈeɪtʃ ˌkwestʃn/	What's your name?	3b, 6b, 8b, 14b, 18b, 20b
Fragewort	question word /ˈkwestʃn wɜːd/	who, what, when, where, why	3b, 6b, 8b, 14b, 18b, 20b
Futur mit *going to*	going to-future /gəʊɪŋ ˈtu: fju:tʃə/	We are going to have a party.	19, 20
Futur mit *will*	will-future /ˈwɪl fju:tʃə/	I'll be a famous fashion designer.	13, 14
Grundform des Verbs (Infinitiv)	infinitive /ɪnˈfɪnətɪv/	be, go, like	1a, 2a, 3a, 5a, 6a, 7a, 10, 11, 13a, 17a, 19a
Häufigkeitsadverb	adverb of frequency /ˌædvɜːb‿əv ˈfriːkwənsi/	always, sometimes, never	12
Hauptsatz	main clause /ˈmeɪn ˌklɔːz/	Tarek goes to the cooking club.	16
Komparativ (1. Vergleichsform)	comparative /kəmˈpærətɪv/	bigger, more expensive, more boring	4
Konsonant (Mitlaut)	consonant /ˈkɒnsənənt/		1a, 5a, 7a
stimmlos	voiceless /ˈvɔɪsləs/	k, p, t	1a, 5a
stimmhaft	voiced /vɔɪst/	g, b, d	1a, 5a

Deutscher Begriff	Englischer Begriff	Beispiele	Grammatik-Kapitel
Kurzantwort	short answer /ˈʃɔːt‿ˌɑːnsə/	Are you happy? Yes, I am.	3a, 6a, 8a, 14a, 18a, 20a
Kurzform	short form /ˈʃɔːt fɔːm/	’m, ’s, isn’t, aren’t	2b, 7, 8a, 10a, 11c, 13, 19
Langform	long form /ˈlɒŋ fɔːm/	am, is, is not, are not	7a, 13a, 19
Modalverb	modal verb /ˈməʊdl ˌvɜːb/	can, must	10, 11
Nebensatz	subordinate clause /səˈbɔːdɪnət ˌklɔːz/	Ava is happy because she got a nice present.	12, 16
Nomen (Substantiv, Hauptwort)	noun /naʊn/	school, book, dog	9b, 15
Objekt (Satzergänzung)	object /ˈɒbdʒɪkt/	Harry loves music.	12
Partizip Perfekt	past participle /ˌpɑːst ˈpɑːtɪsɪpl/	played, been, gone	17, 18
Perfekt	present perfect /ˌpreznt ˈpɜːfɪkt/	have played, has been, have gone	17, 18
Plural (Mehrzahl)	plural /ˈplʊərəl/	books, apples, children	9b
s-Form (des Verbs)	s-form /ˈes fɔːm/	likes, goes, does	5a
Singular (Einzahl)	singular /ˈsɪŋgjʊlə/	one house, one apple	9b
Subjekt (Satzgegenstand)	subject /ˈsʌbdʒekt/	Harry loves music.	3, 6, 12
Superlativ (2. Vergleichsform)	superlative /suːˈpɜːlətɪv/	(the) biggest, (the) most expensive	4
Verb (Tätigkeitswort)	verb /vɜːb/		
regelmäßig	regular /ˈregjʊlə/	play, like	1a, 17a
unregelmäßig	irregular /ɪˈregjʊlə/	be, go	1b, 17a
Vergangenheitsform	past form /ˈpɑːst fɔːm/	was, were, visited	2a, 10a
Verlaufsform der Gegenwart	present progressive /ˌpreznt prəʊˈgresɪv/	We are having a party.	7, 8
Verneinung	negation /nɪˈgeɪʃn/	I don’t like carrots.	2, 5b, 7b, 9, 11, 13b, 17b, 19b
verneint, negativ	negative /ˈnegətɪv/		
Vokal (Selbstlaut)	vowel /ˈvaʊəl/	a, e, i , o, u	1a, 5a, 7a

1 THE SIMPLE PAST: POSITIVE STATEMENTS
Die einfache Vergangenheit: bejahte Aussagen

Das *simple past* verwendest du, wenn du über etwas sprechen willst, das in der Vergangenheit liegt und abgeschlossen ist, also zum Beispiel wenn du erzählst, was du in den Ferien gemacht hast. Es gibt regelmäßige und unregelmäßige Verben.

a) Regelmäßige Verben

DIGITAL+ video 21, 22

Das *simple past* der regelmäßigen Verben bildest du, indem du die Endung *-ed* an die Grundform anhängst:

stay + ***ed*** → *stay**ed*** /steɪd/
look + ***ed*** → *look**ed*** /lʊkt/
visit + ***ed*** → *visit**ed*** /ˈvɪzɪtɪd/

Die Formen sind bei allen Personen gleich.

Achte auf die Aussprache der Endung *-ed*:
- Nach stimmhaften (weichen) Konsonanten oder Vokalen: /-d/
- Nach stimmlosen (harten) Konsonanten: /-t/
- Nach /t/ oder /d/: /-ɪd/

Achte auf folgende Besonderheiten bei der Rechtschreibung:

Endet die Grundform des Verbs auf *-e*, dann wird nur *-d* angehängt.
*arriv**e*** → *arriv**ed*** /əˈraɪvd/

Endet das Verb auf einen kurzen betonten **Vokal + Konsonant**, dann wird der Konsonant verdoppelt.
*sto**p*** → *sto**pped*** /stɒpt/

Endet das Verb auf **Konsonant + y**, dann wird aus dem *-y* ein *-i* und die Endung lautet *-ied*.
*tid**y*** → *tid**ied*** /ˈtaɪdid/

b) Unregelmäßige Verben

Die unregelmäßigen Verben haben im *simple past* eine eigene Form, die du lernen musst.

have → ***had***	*Tarek **had** a great holiday.*
go → ***went***	*He **went** to Wales with his father.*
do → ***did***	*They **did** lots of things together.*

Das Verb *be* hat als einziges Verb zwei Formen im *simple past*: *was* und *were*.
*I / he / she / it **was** – you / we / they **were***

*I **was** in London last week.*
*My grandparents **were** in London two years ago.*

Eine Liste mit unregelmäßigen Verben findest du auf S. 247–248.

2 THE SIMPLE PAST: NEGATIVE STATEMENTS
Die einfache Vergangenheit: verneinte Aussagen

Wenn du sagen willst, was in der Vergangenheit nicht passiert ist, bildest du bei den meisten Verben die Verneinung mit *didn't*.
Bei Sätzen mit *was* oder *were* hängst du jedoch nur *not* bzw. *n't* an die Formen *was* oder *were* an.

a) Verneinte Aussagesätze mit *didn't*

DIGITAL+ video 21, 22

Sätze im *simple past* verneinst du im Allgemeinen mit *didn't (= did not)*.
Didn't ist die Vergangenheitsform von *don't* und *doesn't*.

Didn't ist bei allen Personen gleich.
Danach kommt dann das Verb in der Grundform.

Bejahte Aussage	Verneinte Aussage
I went to Paris last year.	I didn't **go** to London last year.
Ava talked to Lily yesterday.	Ava didn't **talk** to Tarek yesterday.

b) Verneinte Aussagesätze mit *was* und *were*

Bei *was* und *were* hängst du nur *not* oder die Kurzform *n't* an, wenn du einen verneinten Satz bilden willst.

Bejahte Aussage	Verneinte Aussage
I was in London last week.	I wasn't in Paris last week.
They were friendly at the hotel.	They weren't friendly at the restaurant.

3 THE SIMPLE PAST: QUESTIONS
Die einfache Vergangenheit: Fragen

Fragen im *simple past* bildest du in den meisten Fällen mit *did*. Eine Ausnahme sind Sätze mit *was* oder *were*.

a) Entscheidungsfragen und Kurzantworten

DIGITAL+ video 21, 22

Bei Entscheidungsfragen im *simple past* stellst du *did* an den Satzanfang. *Did* ist bei allen Personen gleich.
Achte auch hier darauf, das Verb danach in der Grundform zu verwenden.
In der Kurzantwort wird *did* wieder aufgegriffen.

Entscheidungsfrage	Kurzantwort	Kurzantwort
Did you go on holiday?	Yes, I did.	No, I didn't.
Did Harry visit his grandparents?	Yes, he did.	No, he didn't.

Bei Fragen mit *was* und *were* brauchst du kein *did*.
Hier steht *was* oder *were* am Satzanfang.
In der Kurzantwort wird *was* bzw. *were* wieder aufgegriffen.

Entscheidungsfrage	Kurzantwort	Kurzantwort
Were your parents in Paris last year?	Yes, they were.	No, they weren't.
Was the weather good?	Yes, it was.	No, it wasn't.

b) Fragen mit Fragewort

Bei Sätzen mit Fragewort steht das Fragewort am Satzanfang. Es steht vor *did*.

What *did you do in the holidays?*
Where *did you go?*

Bei Fragen mit *who* braucht man kein zusätzliches *did*, wenn *who* nach dem Subjekt fragt.

Who *went to Poland?* - ***Ava*** *went to Poland.*

Bei Fragen mit *was* oder *were* brauchst du ebenfalls kein *did*.

How *was your holiday?*
What *were your favourite places?*

4 THE COMPARISON OF ADJECTIVES
Die Steigerung von Adjektiven

Wenn du Personen oder Dinge näher beschreiben möchtest, verwendest du Adjektive. Wenn du Personen oder Dinge miteinander vergleichen möchtest, kannst du diese Adjektive steigern. Die erste Steigerungsform heißt Komparativ, die zweite Steigerungsform heißt Superlativ.

a) Steigerung von Adjektiven mit *-er* und *-est*

DIGITAL+ video 23

Einsilbige Adjektive (z. B. *cheap* und *old*) werden durch das Anhängen von *-er* und *-est* gesteigert.

Bei manchen Adjektiven ändert sich die Schreibweise.

Auch einige zweisilbige Adjektive können mit *-er* und *-est* gesteigert werden, z. B. Adjektive, die auf *-er*, *-le*, *-ow* und *-y* enden. Vorsicht: Bei Adjektiven auf *-y* wird dabei aus dem *-y* ein *-i*.

Einige Adjektive haben unregelmäßige Steigerungsformen. Diese Formen musst du wie Vokabeln lernen.

	Komparativ	Superlativ
cheap	cheaper	(the) cheapest
old	older	(the) oldest
big	bigger	(the) biggest
nice	nicer	(the) nicest
clever	cleverer	(the) cleverest
easy	easier	(the) easiest
good	better	(the) best
bad	worse	(the) worst

b) Steigerung von Adjektiven mit *more* und *most*

Mehrsilbige Adjektive werden mit *more* und *most* gesteigert.
Du stellst dabei *more* oder *most* vor das Adjektiv. Das Adjektiv bleibt unverändert.

	Komparativ	Superlativ
useful	more useful	(the) most useful
beautiful	more beautiful	(the) most beautiful
interesting	more interesting	(the) most interesting

c) Vergleichssätze

Willst du Personen oder Dinge miteinander vergleichen, dann benutzt du den Komparativ mit *than*.

Noah is older than Ava.

The jacket is more expensive than the T-shirt.

Sind die Eigenschaften gleich, benutzt du *as … as*.

Lily is as old as Harry.

The jeans are as expensive as the jacket.

5 THE SIMPLE PRESENT: STATEMENTS (REVISION)
Die einfache Gegenwart: Aussagen *(revision)*

Das *simple present* verwendest du,
- wenn jemand etwas regelmäßig tut oder wenn etwas regelmäßig stattfindet,
- wenn etwas über längere Zeit oder allgemein gültig ist.

a) Bejahte Aussagesätze im *simple present*

DIGITAL+ video 24

Das *simple present* hat meistens die gleiche Form wie die Grundform des Verbs.

*I **love** Christmas. I always **celebrate** it with my family.*

Nur in der 3. Person Singular *(he, she, it)* hängst du ein *-s* an.

*My little brother **loves** Christmas, too.*
*He always **gets** a lot of presents.*

Achte auf die Aussprache des -s:
- Nach stimmhaften (weichen) Konsonanten oder Vokalen klingt es wie das Summen einer Biene: /z/
- Nach stimmlosen (harten) Konsonanten klingt es wie das Zischen einer Schlange: /-s/

Vorsicht: Es gibt bei der s-Form in der 3. Person Singular einige Besonderheiten bei der Rechtschreibung:

- Endet das Verb mit *-ss, -sh, -ch oder -x*, hängst du in der 3. Person Singular ein *-es* an:
  watch → *watch**es***
- Auch bei *do* und *go* fügst du in der 3. Person Singular *-es* an. Beachte die Aussprache:
  *do**es*** wird /dʌz/ ausgesprochen, *go**es*** wird /gəʊz/ ausgesprochen.
- Bei Verben, die auf *-y* enden (zum Beispiel *worry*), gilt: Steht ein Konsonant vor dem *-y*, so wird das *-y* in der 3. Person Singular zu *-i* und du hängst *-es* an:
  worry → *worr**ies***

b) Verneinte Aussagesätze im *simple present*

Für die Verneinung fügst du in den meisten Fällen *don't (= do not)* bzw. bei der 3. Person Singular *doesn't (= does not)* ein.

*I **don't** celebrate Christmas.*
*The Chinese New Year **doesn't** take place on the same day every year.*

Bei der Verneinung von Sätzen mit *be, can* oder *have got* brauchst du *don't* oder *doesn't* nicht.

*Diwali **isn't** a Christian festival.*
*I **can't** go to my granny's place for Easter this year.*
*We **haven't got** a Christmas tree at home.*

6 THE SIMPLE PRESENT: QUESTIONS (REVISION)
Die einfache Gegenwart: Fragen *(revision)*

Auf Entscheidungsfragen antwortest du meistens mit einer Kurzantwort. Fragen mit Fragewort beginnen zum Beispiel mit *what, where* oder *when*.

a) Entscheidungsfragen und Kurzantworten im *simple present*

DIGITAL+ video 24

Wenn du Entscheidungsfragen im *simple present* stellen möchtest, musst du in den meisten Fällen *do* oder *does* an den Satzanfang stellen. Das Hauptverb, das dann folgt, steht immer in der Grundform, auch bei der 3. Person Singular. Das -s steckt schon in *does*.
In den Kurzantworten wird *do* oder *does* aufgegriffen.

Entscheidungsfrage	Kurzantwort	Kurzantwort
Do you celebrate Eid?	Yes, I do.	No, I don't.
Does your little sister like her presents?	Yes, she does.	No, she doesn't.

Bei Fragen mit dem Verb *be* steht kein *do* oder *does* am Satzanfang, hier steht dann die entsprechende Form von *be*, also *am, are* oder *is*.

***Are** you from London? – Yes, I **am**./No, I'**m** not.*

b) Fragen mit Fragewort im *simple present*

Bei Fragen mit Fragewort steht das Fragewort am Satzanfang.
Es steht vor *do* oder *does*.

***What** do you think about the party? – It's great!*
***Where** do you celebrate Hanukkah? – We celebrate it at home.*
***When** does the party start? – It starts at 7pm.*

Bei Fragen mit *who* braucht man kein zusätzliches *do* oder *does*, wenn *who* nach dem Subjekt fragt:
***Who** decorates the house? – **My parents** always decorate the house.*
***Who** likes Easter eggs? – **The children** like Easter eggs.*

7 THE PRESENT PROGRESSIVE: STATEMENTS (REVISION)
Die Verlaufsform der Gegenwart: Aussagen *(revision)*

Das *present progressive* verwendest du, wenn du beschreiben möchtest, was gerade passiert. Du kannst es aber auch verwenden, um über Pläne für die (nähere) Zukunft zu sprechen.

a) Bejahte Aussagesätze im *present progressive*

DIGITAL+ video 25

So bildest du das *present progressive*:

Form von *be (am, is, are)* + Grundform des Verbs + Endung ***-ing***.

	Langform	Kurzform	
Singular	I am	I'm	having a party.
	You are	You're	
	He/She/It is	He's/She's/It's	
Plural	We are	We're	
	You are	You're	
	They are	They're	

Endet das Verb auf ein stummes *-e*, dann fällt das *-e* in der *ing*-Form weg.

*writ**e** → writ**ing*** *Lily is writ**ing** a birthday card.*
*danc**e** → danc**ing*** *Harry is danc**ing**.*

Endet das Verb auf einem kurzen betonten Vokal + Konsonant, wird der Konsonant verdoppelt.

*put → pu**tt**ing* *Tarek is pu**tt**ing food on the table.*
*run → ru**nn**ing* *Ava is ru**nn**ing.*

b) Verneinte Aussagesätze im *present progressive*

Für die Verneinung fügst du *not* hinter der Form von *be* ein. Hier wird dann oft die Kurzform verwendet:

*I **am not** making pizza.*	*I'**m not** making pizza.*
*Harry **is not** dancing.*	*Harry **isn't** dancing.*
*They **are not** watching TV.*	*They **aren't** watching TV.*

8 THE PRESENT PROGRESSIVE: QUESTIONS (REVISION)
Die Verlaufsform der Gegenwart: Fragen *(revision)*

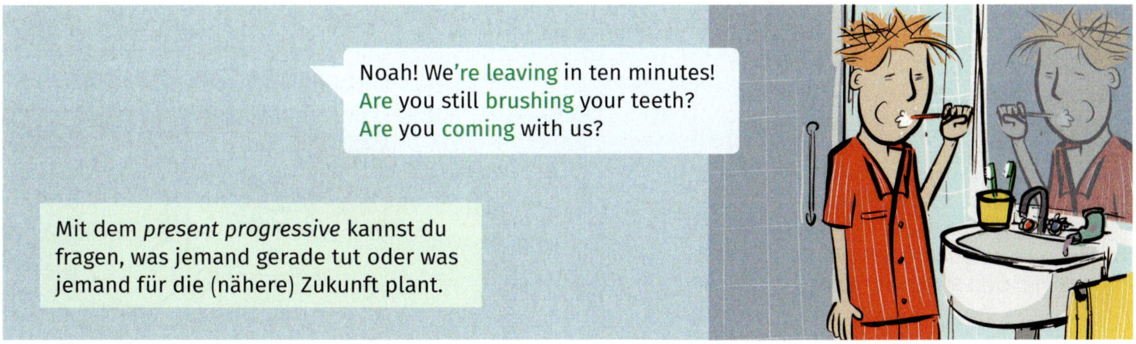

Mit dem *present progressive* kannst du fragen, was jemand gerade tut oder was jemand für die (nähere) Zukunft plant.

a) Entscheidungsfragen und Kurzantworten im *present progressive*

DIGITAL+ video 25

Entscheidungsfragen im *present progressive* bildest du, indem du die Form von *be* (also *am, is* oder *are*) an den Satzanfang stellst.
In den Kurzantworten wird die Form von *be* aufgegriffen.
In verneinten Kurzantworten verwendet man meistens die Kurzformen.

Entscheidungsfrage	Kurzantwort	Kurzantwort
Are you going to the party next weekend?	Yes, I am.	No, I'm not.
Is your brother coming?	Yes, he is.	No, he isn't.
Are your friends staying at home?	Yes, they are.	No, they aren't.

b) Fragen mit Fragewort im *present progressive*

Bei Fragen mit Fragewort steht das Fragewort am Satzanfang:

What *are you doing next weekend?*
Where *are you going tomorrow?*
When *is your friend coming for a visit?*

9 QUANTIFIERS
Mengenangaben

Mengenangaben wie *some* und *any* verwendest du, wenn du keine genaue Menge oder Anzahl von etwas angeben möchtest. Auch *much* (viel) und *many* (viele) sind Mengenangaben.

a) Die Mengenangaben *some* und *any*

DIGITAL+ video 26

Some und *any* bedeuten auf Deutsch so viel wie „einige", „ein paar" oder „etwas". In bejahten Aussagesätzen benutzt du *some*.

*There are **some** apples in the kitchen.*
*I need **some** milk for my cornflakes.*

In verneinten Aussagesätzen und in den meisten Fragen verwendest du *any*. Die Mengenangabe *not ... any* bedeutet „kein" oder „keine".

*Are there **any** apples?*	*We have**n't** got **any** apples.*
*Have you got **any** milk?*	*There is**n't** **any** milk.*

Wenn du höflich um etwas bittest oder etwas anbietest, benutzt du *some* auch in Fragen:

*Can I have **some** milk, please?*
*Would you like **some** tea?*

b) Die Mengenangaben *much, many* und *a lot of*

Much (auf Deutsch "viel") wird mit Nomen verwendet, die nicht zählbar sind (z. B. *water, milk, juice, time, money, ...*). Die Nomen stehen daher in der Einzahl.

*We haven't got **much** milk.*
*How **much** money have we got?*

Many (auf Deutsch "viele") wird dagegen mit Nomen verwendet, die zählbar sind (z. B. *apples, eggs, tomatoes, ...*). Die Nomen stehen in der Mehrzahl.

*We haven't got **many** apples.*
*How **many** tomatoes have we got?*

Much und *many* werden vor allem in Fragen und verneinten Aussagesätzen verwendet, in bejahten Aussagesätzen eher *a lot of* oder *lots of*. Hier braucht man nicht zwischen zählbaren und nicht zählbaren Nomen zu unterscheiden.

*We need **lots of** juice and **lots of** snacks for the party.*

10 THE MODAL VERBS MUST AND MUSTN'T
Die Modalverben *must* und *mustn't*

Mit *must* kannst du sagen, was jemand tun muss.
Mit *mustn't* kannst du sagen, was jemand nicht tun darf.

a) *Must*

Must bedeutet „müssen". Die Form steht mit der Grundform des Hauptverbs zusammen und ist bei allen Personen gleich.

Students ***must*** *wear the correct school uniform.*
Harry ***must*** *wear a tie.*

In der Regel kannst du *must* auch durch *have to* bzw. *has to* ersetzen.

Students ***have to*** *wear the correct school uniform.*
Harry ***has to*** *wear a tie.*

Must hat keine eigene Vergangenheitsform.
Daher wird die *simple past*-Form von *have to* benutzt.

Yesterday, Ava ***had to*** *tidy her room.*

Wenn du sagen willst, was jemand nicht tun muss, benutzt du *don't have to* bzw. *doesn't have to*.

Today, Ava ***doesn't have to*** *tidy it again.*

Mit *needn't* (Kurzform von *need not*) kannst du ebenfalls ausdrücken, dass jemand etwas nicht tun muss.

Today, Ava ***needn't*** *tidy it again.*

b) *Mustn't*

Mustn't bedeutet „nicht dürfen". Mit *mustn't* kannst du also sagen, was jemand nicht tun darf. Es steht mit der Grundform des Hauptverbs zusammen und ist bei allen Personen gleich.

Ava ***mustn't*** *listen to music when she does her homework.*
Students ***must not*** *run in the school building.*

11 THE MODAL VERBS CAN, BE ALLOWED TO AND MAY
Die Modalverben *can, be allowed to* und *may*

Mit *can, be allowed to* und *may* kannst du ausdrücken, dass etwas erlaubt oder nicht erlaubt ist.

a) *Can*

Can bedeutet nicht nur „können" sondern auch „dürfen".
Die Form ist bei allen Personen gleich und steht mit der Grundform des Verbs.
Die Verneinung *can't* kannst du verwenden, um darüber zu sprechen, was nicht erlaubt ist.

We ***can*** *bring our mobiles to school, but we* ***can't*** *use them during lessons.*

Mit *can* kannst du auch um Erlaubnis fragen.

Dad, ***can*** *I go outside and play football with my friends? – Yes, you* ***can****, but only for an hour.*

b) *Be allowed to*

Auch *be allowed to* heißt „dürfen". Hier musst du die Form von *be* an die jeweilige Person anpassen. Für die Verneinung wird *not* eingefügt.

Students ***are allowed to*** *bring their own lunch, but they* ***are not allowed to*** *eat in the classrooms.*
*I'****m allowed to*** *stay out until eight o'clock in the evening.*
My little brother ***is not allowed to*** *watch TV after seven o'clock.*

Fragen mit *be allowed to* stellst du so:

Are *you* ***allowed to*** *bring your mobiles to school? – Yes, we are. / No, we aren't.*
What ***are*** *you* ***allowed to*** *do during break?*

c) *May*

Mit *may* und *may not* kannst du ebenfalls sagen, was jemand tun darf bzw. nicht tun darf.
Die Form ist bei allen Personen gleich und steht mit der Grundform des Verbs.
Für *may* gibt es keine Kurzform.

You ***may*** *use your mobiles at lunch break.*
You ***may not*** *use your mobiles during lessons.*

Mit *may* kannst du auch höflich um Erlaubnis bitten.

May *I open the window, please?*

12 WORD ORDER IN STATEMENTS (REVISION)
Die Wortstellung im Aussagesatz *(revision)*

Aussagesätze werden im Englischen nach einem bestimmten Muster gebildet.

Subjekt, Verb und Objekt stehen in englischen Aussagesätzen immer in dieser Reihenfolge:

Subjekt – Verb – Objekt (S – V – O).

Danach können noch weitere Ergänzungen wie z. B. Orts- oder Zeitangaben folgen. Wenn ein Satz eine Orts- und eine Zeitangabe enthält, nennt man erst den Ort und dann die Zeit.

Subjekt	Verb	Objekt	Ortsangabe	Zeitangabe
Tarek	loves	cooking.		
He	cooks		in the school kitchen	every Tuesday.
The friends	play	football	in the park	on Saturdays.
Ava	sees	her friends	at school	every day.
Tarek	meets	his uncle		on Thursdays.

Die Reihenfolge „Subjekt – Verb – Objekt" gilt im Englischen auch in Nebensätzen.

Nebensatz im Englischen
Tarek goes to the cooking club because **he loves cooking**. S V O

Nebensatz im Deutschen
Tarek geht in die Koch-AG, weil **er Kochen liebt**. S O V

Beachte auch die Position von Häufigkeitsadverbien wie *always, usually, often, sometimes* oder *never*. Das Häufigkeitsadverb steht fast immer vor dem Verb.

*We **often play** football in the park.*

Das Häufigkeitsadverb steht hinter der Form von *be*.

*My friend **is often** late.*

13 THE WILL-FUTURE: STATEMENTS
Das Futur mit *will*: Aussagen

Wenn du über die Zukunft sprechen möchtest, kannst du das *will-future* verwenden. Damit kannst du zum Beispiel Vermutungen ausdrücken und Vorhersagen machen.

a) Bejahte Aussagesätze im *will-future*

DIGITAL+ video 27

Das *will-future* bildest du mit *will* und der Grundform des Verbs.
Auch *will* hat eine Kurzform. Sie lautet *'ll*.
Die Kurzformen verwendet man meistens beim Sprechen,
die Langformen verwendet man meist, wenn man etwas schreibt.
Die Form *will* ist bei allen Personen gleich.

	Langform	Kurzform			
Singular	I will	I'll	be	famous.	*Ich werde ...*
	You will	You'll			*Du wirst ... / Sie werden ...*
	He/She/It will	He's/She's/It'll			*Er/Sie/Es wird ...*
Plural	We will	We'll			*Wir werden ...*
	You will	You'll			*Ihr werdet ... / Sie werden ...*
	They will	They'll			*Sie werden ...*

b) Verneinte Aussagesätze im *will-future*

Für die Verneinung fügst du *not* hinter *will* ein.
Die Kurzform von *will not* ist *won't*.
Won't ist bei allen Personen gleich.

I ***won't*** *have a regular job.*
Lily ***won't*** *live in London when she is older.*
There ***won't*** *be any more cars in the future.*

14 THE WILL-FUTURE: QUESTIONS
Das Futur mit *will*: Fragen

Bei Entscheidungsfragen im *will-future* steht *will* am Satzanfang.

a) Entscheidungsfragen und Kurzantworten im *will-future*

DIGITAL+ video 27

In Entscheidungsfragen stellst du *will* an den Satzanfang.
Du verwendest *will* bzw. *won't* auch in den Kurzantworten.

Entscheidungsfrage	Kurzantwort	Kurzantwort
Will I be a famous fashion designer?	Yes, you will.	No, you won't.
Will you live in New York?	Yes, I will.	No, I won't.
Will Harry be rich?	Yes, he will.	No, he won't.

b) Fragen mit Fragewort im *will-future*

Bei Fragen mit Fragewort stellst du auch beim *will-future* das Fragewort an den Satzanfang.

Where *will you live?*
What *will Lily's job be?*
How *will we live in twenty years?*

15 ADVERBS OF MANNER
Adverbien der Art und Weise

Wenn du beschreiben möchtest, wie jemand etwas tut oder wie etwas geschieht, kannst du Adverbien der Art und Weise benutzen.

DIGITAL+ video 28

Adjektive kennst du bereits, sie beziehen sich auf Nomen, also darauf, wie jemand oder etwas ist. Adjektive beschreiben also Eigenschaften.

Adverbien der Art und Weise beziehen sich dagegen auf Verben und beschreiben, wie jemand etwas tut oder wie etwas geschieht. Diese Adverbien beschreiben also Tätigkeiten.

Adjektiv: *The children are* ***careful****.*

Adverb: *The children walk* ***carefully****.*

Ein Adverb der Art und Weise bildest du, indem du an das Adjektiv die Endung *-ly* anhängst.

Adjektiv	Adverb
loud	loud**ly**
bad	bad**ly**
slow	slow**ly**

Manchmal ändert sich die Schreibweise, wenn *-ly* angehängt wird:
-y wird zu *-ily*
-le wird zu *-ly*
-l wird zu *-lly*.
-ic wird zu *-ically*

Adjektiv	Adverb
easy	eas**ily**
terrible	terrib**ly**
beautiful	beautiful**ly**
fantastic	fantast**ically**

Einige Adverbien haben Sonderformen, die du wie Vokabeln lernen musst. Manche Adjektive und Adverbien sind gleich.

Adjektiv	Adverb
good	**well**
fast	**fast**
hard	**hard**

Vorsicht: Nach einigen Verben der Sinneswahrnehmung (z. B. *look* und *feel*) verwendet man kein Adverb, sondern ein Adjektiv.

The house ***looks interesting****.*
Kate and Jonathan ***feel great****.*

16 LINKING WORDS
Verbindung von Sätzen mit *linking words*

Linking words sind Verbindungswörter, die Sätze oder Teile eines Satzes miteinander verbinden. Sie können helfen, einen Text zu strukturieren und ihn stilistisch zu verbessern.

Mit Hilfe von *linking words* kannst du unter anderem Inhalte in einem Text ordnen, Kontraste herstellen oder Gründe angeben.

Zu den *linking words* gehören z. B. die Konjunktionen *and*, *or* und *but*. Diese verbinden Hauptsätze miteinander. Vor der Konjunktion steht dann in der Regel ein Komma.

1. Hauptsatz		**2. Hauptsatz**	
Jonathan's new watch had a bright torch,	**and**	it could also tell the time, date and year.	***... und ...***
The children had to find a way back,	**or**	they would have to stay in the future.	***... oder ...***
They tried to change the year on the watch,	**but**	the watch simply changed it back to 2128.	***... aber ...***

Andere Konjunktionen verbinden einen Hauptsatz mit einem Nebensatz, z. B. *because* und *when*. Beachte, dass in diesem Fall – anders als im Deutschen – kein Komma vor der Konjunktion steht.

Hauptsatz		**Nebensatz**	
Jonathan and Kate realized	**that**	they were in the future.	***... dass ...***
They needed help	**so**	they went back to Kate's house.	***... also ...***
The children hid in the bushes	**because**	they wanted to see who lived in the house.	***... weil ...***
They were surprised	**when**	they saw Georgia.	***... als ...***
They said goodbye to Georgia	**before**	they went home.	***... bevor ...***
Now they have to write a letter	**so that**	Georgia can find it in the future.	***... sodass ...***

17 THE PRESENT PERFECT: STATEMENTS
Das Perfekt: Aussagen

Das *present perfect* verwendest du, wenn etwas irgendwann in einem Zeitraum von der Vergangenheit bis zur Gegenwart passiert ist. Der genaue Zeitpunkt ist dabei nicht wichtig.
Du verwendest es auch, wenn ein Vorgang in der Vergangenheit noch Auswirkungen auf die Gegenwart hat.

a) Bejahte Aussagesätze im *present perfect*

DIGITAL+ video 29

Das *present perfect* bildest du mit *have / has* + Partizip Perfekt *(past participle)*. Statt *have* bzw. *has* kannst du auch die entsprechende Kurzform benutzen.

I ***have cleaned*** *the kitchen.*
*I****'ve done*** *the shopping.*
He ***has finished*** *his homework.*
*He****'s tidied*** *his room.*

Bei regelmäßigen Verben bildest du das Partizip Perfekt, indem du an die Grundform des Verbs die Endung *-ed* anhängst. Beachte auch die Besonderheiten bei der Schreibung und Aussprache der *ed*-Endungen (siehe Grammatik-Kapitel 1 auf Seite 174).

Grundform	*simple past*	*past participle*
clean	cleaned	clean**ed**
help	helped	help**ed**
play	played	play**ed**
tidy	tidied	tidi**ed**
visit	visited	visit**ed**

Die Formen der unregelmäßigen Verben musst du wie Vokabeln auswendig lernen.

Auf S. 247–248 findest du eine Liste mit unregelmäßigen Verben.

Grundform	*simple past*	*past participle*
be	was / were	**been**
do	did	**done**
have	had	**had**
buy	bought	**bought**

b) Verneinte Aussagesätze im *present perfect*

Die Verneinung bildest du mit *have not / has not* + Partizip Perfekt bzw. mit den Kurzformen *haven't / hasn't* + Partizip Perfekt.

I ***have not cleaned*** *the kitchen yet.*
He ***hasn't finished*** *his homework.*
We ***haven't been*** *to Paris yet.*

18 THE PRESENT PERFECT: QUESTIONS
Das Perfekt: Fragen

Mit einer Entscheidungsfrage im *present perfect* kannst du z. B. fragen, ob jemand etwas irgendwann in der Vergangenheit schon einmal gemacht hat. Der genaue Zeitpunkt ist dabei nicht so wichtig.

a) Fragen und Kurzantworten im *present perfect*

DIGITAL+ video 29

Entscheidungsfragen im *present perfect* bildest du, indem du *have* bzw. *has* an den Satzanfang stellst.

Entscheidungsfrage	Kurzantwort	Kurzantwort
Have you ever been to London?	Yes, I have.	No, I haven't.
Has Ava bought a new book?	Yes, she has.	No, she hasn't.
Have the children finished their homework?	Yes, they have.	No, they haven't.

b) Fragen mit Fragewort im *present perfect*

Bei Fragen mit Fragewort steht das Fragewort am Satzanfang.

What *have you done?*
Where *have you been?*
Why *hasn't she called yet?*

c) Adverbien der unbestimmten Zeit

Beim *present perfect* ist es nicht wichtig, wann genau in der Vergangenheit etwas passiert ist. Man betrachtet stattdessen den Zeitraum von der Vergangenheit bis zur Gegenwart. Daher werden bei Fragen und Aussagen im *present perfect* häufig Adverbien der unbestimmten Zeit verwendet, z. B. *ever* (= jemals), *never* (= nie), *already* (= schon), *just* (= gerade) und *not yet* (= noch nicht).

Die meisten Adverbien stehen dann direkt vor dem Partizip Perfekt.

*Have you **ever** been to London? – No, I've **never** been there.*
*Has Ava **already** taken Ollie for a walk? – Yes, she has **just** come back.*

Beachte die Ausnahme: *yet* steht am Satzende.

*Have you ever been to London Zoo? – No, I have**n't** been there **yet**.*

19 THE GOING TO-FUTURE: STATEMENTS
Das Futur mit *going to*: Aussagen

Das Futur mit *going to* kannst du verwenden, um über Pläne für die Zukunft zu sprechen.
Man verwendet es auch bei Ereignissen, die wahrscheinlich eintreten werden.

a) Aussagesätze im *going to-future*

DIGITAL+ video 30

Im Deutschen gibt es keine Zeitform, die dem *going to-future* entspricht.
Du hast aber verschiedene Möglichkeiten, es im Deutschen wiederzugeben.

Englisch	Deutsch
I'**m going to do** a drama workshop.	Ich **werde** einen Theaterworkshop **machen**. Ich **möchte/will** einen Theaterworkshop **machen**. Ich **plane/habe vor**, einen Theaterworkshop **zu machen**.

Du bildest das Futur mit *going to* mit einer Form von *be* + *going to* + Grundform des Verbs.

	Langform	Kurzform			
Singular	I am	I'm	going to	do	a drama workshop.
	You are	You're			
	He/She is	He's/She's			
Plural	We are	We're			
	You are	You're			
	They are	They're			

b) Verneinung im *going to-future*

Für die Verneinung stellst du *not* hinter die Form von *be*. Oft benutzt man Kurzformen.

	Langform	Kurzform			
Singular	I am not	I'm not	going to	do	a cooking workshop.
	You are not	You aren't			
	He/She is not	He/She isn't			
Plural	We are not	We aren't			
	You are not	You aren't			
	They are not	They aren't			

20 THE GOING TO-FUTURE: QUESTIONS
Das Futur mit *going to*: Fragen

Mit einer Frage im *going to-future* kannst du z. B. danach fragen, was jemand für die nächsten Ferien plant.

a) Entscheidungsfragen und Kurzantworten im *going to-future*

DIGITAL+ video 30

Bei Entscheidungsfragen rückt im *going to-future* die Form von *be (am, is, are)* an den Satzanfang. In der Kurzantwort steht dann die entsprechende Form von *be*.

Entscheidungsfrage	Kurzantwort	Kurzantwort
Are you going to do a cooking workshop?	Yes, I am.	No, I'm not.
Is Ava going to visit her grandmother?	Yes, she is.	No, she isn't.
Are the children going to act in a play?	Yes, they are.	No, they aren't.

b) Fragen mit Fragewort im *going to-future*

Bei Fragen mit Fragewort steht das Fragewort an erster Stelle.

What *are you going to do in the holidays?*
When *is the workshop going to start?*
Where *is it going to take place?*

Nach Vokabeln suchen

Alphabetische Wortliste (*Dictionary*): Du suchst nach der Bedeutung eines einzelnen englischen Wortes, das im Textbook vorgekommen ist? Dann nutze die alphabetische Wortliste ab Seite 221. Hier findest du auch die Wörter aus der *Story*, aus den Projekten, aus den *Wordbanks* und von den *Get together-* und *Challenge*-Seiten. Einige englische Wörter, die im Englischen und im Deutschen gleich sind, findest du auf Seite 196.

Wortlisten nach Kapiteln (*Vocabulary*): Du möchtest die Vokabeln zu einem ganzen Abschnitt im Buch lernen? Dann nutze die chronologische Wortliste ab Seite 197. Nach Kapiteln und Seitenzahlen sortiert findest du hier alle Wörter, die neu im Buch vorkommen.

Vokabeln finden
Hier siehst du, zu welcher Aufgabe eines Kapitels die Vokabeln gehören. Die Seitenzahl hilft dabei.

Wichtige Vokabeln erkennen
Wichtige Vokabeln sind fett schwarz gedruckt und farbig markiert. Die solltest du dir merken.

Vokabeln richtig aussprechen
Die Lautschrift zeigt dir, wie die Wörter richtig ausgesprochen werden.

Unit

p. 36, 1	**englische Vokabel** /Lautschrift/	deutsche Übersetzung
	englische Vokabel /Lautschrift/	deutsche Übersetzung
	englische Vokabel /Lautschrift/	deutsche Übersetzung
	englische Vokabel /Lautschrift/	deutsche Übersetzung
	englische Vokabel /Lautschrift/	deutsche Übersetzung
	englische Vokabel /Lautschrift/	deutsche Übersetzung
	englische Vokabel /Lautschrift/	deutsche Übersetzung
	englische Vokabel *(Hinweis)* /Lautschrift/	deutsche Übersetzung

Beispielsätze und Bilder helfen dir dabei, dir Vokabeln einzuprägen.

In farbigen Kästen findest du nützliche Informationen.

Passiver Wortschatz
Vokabeln, die nicht zum Lernwortschatz gehören, sind grau gedruckt. Die brauchst du dir nicht zu merken.

Besondere Hinweise
Zu einigen Vokabeln findest du Angaben, die dir wichtige Hinweise zu ihrem Gebrauch geben:

(pl)	Das Wort kommt hier in seiner Pluralform vor bzw. hat eine unregelmäßige Pluralform.
(no pl)	Dieses Wort hat keine Pluralform.
(informal)	Dieses Wort oder dieser Ausdruck ist umgangssprachlich.
(AE)	Dieses Wort oder dieser Ausdruck kommt aus dem amerikanischen Englisch.
(irr)	Dieses Verb ist unregelmäßig. Du findest eine Liste mit unregelmäßigen Verben auf Seite 247.

Die richtige Aussprache

Im Englischen spricht man Wörter oft anders aus als man sie schreibt.
Die Aussprache der Wörter wird mithilfe der Lautschrift in jedem Wörterbuch angegeben.
Man kann so auch neue Wörter richtig aussprechen, ohne sie vorher gehört zu haben.
Die Lautschrift ist eine Schrift, deren Symbole jeden Laut genau bezeichnen.
Hier ist eine Liste mit den Symbolen dieser Lautschrift zusammen mit Beispielwörtern.

The English alphabet

a	/eɪ/
b	/biː/
c	/siː/
d	/diː/
e	/iː/
f	/ef/
g	/dʒiː/
h	/eɪtʃ/
i	/aɪ/
j	/dʒeɪ/
k	/keɪ/
l	/el/
m	/em/
n	/en/
o	/əʊ/
p	/piː/
q	/kjuː/
r	/ɑː/
s	/es/
t	/tiː/
u	/juː/
v	/viː/
w	/ˈdʌbljuː/
x	/eks/
y	/waɪ/
z	/zed/

English sounds

Vokale

/ɑː/	**arm**
/ʌ/	**but**
/e/	**desk**
/ə/	**a, an**
/ɜː/	**girl, bird**
/æ/	**apple**
/ɪ/	**in, it**
/i/	**happy**
/iː/	**easy, eat**
/ɒ/	**orange, sorry**
/ɔː/	**all, call**
/ʊ/	**look**
/u/	**January**
/uː/	**boot**

Doppellaute

/aɪ/	**eye, by, buy**
/aʊ/	**our**
/eə/	**air, there**
/eɪ/	**take, they**
/ɪə/	**here**
/ɔɪ/	**boy**
/əʊ/	**go, old**
/ʊə/	**tour**

Konsonanten

/b/	**bag, club**
/d/	**duck, card**
/f/	**fish, laugh**
/g/	**get, dog**
/h/	**hot**
/j/	**you**
/k/	**can, duck**
/l/	**lot, small**
/m/	**more, mum**
/n/	**now, sun**
/ŋ/	**song, long**
/p/	**present, top**
/r/	**red, around**
/s/	**sister, class** *(stimmlos)*
/z/	**nose, dogs** *(stimmhaft)*
/t/	**time, cat**
/ʒ/	**television**
/dʒ/	**sausage**
/ʃ/	**fresh**
/tʃ/	**child, cheese**
/ð/	**these, mother** *(stimmhaft)*
/θ/	**bathroom, think** *(stimmlos)*
/v/	**very, have**
/w/	**what, word**

Betonungszeichen für die folgende Silbe

/ˈ/	**Hauptbetonung**
/ˌ/	**Nebenbetonung**

Bekannte Wörter

Viele Wörter sind im Englischen und im Deutschen so gut wie gleich. Manche unterscheiden sich nur durch die Groß- bzw. Kleinschreibung – im Englischen werden die meisten Nomen kleingeschrieben. Viele dieser Wörter, die in deinem Buch vorkommen, findest du hier. Bei denen, die anders ausgesprochen werden als im Deutschen, ist die Lautschrift farbig hervorgehoben.

ABC /ˌeɪbiːˈsiː/
action /ˈækʃn/
adverb /ˈædvɜːb/
alien /ˈeɪliən/
aluminium /ˌæləˈmɪniəm/
anti- /ˈænti/
app /æp/
aquarium /əˈkweəriəm/
argument /ˈɑːgjʊmənt/
arm /ɑːm/
astronaut /ˈæstrəˌnɔːt/
audio /ˈɔːdiəʊ/
baby /ˈbeɪbi/
back flip /ˈbæk flɪp/
ball /bɔːl/
band /bænd/
basketball /ˈbɑːskɪtˌbɔːl/
blog /blɒg/
blond /blɒnd/
bus /bʌs/
café, cafeteria /ˈkæfeɪ, ˌkæfəˈtɪəriə/
camping /ˈkæmpɪŋ/
CD /ˌsiːˈdiː/
clever /ˈklevə/
clip /klɪp/
coach /kəʊtʃ/
collage /ˈkɒlɑːʒ/
computer /kəmˈpjuːtə/
cool /kuːl/
designer /dɪˈzaɪnə/
digital /ˈdɪdʒɪtl/
drama /ˈdrɑːmə/
dress code /ˈdres kəʊd/
email /ˈiːmeɪl/
etc. (= etcetera) /et ˈsetrə/
fair /feə/
fan /fæn/
film /fɪlm/
finger /ˈfɪŋgə/
fitness /ˈfɪtnəs/
flyer /ˈflaɪə/
form /fɔːm/
generation /ˌdʒenəˈreɪʃn/
golden /ˈgəʊldn/
hammer /ˈhæmə/
hand /hænd/
hey, hi /heɪ, haɪ/
hieroglyph /ˈhaɪrəglɪf/
hockey /ˈhɒki/
horror /ˈhɒrə/
hotel /həʊˈtel/
info /ˈɪnfəʊ/
instrument /ˈɪnstrʊmənt/
Internet /ˈɪntəˌnet/
interview /ˈɪntəˌvjuː/
jeans /dʒiːnz/
kiwi /ˈkiːwiː/
laptop /ˈlæpˌtɒp/
live /laɪv/
live stream /ˌlaɪv ˈstriːm/
mailbox /ˈmeɪlˌbɒks/
make-up /ˈmeɪkʌp/
marathon /ˈmærəθn/
marshmallow /ˈmɑːʃˌmæləʊ/
material /məˈtɪəriəl/
million /ˈmɪljən/
mini /ˈmɪni/
minute /ˈmɪnɪt/
modern /ˈmɒdən/
moment /ˈməʊmənt/
moor /mʊə/
museum /mjuːˈziːəm/
musical /ˈmjuːzɪkl/
name /neɪm/
national /ˈnæʃnəl/
nest /nest/
OK (= okay) /ˌəʊˈkeɪ/
online /ˈɒnlaɪn/
parade /pəˈreɪd/
park /pɑːk/
partner /ˈpɑːtnə/
party /ˈpɑːti/
patient /ˈpeɪʃnt/
person /ˈpɜːsn/
piercing /ˈpɪərsɪŋ/
pilot /ˈpaɪlət/
pink /pɪŋk/
plan /plæn/
planet /ˈplænɪt/
playlist /ˈpleɪˌlɪst/
podcast /ˈpɒdˌkɑːst/
popcorn /ˈpɒpkɔːn/
post /pəʊst/
poster /ˈpəʊstə/
problem /ˈprɒbləm/
quiz /kwɪz/
region /ˈriːdʒn/
religion /rɪˈlɪdʒn/
reporter /rɪˈpɔːtə/
rest /rest/
restaurant /ˈrestrɒnt/
ring /rɪŋ/
rock /rɒk/
rose /rəʊz/
sand /sænd/
sandwich /ˈsænwɪdʒ/
science fiction /ˌsaɪəns ˈfɪkʃn/
shorts /ʃɔːts/
show /ʃəʊ/
sightseeing /ˈsaɪtˌsiːɪŋ/
signal /ˈsɪgnl/
situation /ˌsɪtʃuˈeɪʃn/
skateboard /ˈskeɪtbɔːd/
smartphone /ˈsmɑːtˌfəʊn/
snack /snæk/
so /səʊ/
sound check /ˈsaʊnd‿tʃek/
souvenir /ˌsuːvəˈnɪə/
spaghetti /spəˈgeti/
star /stɑː/
stress /stres/
stunt man /ˈstʌnt mæn/
symbol /ˈsɪmbl/
tablet /ˈtæblət/
talent /ˈtælənt/
taxi /ˈtæksi/
team /tiːm/
teenager /ˈtiːnˌeɪdʒə/
test /test/
text /tekst/
ticket /ˈtɪkɪt/
toaster /ˈtəʊstə/
toffee /ˈtɒfi/
tour, tourist /tʊə, ˈtʊərɪst/
tradition /trəˈdɪʃn/
tunnel /ˈtʌnl/
unboxing /ˌʌnˈbɒksɪŋ/
undercover /ˌʌndəˈkʌvə/
uniform /ˈjuːnɪfɔːm/
upcycling /ˈʌpˌsaɪklɪŋ/
vase /vɑːz/
verb /vɜːb/
video chat, video clip /ˈvɪdiəʊ tʃæt, ˈvɪdiəʊ klɪp/
virus /ˈvaɪrəs/
volleyball /ˈvɒlibɔːl/
warm /wɔːm/
webcode /ˈwebˌkəʊd/
website /ˈwebˌsaɪt/
wild /waɪld/
winter /ˈwɪntə/
workshop /ˈwɜːkˌʃɒp/
zoo /zuː/

p. 6	**board game** /ˈbɔːd ɡeɪm/	(das) Brettspiel

Unit 1 | Part A Holiday fun

p. 8, 1	(to) **go abroad** *(irr)* /ˌɡəʊ‿əˈbrɔːd/	ins Ausland gehen / fahren
	the USA (= United States of America) /ðə ˌju‿es‿ˈeɪ, juːˌnaɪtɪd ˌsteɪts‿əv‿əˈmerɪkə/	(die) USA, (die) Vereinigten Staaten von Amerika
	plane /pleɪn/	(das) Flugzeug
	view /vjuː/	(die) (Aus)sicht
	(to) **learn** *(irr)* /lɜːn/	lernen
	just /dʒʌst/	einfach, wirklich
	(you) guys *(pl, informal)* /ɡaɪz/	Leute *(umgangssprachl.)*
	(to) **spend** *(irr)* /spend/	verbringen *(Zeit)*, ausgeben *(Geld)*
	seaside /ˈsiːˌsaɪd/	(die) (Meeres)küste, (das) Meer
	(to) **go swimming** *(irr)* /ˌɡəʊ ˈswɪmɪŋ/	schwimmen gehen
	(to) **make friends (with)** *(irr)* /ˌmeɪk ˈfrendz/	sich anfreunden (mit)
	(to) **like doing something** /laɪk ˈduːɪŋ ˌsʌmθɪŋ/	etwas gern tun
	(to) **visit** /ˈvɪzɪt/	besuchen
	relative /ˈrelətɪv/	(der/die) Verwandte
	(to) **do sports** *(irr)* /ˌduː ˈspɔːts/	Sport treiben
	adventure park /ədˈventʃə pɑːk/	(der) Erlebnispark
	grandpa *(informal)* /ˈɡrænˌpɑː/	(der) Opa
	(to) **hike** /haɪk/	wandern
	mountaintop /ˈmaʊntɪnˌtɒp/	(der) Berggipfel
	spectacular /spekˈtækjʊlə/	atemberaubend, spektakulär
	outdoor /ˌaʊtˈdɔː/	im Freien
	seashell /ˈsiːˌʃel/	(die) Muschel
	day trip /ˈdeɪ trɪp/	(der) Tagesausflug
p. 9, 2	(to) **go riding** *(irr)* /ˌɡəʊ ˈraɪdɪŋ/	reiten gehen
	lazy /ˈleɪzi/	faul
	horse /hɔːs/	(das) Pferd
	at first /ət ˈfɜːst/	zuerst
	not anywhere /ˌnɒt‿ˈeniˌweə/	nirgendwo
	(to) **stand** *(irr)* /stænd/	stehen
	grass /ɡrɑːs/	(das) Gras
	farm /fɑːm/	(der) Bauernhof
	(to) **leave** *(irr)* /liːv/	verlassen, abfahren
	(to) **change one's mind** /ˌtʃeɪndʒ wʌnz ˈmaɪnd/	seine Meinung ändern
	yesterday /ˈjestədeɪ/	gestern
	cow /kaʊ/	(die) Kuh
	for the first time /fə ðə ˈfɜːst‿taɪm/	zum ersten Mal
	actually /ˈæktʃuəli/	eigentlich; tatsächlich

She is sitting on a **plane**.

Many people **spend** a lot of time shopping. They also **spend** money when they go shopping.

stayed /steɪd/ blieb(en)
took /tʊk/ nahm(en)
was/were /wɒz/wɜː/ war/waren
went /went/ ging(en)
hiked /haɪkt/ wanderte(n)
learnt /lɜːnt/ lernte(n)
loved /lʌvd/ liebte(n)
spent /spent/ verbrachte(n)
played /pleɪd/ spielte(n)
collected /kəˈlektɪd/ sammelte(n)

horse

had /hæd/ hatte(n)
didn't want to /ˌdɪdnt ˈwɒnt‿tə/ wollte(n) nicht
stood /stʊd/ stand(en)
ate /et/eɪt/ aß(en)
arrived /əˈraɪvd/ kam(en) an
What did you say? /ˌwɒt‿dɪd jə ˈseɪ/ Was sagtest du/sagtet ihr?
Did you change your mind? /ˌdɪd jə ˌtʃeɪndʒ jɔː ˈmaɪnd/ Hast du deine / Habt ihr eure Meinung geändert?
milked /mɪlkt/ molk(en)
liked /laɪkt/ mochte(n)
made /meɪd/ machte(n)
thought /θɔːt/ dachte(n)

	(to) **be good at something** *(irr)* /ˌbiː ˈgʊd‿æt ˌsʌmθɪŋ/	gut in etwas sein	
	fresh /freʃ/	frisch, neu	
	(to) **be afraid of** *(irr)* /ˌbi‿əˈfreɪd‿əv/	Angst haben vor	to **be afraid of** = to be scared of
	anyway /ˈeniweɪ/	jedenfalls	
	stuff *(informal)* /stʌf/	(das) Zeug	
	(to) **go cycling** *(irr)* /ˌgəʊ ˈsaɪklɪŋ/	Rad fahren gehen	
	... ago /əˈgəʊ/	vor ...	
	chicken /ˈtʃɪkɪn/	(das) Huhn	 **chicken**
	at least /ət ˈliːst/	mindestens, wenigstens	**at least** two = two or more
	grandma *(informal)* /ˈgrænˌmɑː/	(die) Oma	
	(to) **milk** /mɪlk/	melken	
	milkshake /ˈmɪlkˌʃeɪk/	(der) Milchshake	
	yummy *(informal)* /ˈjʌmi/	lecker	
p. 10, 3	**delicious** /dɪˈlɪʃəs/	köstlich, lecker	A nice cake is **delicious**.
	(to) **drive** *(irr)* /draɪv/	fahren	
	positive /ˈpɒzətɪv/	positiv	
	negative /ˈnegətɪv/	negativ	**negative** ≠ **positive**
	Rome /rəʊm/	Rom	
	Italian /rəʊm/	(der/die) Italiener/in; italienisch	
	Egypt /ˈiːdʒɪpt/	Ägypten	
p. 11, 5	(to) **move something** /ˈmuːv ˌsʌmθɪŋ/	etwas wegräumen, etwas woanders hinstellen	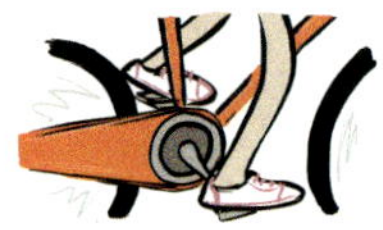
	(to) **move** /muːv/	umziehen	
	(to) **cycle** /ˈsaɪkl/	Rad fahren, radeln	to **cycle**
	all the time /ˌɔːl ðə ˈtaɪm/	die ganze Zeit	
	grandparents *(pl)* /ˈgrænˌpeərənts/	(die) Großeltern	
	a couple of /ə ˈkʌpl‿əv/	einige, ein paar	**a couple of** = some
	See you (soon)! /ˌsiː juː ˈsuːn/	Bis bald!	
	(to) **renovate** /ˈrenəveɪt/	renovieren	
	picnic /ˈpɪknɪk/	(das) Picknick	
p. 12, 6	**amazing** *(informal)* /əˈmeɪzɪŋ/	toll	
	space /speɪs/	(der) Raum, (der) Platz	The **castle** is very big and old.
	castle /ˈkɑːsl/	(die) Burg, (das) Schloss	
	thousand /ˈθaʊznd/	tausend	
	Roman /ˈrəʊmən/	(der/die) Römer/in; römisch	
	difficult /ˈdɪfɪklt/	schwierig, schwer	
	hard /hɑːd/	hart, schwierig	**hard** = **difficult**
	(to) **compare** /kəmˈpeə/	vergleichen	
	And so do I. /ænd ˌsəʊ du‿ˈaɪ/	Ich auch.	
	sock /sɒk/	(die) Socke	a pair of **socks** 
	What was that like? /ˌwɒt wɒz ðæt ˈlaɪk/	Wie war das?	
	open-air /ˌəʊpən‿ˈeə/	im Freien	

	roundhouse /ˈraʊnd,haʊs/	(das) Rundhaus	
	farmhouse /ˈfɑːm,haʊs/	(das) Bauernhaus	
	guide /gaɪd/	(der) Führer *(Buch)*; (der/die) Führer/in	A **guide** can be a person or a book.
	fort /fɔːt/	(das) Fort, (die) Festung	
	Norman /ˈnɔːmən/	(der/die) Normanne/Normannin	
	Welsh /welʃ/	walisisch	
	harder /ˈhɑːdə/	schwieriger	
p. 13, 7	**airport** /ˈeəpɔːt/	(der) Flughafen	There are usually lots of planes at an **airport**.
	(to) **catch up with** *(irr)* /ˌkætʃ‿ˈʌp wɪð/	*sich nach längerer Zeit (auch virtuell) mit jemandem treffen, um sich auf den neusten Stand zu bringen*	
p. 13, 8	**around** /əˈraʊnd/	um, herum, umher	
p. 14, 9	(to) **have (a lot of) fun** *(irr)* /ˌhæv‿ə ˌlɒt‿əv‿ˈfʌn/	(viel) Spaß haben	He loves dancing. He **is having a lot of fun**.
	as well /ˌəz‿ˈwel/	auch	
	could /kʊd/	*Vergangenheitsform von can*	
	yours /jɔːz/	deine(r,s), eure(r,s), Ihre(r,s)	
	camp /kæmp/	(das) (Zelt)lager	
	by /baɪ/	bei, an	
	for *(+ Zeitraum)* /fɔː/	... lang	When you work from 4 to 5, you work **for** an hour.
	(to) **meet** *(irr)* /miːt/	kennenlernen	
	along /əˈlɒŋ/	entlang	
	(to) **post** /pəʊst/	posten, bekannt geben	
	about /əˈbaʊt/	ungefähr	
	mile /maɪl/	(die) Meile	1 **mile** is about 1.6 kilometres.
	down /daʊn/	hinunter; (nach) unten	
	hill /hɪl/	(der) Hügel	
	bike /baɪk/	(das) Fahrrad	
	travel /ˈtrævl/	(die) Reise	
	a few /ə ˈfjuː/	einige, wenige	
	through /θruː/	durch	
	(to) **taste** /teɪst/	schmecken	Chocolate usually **tastes** sweet.
	(to) **go hiking** *(irr)* /ˌgəʊ ˈhaɪkɪŋ/	wandern gehen	
	might /maɪt/	könnte(st,n,t)	
	(to) **check out** *(informal)* /ˌtʃek‿ˈaʊt/	sich ansehen; ausprobieren	
	B&B (= bed and breakfast) /ˌbed‿ən ˈbrekfəst/	(die) Frühstückspension	
	(to) **rent** /rent/	mieten	
	(to) **get lost** *(irr)* /ˌget ˈlɒst/	sich verirren	
	tart /tɑːt/	(das) Törtchen	
p. 15, 11	**diary entry** /ˈdaɪəri‿ˌentri/	(der) Tagebucheintrag	You make a **diary entry** to write about your day.
	horrible /ˈhɒrəbl/	schrecklich, gemein	
	melody /ˈmelədi/	(die) Melodie	
p. 16, 12	**afterwards** /ˈɑːftəwədz/	anschließend, später	

	very much /ˌveri ˈmʌtʃ/	sehr	
	during /ˈdjʊərɪŋ/	während	
	busy /ˈbɪzi/	bewegt, ereignisreich	There is lots to do on a **busy** day.
	strange /streɪndʒ/	sonderbar, merkwürdig	
	unfortunately /ʌnˈfɔːtʃnətli/	unglücklicherweise	
	nice /naɪs/	*hier:* lecker	
p. 16, 13	**adjective** /ˈædʒɪktɪv/	(das) Adjektiv	'Good' is an **adjective**.
	more interesting /ˌmɔːr‿ˈɪntrəstɪŋ/	interessanter	
p. 17, 14	**real** /rɪəl/	wirklich, echt	
	(to) **organize (= organise)** /ˈɔːɡənaɪz/	organisieren	
	careful /ˈkeəfl/	vorsichtig	
	especially /ɪˈspeʃli/	besonders, vor allem	
	tip /tɪp/	(der) Tipp	
	fun /fʌn/	lustig, witzig	
	polite /pəˈlaɪt/	höflich	The man is very **polite**.
	(to) **respect** /rɪˈspekt/	respektieren	
	culture /ˈkʌltʃə/	(die) Kultur	
	opinion /əˈpɪnjən/	(die) Meinung, (die) Ansicht	Your **opinion** is what you think.
	title /ˈtaɪtl/	(der) Titel, (die) Überschrift	
	(to) **recommend** /ˌrekəˈmend/	empfehlen	
	(to) **publish** /ˈpʌblɪʃ/	veröffentlichen, herausgeben	
	(to) **comment on** /ˈkɒment‿ɒn/	kommentieren	When you **comment on** something, you give your **opinion**.
	writing style /ˈraɪtɪŋ staɪl/	(der) Schreibstil	
	gallery walk /ˈɡæləri wɔːk/	*(die) Gruppendiskussion in Stationsarbeit*	

Unit 1 | Part B Sightseeing in London

p. 18, 1	**sound** /saʊnd/	(das) Geräusch, (der) Klang	A **sound** is anything that you can hear.
	(to) **come to mind** *(irr)* /ˌkʌm tə ˈmaɪnd/	einfallen	
p. 19, 1	(to) **go with** *(irr)* /ˌɡəʊ ˈwɪθ/	gehören zu, passen zu	
	tall /tɔːl/	groß	
	Europe /ˈjʊərəp/	(das) Europa	Germany, France and Spain are countries in **Europe**.
	popular /ˈpɒpjʊlə/	beliebt	
	attraction /əˈtrækʃn/	(die) Attraktion	
	the UK (= United Kingdom) /ðə ˌjuː ˈkeɪ, juːˌnaɪtɪd ˈkɪŋdəm/	(das) Vereinigte Königreich	
	top /tɒp/	(das) obere Ende, (die) Spitze	
	until /ənˈtɪl/	bis	A car needs four **wheels** to drive.
	wheel /wiːl/	(das) Rad	
	palace /ˈpæləs/	(der) Palast	
	British /ˈbrɪtɪʃ/	britisch	
	king /kɪŋ/	(der) König	
	queen /kwiːn/	(die) Königin	

heart /hɑːt/	(das) Herz	**heart** 
although /ɔːlˈðəʊ/	obwohl	
home /həʊm/	(das) Zuhause, (das) Haus	
royal /ˈrɔɪəl/	königlich	
bell /bel/	(die) Glocke	
tower /ˈtaʊə/	(der) Turm	
parliament /ˈpɑːləmənt/	(das) Parlament	
river /ˈrɪvə/	(der) Fluss	**river** → 
stair /steə/	(die) Stufe	
(to) **get** *(irr)* /get/	kommen, gelangen	
ugly /ˈʌgli/	hässlich	**ugly** ≠ beautiful
building /ˈbɪldɪŋ/	(das) Gebäude	
as … as /æz æz/	so … wie	A hamster is not **as** big **as** a dog.
entry /ˈentri/	(der) Eintritt	
free /friː/	frei, kostenlos	
(to) **discover** /dɪˈskʌvə/	entdecken	The name of our planet is **Earth**.
earth /ɜːθ/	(die) Erde	
huge /hjuːdʒ/	riesig	Museums often have special **exhibitions**.
exhibition /ˌeksɪˈbɪʃn/	(die) Ausstellung	
moving /ˈmuːvɪŋ/	beweglich	
model /ˈmɒdl/	(das) Modell	
large /lɑːdʒ/	groß	
ever /ˈevə/	jemals	
(to) **exist** /ɪgˈzɪst/	existieren	
the public /ðə ˈpʌblɪk/	die Öffentlichkeit	
today /təˈdeɪ/	heutzutage	
than /ðæn/	als *(bei Vergleich)*	
species (*pl* **species**) /ˈspiːʃiːz, ˈspiːʃiːz/	(die) Art, (die) Spezies	
adult /ˈædʌlt/	(der/die) Erwachsene	
ferris wheel /ˈferɪs ˌwiːl/	(das) Riesenrad	
viewing point /ˈvjuːɪŋ pɔɪnt/	(der) Aussichtspunkt	
clock tower /ˈklɒk ˌtaʊə/	(der) Uhrenturm	
Thames /temz/	(die) Themse	
lift /lɪft/	(der) Aufzug	
skyscraper /ˈskaɪˌskreɪpə/	(der) Wolkenkratzer	
the Natural History Museum /ðə ˌnætʃərəl ˈhɪstəri mjuːˌziːəm/	(das) Naturkundemuseum	
dinosaur /ˈdaɪnəˌsɔː/	(der) Dinosaurier	
skeleton /ˈskelɪtn/	(das) Skelett	
p. 20 **bridge** /brɪdʒ/	(die) Brücke	
better /ˈbetə/	besser	
the best /ðə ˈbest/	am besten	good ➡ **better** ➡ **the best**
worse /wɜːs/	schlechter, schlimmer	

higher /ˈhaɪə/ höher
bigger / ˈbɪgə/ größer

the tallest /ðə ˈtɔːlɪst/ der/die/das größte; am größten
the most popular /ðə ˌməʊst ˈpɒpjʊlə/ der/die/das beliebteste; am beliebtesten
the highest /ðə ˈhaɪɪst/ der/die/das höchste; am höchsten
the most famous /ðə ˌməʊst ˈfeɪməs/ der/die/das berühmteste; am berühmtesten
the ugliest /ði‿ˈʌgliɪst/ der/die/das hässlichste; am hässlichsten
the largest /ðə ˈlɑːdʒɪst/ der/die/das größte; am größten
the oldest /ði‿ˈəʊldɪst/ der/die/das älteste; am ältesten

	the worst /ðə 'wɜːst/	der/die/das schlechteste/schlimmste; am schlechtesten/schlimmsten	bad ➡ **worse** ➡ **the worst**
p. 20, 2	**comparison** /kəm'pærɪsn/	(der) Vergleich	
	young /jʌŋ/	jung	**young** ≠ old
	leg /leg/	(das) Bein	
p. 20, 3	(to) **pay attention (to)** *(irr)* /ˌpeɪ‿ə'tenʃn tʊ/	aufpassen, achten auf	
	spelling /'spelɪŋ/	(das) Buchstabieren, (die) Rechtschreibung	
	comparative /kəm'pærətɪv/	(der) Komparativ	
	superlative /sʊ'pɜːlətɪv/	(der) Superlativ	
p. 22, 5	**timetable** /'taɪmteɪbl/	(der) Fahrplan	A **timetable** tells you what time a bus or train arrives.
	mobile (phone) /'məʊbaɪl/	(das) Handy	
	journey /'dʒɜːni/	(die) Reise, (die) Fahrt	A **journey** is a trip.
	(to) **take** *(irr)* /teɪk/	dauern	
	(to) **change lines** /ˌtʃeɪndʒ 'laɪnz/	umsteigen	
	platform /'plætˌfɔːm/	(der) Bahnsteig, (die) Plattform	
	towards /tə'wɔːdz/	in Richtung, zu; gegenüber	
	metre /'miːtə/	(der) Meter	**m** = **metre(s)** Meter **min** = **minute(s)** Minute(n) **sec** = **second(s)** Sekunde(n)
	the Tube /ðə 'tjuːb/	(die) (Londoner) U-Bahn	
	Day Travelcard /'deɪ ˌtrævlkɑːd/	(die) Tageskarte	
	(to) **depart** /dɪ'pɑːt/	abfahren	
p. 22, 6	(to) **follow** /'fɒləʊ/	folgen, verfolgen	
	directions *(pl)* /dɪ'rekʃnz/	*hier:* (die) Wegbeschreibungen	
	straight on /ˌstreɪt‿'ɒn/	geradeaus	↑ **straight on**
	(to) **turn** /tɜːn/	abbiegen	
	left /left/	links, nach links	← **left**
	onto /'ɒntə/	auf, in	
	right /raɪt/	rechts, nach rechts	**right** →
	past /pɑːst/	vorbei, vorüber	
	(to) **cross** /krɒs/	überqueren	xxx am Ende einer Nachricht = kisses = Küsschen
	(to) **give directions** *(irr)* /ˌgɪv daɪ'rekʃnz/	den Weg beschreiben	
	(to) **walk on** /ˌwɔːk‿'ɒn/	weiterlaufen	
	(to) **guide** /gaɪd/	führen, leiten	
p. 23, 8	**expensive** /ɪk'spensɪv/	teuer	If something is **expensive**, you have to pay a lot of money for it.
	less /les/	weniger	
	capsule /'kæpsjuːl/	(die) Kapsel	
Land und Leute 1	**raven** /'reɪvn/	(der) Rabe	
p. 24, 9	**flower** /'flaʊə/	(die) Blume	
	hundred /'hʌndrəd/	Hundert	
	entertainment /ˌentə'teɪnmənt/	(die) Unterhaltung	
	musician /mjʊ'zɪʃn/	(der/die) Musiker/in	A piano player is a **musician**.
	round /raʊnd/	(um ...) herum	
	corner /'kɔːnə/	(die) Ecke	

A piano player is a **musician**.

	entrance /ˈentrəns/	(der) Eingang, (der) Eintritt	The **present** is the time now.
	present /ˈpreznt/	(die) Gegenwart	
	combination /ˌkɒmbɪˈneɪʃn/	(die) Kombination, (die) Mischung	
	opening times *(pl)* /ˈəʊpənɪŋ taɪmz/	(die) Öffnungszeiten	
	underground /ˈʌndəˌgraʊnd/	(die) U-Bahn	
	acrobat /ˈækrəbæt/	(der/die) Akrobat/in	3/4 = three quarters /ˌθriː ˈkwɔːtəz/ dreiviertel
	(to) **be worth a visit** *(irr)* /ˌbiː ˌwɜːθ‿ə ˈvɪzɪt/	einen Besuch wert sein	
	must /mʌst/	(das) Muss	
	magical /ˈmædʒɪkl/	magisch	
	time travelling /ˈtaɪm ˌtrævlɪŋ/	(das) Zeitreisen	
	(to) **take a selfie** *(irr)* /ˌteɪk‿ə ˈselfi/	ein Selfie machen	
	wax statue /ˈwæks ˌstætʃuː/	(die) Wachsfigur	
p. 25, 10	**glass** /glɑːs/	(das) Glas	**glass**
	below /bɪˈləʊ/	unten, unter	
	height /haɪt/	(die) Höhe	A **visitor** is a person who visits a person or a place.
	visitor /ˈvɪzɪtə/	(der/die) Besucher/in	
	walkway /ˈwɔːkˌweɪ/	(der) (Fuß)weg	
p. 26, 12	**possibility** /ˌpɒsəˈbɪləti/	(die) Möglichkeit	
	stadium *(pl* **stadiums** *or* **stadia***)* /ˈsteɪdiəm, ˈsteɪdiəmz, ˈsteɪdiə/	(das) Stadion	
p. 26, 13	**concert** /ˈkɒnsət/	(das) Konzert	
	whole /həʊl/	ganz, gesamt	**whole** = 100%
	blue whale /bluː ˈweɪl/	(der) Blauwal	
	(to) **unscramble** /ʌnˈskræmbl/	in die richtige Reihenfolge bringen	
	(to) **move in** /ˌmuːv‿ˈɪn/	einziehen	
p. 27, 14	**day out** /ˌdeɪ‿ˈaʊt/	*(der) Ausflugstag*	
	theme /θiːm/	(das) Thema	If something is **for free**, it doesn't cost anything.
	for free /fə ˈfriː/	gratis	
	(to) **enter** /ˈentə/	eingeben	A **draft** is something like a plan.
	draft /drɑːft/	(der) Entwurf	
	search engine /ˈsɜːtʃ‿ˌendʒɪn/	(die) Suchmaschine	

Unit 2 | Part A Festivals and traditions

p. 31	**celebration** /ˌseləˈbreɪʃn/	(die) Feier	A **festival** is a big, public **celebration**.
	festival /ˈfestɪvl/	(das) Fest, (das) Festival	
	holiday /ˈhɒlɪdeɪ/	(der) Feiertag	
	(to) **celebrate** /ˈseləˌbreɪt/	feiern	
	Bonfire Night /ˈbɒnˌfaɪə ˌnaɪt/	*brit. Gedenkfest am 5. November*	
p. 32, 1	**following** /ˈfɒləʊɪŋ/	folgende(r,s)	**following** = next
p. 33, 1	**Easter** /ˈiːstə/	(das) Ostern	
	religious /rəˈlɪdʒəs/	religiöse(r,s)	
	Christian /ˈkrɪstʃən/	(der/die) Christ/in; christlich	
	spring /sprɪŋ/	(der) Frühling	

(to) **believe (in)** /bɪˈliːv‿ɪn/	glauben (an)	
(to) **hide** *(irr)* /haɪd/	(sich) verstecken	
traditional /trəˈdɪʃnəl/	traditionell	
Muslim /ˈmʊzləm/	(der/die) Muslim/in; muslimisch	
all over the world /ˌɔːl‿ˌəʊvə ðə ˈwɜːld/	auf der ganzen Welt	**all over the world** = everywhere in the world
mosque /mɒsk/	(die) Moschee	
prayer /preə/	(das) Gebet	
Hinduism /ˈhɪnduˌɪzm/	Hinduismus	**Hinduism** is a religion.
(to) **stand for** *(irr)* /ˈstænd fɔː/	stehen für	
victory /ˈvɪktri/	(der) Sieg	
darkness /ˈdɑːknəs/	(die) Dunkelheit	
decoration /ˌdekəˈreɪʃn/	(die) Dekoration, (der) Schmuck	
(to) **light** *(irr)* /laɪt/	anzünden	
Chinese /ˌtʃaɪˈniːz/	(der/die) Chinese/Chinesin; chinesisch	
New Year /ˌnjuː ˈjɪə/	(das) Neujahr	
(to) **take place** *(irr)* /ˌteɪk ˈpleɪs/	stattfinden	
(to) **depend on** /dɪˈpend‿ɒn/	abhängen von	
(to) **last** /lɑːst/	(an)dauern	
(to) **end** /end/	enden; beenden	
lantern /ˈlæntən/	(die) Laterne	
dragon /ˈdrægən/	(der) Drache	**dragon**
costume /ˈkɒstjuːm/	(das) Kostüm	
dancer /ˈdɑːnsə/	(der/die) Tänzer/in	
fireworks *(pl)* /ˈfaɪəˌwɜːks/	(das) Feuerwerk	
Jewish /ˈdʒuːɪʃ/	jüdisch	
night /naɪt/	(die) Nacht, (der) Abend	It is dark at **night**.
beginning /bɪˈgɪnɪŋ/	(der) Anfang, (der) Beginn	**beginning** = start
(to) **have in common** *(irr)* /ˌhæv‿ɪn ˈkɒmən/	gemeinsam haben	
Easter egg hunt /ˈiːstər‿eg ˌhʌnt/	Ostereiersuche	
Easter bunny /ˈiːstə ˌbʌni/	Osterhase	
Easter egg roll /ˈiːstər‿eg ˌrəʊl/	*Ostereierrollen*	
daylight *(no pl)* /ˈdeɪˌlaɪt/	(das) Tageslicht	
sunset /ˈsʌnˌset/	(der) Sonnenuntergang	
good /gʊd/	(das) Gute	
evil /ˈiːvl/	(das) Böse	
candle holder /ˈkændl ˌhəʊldə/	(der) Kerzenständer	
p. 34, 2 **Christmas** /ˈkrɪsməs/	(das) Weihnachten	At **Christmas**, many Christians go to **church**.
church /tʃɜːtʃ/	(die) Kirche	
not anything /ˌnɒt‿ˈeniˌθɪŋ/	nichts	
p. 34, 3 (to) **inform** /ɪnˈfɔːm/	informieren	You can find lots of words in a **dictionary**.
dictionary /ˈdɪkʃənri/	(das) Lexikon, (das) Wörterbuch	
full of /ˈfʊl‿əv/	voller	

	(to) **go together** *(irr)* /ˌɡəʊ təˈɡeðə/	zusammenpassen	
	(to) **underline** /ˌʌndəˈlaɪn/	unterstreichen	
p. 35, 4	**grape** /ɡreɪp/	(die) (Wein)traube	A **grape** is a fruit.
	(good) luck /lʌk/	(das) Glück	
	(to) **change** /tʃeɪndʒ/	(sich) ändern, verändern	
	India /ˈɪndiə/	Indien	
	Spain /speɪn/	Spanien	
	first footing /ˌfɜːst ˈfʊtɪŋ/	*(das) Abstatten eines Neujahrsbesuchs (schottische Tradition)*	
	midnight /ˈmɪdˌnaɪt/	(die) Mitternacht	
	Scottish /ˈskɒtɪʃ/	schottisch	
	New Year's Eve /ˌnjuː jɪəz‿ˈiːv/	(das) Silvester	
p. 36, 6	**probably** /ˈprɒbəbli/	wahrscheinlich	
	Ireland /ˈaɪələnd/	Irland	
	northern /ˈnɔːðən/	nördlich, Nord-	
	ghost /ɡəʊst/	(der) Geist, (das) Gespenst	**ghost** 
	scary /ˈskeəri/	Furcht erregend	
	(to) **offer** /ˈɒfə/	anbieten	
	(to) **rule** /ruːl/	herrschen, regieren	
	Britain /ˈbrɪtn/	Großbritannien	**Britain** = England, Scotland and Wales
	(to) **mix** /mɪks/	sich (ver)mischen	
	century /ˈsentʃəri/	(das) Jahrhundert	
	sweet /swiːt/	(die) Süßigkeit	Most children love **sweets**.
	inspiration /ˌɪnspəˈreɪʃn/	(die) Inspiration, (die) Idee	
	Celtic /ˈkeltɪk/	keltisch	
	Celt /kelt/	(der/die) Kelte/Keltin	
	bonfire /ˈbɒnˌfaɪə/	(das) (Freuden)feuer	**bonfire** 
	(to) **come together** *(irr)* /ˌkʌm təˈɡeðə/	zusammenkommen	
	the dead *(pl)* /ðə ˈded/	die Toten *(pl)*	
	trick-or-treating /ˌtrɪk‿ɔː ˈtriːtɪŋ/	*(das) Spiel zu Halloween, bei dem die Kinder von Tür zu Tür gehen und entweder Süßigkeiten bekommen oder einen Streich spielen*	
	(to) **honour** /ˈɒnə/	ehren	
	goddess /ˈɡɒdes/	(die) Göttin	
	apple bobbing /ˈæpl ˌbɒbɪŋ/	*(das) Apfelfischen*	
	All Hallows' Day /ˌɔːl ˈhæləʊz deɪ/	Allerheiligen	
	saint /seɪnt/	(der/die) Heilige	
	All Hallows' Eve /ˌɔːl ˌhæləʊz‿ˈiːv/	*(der) Abend vor Allerheiligen*	
	Catholic /ˈkæθlɪk/	(der/die) Katholik/in; katholisch	
	Irish /ˈaɪrɪʃ/	irisch	
	(to) **carve** /kɑːv/	schnitzen	
	jack-o'-lantern /ˌdʒæk‿ə ˈlæntən/	(die) Kürbislaterne	**jack-o'-lantern**
	(to) **dress up** /ˌdres‿ˈʌp/	(sich) verkleiden	

	(to) **scare away** /ˌskeər‿əˈweɪ/	verscheuchen	
p. 37, 6	**surprising** /səˈpraɪzɪŋ/	überraschend	
	timeline /ˈtaɪmlaɪn/	(die) Zeitachse	
p. 38, 7	**commercial** /kəˈmɜːʃl/	kommerziell, profitorientiert	
	stupid /ˈstjuːpɪd/	dumm, blöd	**stupid** ≠ intelligent
	(to) **mean** *(irr)* /miːn/	meinen; bedeuten	
	character /ˈkærəktə/	(die) Figur, (der) Charakter	**Characters** are the people in a book or film.
	all kinds of /ˌɔːl ˈkaɪndz‿əv/	alle möglichen	
	out of /ˈaʊt‿əv/	aus	
	pumpkin /ˈpʌmpkɪn/	(der) Kürbis	**pumpkin** 
	Trick or treat! /ˌtrɪk‿ɔː ˈtriːt/	*etwa:* Süßes oder es gibt Saures!	
	(to) **play a trick on somebody** /ˌpleɪ‿ə ˈtrɪk‿ɒn ˌsʌmbədi/	jemandem einen Streich spielen	
	mummy /ˈmʌmi/	(die) Mumie	
	(to) **wrap** /ræp/	einwickeln	
	toilet paper /ˈtɔɪlət ˌpeɪpə/	(das) Toilettenpapier	
p. 39, 7	**pro** /prəʊ/	(der) Vorteil, (das) Pro	**Pro** and **con** are opposites.
	con /kɒn/	(der) Nachteil, (das) Kontra	
p. 39, 8	**the other one** /ði‿ˈʌðə wʌn/	der/die/das andere	
p. 39, 9	(to) **fill** /fɪl/	füllen	
	inside /ˈɪnˌsaɪd/	innen, drinnen, hinein	
	piece /piːs/	(das) Stück, (der) Teil	
	(to) **cut** *(irr)* /kʌt/	schneiden	You need a knife or scissors to **cut**.
	(to) **make sure** *(irr)* /ˌmeɪk ˈʃɔː/	darauf achten, dass ...	
	apart /əˈpɑːt/	auseinander	**apart** = not together
	glass jar /ˈglɑːs dʒɑː/	(das) Glasgefäß	
	tape /teɪp/	(das) Klebeband	
	pair /peə/	(das) Paar	
	googly eyes *(pl)* /ˌguːgli‿ˈaɪz/	*(die) Wackelaugen*	
	LED candle /ˌel‿iː ˌdiː ˈkændl/	(die) LED-Kerze	
	garland /ˈgɑːlənd/	(der) Kranz, (die) Girlande	
	(to) **fold** /fəʊld/	falten	
	cm (= centimetre) /ˌsiː ˈem, ˈsentɪˌmiːtə/	(der) Zentimeter	
	section /ˈsekʃn/	(das) Teil, (das) Stück, (der) Abschnitt	
	the top /tɒp/	der/die/das oberste	
	(to) **cut out** *(irr)* /ˌkʌt‿ˈaʊt/	ausschneiden	
p. 40, 11	**category** /ˈkætəgri/	(die) Kategorie	
	country /ˈkʌntri/	(das) Land	You can see trees in the **background** of this picture.
p. 41, 12	**background** /ˈbækˌgraʊnd/	(der) Hintergrund	
	(to) **put up** *(irr)* /ˌpʊt‿ˈʌp/	aufhängen, aufstellen	

Unit 2 | Part B Let's celebrate!

p. 42, 1	**role** /rəʊl/	(die) Rolle	

	(to) **join in** /ˌdʒɔɪn‿ˈɪn/	sich beteiligen an, mitmachen bei	
	stall /stɔːl/	(der) Stand	
	(to) **take a ride** *(irr)* /ˌteɪk‿ə ˈraɪd/	*hier:* Karussell fahren	
	funfair /ˈfʌnˌfeə/	(der) Vergnügungspark, (die) Kirmes	
	painting /ˈpeɪntɪŋ/	(das) Anmalen	
p. 43, 2	**may** /meɪ/	können, dürfen	
	(to) **have a look at** *(irr)* /ˌhæv‿ə ˈlʊk‿ət/	sich ansehen	**to have a look at** = to look at
	quite /kwaɪt/	ziemlich	
	that /ðæt/	so	
	out /aʊt/	draußen	If the weather is good, the children can play **out** in the garden.
	..., are we? /ˈɑː wiː/	*hier:* ..., nicht wahr?	
	cold /kəʊld/	(die) Kälte	
	(to) **queue** /kjuː/	Schlange stehen	
	phew *(informal)* /fjuː/	puh	
	right now /ˌraɪt ˈnaʊ/	jetzt, im Moment	**right now** = at the moment
	excuse /ɪkˈskjuːs/	(die) Entschuldigung, (die) Ausrede	
	toffee apple /ˈtɒfi ˌæpl/	(der) kandierte Apfel	
p. 44, 3	**lab (= laboratory)** /læb, ləˈbɒrətri/	(das) Labor	
p. 44, 5	**stress** /stres/	(die) Betonung	
	syllable /ˈsɪləbl/	(die) Silbe	
p. 45, 6	**almost** /ˈɔːlməʊst/	fast, beinahe	If it is **almost** your birthday, then it is your birthday in a few days.
	not yet /nɒt ˈjet/	noch nicht	
	definitely /ˈdefnətli/	eindeutig, definitiv	
	hot /hɒt/	heiß	
	wood /wʊd/	(das) Holz	
	fire /ˈfaɪə/	(das) Feuer	
	(to) **cook** /kʊk/	braten, backen	
	(to) **be going to** *(irr)* /ˌbiː ˈgəʊɪŋ tʊ/	werden	
	love /lʌv/	viele Grüße, alles Liebe *(in Briefen)*	At the end of a letter you can write "**love**" and then your name.
	sparkler /ˈspɑːklə/	(die) Wunderkerze	
	s'more *(AE)* /smɔː/	*(das/der) Sandwich aus süßen Kräckern mit getoasteten Marshmallows und Schokolade*	Der Name *s'more* für den beliebten Lagerfeuersnack kommt wahrscheinlich einfach von „*some more*".
	forever /fərˈevə/	ewig	
	recipe /ˈresəpi/	(das) Rezept	
	hot chocolate /ˌhɒt ˈtʃɒklət/	(der) heiße Kakao	
	jacket potato (*pl* **jacket potatoes**) /ˌdʒækɪt pəˈteɪtəʊ, ˌdʒækɪt pəˈteɪtəʊz/	(die) Folienkartoffel	
p. 46, 7	**sugar** /ˈʃʊgə/	(der) Zucker	**Sugar** is sweet.
	bowl /bəʊl/	(die) Schüssel, (die) Schale	**bowl** 
	(to) **cover** /ˈkʌvə/	bedecken	
	(to) **remove** /rɪˈmuːv/	entfernen	
	(to) **push** /pʊʃ/	schieben, stoßen	
	sheet /ʃiːt/	(das) Blatt, (der) Bogen	

	by /baɪ/ *(+ Verbform mit -ing)*	indem
	a little /ə ˈlɪtl/	ein bisschen
	should /ʃʊd/	sollte(st, n,t)
	(to) **leave** *(irr)* /liːv/	(übrig) lassen; zurücklassen
	order /ˈɔːdə/	(die) Reihenfolge, (die) Ordnung
	boiling /ˈbɔɪlɪŋ/	kochend
	(to) **dry** /draɪ/	trocknen
	stalk /stɔːk/	(der) Stängel, (der) Stiel
	wooden /ˈwʊdn/	Holz-, hölzern
	skewer /ˈskjuːə/	(der) Spieß
	baking paper /ˈbeɪkɪŋ ˌpeɪpə/	(das) Backpapier
	pot /pɒt/	(der) Topf
	(to) **melt** /melt/	schmelzen
	(to) **boil** /bɔɪl/	kochen *(Flüssigkeit)*
	(to) **test** /test/	prüfen, testen
	instantly /ˈɪnstəntli/	sofort
	(to) **cool** /kuːl/	abkühlen
p. 47, **8**	**safety** /ˈseɪfti/	(die) Sicherheit
Land und Leute 3	**Guy** /gaɪ/	*(die) Guy Fawkes-Puppe*
p. 48, **9**	**reaction** /riˈækʃn/	(die) Reaktion
	suggestion /səˈdʒestʃn/	(der) Vorschlag
p. 48, **10**	**reason** /ˈriːzn/	(der) Grund
	rhyme /raɪm/	(der) Reim
	gunpowder *(no pl)* /ˈgʌnˌpaʊdə/	(das) Schießpulver
	treason /ˈtriːzn/	(der) (Landes)verrat
	plot /plɒt/	(die) Verschwörung
	(to) **be forgot** *(irr, poet.)* /ˌbiː fəˈgɒt/	vergessen werden *(poetisch)*
	(to) **look up** /ˌlʊk‿ˈʌp/	nach oben sehen, aufschauen
	aloud /əˈlaʊd/	laut
	by heart /ˌbaɪ ˈhɑːt/	auswendig
p. 48, **11**	**acrostic** /əˈkrɒstɪk/	(das) Akrostichon, (der) Leistenvers
	noisy /ˈnɔɪzi/	laut
p. 49, **12**	**earlier** /ˈɜːliə/	vorhin, früher
	(to) **roast** /rəʊst/	rösten, braten
	(to) **grill** /grɪl/	grillen
	sausage /ˈsɒsɪdʒ/	(die) Wurst, (das) Würstchen
	CU! (= **See you!**) *(informal)* /ˈsiː juː/	Bis bald!
p. 50, **14**	**discussion** /dɪˈskʌʃn/	(die) Diskussion
	contest /ˈkɒntest/	(der) Wettbewerb
p. 50, **15**	**healthy** /ˈhelθi/	gesund
	checklist /ˈtʃeklɪst/	(die) Checkliste
	crisps *(pl)* /krɪsps/	(die) Chips
	lemonade /ˌleməˈneɪd/	(die) Limonade

a little ≠ a lot

g (= gram) /græm/
(das) Gramm
tbsp (= tablespoon) /ˈteɪblspuːn/
(der) EL (= Esslöffel)
ml (= millilitre) /ˈmɪlɪˌliːtə/
(der) Milliliter
°C (= degree Celsius) /dɪˌgriː ˈselsiəs/
(das) Grad Celsius

A **suggestion** is an idea or plan that you tell somebody for them to think about.

People often **grill sausages** in the garden in summer.

A **healthy** person doesn't need a doctor.

p. 51, 16	**autumn** /ˈɔːtəm/	(der) Herbst	
	somewhere /ˈsʌmweə/	irgendwo	**to discuss** = to talk about something with someone
	(to) **discuss** /dɪˈskʌs/	besprechen, diskutieren	
	placemat /ˈpleɪsmæt/	Platzdeckchen *(Methode)*	

Unit 3 | Part A Getting along

p. 55	(to) **get along** *(irr)* /ˌget‿əˈlɒŋ/	sich verstehen	When you **take care of** someone, you look after them.
	(to) **take care of** *(irr)* /ˌteɪk‿ˈkeər‿əv/	sich kümmern um	
p. 56, 1	**respect** /rɪˈspekt/	(der) Respekt	
	must /mʌst/	müssen	
	(to) **report** /rɪˈpɔːt/	sich melden	
	mustn't (= must not) /ˈmʌsnt, mʌst ˈnɒt/	nicht dürfen	
	(to) **run** *(irr)* /rʌn/	laufen, rennen	
	(to) **be allowed (to)** *(irr)* /ˌbi‿əˈlaʊd‿tə/	erlaubt sein	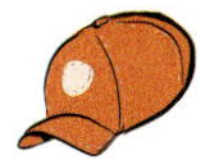
	cap /kæp/	(die) Mütze, (die) Cap	**cap**
	school grounds *(pl)* /ˈskuːl ˌgraʊndz/	(das) Schulgelände	
	(to) **enter** /ˈentə/	betreten	
	(to) **knock** /nɒk/	klopfen	(to) be in trouble /biː‿ɪn ˈtrʌbl/ in Schwierigkeiten sein
	dangerous /ˈdeɪndʒərəs/	gefährlich	(to) get into trouble /ˌget‿ɪntʊ ˈtrʌbl/ in Schwierigkeiten geraten
	headteacher /ˌhedˈtiːtʃə/	(der/die) Schulleiter/in, (der/die) Rektor/in	
	lunchtime /ˈlʌntʃtaɪm/	(die) Mittagszeit, (die) Mittagspause	
	hat /hæt/	(der) Hut	
p. 57, 1	(to) **break** *(irr)* /breɪk/	brechen, zerbrechen, kaputt machen	
	bored /bɔːd/	gelangweilt	
	trouble /ˈtrʌbl/	(der) Ärger, (die) Schwierigkeiten	
	mark /mɑːk/	(die) Note, (die) Zensur	
	(to) **shout at somebody** /ˈʃaʊt‿ət ˌsʌmbədi/	jemanden anschreien	When you **shout at somebody**, you are loud.
p. 57, 2	**in my opinion** /ɪn ˈmaɪ‿əˌpɪnjən/	meiner Meinung nach	
p. 58, 5	**knee** /niː/	(das) Knie	
	silent letter /ˌsaɪlənt ˈletə/	(der) stumme Laut	
	(to) **circle** /sɜːkl/	einkreisen	
p. 59, 6	(to) **express** /ɪkˈspres/	ausdrücken	
	style /staɪl/	(der) Stil	
	shoe /ʃuː/	(der) Schuh	a pair of **shoes**
	jewellery *(no pl)* /ˈdʒuːəlri/	(der) Schmuck	
Land und Leute 4	**casual** /ˈkæʒuəl/	lässig	
p. 60, 7	(to) **feel** *(irr)* /fiːl/	(sich) fühlen	
	angry /ˈæŋgri/	zornig, wütend	
	sad /sæd/	traurig	He is always very **tired** in the mornings.
	tired /ˈtaɪəd/	müde	
	annoyed /əˈnɔɪd/	verärgert	

	worried /ˈwʌrid/	beunruhigt, besorgt	
	scared /skeəd/	verängstigt, ängstlich	
	relaxed /rɪˈlækst/	entspannt	
p. 61, 8	**solution** /səˈluːʃn/	(die) Lösung	
p. 61, 9	**sign** /saɪn/	(das) Zeichen, (das) Schild	 **sign**
	friendship /ˈfrenʃɪp/	(die) Freundschaft	
	silly /ˈsɪli/	albern, dumm	
p. 62, 10	**diary** /ˈdaɪəri/	(das) Tagebuch	
	by /baɪ/	*hier:* (spätestens) bis	
	while /waɪl/	während	
	(to) **finish** /ˈfɪnɪʃ/	beenden, enden	
	meeting /ˈmiːtɪŋ/	(die) Versammlung, (das) Treffen	
	side /saɪd/	(die) Seite	
	strict /strɪkt/	streng	
	TV (= television) /ˌtiː ˈviː, ˈtelɪˌvɪʒn/	(das) Fernsehen, (der) Fernseher	 **TV**
	(to) **stay out** /ˌsteɪ‿ˈaʊt/	ausbleiben, wegbleiben	
p. 63, 11	**early** /ˈɜːli/	früh	**early** ≠ late
	not anymore /ˌnɒt‿ˌeni ˈmɔː/	nicht mehr	
	(to) **work** /wɜːk/	funktionieren	
	(to) **interrupt** /ˌɪntəˈrʌpt/	unterbrechen	
	(to) **stick to** *(irr)* /ˈstɪk tʊ/	*hier:* sich halten an	
p. 63, 12	**door** /dɔː/	(die) Tür	 **door**
p. 64, 13	(to) **go out** *(irr)* /ˌgəʊ‿ˈaʊt/	(hinaus)gehen, ausgehen	
p. 64, 14	(to) **stay up (late)** /ˌsteɪ‿ˌʌp ˈleɪt/	(lange) aufbleiben	
	helmet /ˈhelmɪt/	(der) Helm	
p. 65, 15	**role play** /ˈrəʊl pleɪ/	(das) Rollenspiel	
	conflict /ˈkɒnflɪkt/	(der) Konflikt	
	(to) **take part in** *(irr)* /ˌteɪk ˈpɑːt‿ɪn/	teilnehmen an	
	against /əˈgenst/	gegen	In a football match, one team plays **against** the other.
	compromise /ˈkɒmprəmaɪz/	(der) Kompromiss	

Unit 3 | Part B Take care!

p. 66, 1	**wildlife** /ˈwaɪldˌlaɪf/	(die) Tier- und Pflanzenwelt, (die) Flora und Fauna	
	centre /ˈsentə/	(das) Zentrum	
	bird /bɜːd/	(der) Vogel	**birds**
	(to) **note** /nəʊt/	beachten, zur Kenntnis nehmen	
	(to) **book** /bʊk/	buchen, reservieren	
	(to) **feed** *(irr)* /fiːd/	füttern	
	closed /kləʊzd/	geschlossen	When a supermarket is **closed**, you cannot go shopping there.
	safe /seɪf/	sicher, ungefährlich	
	forest /ˈfɒrɪst/	(der) Wald	
	path /pɑːθ/	(der) Weg, (der) Pfad	

	runner /ˈrʌnə/	(der/die) Läufer/in	If you **hire** something, it is not yours.
	(to) **hire** /ˈhaɪə/	mieten	
	lead /liːd/	(die) Leine	
	all year round /ˌɔːl ˈjɪə raʊnd/	das ganze Jahr lang	
	fox /fɒks/	(der) Fuchs	
	deer /dɪə/	(der) Hirsch, (das) Reh	
	squirrel /ˈskwɪrəl/	(das) Eichhörnchen	**squirrel**
	feeding time /ˈfiːdɪŋ taɪm/	(die) Fütterungszeit	
	parking /ˈpɑːkɪŋ/	(das) Parken	
	flag /flæg/	(die) Fahne, (die) Flagge	
	at all times /æt‿ˌɔːl ˈtaɪmz/	jederzeit, immer	
	barbecue /ˈbɑːbɪˌkjuː/	(der) Grill, (die) Grillparty	
	sun cream /ˈsʌn kriːm/	(die) Sonnenschutzcreme	**Sun (= Sunday)** /ˈsʌndeɪ/ (der) Sonntag
	walker /ˈwɔːkə/	(der/die) Spaziergänger/in	
	cyclist /ˈsaɪklɪst/	(der/die) Radfahrer/in	
	horse rider /ˈhɔːs ˌraɪdə/	(der/die) Reiter/in	
	information point /ˌɪnfəˈmeɪʃn pɔɪnt/	(die) Informationsstelle	
	horse riding /ˈhɔːs ˌraɪdɪŋ/	(das) Reiten	A **national park** is an area of nature that is especially beautiful.
p. 67, 1	**national park** /ˌnæʃnl ˈpɑːk/	(der) Nationalpark	
	countryside /ˈkʌntriˌsaɪd/	(das) Land, (die) Landschaft	
	(to) **explore** /ɪkˈsplɔː/	erforschen, untersuchen	
	(to) **take away** *(irr)* /ˌteɪk‿əˈweɪ/	wegnehmen, mitnehmen	
	suddenly /ˈsʌdnli/	plötzlich	
	gate /geɪt/	(das) Tor	**gate**
	nothing /ˈnʌθɪŋ/	nichts	
	but /bʌt/	außer	
	photograph /ˈfəʊtəˌgrɑːf/	(die) Fotografie, (das) Foto	**photograph** = photo
	appropriate /əˈprəʊpriət/	angemessen, passend	
	campsite /ˈkæmpˌsaɪt/	(der) Campingplatz	
	footprint /ˈfʊtˌprɪnt/	(der) Fußabdruck	
	(to) **go camping** *(irr)* /ˌgəʊ ˈkæmpɪŋ/	zelten gehen	
p. 67, 2	**the ones** /ðə ˈwʌnz/	diejenigen; diese	
p. 68, 4	**car park** /ˈkɑː pɑːk/	(der) Parkplatz	
p. 69, 6	**letter** /ˈletə/	(der) Brief	**letter**
	year /jɪə/	(das) Schuljahr, (die) Klasse	
	trip /trɪp/	(der) Ausflug, (die) Fahrt	A **jacket** is a piece of clothing.
	jacket /ˈdʒækɪt/	(die) Jacke	
	(to) **return** /rɪˈtɜːn/	zurückgeben	
	permission /pəˈmɪʃn/	(die) Erlaubnis, (die) Genehmigung	Rd (= road) /rəʊd/ (die) Straße *(bei Adressangaben)*
	payment /ˈpeɪmənt/	(die) Bezahlung	
	written /ˈrɪtn/	schriftlich	
	(to) **look forward to** /ˌlʊk ˈfɔːwəd‿tʊ/	sich freuen auf	

	yours sincerely /ˌjɔ:z sɪnˈsɪəli/	mit freundlichen Grüßen *(am Ende eines formellen Briefes)*	
	field trip /ˈfi:ld‿trɪp/	(die) Exkursion	
	packed lunch /ˌpækt ˈlʌntʃ/	(das) Lunchpaket	
	slip /slɪp/	(der) Zettel	
	educational /ˌedjʊˈkeɪʃnəl/	lehrreich	
	full /fʊl/	voll, vollständig	
p. 70, 7	**job** /dʒɒb/	(die) Aufgabe, (der) Beruf	
	(to) **protect** /prəˈtekt/	beschützen	
	hedgehog /ˈhedʒˌhɒg/	(der) Igel	
	bee /bi:/	(die) Biene	
	busy /ˈbɪzi/	belebt, verkehrsreich	There is a lot of traffic on a **busy** street.
	dry /draɪ/	trocken	
	leaf (*pl* **leaves**) /li:f, li:vz/	(das) Blatt	
	(to) **produce** /prəˈdju:s/	herstellen	
	This way, please. /ˈðɪs weɪ ˌpli:z/	Hier entlang, bitte.	
	nail /neɪl/	(der) Nagel	
	food /fu:d/	*hier:* (das) Futter	
	honeybee /ˈhʌniˌbi:/	(die) Honigbiene	
	honey /ˈhʌni/	(der) Honig	
p. 71, 7	**ground** /graʊnd/	(der) Boden	He finds something on the **ground**.
	plant /plɑ:nt/	(die) Pflanze	
	danger /ˈdeɪndʒə/	(die) Gefahr	
	(to) **destroy** /dɪˈstrɔɪ/	zerstören	
	(to) **grow** *(irr)* /grəʊ/	anbauen	
	friendly /ˈfrendli/	freundlich	
	flat /flæt/	(die) Wohnung	A **flat** is usually smaller than a house.
	project /ˈprɒdʒekt/	(das) Projekt	
	(to) **include** /ɪnˈklu:d/	beinhalten; einbeziehen	
	(to) **pollinate** /ˈpɒləneɪt/	bestäuben	
p. 73, 10	**instruction** /ɪnˈstrʌkʃn/	(die) Anweisung, (die) Instruktion	You need **instructions** that tell you how to build something or how to do something.
	half (*pl* **halves**) /hɑ:f, hɑ:vz/	(die) Hälfte	
	string /strɪŋ/	(die) Schnur, (die) Kordel	
	(to) **hang (up)** *(irr)* /ˌhæŋ‿ˈʌp/	aufhängen	Many teenagers **hang up** posters of singers on the walls of their rooms.
	feeder /ˈfi:də/	(die) Futterstation	
	birdseed /ˈbɜ:dˌsi:d/	(das) Vogelfutter	
	nut /nʌt/	(die) Nuss	
	dried fruit /ˌdraɪd ˈfru:t/	(das) getrocknete Obst, (das) Dörrobst	
	fat /fæt/	(das) Fett	
	coconut /ˈkəʊkəˌnʌt/	(die) Kokosnuss	**coconut**
	yoghurt pot /ˈjɒgət pɒt/	(der) Joghurtbecher	
p. 73, 11	**environment** /ɪnˈvaɪrənmənt/	(die) Umwelt, (die) Umgebung	

p. 74, 12	**wall** /wɔːl/	(die) Wand	
	ice /aɪs/	(das) Eis	
	off /ɒf/	von; hinunter, herunter	
	arts and crafts /ˌɑːrts‿ən ˈkrɑːfts/	(das) Basteln, (die) Bastelarbeit	
	insect /ˈɪnsekt/	(das) Insekt	
	balcony /ˈbælkəni/	(der) Balkon	
	overnight /ˌəʊvəˈnaɪt/	über Nacht	
	freezer /ˈfriːzə/	(der) Gefrierschrank	
p. 74, 13	**exercise** /ˈeksəsaɪz/	(die) Übung	
	(to) **notice** /ˈnəʊtɪs/	bemerken; wahrnehmen	
p. 75, 14	**expert** /ˈekspɜːt/	(der/die) Experte/Expertin	An **expert** is a person who knows a lot about a topic.
	brochure /ˈbrəʊʃə/	(die) Broschüre	

Unit 4 | Part A My dreams

p. 79	**future** /ˈfjuːtʃə/	(die) Zukunft	
	adventure /ədˈventʃə/	(das) Abenteuer	An **adventure** is an exciting experience.
	to /tʊ/	*hier:* für	
p. 80, 1	**will** /wɪl/	werden	
	(to) **film** /fɪlm/	drehen, filmen	to **film** = to make a film
	public /ˈpʌblɪk/	öffentlich	
	(to) **hand in** /ˌhænd‿ˈɪn/	einreichen, abgeben	
	either ... or ... /ˌaɪðə ˈɔː/	entweder ... oder ...	
	opening /ˈəʊpnɪŋ/	(die) Öffnung	
p. 80, 2	**drawing** /ˈdrɔːɪŋ/	(die) Zeichnung	
	whatever /wɒtˈevə/	was (auch immer)	
	'll (= will) /l, wɪl/	werden	
	(to) **leave** *(irr)* /liːv/	hinterlassen	If I **leave** my email adress with someone, I give it to them so they can send me an email later.
	(to) **contact** /ˈkɒntækt/	sich in Verbindung setzen mit	
p. 81, 2	**won't** /wəʊnt/	nicht werden	
	fashion /ˈfæʃn/	(die) Mode	
	engineer /ˌendʒɪˈnɪə/	(der/die) Ingenieur/in	
	(to) **grow up** *(irr)* /ˌɡrəʊ‿ˈʌp/	erwachsen sein, erwachsen werden	
	(to) **invent** /ɪnˈvent/	erfinden	
	regular /ˈregjʊlə/	üblich, normal	
	singer /ˈsɪŋə/	(der/die) Sänger/in	
	exactly /ɪgˈzækli/	genau	
	rather than /ˈrɑːðə ðæn/	anstatt	
	honest /ˈɒnɪst/	ehrlich	
	customer /ˈkʌstəmə/	(der/die) Kunde/Kundin	A **customer** is a person who buys something.
	technology /tekˈnɒlədʒi/	(die) Technologie, (die) Technik	
	and so on /ænd ˈsəʊ‿ɒn/	und so weiter	
	fancy /ˈfænsi/	nobel	
	play a stage /ˌpleɪ‿ə ˈsteɪdʒ/	auf einer Bühne spielen	

	Go big or go home. *(AE)* /ˌgəʊ ˌbɪg‿ɔ: ˌgəʊ ˈhəʊm/	Ganz oder gar nicht.
	chef /ʃef/	(der/die) Koch/Köchin
	mate *(informal)* /meɪt/	(der) Kumpel
	We'll see about that! /wi:l ˈsi:‿əˌbaʊt ðæt/	Das werden wir sehen.
	(to) **be lucky** *(irr)* /ˌbi: ˈlʌki/	Glück haben
p. 82, 3	**future** /ˈfju:tʃə/	zukünftig
p. 82, 4	(to) **be married** *(irr)* /ˌbi: ˈmærid/	verheiratet sein
p. 83, 6	**firefighter** /ˈfaɪəˌfaɪtə/	(der/die) Feuerwehrmann/-frau
	(to) **fight** *(irr)* /faɪt/	bekämpfen; ankämpfen gegen
	police officer /pəˈli:s‿ˌɒfɪsə/	(der/die) Polizeibeamte/Polizeibeamtin
	ill /ɪl/	krank
	(to) **repair** /rɪˈpeə/	reparieren
	(to) **act** /ækt/	handeln; spielen
	stage /steɪdʒ/	(die) Bühne
	actor/actress /ˈæktə, ˈæktrəs/	(der/die) Schauspieler/in
	mechanic /mɪˈkænɪk/	(der/die) Mechaniker/in
	nurse /nɜ:s/	(die) Krankenschwester, (der) Krankenpfleger
	hairdresser /ˈheəˌdresə/	(der/die) Friseur/in
	vet /vet/	(der/die) Tierarzt/-ärztin
	(to) **colour** /ˈkʌlə/	färben
	(to) **arrest** /əˈrest/	verhaften
	criminal /ˈkrɪmɪnl/	(der/die) Verbrecher/in
p. 84, 7	(to) **earn** /ɜ:n/	verdienen
	concept /ˈkɒnsept/	(der) Entwurf, (das) Konzept
p. 84, 8	**shop assistant** /ˈʃɒp‿əˌsɪstnt/	(der/die) Verkäufer/in
	hospital /ˈhɒspɪtl/	(das) Krankenhaus
	baker /ˈbeɪkə/	(der/die) Bäcker/in
p. 85, 9	**similar** /ˈsɪmɪlə/	ähnlich
	photographer /fəˈtɒgrəfə/	(der/die) Fotograf/in
	zoologist /zuˈɒlədʒɪst/	(der/die) Zoologe/Zoologin
	racing driver /ˈreɪsɪŋ ˌdraɪvə/	(der/die) Rennfahrer/in
p. 85, 10	**invention** /ɪnˈvenʃn/	(die) Erfindung
	inventor /ɪnˈventə/	(der/die) Erfinder/in
p. 87, 13	(to) **fly** *(irr)* /flaɪ/	fliegen
	smart /smɑ:t/	schlau, clever
	(to) **go shopping** *(irr)* /ˌgəʊ ˈʃɒpɪŋ/	einkaufen gehen
	(to) **be able to do something** *(irr)* /ˌbi‿ˌeɪbl tə ˈdu: ˌsʌmθɪŋ/	etwas tun können
	table /ˈteɪbl/	(die) Tabelle
	prediction /prɪˈdɪkʃn/	(die) Vorhersage, (die) Prophezeiung
	solar-powered /ˈsəʊlə ˌpaʊəd/	solarbetrieben

The **firefighters are fighting** a fire.

They are sitting on a **stage**.

You take your pet to a **vet** if it is **ill**.

To **earn** money means that you get money for the work that you do.

Nurses usually work in **hospitals**.

She **goes shopping** to buy food.

A **table** is a list of facts or numbers.

	helicopter /ˈhelɪˌkɒptə/	(der) Hubschrauber
	VR (= virtual reality) /ˌviː ˈɑː, ˌvɜːtʃʊəl riˈæləti/	(die) virtuelle Realität
	glasses *(pl)* /ˈglɑːsɪz/	(die) Brille
	fridge /frɪdʒ/	(der) Kühlschrank
	hologram /ˈhɒləgræm/	(das) Hologramm
	(to) **come true** *(irr)* /ˌkʌm ˈtruː/	wahr werden
p. 87, **14**	**wonderful** /ˈwʌndəfl/	wunderbar, wundervoll
	plastic /ˈplæstɪk/	(das) Plastik
	verse /vɜːs/	(die) Strophe, (der) Vers
	robot /ˈrəʊbɒt/	(der) Roboter
	flying /ˈflaɪɪŋ/	fliegend
p. 88, **15**	**vegetarian** /ˌvedʒəˈteəriən/	(der/die) Vegetarier/in; vegetarisch
p. 88, **16**	**odd one out** /ˌɒd wʌn‿ˈaʊt/	*(das) Wort, das nicht zu den anderen passt*
p. 88, **17**	**rhyming pair** /ˈraɪmɪŋ peə/	(das) Reimpaar
p. 89, **18**	**travelling** /ˈtrævlɪŋ/	(das) Reisen

The children are wearing **glasses**.

A **verse** is a group of words or sentences that are part of a poem or song.

Many people love **travelling** in their holidays.

Unit 4 | Part B Stories

p. 90, **1**	**proud, proudly** /praʊd, ˈpraʊdli/	stolz
	(to) **give** *(irr)* /gɪv/	angeben, mitteilen
	a /ə/	pro
	watch /wɒtʃ/	(die) (Armband)uhr
	interested /ˈɪntrəstɪd/	interessiert
	(to) **wake up** *(irr)* /ˌweɪk‿ˈʌp/	aufwachen
	dark /dɑːk/	(die) Dunkelheit
	bright, brightly /braɪt, ˈbraɪtli/	hell, strahlend
	torch /tɔːtʃ/	(die) Taschenlampe
	single /ˈsɪŋgl/	einzelne(r,s)
	well /wel/	gut
	except /ɪkˈsept/	außer
	dark /dɑːk/	dunkel
	stairs *(pl)* /steəz/	(die) Treppe
	carefully /ˈkeəfli/	vorsichtig
	(to) **wonder** /ˈwʌndə/	sich fragen
	clearly /ˈklɪəli/	klar, deutlich
	(to) **read something to somebody** *(irr)* /ˈriːd ˌsʌmθɪŋ tʊ ˌsʌmbədi/	jemandem etwas vorlesen
	politely /pəˈlaɪtli/	höflich
	(to) **glow** /gləʊ/	leuchten, glühen
	(to) **shine** *(irr)* /ʃaɪn/	scheinen
	bit /bɪt/	(der/das) Teil, (das) Stück
	cellar /ˈselə/	(der) Keller
	(to) **watch out** /ˌwɒtʃ‿ˈaʊt/	aufpassen
	spider /ˈspaɪdə/	(die) Spinne

He is looking at his **watch**.

There are **stairs** at the entrance to the underground station.

to **wonder** = to think about

	(to) **light up** *(irr)* /ˌlaɪt‿ˈʌp/	aufleuchten	A **slow** animal walks **slowly**. 
p. 91, 1	**slow, slowly** /sləʊ, ˈsləʊli/	langsam	
	(to) **disappear** /ˌdɪsəˈpɪə/	verschwinden	
	next /nekst/	dann, als Nächstes	
	(to) **be proud of** *(irr)* /ˌbiː ˈpraʊd‿əv/	stolz sein auf	
p. 92, 2	**(to) laugh** /lɑːf/	lachen	
p. 93, 4	**wet** /wet/	nass	**wet** ≠ dry
	in the end /ˌɪn ði‿ˈend/	am Ende, schließlich	
	(to) **realize (= realise)** /ˈrɪəlaɪz/	sich bewusst sein, erkennen	An **excited** person is not calm.
	excited /ɪkˈsaɪtɪd/	aufgeregt	
	sick /sɪk/	krank	
	surprised /səˈpraɪzd/	überrascht, erstaunt	
	slide /slaɪd/	(die) Rutsche	
p. 94, 5	**simply** /ˈsɪmpli/	einfach	**simply** = just
	rather /ˈrɑːðə/	eher	
	used to *(+ infinitive)* /ˈjuːst‿tuː/	früher *(+ Vergangenheitsform)*	I **used to *be*** ... = ***Früher war*** ich ...
	(to) **become** *(irr)* /bɪˈkʌm/	werden	
	clear /klɪə/	klar, deutlich	**clear** = easy to understand
	completely /kəmˈpliːtli/	völlig, absolut	
	(to) **open** /ˈəʊpən/	sich öffnen, aufgehen	to **open** ≠ to close
	(to) **smile** /smaɪl/	lächeln	
	object /ˈɒbdʒekt/	(der) Gegenstand, (das) Objekt	A book is an **object**.
	paper /ˈpeɪpə/	(das) Papier	
	(to) **freak out** *(informal)* /ˌfriːk‿ˈaʊt/	ausflippen, ausrasten	
	calm /ˈkɑːmli/	ruhig, gelassen	
	oh dear *(informal)* /əʊ ˈdɪə/	oje	
	bush /bʊʃ/	(der) Busch	
	silently /ˈsaɪləntli/	lautlos, schweigend	
	compass /ˈkʌmpəs/	(der) Kompass	
	owner /ˈəʊnə/	(der/die) Besitzer/in	
	(to) **get** *(irr)* /get/	*hier:* bringen	
	thank God /ˌθæŋk ˈgɒd/	Gott sei Dank	
p. 95, 5	(to) **reply** /rɪˈplaɪ/	antworten, erwidern	Bikes, cars and buses are all forms of **transport**.
	transport /ˈtrænspɔːt/	(der) Transport, (das) Verkehrsmittel	
	(to) **get** *(irr)* /get/	werden	
	so that /ˈsəʊ ðæt/	damit	
	heading /ˈhedɪŋ/	(die) Überschrift, (der) Titel	The first sentence of a **paragraph** always starts on a new line.
	paragraph /ˈpærəˌgrɑːf/	(der) Absatz, (der) Abschnitt	
	virtual /ˈvɜːtʃʊəl/	virtuell	
	obviously /ˈɒbviəsli/	offensichtlich	
	no more /ˌnəʊ ˈmɔː/	nicht mehr	
p. 96, 8	**quickly** /ˈkwɪkli/	schnell	**quickly** = fast
p. 96, 9	**machine** /məˈʃiːn/	(die) Maschine, (der) Apparat	

Land und Leute 6	**time machine** /ˈtaɪm‿məˌʃiːn/	(die) Zeitmaschine	
p. 98, 12	**camera** /ˈkæmrə/	(die) Kamera, (der) Fotoapparat	**camera**
	linking word /ˈlɪŋkɪŋ wɜːd/	(das) Verbindungswort	
p. 98, 13	(to) **improve** /ˈendɪŋ/	verbessern; besser werden	
	ending /ˈendɪŋ/	(das) Ende, (der) Schluss	**ending** ≠ beginning
	(to) **get up** *(irr)* /ˌget‿ˈʌp/	aufstehen	
	(to) **expect** /ɪkˈspekt/	erwarten	
	noise /nɔɪz/	(das) Geräusch, (der) Lärm	A **noise** is a loud sound.
	bracket /ˈbrækɪt/	(die) Klammer	
	stormy /ˈstɔːmi/	stürmisch	
p. 99, 14	**somebody** /ˈsʌmbədi/	jemand, irgendwer	**somebody** = someone
	(to) **put together** *(irr)* /ˌpʊt‿təˈgeðə/	zusammenstellen, zusammensetzen	

Unit 5 | Part A A trip to the museum

p. 103	**play** /pleɪ/	(das) Spiel, (das) (Theater)stück	A **play** is a piece of writing for actors to perform.
	out and about /ˌaʊt‿ən‿əˈbaʊt/	unterwegs	
p. 104, 2	**ancient** /ˈeɪnʃnt/	alt, antik	An **ancient** tradition is a very old tradition.
	pair /peə/	(das) Paar	a **pair** of jeans 
	collection /kəˈlekʃn/	(die) Sammlung	
	theatre /ˈθɪətə/	(das) Theater	
	(to) **step** /step/	treten, steigen	
	right /raɪt/	genau, direkt	**so** *(+ Verb)* /səʊ/ … auch Do you think … is / are a piece of art? Glaubst du, dass … ein Kunstwerk ist / sind? **So does the museum.** Das Museum auch. **So do I.** Ich auch
	himself /hɪmˈself/	selbst; sich (selbst)	
	Dr (= Doctor) /ˈdɒktə/	Dr. (= Doktor)	
	Egyptian /ɪˈdʒɪpʃn/	ägyptisch	
	trainer /ˈtreɪnə/	(der) Turnschuh	
	piece of art /ˌpiːs‿əv‿ˈɑːt/	(das) Kunstwerk	
	so + *Verb* /səʊ/	… auch	
	detective /dɪˈtektɪv/	(der/die) Detektiv/in	
	pipe /paɪp/	(die) Pfeife	
	microscope /ˈmaɪkrəˌskəʊp/	(das) Mikroskop	
	violin /ˌvaɪəˈlɪn/	(die) Violine, (die) Geige	
	assistant /əˈsɪstnt/	(der/die) Assistent/in	
p. 105, 3	**just** /dʒʌst/	gerade	
	rain /reɪn/	(der) Regen	
	so far /ˈsəʊ fɑː/	bisher	If you have read 100 books **so far**, you have read 100 books until now.
	(to) **solve** /sɒlv/	lösen	
	case /keɪs/	(der) Fall	
	(to) **suggest** /səˈdʒest/	vorschlagen	
	school trip /ˈskuːl ˌtrɪp/	(der) Schulausflug	
	smelly /ˈsmeli/	übel riechend	
	clever /ˈklevə/	klug, schlau	
	sir/Sir /sɜː/	Sir; Herr *(Anrede vor Vornamen)*	

	erm *(informal)* /ɜ:m/	ähm	
p. 106, **5**	(to) **call** /kɔ:l/	anrufen	
	the Science Museum /ðə ˈsaɪəns mju:ˌzi:əm/	(das) Naturwissenschaftsmuseum	
	Indian /ˈɪndiən/	Inder/in; indisch	
p. 107, **6**	**blood** /blʌd/	(das) Blut	
	all over /ˌɔ:l‿ˈəʊvə/	überall	
	head /hed/	(der) Kopf	
	newspaper /ˈnju:zˌpeɪpə/	(die) Zeitung	
	fingerprint /ˈfɪŋgəˌprɪnt/	(der) Fingerabdruck	
	chemistry /ˈkemɪstri/	(die) Chemie	
	wax model /ˈwæksˌmɒdl/	(das) Wachsmodell	
p. 108, **7**	**description** /dɪˈskrɪpʃn/	(die) Beschreibung	
	telephone /ˈtelɪˌfəʊn/	(das) Telefon	
	type /taɪp/	(die) Art	
	telescope /ˈtelɪˌskəʊp/	(das) Teleskop	
	space capsule /ˈspeɪs ˌkæpsju:l/	(die) Weltraumkapsel	
	overstuffed /ˌəʊvəˈstʌft/	*zu prall ausgestopft*	
	walrus (*pl* **walrus** *or* **walruses**) /ˈwɔ:lrəs, ˈwɔ:lrəs, ˈwɔ:lrəsɪz/	(das) Walross	
	vehicle /ˈvi:ɪkl/	(das) Fahrzeug	
	playzone /ˈpleɪˌzəʊn/	*(der) Spielbereich*	
	coin /kɔɪn/	(die) Münze	
p. 109, **8**	**announcement** /əˈnaʊnsmənt/	(die) Mitteilung, (die) Durchsage	
p. 109, **9**	**everyday** /ˈevriˌdeɪ/	alltäglich, Alltags-	
	hockey stick /ˈhɒki stɪk/	(der) Hockeyschläger	
p. 110, **11**	**screen** /skri:n/	(der) Bildschirm	Looking at a **screen** can be bad for your eyes.
	wrong /rɒŋ/	falsch	
	(to) **make up** *(irr)* /ˌmeɪk‿ˈʌp/	erfinden, sich ausdenken	to **make up** = to think of
	snail /sneɪl/	(die) Schnecke	
	snake /sneɪk/	(die) Schlange	
	frogs' legs *(pl)* /ˈfrɒgz legz/	(die) Froschschenkel	
p. 111, **11**	**bat** /bæt/	(die) Fledermaus	
p. 111, **12**	**kg (= kilogram)** /ˈkɪləˌgræm/	(das) Kilogramm	1 **kilogram** = 1,000 grams
	design /dɪˈzaɪn/	(der) Entwurf, (das) Design	
	since /sɪns/	seit	
	masterpiece /ˈmɑ:stəˌpi:s/	(das) Meisterwerk	
	painted /ˈpeɪntɪd/	bemalt, farbig	
	(to) **sculpt** /skʌlpt/	modellieren	
	(to) **weigh** /weɪ/	wiegen	
	lamp /læmp/	(die) Lampe	 **lamp**
	creativity /ˌkri:eɪˈtɪvəti/	(die) Kreativität	
	functional /fʌŋkʃnəl/	funktional	
	stripe /straɪp/	(der) Streifen	

I've looked (= I have looked) /ˌaɪv ˈlʊkt, ˌaɪ hæv ˈlʊkt/ ich habe geguckt
I've found /ˌaɪv ˈfaʊnd/ ich habe gefunden
Haven't you been ...? /ˌhævnt jə ˈbi:n/ Bist du nicht ... gewesen?
Have you ever seen ...? /ˌhæv jə ˌevə ˈseen/ Hast du jemals ... gesehen?
No, I haven't. /ˌnəʊ‿aɪ ˈhævnt/ Nein.
They have put together ... /ˌðeɪ hæv ˌpʊt‿təˈgeðə/ sie haben ... zusammengestellt
I've never been /ˌaɪv ˈnevə ˌbi:n/ ich bin nie gewesen
we've read /ˌwi:v ˈred/ wir haben gelesen

	athlete /ˈæθliːt/	(der/die) Athlet/in	
	tune /tjuːn/	(die) Melodie	
	musical /ˈmjuːzɪkl/	musikalisch	
p. 112, 13	(to) **open** /ˈəʊpən/	eröffnen	
	(to) **put on display** *(irr)* /ˌpʊt‿ɒn dɪˈspleɪ/	ausstellen	The school **puts** lots of notes **on display** on a noticeboard.
p. 112, 14	**soft toy** /ˌsɒft‿ˈtɔɪ/	(das) Kuscheltier	
p. 113, 15	**catalogue** /ˈkætəlɒg/	(der) Katalog	

Unit 5 | Part B A play

A **youth club** is a place where young people can meet and take part in activities.

A stage is the part of a theatre where the **performance** takes place.

p. 114, 1	**What's on?** *(informal)* /ˌwɒts‿ˈɒn/	Was ist los?	
	youth club /ˈjuːθ ˌklʌb/	(der) Jugendklub	
	programme /ˈprəʊgræm/	(das) Programm	
	course /kɔːs/	(der) Kurs	
	drama /ˈdrɑːmə/	Theater-, Schauspiel-	
	(to) **perform** /pəˈfɔːm/	aufführen; durchführen	
	practice /ˈpræktɪs/	(die) Übung, (das) Training	
	(to) **throw away** *(irr)* /ˌθrəʊ‿əˈweɪ/	wegwerfen	
	further /ˈfɜːðə/	weiter	
	climbing /ˈklaɪmɪŋ/	(das) Klettern	
	professional /prəˈfeʃnəl/	professionell, beruflich	
p. 115, 2	**performance** /pəˈfɔːməns/	(die) Aufführung, (die) Leistung	
	singing /ˈsɪŋɪŋ/	(das) Singen, (der) Gesang	
	acting /ˈæktɪŋ/	(das) Schauspielern	
	lighting /ˈlaɪtɪŋ/	(die) Beleuchtung	
	prop /prɒp/	(die) Requisite	
	(to) **save** /seɪv/	*hier:* zurücklegen lassen	
p. 116, 6	(to) **take turns** *(irr)* /ˌteɪk ˈtɜːnz/	sich abwechseln	
p. 117, 7	**no one** /ˈnəʊ wʌn/	keiner	**no one** = nobody
	(to) **scare** /skeə/	erschrecken	
	(to) **move out** /ˌmuːv‿ˈaʊt/	ausziehen	
p. 117, 8	**leader** /ˈliːdə/	(der/die) Leiter/in	
	subject /ˈsʌbdʒɪkt/	(das) Thema, (der) Betreff *(in Emails)*	
	deadline /ˈdedˌlaɪn/	(der) letzte Termin, (die) Deadline	
	(to) **sign up** /ˌsaɪn‿ˈʌp/	sich anmelden	
p. 118, 9	**finding** /ˈfaɪndɪŋ/	(die) Entdeckung, (das) Ergebnis	
p. 119, 11	**lonely** /ˈləʊnli/	einsam	A **lonely** person is unhappy because **no one** else is there.
	sort /sɔːt/	(die) Sorte, (die) Art	
	script /skrɪpt/	(das) Drehbuch, (das) Skript	
	inspector /ɪnˈspektə/	(der/die) Inspektor/in	
p. 120, 12	**chain** /tʃeɪn/	(die) Kette	
	(to) **go away** *(irr)* /ˌgəʊ‿əˈweɪ/	weggehen, verschwinden	to **go away** = to disappear
	voice /vɔɪs/	(die) Stimme	

	disappointed /ˌdɪsəˈpɔɪntɪd/	enttäuscht
	(to) **stop** /stɒp/	aufhören
	frustrated /frʌˈstreɪtɪd/	frustriert
	impossible /ɪmˈpɒsəbl/	unmöglich
	poor /pɔː/	arm
	(to) **cry** /kraɪ/	weinen, schreien
	(to) **rattle** /ˈrætl/	klappern, rasseln
	sleepy /ˈsliːpi/	schläfrig
	(to) **clang** /klæŋ/	scheppern, klappern
	(to) **clonk** /klɒŋk/	scheppern, klappern
	(to) **frighten** /ˈfraɪtn/	erschrecken
	laughter /ˈlɑːftə/	(das) Gelächter, (das) Lachen
	(to) **get back to sleep** *(irr)* /ˌget ˌbæk tə ˈsliːp/	wieder einschlafen
	(to) **frighten away** /ˌfraɪtn‿əˈweɪ/	verscheuchen
	(to) **stumble** /ˈstʌmbl/	stolpern
	(to) **fall down** *(irr)* /ˌfɔːl ˈdaʊn/	hinfallen
	crash /kræʃ/	*hier:* Krach, Getöse
	(to) **enter** /ˈentə/	*hier:* auftreten
p. 121, 12	**Well done!** /ˌwel ˈdʌn/	Gut gemacht!
	gone /gɒn/	weg
	full /fʊl/	voll, vollständig
	(to) **react (to)** /riˈækt/	reagieren (auf)
	(to) **run away** *(irr)* /ˌrʌn‿əˈweɪ/	weglaufen
	dramatic reading /drəˌmætɪk ˈriːdɪŋ/	(die) szenische Lesung
p. 121, 13	**ghostly** /ˈgəʊsli/	geisterhaft, gespenstisch
p. 122, 15	(to) **pronounce** /prəˈnaʊns/	aussprechen
	feeling /ˈfiːlɪŋ/	(das) Gefühl
	(to) **match** /mætʃ/	passen zu
p. 122, 16	**mood** /muːd/	(die) Laune, (die) Stimmung
p. 123, 17	**cue card** /ˈkjuː kɑːd/	*(die) Stichwortkarte*

The boy **is crying** for help.

gone = away from a place

The teacher is in a bad **mood**.

Hier findest du alphabetisch sortiert alle Wörter aus dem vorliegenden Buch mit der Angabe der Seite *(p.)*, auf der das Wort das erste Mal vorkommt oder auf der es zum Lernwort gemacht wird. Die Zahl hinter dem Komma bezeichnet die Aufgabe auf der Seite.
Lernwörter aus dem vorigen Band sind mit „NHG 5" markiert.
Die **fett** gedruckten Lernwörter solltest du dir merken.
Folgende Abkürzungen werden verwendet: *(pl)* = (unregelmäßige) Mehrzahlform, *(no pl)* = keine Mehrzahlform, *(irr)* = unregelmäßiges Verb, *(AE)* = amerikanisches Englisch
(informal) bedeutet: Dieses Wort oder dieser Ausdruck ist umgangssprachlich.

A

a, an /ə/eɪ, ən/ ein(e) NHG 5
a /ə/ pro p. 90, 1
(to) be able to do something *(irr)* /ˌbi‿ˌeɪbl tə ˈduː ˌsʌmθɪŋ/ etwas tun können p. 87, 13
about /əˈbaʊt/ über; an NHG 5; ungefähr p. 14, 9
(to) **be about** *(irr)* /ˌbi‿əˈbaʊt/ gehen um; handeln von NHG 5
above /əˈbʌv/ über NHG 5
(to) **go abroad** /ˌɡəʊ‿əˈbrɔːd/ ins Ausland gehen, ins Ausland fahren p. 8, 1
acrobat /ˈækrəbæt/ Akrobat/in p. 24, 9
acrostic /əˈkrɒstɪk/ Akrostichon; Leistenvers p. 48, 11
(to) **act** /ækt/ handeln; spielen p. 83, 6
(to) **act out** /ˌækt‿ˈaʊt/ nachspielen; vorspielen NHG 5
acting /ˈæktɪŋ/ Schauspielern p. 115, 2
action /ˈækʃn/ Handlung NHG 5
(to) activate /ˈæktɪveɪt/ aktivieren p. 8, 1
activity /ækˈtɪvəti/ Aktivität NHG 5
actor / actress /ˈæktə, ˈæktrəs/ Schauspieler/in p. 83, 6
actually /ˈæktʃuəli/ eigentlich; tatsächlich p. 9, 2
(to) **add** /æd/ hinzufügen NHG 5
address /əˈdres/ Adresse NHG 5
address /əˈdres/ adressieren p. 30
adjective /ˈædʒɪktɪv/ Adjektiv p. 16, 13
adult /ˈædʌlt/ Erwachsene/r p. 19, 1
adventure /ədˈventʃə/ Abenteuer p. 79
adventure park /ədˈventʃə pɑːk/ Erlebnispark p. 8, 1
adverb of manner /ˌædvɜːb‿əv ˈmænə/ Adverb der Art und Weise p. 92
(to) **be afraid of** /ˌbi‿əˈfreɪd‿əv/ Angst haben vor p. 9, 2
after /ˈɑːftə/ nach NHG 5
after that /ˌɑːftə ˈðæt/ danach p. 169
afternoon /ˌɑːftəˈnuːn/ Nachmittag NHG 5
afterwards /ˈɑːftəwədz/ anschließend; später p. 16, 12
again /əˈɡen/ wieder; noch einmal NHG 5
against /əˈɡenst/ gegen p. 65, 15
age /eɪdʒ/ Alter p. 28
... ago /əˈɡəʊ/ vor ... p. 9, 2
air /eə/ Luft p. 53
airport /ˈeəpɔːt/ Flughafen p. 13, 7
alien /ˈeɪliən/ Außerirdische/r p. 102
all /ɔːl/ alle; alles; ganz; völlig NHG 5
All Hallows' Day /ˌɔːl ˈhæləʊz deɪ/ Allerheiligen p. 36, 6
All Hallows' Eve /ˌɔːl ˌhæləʊz‿ˈiːv/ *Abend vor Allerheiligen* p. 36, 6
all kinds of /ˌɔːl ˈkaɪndz‿əv/ alle möglichen p. 38, 7
all over /ˌɔːl‿ˈəʊvə/ überall p. 107, 6
all over the world /ˌɔːl‿ˌəʊvə ðə ˈwɜːld/ auf der ganzen Welt p. 33, 1
all the time /ˌɔːl ðə ˈtaɪm/ die ganze Zeit p. 11, 5
all year round /ˌɔːl ˈjɪə raʊnd/ das ganze Jahr lang p. 66, 1
(to) **be allowed (to)** /ˌbi‿əˈlaʊd‿tə/ erlaubt sein, dürfen p. 56, 1
almost /ˈɔːlməʊst/ fast; beinahe p. 45, 6
alone /əˈləʊn/ allein NHG 5
along /əˈlɒŋ/ entlang p. 14, 9
aloud /əˈlaʊd/ laut p. 48, 10
already /ɔːlˈredi/ schon; bereits NHG 5
also /ˈɔːlsəʊ/ auch NHG 5
although /ɔːlˈðəʊ/ obwohl p. 19, 1
always /ˈɔːlweɪz/ immer NHG 5
am (= ante meridiem) /ˌeɪˈem, ˌænti məˈrɪdiəm/ morgens, vormittags *(hinter Uhrzeit zwischen Mitternacht und 12 Uhr mittags)* NHG 5
amazing *(informal)* /əˈmeɪzɪŋ/ toll p. 12, 6
American /əˈmerɪkən/ Amerikaner/in; amerikanisch p. 148
analytically /ˌænəˈlɪtɪkli/ analytisch p. 127
ancient /ˈeɪnʃnt/ alt; antik p. 104, 2
and /ænd/ und NHG 5
And so do I. /ænd ˌsəʊ du‿ˈaɪ/ Ich auch. p. 12, 6
and so on /ænd ˈsəʊ‿ɒn/ und so weiter p. 81, 2
angry /ˈæŋɡri/ zornig, wütend p. 60, 7
animal /ˈænɪml/ Tier NHG 5
announcement /əˈnaʊnsmənt/ Mitteilung; Durchsage p. 109, 8
annoyed /əˈnɔɪd/ genervt p. 60, 7
another /əˈnʌðə/ noch ein/e; ein/e andere/r, ein anderes NHG 5
answer /ˈɑːnsə/ Antwort; (be)antworten NHG 5
any /ˈeni/ (irgend)ein(e) NHG 5
anything /ˈeniˌθɪŋ/ irgendetwas NHG 5
anyway /ˈeniweɪ/ jedenfalls p. 9, 2
apart /əˈpɑːt/ auseinander p. 39, 9
(to) appear /əˈpɪə/ erscheinen, auftauchen p. 138
apple /ˈæpl/ Apfel NHG 5
apple bobbing /ˈæpl ˌbɒbɪŋ/ *Apfelfischen* p. 36, 6
(to) apply /əˈplaɪ/ anwenden p. 8, 1
appropriate /əˈprəʊpriət/ angemessen; passend p. 67, 1

April /ˈeɪprəl/ April NHG 5
..., are we? /ˈɑː wiː/ *hier:* ..., nicht wahr? p. 43, 2
area /ˈeəriə/ Gebiet; Region NHG 5
around /əˈraʊnd/ um; herum; umher p. 13, 8
around the world /əˌraʊnd ðə ˈwɜːld/ weltweit, überall auf der Welt p. 102
(to) arrest /əˈrest/ verhaften p. 83, 6
arrival /əˈraɪvl/ Ankunft p. 135
(to) **arrive** /əˈraɪv/ ankommen NHG 5
art /ɑːt/ Kunst NHG 5
piece of art /ˌpiːs‿əv‿ˈɑːt/ Kunstwerk p. 104, 2
article /ˈɑːtɪkl/ Artikel NHG 5
arts and crafts /ˌɑːrts‿ən ˈkrɑːfts/ Basteln; Bastelarbeit p. 74, 12
as /əz/ als; wie; während NHG 5
as /əz/ weil; da p. 54
as ... as /æz ... æz/ so ... wie p. 19, 1
as well /ˌəz‿ˈwel/ auch p. 14, 9
(to) **ask** /ɑːsk/ fragen; bitten NHG 5
(to) **ask questions** /ˌɑːsk‿ˈkwestʃnz/ Fragen stellen NHG 5
aspect /ˈæspekt/ Aspekt; Gesichtspunkt p. 146
assembly /əˈsembli/ (Schüler)versammlung NHG 5
assistant /əˈsɪstnt/ Assistent/in p. 104, 2
at /æt/ an; in; bei; um NHG 5
at all times /ˌæt‿ɔːl ˈtaɪmz/ jederzeit, immer p. 66, 1
at first /ət ˈfɜːst/ zuerst p. 9, 2
at home /ˌæt ˈhəʊm/ zu Hause NHG 5
at least /ət ˈliːst/ mindestens; wenigstens p. 9, 2
at night /ˌæt ˈnaɪt/ nachts p. 138
at/in the back /ˌæt/ˌɪn ðə ˈbæk/ hinten NHG 5
at the end /ˌæt ði‿ˈend/ am Ende p. 130
at/in the front /ˌæt/ˌɪn ðə ˈfrʌnt/ vorne NHG 5
at the time /ˌæt‿ðə ˈtaɪm/ damals; zu dem Zeitpunkt p. 30
at the top /ˌæt‿ðə ˈtɒp/ oben p. 52
athlete /ˈæθliːt/ Athlet/in p. 111, 12
(to) **do athletics** *(irr)* /ˌduː‿æθˈletɪks/ Leichtathletik machen NHG 5
(to) attack /əˈtæk/ angreifen p. 28
(to) **pay attention (to)** *(irr)* /ˌpeɪ‿əˈtenʃn tʊ/ aufpassen; achten auf p. 20, 3
attraction /əˈtrækʃn/ Attraktion p. 19, 1
August /ˈɔːgəst/ August NHG 5
aunt /ɑːnt/ Tante NHG 5
author /ˈɔːθə/ Autor/in p. 127
autumn /ˈɔːtəm/ Herbst p. 51, 16
avenue /ˈævəˌnjuː/ Allee; Straße p. 54
awake /əˈweɪk/ wach p. 77
away /əˈweɪ/ weg NHG 5
awesome *(AE, informal)* /ˈɔːsm/ super p. 54

B

back /bæk/ zurück NHG 5
at/in the back /ˌæt/ˌɪn ðə ˈbæk/ hinten NHG 5
back /bæk/ Rücken p. 53
background /ˈbækˌgraʊnd/ Hintergrund p. 41, 12
backyard *(AE)* /ˌbækˈjɑːd/ Garten p. 54
bad /bæd/ schlecht; schlimm NHG 5
bag /bæg/ Tasche; Tüte NHG 5
(to) **bake** /beɪk/ backen NHG 5
baker /ˈbeɪkə/ Bäcker/in p. 84, 8
baking paper /ˈbeɪkɪŋ ˌpeɪpə/ Backpapier p. 46, 7
balcony /ˈbælkəni/ Balkon p. 74, 12
balloon /bəˈluːn/ Luftballon NHG 5
banana /bəˈnɑːnə/ Banane NHG 5
banana skin /bəˈnɑːnə skɪn/ Bananenschale p. 101
barbecue /ˈbɑːbɪˌkjuː/ Grill; Grillparty p. 66, 1
bat /bæt/ Fledermaus p. 111, 11
bathroom /ˈbɑːθˌruːm/ Badezimmer NHG 5
(to) **be** *(irr)* /biː/ sein NHG 5
(to) **be able to do something** *(irr)* /ˌbi‿ˌeɪbl tə ˈduː ˌsʌmθɪŋ/ etwas tun können p. 87, 13
(to) **be about** *(irr)* /ˌbi‿əˈbaʊt/ gehen um; handeln von NHG 5
(to) **be afraid of** *(irr)* /ˌbi‿əˈfreɪd‿əv/ Angst haben vor p. 9, 2
(to) **be allowed (to)** *(irr)* /ˌbi‿əˈlaʊd‿tə/ erlaubt sein, dürfen p. 56, 1
(to) be asleep *(irr)* /ˌbi‿əˈsliːp/ schlafen p. 77
(to) be born *(irr)* /biː ˈbɔːn/ geboren werden p. 127
(to) be forgot *(irr, poet.)* /ˌbiː fəˈgɒt/ vergessen werden *(poetisch)* p. 48, 10
(to) **be good at doing something** *(irr)* /ˌbiː gʊd‿ət ˈduːɪŋ ˌsʌmθɪŋ/ gut darin sein, etwas zu tun NHG 5
(to) **be good at something** *(irr)* /ˌbiː ˈgʊd‿æt ˌsʌmθɪŋ/ gut in etwas sein p. 9, 2
(to) **be (good/great) fun** *(irr)* /ˌbiː ˌgʊd/ˌgreɪt ˈfʌn/ (viel / großen) Spaß machen NHG 5
(to) be lucky *(irr)* /ˌbiː ˈlʌki/ Glück haben p. 81, 2
(to) **be one's turn** *(irr)* /ˌbiː wʌnz ˈtɜːn/ an der Reihe sein NHG 5
(to) **be proud of** *(irr)* /ˌbiː ˈpraʊd‿əv/ stolz sein auf p. 91, 1
(to) **be right** *(irr)* /ˌbiː ˈraɪt/ recht haben NHG 5
Be safe! /ˌbiː ˈseɪf/ Sei vorsichtig! p. 28
(to) be worth a visit *(irr)* /ˌbiː ˌwɜːθ‿ə ˈvɪzɪt/ einen Besuch wert sein p. 24, 9
beach /biːtʃ/ Strand NHG 5
(to) beat *(irr)* /biːt/ schlagen p. 77
beautiful /ˈbjuːtəfl/ schön NHG 5
because /bɪˈkɒz/ weil; da NHG 5
(to) **become** *(irr)* /bɪˈkʌm/ werden p. 94, 5
(to) become friends *(irr)* /bɪˌkʌm ˈfrendz/ sich anfreunden p. 29
bed /bed/ Bett NHG 5
B&B (= bed and breakfast) /ˌbed‿ən ˈbrekfəst/ Frühstückspension p. 14, 9
bedroom /ˈbedruːm/ Schlafzimmer NHG 5
bee /biː/ Biene p. 70, 7
before /bɪˈfɔː/ bevor; zuvor, vorher; vor NHG 5
(to) **begin** *(irr)* /bɪˈgɪn/ anfangen; beginnen NHG 5
beginning /bɪˈgɪnɪŋ/ Anfang; Beginn p. 33, 1
behind /bɪˈhaɪnd/ hinter NHG 5
(to) **believe (in)** /bɪˈliːv‿ɪn/ glauben (an) p. 33, 1

bell /bel/ Glocke p. 19, 1
below /bɪˈləʊ/ unten, unter p. 25, 10
best /best/ beste(r, s) NHG 5
the best /ðə ˈbest/ der/die/das beste NHG 5; am besten p. 20
(to) **like best** /ˌlaɪk ˈbest/ am liebsten mögen NHG 5
better /ˈbetə/ besser p. 20
between /bɪˈtwiːn/ zwischen NHG 5
big /bɪg/ groß NHG 5
bike /baɪk/ Fahrrad p. 14, 9
(to) **ride a bike** /ˌraɪd‿ə ˈbaɪk/ Fahrrad fahren NHG 5
bin /bɪn/ Abfalleimer NHG 5
bird /bɜːd/ Vogel p. 66, 1
birdseed /ˈbɜːdˌsiːd/ Vogelfutter p. 73, 10
birth /bɜːθ/ Geburt p. 128
birthday /ˈbɜːθdeɪ/ Geburtstag NHG 5
Happy birthday (to you)! /ˌhæpi ˈbɜːθdeɪ tʊ juː/ Herzlichen Glückwunsch zum Geburtstag! NHG 5
biscuit /ˈbɪskɪt/ Keks NHG 5
a bit /ə ˈbɪt/ ein bisschen NHG 5
bit /bɪt/ Teil; Stück p. 90, 1
black /blæk/ schwarz NHG 5
blood /blʌd/ Blut p. 107, 6
blue /bluː/ blau NHG 5
blue whale /bluː ˈweɪl/ Blauwal p. 26, 13
board /bɔːd/ Tafel; Brett NHG 5
on board /bɔːd/ an Bord p. 102
board game /ˈbɔːd geɪm/ Brettspiel p. 6
boat /bəʊt/ Boot NHG 5
apple bobbing /ˈæpl ˌbɒbɪŋ/ *Apfelfischen* p. 36, 6
body /ˈbɒdi/ Körper NHG 5
(to) boil /bɔɪl/ kochen *(Flüssigkeit)* p. 46, 7
boiling /ˈbɔɪlɪŋ/ kochend p. 46, 7
bonfire /ˈbɒnˌfaɪə/ (Freuden)feuer p. 36, 6
Bonfire Night /ˈbɒnˌfaɪə ˌnaɪt/ *brit. Gedenkfest am 5. November* p. 31
book /bʊk/ Buch NHG 5; buchen, reservieren p. 66, 1
bookshelf /ˈbʊkˌʃelf/ Bücherregal NHG 5
bored /bɔːd/ gelangweilt p. 57, 1
boring /ˈbɔːrɪŋ/ langweilig NHG 5

(to) **borrow** /ˈbɒrəʊ/ (aus)leihen NHG 5
both /bəʊθ/ beide p. 124
bottle /ˈbɒtl/ Flasche NHG 5
message in a bottle /ˌmesɪdʒ‿ɪn‿ə ˈbɒtl/ Flaschenpost p. 30
(to) **bow** /baʊ/ sich verbeugen p. 53
bowl /bəʊl/ Schüssel; Schale p. 46, 7
box /bɒks/ Kasten; Kiste NHG 5
boy /bɔɪ/ Junge NHG 5
bracket /ˈbrækɪt/ Klammer p. 98, 13
break /breɪk/ Pause NHG 5
(to) **break *(irr)*** /breɪk/ brechen; zerbrechen; kaputt machen p. 57, 1
breakfast /ˈbrekfəst/ Frühstück NHG 5
(to) breathe /briːð/ atmen; *hier:* speien p. 100
bridge /brɪdʒ/ Brücke p. 20
bright, brightly /braɪt,ˈbraɪtli/ hell; strahlend p. 90, 1
brilliant /ˈbrɪljənt/ genial, klasse NHG 5
(to) **bring *(irr)*** /brɪŋ/ mitbringen NHG 5
Britain /ˈbrɪtn/ Großbritannien p. 36, 6
British /ˈbrɪtɪʃ/ britisch p. 19, 1
brochure /ˈbrəʊʃə/ Broschüre p. 75, 14
brother /ˈbrʌðə/ Bruder NHG 5
brown /braʊn/ braun NHG 5
(to) **brush one's teeth** /ˌbrʌʃ wʌnz ˈtiːθ/ sich die Zähne putzen NHG 5
(to) bubble /ˈbʌbl/ blubbern; sprudeln p. 78
(to) **build *(irr)*** /bɪld/ bauen NHG 5
building /ˈbɪldɪŋ/ Gebäude p. 19, 1
bump /bʌmp/ dumpfer Schlag p. 77
Easter bunny /ˈiːstə ˌbʌni/ Osterhase p. 33, 1
bush /bʊʃ/ Busch p. 94, 5
busy /ˈbɪzi/ beschäftigt NHG 5; bewegt, ereignisreich p. 16, 12; belebt; verkehrsreich p. 70, 7
but /bʌt/ aber NHG 5; außer p. 67, 1
(to) butter /ˈbʌtə/ buttern p. 78
button /ˈbʌtən/ Knopf p. 77
(to) **buy *(irr)*** /baɪ/ kaufen NHG 5
by /baɪ/ von; mit NHG 5; bei, an p. 14, 9; (spätestens) bis p. 62, 10

by *(+ Verbform mit -ing)* /baɪ/ indem p. 46, 7
by heart /ˌbaɪ ˈhɑːt/ auswendig p. 48, 10
bye /baɪ/ tschüs(s) NHG 5

C

cage /keɪdʒ/ Käfig NHG 5
cake /keɪk/ Kuchen NHG 5
calculator /ˈkælkjʊˌleɪtə/ Taschenrechner NHG 5
calendar /ˈkælɪndə/ Kalender NHG 5
(to) **call** /kɔːl/ anrufen p. 106, 5
call /kɔːl/ Anruf; Gespräch; anrufen, rufen p. 52
(to) **be called** /ˌbiː ˈkɔːld/ heißen, genannt werden NHG 5
calm /ˈkɑːmli/ ruhig, gelassen p. 94, 5
camera /ˈkæmrə/ Kamera; Fotoapparat p. 98, 12
camp /kæmp/ (Zelt)lager p. 14, 9
camper van /ˈkæmpə væn/ Wohnwagen p. 29
go camping /ˌgəʊ ˌkæmpɪŋ/ zelten gehen p. 67, 1
campsite /ˈkæmpˌsaɪt/ Campingplatz p. 67, 1
can /kæn/ können NHG 5
can't (= cannot) /kɑːnt, ˈkænɒt/ nicht können NHG 5
candle /ˈkændl/ Kerze NHG 5
LED candle /ˌel‿iː ˌdiː ˈkændl/ LED-Kerze p. 39, 9
candle holder /ˈkændl ˌhəʊldə/ Kerzenständer p. 33, 1
candy *(AE, no pl)* /ˈkændi/ Süßigkeiten p. 54
cap /kæp/ Mütze, Cap p. 56, 1
capital /ˈkæpɪtl/ Hauptstadt p. 147
capsule /ˈkæpsjuːl/ Kapsel p. 23, 8
space capsule /ˈspeɪs ˌkæpsjuːl/ Weltraumkapsel p. 108, 7
car /kɑː/ Auto NHG 5
car park /ˈkɑː pɑːk/ Parkplatz p. 68, 4
card /kɑːd/ Karte NHG 5
(to) **take care of** /ˌteɪk‿ˈkeər‿əv/ sich kümmern um p. 55
careful /ˈkeəfl/ vorsichtig p. 17, 14
carefully /ˈkeəfli/ vorsichtig p. 90, 1
carrot /ˈkærət/ Möhre; Karotte NHG 5

(to) carry /ˈkæri/ tragen p. 129
(to) carry on /ˌkæri‿ˈɒn/ *hier:* weitergehen p. 131
(to) carve /kɑːv/ schnitzen p. 36, 6
case /keɪs/ Fall p. 105, 3
castle /ˈkɑːsl/ Burg; Schloss p. 12, 6
casual /ˈkæʒuəl/ lässig Land und Leute 4
cat /kæt/ Katze NHG 5
catalogue /ˈkætəlɒg/ Katalog p. 113, 15
(to) **catch** *(irr)* /kætʃ/ fangen NHG 5
(to) catch up with *(irr)* /ˌkætʃ‿ˈʌp wɪð/ *sich nach längerer Zeit (auch virtuell) mit jemandem treffen, um sich auf den neusten Stand zu bringen* p. 13, 7
category /ˈkætəgri/ Kategorie p. 40, 11
Catholic /ˈkæθlɪk/ Katholik/in; katholisch p. 36, 6
cave /keɪv/ Höhle p. 53
(to) **celebrate** /ˈseləˌbreɪt/ feiern p. 31
celebration /ˌseləˈbreɪʃn/ Feier p. 31
cellar /ˈselə/ Keller p. 90, 1
Celt /kelt/ Kelte/Keltin p. 36, 6
Celtic /ˈkeltɪk/ keltisch p. 36, 6
centre /ˈsentə/ Zentrum p. 66, 1
shopping centre /ˈʃɒpɪŋ ˌsentə/ Einkaufszentrum NHG 5
century /ˈsentʃəri/ Jahrhundert p. 36, 6
chain /tʃeɪn/ Kette p. 120, 12
chair /tʃeə/ Stuhl NHG 5
challenge /ˈtʃæləndʒ/ Herausforderung NHG 5
change /tʃeɪndʒ/ Wechselgeld NHG 5; (sich) ändern; verändern p. 35, 4
(to) change /tʃeɪndʒ/ *hier:* umstellen p. 78
(to) **change lines** /ˌtʃeɪndʒ ˈlaɪnz/ umsteigen p. 22, 5
(to) **change one's mind** /ˌtʃeɪndʒ wʌnz ˈmaɪnd/ seine Meinung ändern p. 9, 2
character /ˈkærəktə/ Figur; Charakter p. 38, 7
(to) **check** /tʃek/ überprüfen; kontrollieren NHG 5
(to) check out /ˌtʃek‿ˈaʊt/ auschecken p. 27, 14
(to) check out *(informal)* /ˌtʃek‿ˈaʊt/ sich ansehen; ausprobieren p. 14, 9
checklist /tʃeklɪst/ Checkliste p. 50, 15
cheese /tʃiːz/ Käse NHG 5
chef /ʃef/ Koch/Köchin p. 81, 2
chemistry /ˈkemɪstri/ Chemie p. 107, 6
(to) chew /tʃuː/ kauen p. 78
chicken /ˈtʃɪkɪn/ Huhn p. 9, 2
child *(pl* **children)** /tʃaɪld, ˈtʃɪldrən/ Kind NHG 5
chilli /ˈtʃɪli/ Chili; Peperoni p. 77
Chinese /ˌtʃaɪˈniːz/ Chinese / Chinesin; chinesisch p. 33, 1
chips *(pl)* /tʃɪps/ Pommes frites NHG 5
chocolate /ˈtʃɒklət/ Schokolade NHG 5
hot chocolate /ˌhɒt ˈtʃɒklət/ heißer Kakao p. 45, 6
(to) **choose** *(irr)* /tʃuːz/ wählen; sich entscheiden NHG 5
chore /tʃɔː/ lästige Aufgabe; Hausarbeit NHG 5
Christian /ˈkrɪstʃən/ Christ/in; christlich p. 33, 1
Christmas /ˈkrɪsməs/ Weihnachten p. 34, 2
church /tʃɜːtʃ/ Kirche p. 34, 2
cinema /ˈsɪnəmə/ Kino NHG 5
(to) circle /sɜːkl/ einkreisen p. 58, 5
city /ˈsɪti/ Stadt; Innenstadt NHG 5
(to) clang /klæŋ/ scheppern, klappern p. 120, 12
class /klɑːs/ Klasse; Unterrichtsstunde NHG 5
classmate /ˈklɑːsˌmeɪt/ Klassenkamerad/in; Mitschüler/in NHG 5
classroom /ˈklɑːsˌruːm/ Klassenzimmer NHG 5
claw /klɔː/ Kralle; Klaue p. 77
clean /kliːn/ sauber NHG 5
(to) **clean (up)** /kliːn, ˌkliːn‿ˈʌp/ sauber machen NHG 5
clear /klɪə/ klar; deutlich p. 94, 5
clearly /ˈklɪəli/ klar; deutlich p. 90, 1
clever /ˈklevə/ klug, schlau p. 105, 3
(to) **climb** /klaɪm/ auf etwas (hinauf)steigen; klettern NHG 5
(to) climb up /ˌklaɪm‿ˈʌp/ hochklettern p. 52
climbing /ˈklaɪmɪŋ/ Klettern p. 114, 1
clock /klɒk/ Uhr NHG 5
clock tower /ˈklɒk ˌtaʊə/ Uhrenturm p. 19, 1
(to) clonk /klɒŋk/ scheppern, klappern p. 120, 12
(to) **close** /kləʊz/ zumachen; schließen NHG 5
close /kləʊs/ nah(e) p. 53
closed /kləʊzd/ geschlossen p. 66, 1
closer /ˈkləʊsə/ näher p. 100
(to) take a closer look at /ˌteɪk‿ə ˌkləʊsə ˈlʊk‿ət/ sich genauer ansehen p. 146
clothes *(pl)* /kləʊðz/ Kleider; Kleidung NHG 5
club /klʌb/ AG; Klub NHG 5
cm (= centimetre) /ˌsiː ˈem, ˈsentɪˌmiːtə/ Zentimeter p. 39, 9
coconut /ˈkəʊkəˌnʌt/ Kokosnuss p. 73, 10
coffee /ˈkɒfi/ Kaffee NHG 5
coin /kɔɪn/ Münze p. 102
cold /kəʊld/ kalt NHG 5
cold /kəʊld/ Kälte p. 43, 2
(to) **collect** /kəˈlekt/ sammeln NHG 5
collection /kəˈlekʃn/ Sammlung p. 104, 2
colour /ˈkʌlə/ Farbe NHG 5
(to) colour /ˈkʌlə/ färben p. 83, 6
combination /ˌkɒmbɪˈneɪʃn/ Kombination; Mischung p. 24, 9
(to) **come** *(irr)* /kʌm/kommen NHG 5
(to) **come back** *(irr)* /ˌkʌm ˈbæk/ zurückkommen NHG 5
(to) come to mind *(irr)* /ˌkʌm tə ˈmaɪnd/ einfallen p. 18, 1
Come on! /ˌkʌm‿ˈɒn/ Komm(t) schon! p. 124
(to) come out *(irr)* /ˌkʌm‿ˈaʊt/ herauskommen p. 77
(to) come together *(irr)* /ˌkʌm təˈgeðə/ zusammenkommen p. 36, 6
(to) come true *(irr)* /ˌkʌm ˈtruː/ wahr werden p. 87, 13
command /kəˈmɑːnd/ Befehl NHG 5
(to) **comment on** /ˈkɒment‿ɒn/ kommentieren p. 17, 14
commercial /kəˈmɜːʃl/ kommerziell, profitorientiert p. 38, 7
(to) **have in common** /ˌhæv‿ɪn ˈkɒmən/ gemeinsam haben p. 33, 1

comparative /kəm'pærətɪv/ Komparativ p. 20, 3
(to) **compare** /kəm'peə/ vergleichen p. 12, 6
comparison /kəm'pærɪsn/ Vergleich p. 20, 2
compass /'kʌmpəs/ Kompass p. 94, 5
competition /ˌkɒmpə'tɪʃn/ Wettbewerb NHG 5
complete /kəm'pliːt/ vervollständigen NHG 5
completely /kəm'pliːtli/ völlig, absolut p. 94, 5
compromise /'kɒmprəmaɪz/ Kompromiss p. 65, 15
con /kɒn/ Nachteil; Kontra p. 39, 7
concept /'kɒnsept/ Entwurf; Konzept p. 84, 7
concert /'kɒnsət/ Konzert p. 26, 13
conflict /'kɒnflɪkt/ Konflikt p. 65, 15
connective /kə'nektɪv/ Bindewort p. 98, 12
construction /kən'strʌkʃn/ Bau p. 102
(to) **contact** /'kɒntækt/ sich in Verbindung setzen mit p. 80, 2
contest /'kɒntest/ Wettbewerb p. 50, 14
(to) **cook** /kʊk/ kochen NHG 5; braten, backen p. 45, 6
cooking /'kʊkɪŋ/ Kochen; Koch- NHG 5
(to) **do the cooking** /ˌduː ðə 'kʊkɪŋ/ kochen NHG 5
(to) cool /kuːl/ abkühlen p. 46, 7
(to) **copy** /'kɒpi/ abschreiben NHG 5
copy /'kɒpi/ Kopie p. 30
corn *(AE)* /kɔːn/ Mais p. 54
corner /'kɔːnə/ Ecke p. 24, 9
correct /kə'rekt/ richtig, korrekt; korrigieren NHG 5
(to) **cost** *(irr)* /kɒst/ kosten NHG 5
costume /'kɒstjuːm/ Kostüm p. 33, 1
could /kʊd/ könnte/könntest/könnten/könntet NHG 5; *Vergangenheitsform von can* p. 14, 9
country /'kʌntri/ Land p. 40, 11
countryside /'kʌntriˌsaɪd/ Land, Landschaft p. 67, 1
a couple of /ə 'kʌpl‿əv/ einige, ein paar p. 11, 5
course /kɔːs/ Kurs p. 114, 1
court /kɔːt/ Platz NHG 5
cousin /'kʌzn/ Cousin/e NHG 5
(to) **cover** /'kʌvə/ bedecken p. 46, 7
cow /kaʊ/ Kuh p. 9, 2
crack *(informal)* /kræk/ *etwa:* knack! p. 77
(to) crack open /ˌkræk‿'əʊpən/ aufbrechen p. 100
crash /kræʃ/ *hier:* Krach; Getöse p. 120, 12
(to) **create** /kri'eɪt/ erschaffen; erzeugen NHG 5
creative /kri'eɪtɪv/ kreativ NHG 5
creativity /ˌkriːeɪ'tɪvəti/ Kreativität p. 111, 12
crime /kraɪm/ Verbrechen p. 127
criminal /'krɪmɪnl/ Verbrecher/in p. 83, 6
crisps *(pl)* /krɪsps/ Chips p. 50, 15
(to) **cross** /krɒs/ überqueren p. 22, 6
(to) **cry** /kraɪ/ weinen; schreien p. 120, 12
CU! (= See you!) *(informal)* /'siː juː/ Bis bald! p. 49, 12
cue card /'kjuː kɑːd/ *Stichwortkarte* p. 123, 17
culture /'kʌltʃə/ Kultur p. 17, 14
cup /kʌp/ Tasse NHG 5
curtain /'kɜːtn/ Vorhang p. 78
customer /'kʌstəmə/ Kunde/Kundin p. 81, 2
(to) **cut** *(irr)* /kʌt/ schneiden p. 39, 9
(to) cut off *(irr)* /ˌkʌt‿'ɒf/ abschneiden p. 78
(to) cut out *(irr)* /ˌkʌt‿'aʊt/ ausschneiden p. 39, 9
(to) **cycle** /'saɪkl/ Rad fahren, radeln p. 11, 5
(to) **go cycling** /ˌgəʊ 'saɪklɪŋ/ Rad fahren gehen p. 9, 2
cyclist /'saɪklɪst/ Radfahrer/in p. 66, 1

D

dad /dæd/ Papa; Vati NHG 5
daily /'deɪli/ täglich NHG 5
(to) **dance** /dɑːns/ tanzen NHG 5
dance /dɑːns/ Tanz p. 101
dancer /'dɑːnsə/ Tänzer/in p. 33, 1
dancing /'dɑːnsɪŋ/ Tanzen NHG 5
danger /'deɪndʒə/ Gefahr p. 71, 7
dangerous /'deɪndʒərəs/ gefährlich p. 56, 1
dark /dɑːk/ dunkel; Dunkelheit p. 90, 1
darkness /'dɑːknəs/ Dunkelheit p. 33, 1
date /deɪt/ Datum NHG 5
daughter /'dɔːtə/ Tochter NHG 5
day /deɪ/ Tag NHG 5
day out /ˌdeɪ‿'aʊt/ *Ausflugstag* p. 27, 14
Day Travelcard /'deɪ ˌtrævlkɑːd/ Tageskarte p. 22, 5
day trip /'deɪ trɪp/ Tagesausflug p. 8, 1
daylight *(no pl)* /'deɪˌlaɪt/ Tageslicht p. 33, 1
the dead /ðə 'ded/ die Toten p. 36, 6
deadline /'dedˌlaɪn/ letzter Termin; Deadline p. 117, 8
dear /dɪə/ liebe/r *(Anrede)* NHG 5
December /dɪ'sembə/ Dezember NHG 5
(to) **decide** /dɪ'saɪd/ entscheiden, sich entscheiden NHG 5
(to) **decorate** /'dekəreɪt/ schmücken; dekorieren NHG 5
decoration /ˌdekə'reɪʃn/ Dekoration; Schmuck p. 33, 1
deer /dɪə/ Hirsch, Reh p. 66, 1
definitely /'defnətli/ eindeutig, definitiv p. 45, 6
delicious /dɪ'lɪʃəs/ köstlich, lecker p. 10, 3
(to) depart /dɪ'pɑːt/ abfahren p. 22, 5
(to) **depend on** /dɪ'pend‿ɒn/ abhängen von p. 33, 1
(to) **describe** /dɪ'skraɪb/ beschreiben NHG 5
description /dɪ'skrɪpʃn/ Beschreibung p. 108, 7
design /dɪ'zaɪn/ entwerfen NHG 5; Entwurf; Design p. 111, 12
desk /desk/ Schreibtisch NHG 5
(to) **destroy** /dɪ'strɔɪ/ zerstören p. 71, 7
detail /'diːteɪl/ Detail; Einzelheit NHG 5
detailed /'diːteɪld/ genau p. 147
(to) detect /dɪ'tekt/ entdecken p. 76
detective /dɪ'tektɪv/ Detektiv/in p. 104, 2
(to) develop /dɪ'veləp/ erarbeiten; entwickeln p. 8, 1

dialogue /ˈdaɪəˌlɒɡ/ Gespräch; Dialog NHG 5
diary /ˈdaɪəri/ Tagebuch p. 62, 10
diary entry /ˈdaɪəri‿ˌentri/ Tagebucheintrag p. 15, 11
dictionary /ˈdɪkʃənri/ Lexikon; Wörterbuch p. 34, 3
(to) die /daɪ/ sterben p. 127
difference /ˈdɪfrəns/ Unterschied p. 148
different /ˈdɪfrənt/ anders; andere(r, s); verschiedene(r, s) NHG 5
difficult /ˈdɪfɪklt/ schwierig; schwer p. 12, 6
dinner /ˈdɪnə/ Abendessen NHG 5
dinosaur /ˈdaɪnəˌsɔː/ Dinosaurier p. 19, 1
directions *(pl)* /dɪˈrekʃnz/ *hier:* Wegbeschreibungen p. 22, 6
(to) **give directions** /ˌɡɪv daɪˈrekʃnz/ den Weg beschreiben p. 22, 6
dirty /ˈdɜːti/ dreckig; schmutzig NHG 5
(to) **disappear** /ˌdɪsəˈpɪə/ verschwinden p. 91, 1
disappointed /ˌdɪsəˈpɔɪntɪd/ enttäuscht p. 120, 12
(to) **discover** /dɪˈskʌvə/ entdecken p. 19, 1
(to) **discuss** /dɪˈskʌs/ besprechen; diskutieren p. 51, 16
discussion /dɪˈskʌʃn/ Diskussion p. 50, 14
dishwasher /ˈdɪʃˌwɒʃə/ Spülmaschine NHG 5
(to) **display** /dɪˈspleɪ/ aushängen; zeigen NHG 5
(to) **put on display** /ˌpʊt‿ɒn dɪˈspleɪ/ ausstellen p. 112, 13
(to) **do** *(irr)* /duː/ tun; machen NHG 5
(to) **do athletics** *(irr)* /ˌduː‿æθˈletɪks/ Leichtathletik machen NHG 5
(to) **do gymnastics** *(irr)* /ˌduː dʒɪmˈnæstɪks/ turnen NHG 5
(to) **do research** *(irr)* /ˌduː rɪˈsɜːtʃ/ recherchieren NHG 5
(to) **do sports** *(irr)* /ˌduː ˈspɔːts/ Sport treiben p. 8, 1
(to) **do the cooking** *(irr)* /ˌduː ðə ˈkʊkɪŋ/ kochen NHG 5
(to) **do the shopping** *(irr)* /ˌduː ðə ˈʃɒpɪŋ/ einkaufen NHG 5
doctor /ˈdɒktə/ Arzt/Ärztin p. 127
dog /dɒɡ/ Hund NHG 5
(to) walk the dog /ˌwɔːk ðə ˈdɒɡ/ den Hund ausführen p. 30
dolphin /ˈdɒlfɪn/ Delfin p. 166
don'ting (= not doing) /ˈdəʊntɪŋ/ *nicht tun* p. 78
door /dɔː/ Tür p. 63, 12
double /ˈdʌbl/ doppelt, Doppel- NHG 5
down /daʊn/ hinunter; (nach) unten p. 14, 9
Dr (= Doctor) /ˈdɒktə/ Dr. (= Doktor) p. 104, 2
draft /drɑːft/ Entwurf p. 27, 14
dragon /ˈdræɡən/ Drache p. 33, 1
dragon tamer /ˈdræɡən ˌteɪmə/ Drachenzähmer/in p. 28
dragon-taming kit /ˈdræɡənˌteɪmɪŋ kɪt/ *Drachenzähm-Ausrüstung* p. 100
drama /ˈdrɑːmə/ Theater-; Schauspiel- p. 114, 1
dramatic reading /drəˌmætɪk ˈriːdɪŋ/ szenische Lesung p. 121, 12
(to) **draw** *(irr)* /drɔː/ zeichnen NHG 5
drawing /ˈdrɔːɪŋ/ Zeichnung p. 80, 2
dream /driːm/ Traum NHG 5
(to) dress up /ˌdres‿ˈʌp/ (sich) verkleiden p. 36, 6
dried fruit /ˌdraɪd ˈfruːt/ Dörrobst; getrocknetes Obst p. 73, 10
drink /drɪŋk/ Trinken; Getränk NHG 5
(to) **drink** *(irr)* /drɪŋk/ trinken NHG 5
(to) **drive** *(irr)* /draɪv/ fahren p. 10, 3
driver /ˈdraɪvə/ Fahrer/in p. 28
dry /draɪ/ trocken p. 70, 7
(to) dry /draɪ/ trocknen p. 28
during /ˈdjʊərɪŋ/ während p. 16, 12

E

each /iːtʃ/ jede(r, s) NHG 5
each other /ˌiːtʃ‿ˈʌðə/ einander NHG 5
ear /ɪə/ Ohr NHG 5
earlier /ˈɜːliə/ vorhin, früher p. 49, 12
early /ˈɜːli/ früh p. 63, 11
(to) **earn** /ɜːn/ verdienen p. 84, 7
earth /ɜːθ/ Erde p. 19, 1
Easter /ˈiːstə/ Ostern p. 33, 1
Easter bunny /ˈiːstə ˌbʌni/ Osterhase p. 33, 1
Easter egg /ˈiːstər‿eɡ/ Osterei p. 137
Easter egg hunt /ˈiːstər‿eɡ ˌhʌnt/ Ostereiersuche p. 33, 1
Easter egg roll /ˈiːstər‿eɡ ˌrəʊl/ Ostereierrollen p. 33, 1
easy /ˈiːzi/ leicht; einfach NHG 5
(to) **eat** *(irr)* /iːt/ essen NHG 5
(to) **edit** /ˈedɪt/ bearbeiten NHG 5
educational /ˌedjʊˈkeɪʃnəl/ lehrreich p. 69, 6
egg /eɡ/ Ei NHG 5
Egypt /ˈiːdʒɪpt/ Ägypten p. 10, 3
Egyptian /ɪˈdʒɪpʃn/ ägyptisch p. 104, 2
either ... or ... /ˌaɪðə ˈɔː/ entweder ... oder ... p. 80, 1
else /els/ anders; sonst NHG 5
emergency /ɪˈmɜːdʒnsi/ Notfall p. 28
emotional /ɪˈməʊʃnəl/ *hier:* gerührt p. 30
(to) **empty** /ˈempti/ ausleeren; ausräumen NHG 5
end /end/ Ende; Schluss NHG 5
(to) **end** /end/ (be)enden p. 33, 1
at the end /ˌæt ðiˈend/ am Ende p. 130
in the end /ˌɪn ði‿ˈend/ am Ende, schließlich p. 93, 4
ending /ˈendɪŋ/ Ende; Schluss p. 98, 13
engineer /ˌendʒɪˈnɪə/ Ingenieur/in p. 81, 2
English /ˈɪŋɡlɪʃ/ Englisch; englisch NHG 5
(to) **enjoy** /ɪnˈdʒɔɪ/ genießen NHG 5
enough /ɪˈnʌf/ genug NHG 5
(to) **enter** /ˈentə/ eingeben p. 27, 14; betreten p. 56, 1
(to) enter /ˈentə/ *hier:* auftreten p. 120, 12
entertainment /ˌentəˈteɪnmənt/ Unterhaltung p. 24, 9
entrance /ˈentrəns/ Eingang; Eintritt p. 24, 9
entry /ˈentri/ Eintritt p. 19, 1
diary entry /ˈdaɪəri‿ˌentri/ Tagebucheintrag p. 15, 11
environment /ɪnˈvaɪrənmənt/ Umwelt; Umgebung p. 73, 11

equipment /ɪ'kwɪpmənt/ Ausrüstung; Ausstattung NHG 5
eraser /ɪ'reɪzə/ Radiergummi NHG 5
erm *(informal)* /ɜ:m/ ähm p. 105, 3
(to) erupt /ɪ'rʌpt/ ausbrechen p. 101
(to) **escape** /ɪ'skeɪp/ fliehen; entkommen NHG 5
especially /ɪ'speʃli/ besonders; vor allem p. 17, 14
Europe /'jʊərəp/ Europa p. 19, 1
even /'i:vn/ selbst; sogar NHG 5
even though /ˌi:vn 'ðəʊ/ obwohl p. 127
evening /'i:vnɪŋ/ Abend NHG 5
event /ɪ'vent/ Ereignis; Veranstaltung NHG 5
ever /'evə/ jemals p. 19, 1
every /'evri/ jede(r, s) NHG 5
everybody /'evriˌbɒdi/ alle; jeder NHG 5
everyday /'evriˌdeɪ/ alltäglich, Alltags- p. 109, 9
everyone /'evriwʌn/ alle; jeder NHG 5
everything /'evriθɪŋ/ alles NHG 5
everywhere /'evriweə/ überall NHG 5
evil /'i:vl/ das Böse p. 33, 1
exactly /ɪg'zækli/ genau p. 81, 2
example /ɪg'zɑ:mpl/ Beispiel NHG 5
for example /fər‿ɪg'zɑ:mpl/ zum Beispiel NHG 5
excellent /'eksələnt/ ausgezeichnet NHG 5
except /ɪk'sept/ außer p. 90, 1
excited /ɪk'saɪtɪd/ aufgeregt p. 93, 4
exciting /ɪk'saɪtɪŋ/ aufregend NHG 5
excuse /ɪk'skju:s/ Entschuldigung; Ausrede p. 43, 2
Excuse me! /ɪk'skju:z ˌmi/ Entschuldigung! NHG 5
exercise /'eksəsaɪz/ Übung p. 74, 13
exercise book /'eksəsaɪz ˌbʊk/ Heft NHG 5
exhibition /ˌeksɪ'bɪʃn/ Ausstellung p. 19, 1
(to) **exist** /ɪg'zɪst/ existieren p. 19, 1
(to) **expect** /ɪk'spekt/ erwarten p. 98, 13
expensive /ɪk'spensɪv/ teuer p. 23, 8
experience /ɪk'spɪəriəns/ Erfahrung NHG 5

experiment /ɪk'sperɪmənt/ Experiment; Versuch NHG 5
expert /'ekspɜ:t/ Experte / Expertin p. 75, 14
(to) **explain** /ɪk'spleɪn/ erklären NHG 5
(to) **explore** /ɪk'splɔ:/ erforschen; untersuchen p. 67, 1
(to) **express** /ɪk'spres/ ausdrücken p. 59, 6
extra /'ekstrə/ zusätzlich NHG 5
eye /aɪ/ Auge NHG 5
googly eyes /ˌgu:gli‿'aɪz/ *Wackelaugen* p. 39, 9

F

face /feɪs/ Gesicht NHG 5
fact /fækt/ Tatsache; Fakt NHG 5
fact file /'fækt faɪl/ Steckbrief NHG 5
(to) fall *(irr)* /fɔ:l/ fallen p. 100
fall *(AE)* /fɔ:l/ Herbst p. 54
(to) fall asleep *(irr)* /ˌfɔ:l‿ə'sli:p/ einschlafen p. 126
(to) fall down *(irr)* /ˌfɔ:l 'daʊn/ hinfallen p. 101
false /fɔ:ls/ falsch NHG 5
family /'fæmli/ Familie NHG 5
famous /'feɪməs/ berühmt NHG 5
fancy /'fænsi/ nobel p. 81, 2
fantastic /fæn'tæstɪk/ fantastisch; super NHG 5
far /fɑ:/ weit NHG 5
far away /ˌfɑ:r‿ə'weɪ/ weit weg p. 100
farm /fɑ:m/ Bauernhof p. 9, 2
farmhouse /'fɑ:mˌhaʊs/ Bauernhaus p. 12, 6
fashion /'fæʃn/ Mode p. 81, 2
fast /fɑ:st/ schnell NHG 5
fast /fɑ:st/ Fastenzeit p. 128
fat /fæt/ Fett p. 73, 10
father /'fɑ:ðə/ Vater NHG 5
Father Christmas /ˌfɑ:ðə 'krɪsməs/ Weihnachtsmann p. 128
favorite *(AE)* /'feɪvrət/ Liebling; Lieblings- p. 54
favourite /'feɪvrət/ Liebling; Lieblings- NHG 5
February /'februəri/ Februar NHG 5
(to) **feed** *(irr)* /fi:d/ füttern p. 66, 1
feedback /'fi:dbæk/ Feedback; Rückmeldung NHG 5

feeder /'fi:də/ Futterstation p. 73, 10
feeding time /'fi:dɪŋ taɪm/ Fütterungszeit p. 66, 1
(to) **feel** *(irr)* /fi:l/ (sich) fühlen p. 60, 7
feeling /'fi:lɪŋ/ Gefühl p. 122, 15
felt-tip /'felt‿tɪp/ Filzstift NHG 5
ferris wheel /'ferɪs ˌwi:l/ Riesenrad p. 19, 1
ferry /'feri/ Fähre p. 29
festival /'festɪvl/ Fest; Festival p. 31
a few /ə 'fju:/ einige; wenige p. 14, 9
field /fi:ld/ Feld NHG 5
field trip /'fi:ld‿trɪp/ Exkursion p. 69, 6
(to) **fight** *(irr)* /faɪt/ bekämpfen; ankämpfen gegen p. 83, 6
(to) **fill** /fɪl/ füllen p. 39, 9
(to) **fill in** /ˌfɪl‿'ɪn/ eintragen, ausfüllen NHG 5
(to) **film** /fɪlm/ drehen, filmen p. 80, 1
final /'faɪnl/ letzte(r, s); endgültig NHG 5
finally /'faɪnli/ schließlich; endlich p. 53
(to) **find** *(irr)* /faɪnd/ finden NHG 5
(to) **find out** *(irr)* /ˌfaɪnd‿'aʊt/ herausfinden NHG 5
finding /'faɪndɪŋ/ Entdeckung; Ergebnis p. 118, 9
fine /faɪn/ in Ordnung, gut NHG 5
fingerprint /'fɪŋgəˌprɪnt/ Fingerabdruck p. 107, 6
(to) **finish** /'fɪnɪʃ/ beenden; enden; fertigstellen p. 62, 10
fire /'faɪə/ Feuer p. 45, 6
firefighter /'faɪəˌfaɪtə/ Feuerwehrmann/-frau p. 83, 6
fireworks *(pl)* /'faɪəˌwɜ:ks/ Feuerwerk p. 33, 1
first /fɜ:st/ erste(r, s); zuerst NHG 5
at first /ət 'fɜ:st/ zuerst p. 9, 2
for the first time /fə ðə 'fɜ:st‿taɪm/ zum ersten Mal p. 91, 1
first footing /ˌfɜ:st 'fʊtɪŋ/ *Abstatten eines Neujahrsbesuchs (schottische Tradition)* p. 35, 4
fish (*pl* **fish** *or* **fishes**) /fɪʃ, fɪʃ, fɪʃɪz/ Fisch NHG 5
(to) **fit** /fɪt/ passen NHG 5
flag /flæg/ Fahne; Flagge p. 66, 1

flame /fleɪm/ Flamme; Feuer p. 100
flat /flæt/ Wohnung p. 71, 7
flexible /ˈfleksəbl/ *hier:* anpassungsfähig p. 135
floor /flɔː/ Fußboden NHG 5
flower /ˈflaʊə/ Blume p. 24, 9
(to) **fly** *(irr)* /flaɪ/ fliegen p. 87, 13
flying /ˈflaɪɪŋ/ fliegend p. 87, 14
(to) **focus on** /ˈfəʊkəs‿ɒn/ sich konzentrieren auf NHG 5
(to) fold /fəʊld/ falten p. 39, 9
folder /ˈfəʊldə/ Mappe; Ordner NHG 5
(to) **follow** /ˈfɒləʊ/ folgen; verfolgen p. 22, 6
following /ˈfɒləʊɪŋ/ folgende(r,s) p. 32, 1
food /fuːd/ Essen NHG 5
food /fuːd/ *hier:* Futter p. 70, 7
foot (*pl* feet) /fʊt, fiːt/ Fuß NHG 5
football /ˈfʊtˌbɔːl/ Fußball NHG 5
footprint /ˈfʊtˌprɪnt/ Fußabdruck p. 67, 1
footstep /ˈfʊtstep/ Schritt p. 77
for /fɔː/ für NHG 5
for *(+ Zeitraum)* /fɔː/ ... lang p. 14, 9
for example /fər‿ɪgˈzɑːmpl/ zum Beispiel NHG 5
for free /fə ˈfriː/ gratis p. 27, 14
for the first time /fə ðə ˈfɜːst‿taɪm/ zum ersten Mal p. 9, 2
forest /ˈfɒrɪst/ Wald p. 66, 1
forever /fərˈevə/ ewig p. 45, 6
(to) **forget** *(irr)* /fəˈget/ vergessen NHG 5
(to) be forgot *(irr, poet.)* /ˌbiː fəˈgɒt/ vergessen werden *(poetisch)* p. 48, 10
fork /fɔːk/ Gabel NHG 5
form /fɔːm/ Klasse NHG 5
fort /fɔːt/ Fort; Festung p. 12, 6
had found /ˌhæd ˈfaʊnd/ gefunden hatte(n) p. 30
fox /fɒks/ Fuchs p. 66, 1
France /frɑːns/ Frankreich NHG 5
(to) freak out *(informal)* /ˌfriːk‿ˈaʊt/ ausflippen, ausrasten p. 94, 5
free /friː/ frei; kostenlos p. 19, 1
free time /friː ˈtaɪm/ Freizeit NHG 5
freezer /ˈfriːzə/ Gefrierschrank p. 74, 12
French /frentʃ/ Französisch NHG 5
fresh /freʃ/ frisch; neu p. 9, 2
Friday /ˈfraɪdeɪ/ Freitag NHG 5
(on) Fridays /ˈfraɪdeɪz/ freitags NHG 5
fridge /frɪdʒ/ Kühlschrank p. 87, 13
friend /frend/ Freund/in NHG 5
friendly /ˈfrendli/ freundlich p. 71, 7
(to) **make friends (with)** *(irr)* /ˌmeɪk ˈfrendz/ sich anfreunden (mit) p. 8, 1
friendship /ˈfrenʃɪp/ Freundschaft p. 61, 9
(to) frighten /ˈfraɪtn/ erschrecken p. 120, 12
(to) frighten away /ˌfraɪtn‿əˈweɪ/ verscheuchen p. 120, 12
frogs' legs *(pl)* /ˈfrɒgz legz/ Froschschenkel p. 110, 11
from /frɒm/ von; aus NHG 5
from all over the world /frəm‿ˌɔːl‿ˌəʊvə ðə ˈwɜːld/ aus der ganzen Welt NHG 5
at/in the front /ˌæt/ˌɪn ðə ˈfrʌnt/ vorne NHG 5
in front of /ˌɪn ˈfrʌnt‿əv/ vor NHG 5
fruit /fruːt/ Frucht; Obst NHG 5
frustrated /frʌˈstreɪtɪd/ frustriert p. 120, 12
full /fʊl/ voll, vollständig p. 121, 12
full of /ˈfʊl‿əv/ voller p. 34, 3
full-time /ˌfʊl ˈtaɪm/ Vollzeit- p. 127
fun /fʌn/ Spaß NHG 5; lustig; witzig p. 17, 14
(to) **be (good/great) fun** *(irr)* /ˌbiː ˌgʊd/ˌgreɪt ˈfʌn/ (viel/großen) Spaß machen NHG 5
(to) **have (a lot of) fun** *(irr)* /ˌhæv‿ə ˌlɒt‿əv‿ˈfʌn/ (viel) Spaß haben p. 14, 9
functional /ˈfʌŋkʃnəl/ funktional p. 111, 12
funfair /ˈfʌnˌfeə/ Vergnügungspark; Kirmes p. 42, 1
funny /ˈfʌni/ lustig; komisch NHG 5
furniture /ˈfɜːnɪtʃə/ Möbel(stück) NHG 5
further /ˈfɜːðə/ weiter p. 114, 1
future /ˈfjuːtʃə/ Zukunft p. 79
future /ˈfjuːtʃə/ zukünftig p. 82, 3

G

g (= gram) /græm/ Gramm p. 46, 7
gallery walk /ˈgæləri wɔːk/ *Gruppendiskussion in Stationsarbeit* p. 17, 14
game /geɪm/ Spiel NHG 5
board game /ˈbɔːd geɪm/ Brettspiel p. 6
gap /gæp/ Lücke NHG 5
garden /ˈgɑːdn/ Garten NHG 5
garland /ˈgɑːlənd/ Kranz; Girlande p. 39, 9
gate /geɪt/ Tor p. 67, 1
general /ˈdʒenrəl/ allgemein p. 146
geography /dʒiːˈɒgrəfi/ Erdkunde NHG 5
German /ˈdʒɜːmən/ Deutsch; deutsch NHG 5
Germany /ˈdʒɜːməni/ Deutschland NHG 5
(to) **get** *(irr)* /get/ bekommen; holen; kaufen NHG 5; kommen; gelangen p. 19, 1; werden p. 95, 5
(to) get *(irr)* /get/ *hier:* bringen p. 94,5
(to) **get along** *(irr)* /ˌget‿əˈlɒŋ/ sich verstehen p. 55
(to) get around *(irr)* /ˌget‿əˈraʊnd/ herumkommen p. 21, 4
(to) get away *(irr)* /ˌget‿əˈweɪ/ wegkommen, flüchten p. 101
(to) get back to sleep *(irr)* /ˌget ˌbæk tə ˈsliːp/ wieder einschlafen p. 120, 12
(to) get hurt *(irr)* /ˌget ˈhɜːt/ sich verletzen p. 100
(to) get into *(irr)* /ˌget‿ˈɪntʊ/ einsteigen in p. 126
(to) get lost *(irr)* /ˌget ˈlɒst/ sich verirren p. 14, 9
(to) get off *(irr)* /ˌget‿ˈɒf/ herunterkommen, absteigen p. 76
(to) get out *(irr)* /ˌget‿ˈaʊt/ *hier:* herausnehmen p. 77
(to) get ready *(irr)* /ˌget ˈredi/ sich fertig machen, sich vorbereiten auf p. 53
(to) **get together** *(irr)* /ˌget‿təˈgeðə/ zusammenkommen NHG 5
(to) **get up** *(irr)* /ˌget‿ˈʌp/ aufstehen p. 98, 13
ghost /gəʊst/ Geist; Gespenst p. 36, 6
ghostly /ˈgəʊsli/ geisterhaft; gespenstisch p. 121, 13

giant /ˈdʒaɪənt/ riesig p. 54
girl /gɜːl/ Mädchen NHG 5
(to) **give** *(irr)* /gɪv/ geben NHG 5; angeben, mitteilen p. 90, 1
(to) give a presentation *(irr)* /ˌgɪv‿ə ˌpreznˈteɪʃn/ eine Präsentation halten p. 147
(to) **give directions** *(irr)* /ˌgɪv daɪˈrekʃnz/ den Weg beschreiben p. 22, 6
give somebody a hug *(irr)* /ˌgɪv ˌsʌmbədi‿ə ˈhʌg/ jemanden umarmen p. 28
glad /glæd/ glücklich, froh p. 126
glass /glɑːs/ Glas p. 25, 10
glass jar /ˈglɑːs ʒɑː/ Glasgefäß p. 39, 9
glasses *(pl)* /ˈglɑːsɪz/ Brille p. 87, 13
(to) glow /gləʊ/ leuchten, glühen p. 90, 1
glue /gluː/ Klebstoff NHG 5
(to) **go** *(irr)* /gəʊ/ gehen; fahren NHG 5
(to) **go abroad** *(irr)* /ˌgəʊ‿əˈbrɔːd/ ins Ausland gehen, ins Ausland fahren p. 8, 1
(to) **go away** *(irr)* /ˌgəʊ‿əˈweɪ/ weggehen; verschwinden p. 120, 12
Go big or go home. *(AE)* /ˌgəʊ ˌbɪg‿ɔː ˌgəʊ ˈhəʊm/ Ganz oder gar nicht. p. 81, 2
(to) go camping *(irr)* /ˌgəʊ ˌkæmpɪŋ/ zelten gehen p. 67, 1
(to) **go cycling** *(irr)* /ˌgəʊ ˈsaɪklɪŋ/ Rad fahren gehen p. 9, 2
(to) go extinct *(irr)* /ˌgəʊ‿ɪkˈstɪŋkt/ aussterben p. 100
(to) **go hiking** *(irr)* /ˌgəʊ ˈhaɪkɪŋ/ wandern gehen p. 14, 9
(to) **go out** *(irr)* /ˌgəʊ‿ˈaʊt/ (hinaus) gehen; ausgehen p. 64, 13
(to) **go riding** *(irr)* /ˌgəʊ ˈraɪdɪŋ/ reiten gehen p. 9, 2
(to) **go shopping** *(irr)* /ˌgəʊ ˈʃɒpɪŋ/ einkaufen gehen p. 87, 13
(to) go to sleep *(irr)* /ˌgəʊ tə ˈsliːp/ schlafen gehen p. 52
(to) **go swimming** *(irr)* /ˌgəʊ ˈswɪmɪŋ/ schwimmen gehen p. 8, 1
(to) go together *(irr)* /ˌgəʊ təˈgeðə/ zusammenpassen p. 34, 3
(to) **go with** *(irr)* /ˌgəʊ ˈwɪθ/ gehören zu; passen zu p. 19, 1
goal /gəʊl/ Tor NHG 5
goal /gəʊl/ Ziel p. 28
thank God /ˌθæŋk ˈgɒd/ Gott sei Dank p. 94, 5
goddess /ˈgɒdes/ Göttin p. 36, 6
(to) goggle (at) /ˈgɒgl/ (an)starren p. 78
(to) **be going to** *(irr)* /ˌbiː ˈgəʊɪŋ tʊ/ werden p. 45, 6
gone /gɒn/ weg p. 121, 12
good /gʊd/ gut NHG 5
good /gʊd/ das Gute p. 33, 1
(to) **be good at something** *(irr)* /ˌbiː ˈgʊd‿æt ˌsʌmθɪŋ/ gut in etwas sein p. 9, 2
I'm good, thanks. /aɪm ˈgʊd ˌθæŋks/ Es geht mir gut, danke. NHG 5
Good luck! /ˌgʊd ˈlʌk/ Viel Glück! p. 28
Good morning! /ˌgʊd ˈmɔːnɪŋ/ Guten Morgen! NHG 5
goodbye /ˌgʊdˈbaɪ/ auf Wiedersehen NHG 5
(to) say goodbye (to somebody) *(irr)* /ˌseɪ gʊdˈbaɪ tə ˌsʌmbədi/ sich von jemandem verabschieden p. 126
googly eyes *(pl)* /ˌguːgli‿ˈaɪz/ *Wackelaugen* p. 39, 9
grammar /ˈgræmə/ Grammatik p. 10
grandfather /ˈgrænˌfɑːðə/ Großvater NHG 5
grandma *(informal)* /ˈgrænˌmɑː/ Oma p. 9, 2
grandmother /ˈgrænˌmʌðə/ Großmutter NHG 5
grandpa *(informal)* /ˈgrænˌpɑː/ Opa p. 8, 1
grandparents *(pl)* /ˈgrænˌpeərənts/ Großeltern p. 11, 5
grape /greɪp/ (Wein)traube p. 35, 4
grass /grɑːs/ Gras p. 9, 2
great /greɪt/ groß; großartig NHG 5
green /griːn/ grün NHG 5
greetings *(pl)* /ˈgriːtɪŋz/ Grüße p. 102
grey /greɪ/ grau NHG 5
(to) grill /grɪl/ grillen p. 49, 12
ground /graʊnd/ Boden p. 71, 7
group /gruːp/ Gruppe NHG 5
(to) **grow** *(irr)* /grəʊ/ anbauen p. 71, 7
(to) grow *(irr)* /grəʊ/ wachsen p. 144
(to) **grow up** *(irr)* /ˌgrəʊ‿ˈʌp/ erwachsen sein / werden p. 81, 2
(to) **guess** /ges/ (er)raten NHG 5
(to) guess /ges/ annehmen; vermuten p. 125
guest /gest/ Gast NHG 5
guide /gaɪd/ Führer *(Buch)*; Führer/in p. 12, 6; führen; leiten p. 22, 6
guitar /gɪˈtɑː/ Gitarre NHG 5
gunpowder *(no pl)* /ˈgʌnˌpaʊdə/ Schießpulver p. 48, 10
Guy /gaɪ/ *Guy Fawkes-Puppe* Land und Leute 3
(you) guys *(pl, informal)* /gaɪz/ Leute *(umgangssprachlich)* p. 8, 1
gym (= gymnasium) /dʒɪm, dʒɪmˈneɪziəm/ Turnhalle NHG 5
(to) **do gymnastics** *(irr)* /ˌduː dʒɪmˈnæstɪks/ turnen NHG 5

H

hair /heə/ Haar; Haare NHG 5
hairdresser /ˈheəˌdresə/ Friseur/in p. 83, 6
half /hɑːf/ halb NHG 5
half (*pl* **halves**) /hɑːf,hɑːvz/ Hälfte p. 73, 10
(to) **hand in** /ˌhænd‿ˈɪn/ einreichen; abgeben p. 80, 1
(to) handle /ˈhændl/ bewältigen, umgehen mit p. 126
handwriting /ˈhændˌraɪtɪŋ/ Handschrift p. 30
(to) **hang (up)** *(irr)* /ˌhæŋ‿ˈʌp/ hängen, aufhängen p. 73, 10
(to) **happen** /ˈhæpən/ geschehen; passieren NHG 5
happy /ˈhæpi/ glücklich NHG 5
Happy birthday (to you)! /ˌhæpi ˈbɜːθdeɪ tʊ juː/ Herzlichen Glückwunsch zum Geburtstag! NHG 5
hard /hɑːd/ hart, schwierig p. 12, 6
hard /hɑːd/ fest; kräftig p. 76
harder /ˈhɑːdə/ schwieriger p. 12, 6
hat /hæt/ Hut p. 56, 1
(to) **hate** /heɪt/ hassen; nicht ausstehen können NHG 5
(to) **have** *(irr)* /hæv/ haben; essen; trinken NHG 5

(to) **have a look at** *(irr)* /ˌhæv‿ə ˈlʊk‿ət/ sich ansehen p. 43, 2

(to) **have (a lot of) fun** *(irr)* /ˌhæv‿ə ˌlɒt‿əv‿ˈfʌn/ (viel) Spaß haben p. 14, 9

(to) **have got** *(irr)* /ˌhæv ˈgɒt/ haben NHG 5

(to) **have in common** *(irr)* /ˌhæv‿ɪn ˈkɒmən/ gemeinsam haben p. 33, 3

(to) **have to** *(irr)* /ˈhæv tə/ müssen NHG 5

he /hiː/ er NHG 5

head /hed/ Kopf p. 107, 6

heading /ˈhedɪŋ/ Überschrift; Titel p. 95, 5

headteacher /ˌhedˈtiːtʃə/ Schulleiter/in; Rektor/in p. 56, 1

healthy /ˈhelθi/ gesund p. 50, 15

(to) **hear** *(irr)* /hɪə/ hören NHG 5

heart /hɑːt/ Herz p. 19, 1

by heart /ˌbaɪ ˈhɑːt/ auswendig p. 48, 10

heavy /ˈhevi/ schwer NHG 5

hedgehog /ˈhedʒˌhɒg/ Igel p. 70, 7

height /haɪt/ Höhe p. 25, 10

helicopter /ˈhelɪˌkɒptə/ Hubschrauber p. 28

hello /həˈləʊ/ hallo NHG 5

helmet /ˈhelmɪt/ Helm p. 64, 14

help /help/ Hilfe; helfen NHG 5

helpful /ˈhelpfl/ hilfreich; nützlich p. 126

her /hɜː/ ihr/ihre; sie NHG 5

here /hɪə/ hier; hierher NHG 5

Here you are! /ˌhɪə ju‿ˈɑː/ Hier, bitte! NHG 5

(to) **hide** *(irr)* /haɪd/ (sich) verstecken p. 33, 1

high /haɪ/ hoch NHG 5

(to) hike /haɪk/ wandern p. 8, 1

(to) **go hiking** *(irr)* /ˌgəʊ ˈhaɪkɪŋ/ wandern gehen p. 14, 9

hill /hɪl/ Hügel p. 14, 9

him /hɪm/ ihm, ihn NHG 5

himself /hɪmˈself/ selbst; sich (selbst) p. 104, 2

Hindu /ˈhɪnduː/ Hindu; hinduistisch; Hindu- p. 128

Hinduism /ˈhɪnduˌɪzm/ Hinduismus p. 33, 1

(to) **hire** /ˈhaɪə/ mieten p. 66, 1

his /hɪz/ sein; seine(r, s) NHG 5

historical /hɪˈstɒrɪkl/ historisch p. 127

history /ˈhɪstri/ Geschichte NHG 5

(to) **hit** *(irr)* /hɪt/ schlagen NHG 5

hockey stick /ˈhɒki stɪk/ Hockeyschläger p. 109, 9

(to) **hold** *(irr)* /həʊld/ (fest)halten NHG 5

(to) hold out *(irr)* /ˌhəʊld‿ˈaʊt/ ausstrecken; hinhalten p. 124

candle holder /ˈkændl ˌhəʊldə/ Kerzenständer p. 33, 1

hole /həʊl/ Loch NHG 5

holiday /ˈhɒlɪdeɪ/ Feiertag p. 31

holiday(s) /ˈhɒlɪdeɪ(z)/ Ferien; Urlaub NHG 5

hologram /ˈhɒləgræm/ Hologramm p. 87, 13

home /həʊm/ nach Hause; zu Hause; daheim NHG 5; Zuhause; Haus p. 19, 1

at home /ˌæt ˈhəʊm/ zu Hause NHG 5

home town /ˈhəʊm ˌtaʊn/ Heimatstadt NHG 5

homework /ˈhəʊmwɜːk/ Hausaufgaben NHG 5

honest /ˈɒnɪst/ ehrlich p. 81, 2

honey /ˈhʌni/ Honig p. 70, 7

honeybee /ˈhʌniˌbiː/ Honigbiene p. 70, 7

(to) **honour** /ˈɒnə/ ehren p. 36, 6

(to) **hope** /həʊp/ hoffen NHG 5

hope /həʊp/ Hoffnung p. 102

horrible /ˈhɒrəbl/ schrecklich; gemein p. 15, 11

horse /hɔːs/ Pferd p. 9, 2

(to) **ride a horse** /ˌraɪd‿ə ˈhɔːs/ reiten NHG 5

horse rider /ˈhɔːs ˌraɪdə/ Reiter/in p. 66, 1

horse riding /ˈhɔːs ˌraɪdɪŋ/ Reiten p. 66, 1

hospital /ˈhɒspɪtl/ Krankenhaus p. 84, 8

hot /hɒt/ heiß p. 45, 6

hot chocolate /ˌhɒt ˈtʃɒklət/ heißer Kakao p. 45, 6

hour /ˈaʊə/ Stunde NHG 5

house /haʊs/ Haus NHG 5

how /haʊ/ wie NHG 5

How are you? /ˌhaʊ‿ˈɑː jʊ/ Wie geht es dir / euch / Ihnen? NHG 5

How much is it? /ˌhaʊ mʌtʃ‿ˈɪz‿ɪt/ Wie viel kostet es? NHG 5

give somebody a hug /ˌgɪvˌsʌmbədi‿ə ˈhʌg/ jemanden umarmen p. 28

huge /hjuːdʒ/ riesig p. 19, 1

human /ˈhjuːmən/ menschlich p. 102

hundred /ˈhʌndrəd/ Hundert p. 24, 9

hungry /ˈhʌŋgri/ hungrig NHG 5

Easter egg hunt /ˈiːstər‿eg ˌhʌnt/ Ostereiersuche p. 33, 1

(to) **hurry (up)** /ˌhʌri‿ˈʌp/ sich beeilen NHG 5

husband /ˈhʌzbənd/ Ehemann NHG 5

I

I /aɪ/ ich NHG 5

And so do I. /ænd ˌsəʊ du‿ˈaɪ/ Ich auch. p. 12, 6

I don't know. /ˌaɪ ˌdəʊnt ˈnəʊ/ Ich weiß es nicht. NHG 5

I don't like ... /ˌaɪ ˈdəʊnt laɪk/ Ich mag ... nicht. NHG 5

I'd like to ... Ich würde gern ... p. 28

I'd love to ... /aɪd ˈlʌv tə/ Ich würde sehr gern ... NHG 5

I'm (= I am) /aɪm, ˈaɪ‿æm/ ich bin, ich heiße NHG 5

ice /aɪs/ Eis p. 74, 12

ice cream /ˈaɪs ˌkriːm/ Eis NHG 5

(to) **ice-skate** /ˈaɪsˌskeɪt/ Schlittschuh laufen NHG 5

ICT (= Information and Communication Technology) /ˌaɪsiːˈtiː, ɪnfəˈmeɪʃn‿ən kəˌmjuːnɪˈkeɪʃn tekˌnɒlədʒi/ Informatik *(Schulfach)* NHG 5

ID (= identification) /ˌaɪˈdiː, aɪˌdentɪfɪˈkeɪʃn/ Ausweis p. 28

idea /aɪˈdɪə/ Idee; Vorstellung NHG 5

(to) identify /aɪˈdentɪfaɪ/ identifizieren p. 28

if /ɪf/ wenn; falls; ob NHG 5

ill /ɪl/ krank p. 83, 6

(to) **imagine** /ɪˈmædʒɪn/ sich etwas vorstellen NHG 5

immune /ɪˈmjuːn/ immun p. 129

important /ɪmˈpɔːtnt/ wichtig NHG 5

impossible /ɪmˈpɒsəbl/ unmöglich p. 120, 12
(to) **improve** /ɪmˈpruːv/ verbessern; besser werden p. 98, 13
in /ɪn/ in; auf NHG 5
in front of /ˌɪn ˈfrʌnt‿əv/ vor NHG 5
in my opinion /ɪn ˈmaɪ‿əˌpɪnjən/ meiner Meinung nach p. 57, 2
in the back /ˌɪn ðə ˈbæk/ hinten NHG 5
in the end /ˌɪn ðiˈ‿end/ am Ende, schließlich p. 93, 4
in the front /ˌɪn ðə ˈfrʌnt/ vorne NHG 5
(to) **include** /ɪnˈkluːd/ beinhalten; einbeziehen p. 71, 7
India /ˈɪndiə/ Indien p. 35, 4
Indian /ˈɪndiən/ Inder/in; indisch p. 106, 5
individual /ˌɪndɪˈvɪdʒuəl/ individuell; einzeln p. 148
(to) infect /ɪnˈfekt/ infizieren p. 129
(to) **inform** /ɪnˈfɔːm/ informieren p. 34, 3
information *(no pl)* /ˌɪnfəˈmeɪʃn/ Informationen NHG 5
information point /ˌɪnfəˈmeɪʃn pɔɪnt/ Informationsstelle p. 66, 1
insect /ˈɪnsekt/ Insekt p. 74, 12
inside /ˈɪnˌsaɪd/ innerhalb NHG 5; innen; drinnen; hinein p. 39, 9
inspector /ɪnˈspektə/ Inspektor/in p. 119, 11
inspiration /ˌɪnspəˈreɪʃn/ Inspiration; Idee p. 36, 6
instantly /ˈɪnstəntli/ sofort p. 46, 7
instead /ɪnˈsted/ stattdessen p. 54
instruction /ɪnˈstrʌkʃn/ Anweisung; Instruktion p. 73, 10
interested /ˈɪntrəstɪd/ interessiert p. 90, 1
interesting /ˈɪntrəstɪŋ/ interessant NHG 5
more interesting /ˌmɔːr‿ˈɪntrəstɪŋ/ interessanter p. 16, 13
(to) interrupt /ˌɪntəˈrʌpt/ unterbrechen p. 63, 11
(to) **interview** /ˈɪntəˌvjuː/ interviewen, befragen NHG 5
into /ˈɪntuː/ in NHG 5
(to) **introduce** /ˌɪntrəˈdjuːs/ einführen; vorstellen NHG 5
introduction /ˌɪntrəˈdʌkʃn/ Einleitung NHG 5
(to) **invent** /ɪnˈvent/ erfinden p. 81, 2
invention /ɪnˈvenʃn/ Erfindung p. 85, 10
inventor /ɪnˈventə/ Erfinder/in p. 85, 10
invitation /ˌɪnvɪˈteɪʃn/ Einladung NHG 5
(to) **invite** /ɪnˈvaɪt/ einladen NHG 5
Ireland /ˈaɪələnd/ Irland p. 36, 6
Irish /ˈaɪrɪʃ/ irisch p. 36, 6
irregular /ɪˈregjʊlə/ unregelmäßig p. 106, 5
it /ɪt/ es NHG 5
it's (= it is) /ɪts, ˈɪt‿ɪz/ es ist, es kostet NHG 5
Italian /ɪˈtæljən/ Italiener/in; italienisch p. 10, 3
Italy /ˈɪtəli/ Italien NHG 5
its /ɪts/ sein(e), ihr(e) *(sächlich)* NHG 5

J

jack-o'-lantern /ˌdʒæk‿ə ˈlæntən/ Kürbislaterne p. 36, 6
jacket /ˈdʒækɪt/ Jacke p. 69, 6
jacket potato (*pl* jacket potatoes) /ˌdʒækɪt pəˈteɪtəʊ, ˌdʒækɪt pəˈteɪtəʊz/ Folienkartoffel p. 45, 6
January /ˈdʒænjuəri/ Januar NHG 5
jewellery *(no pl)* /ˈdʒuːəlri/ Schmuck p. 59, 6
Jewish /ˈdʒuːɪʃ/ jüdisch p. 33, 1
job /dʒɒb/ Aufgabe; Beruf p. 70, 7
(to) **join** /dʒɔɪn/ mitmachen (bei) NHG 5
(to) join /dʒɔɪn/ sich zu jemandem gesellen p. 100
(to) **join in** /ˌdʒɔɪn‿ˈɪn/ sich beteiligen an; mitmachen bei p. 42, 1
journey /ˈdʒɜːni/ Reise; Fahrt p. 22, 5
(to) juggle /ˈdʒʌgl/ jonglieren p. 101
juice /dʒuːs/ Saft NHG 5
July /dʒʊˈlaɪ/ Juli NHG 5
(to) **jump** /dʒʌmp/ springen NHG 5
June /dʒuːn/ Juni NHG 5
just /dʒʌst/ nur; bloß NHG 5; einfach; wirklich p. 8, 1; gerade p. 105, 3
just /dʒʌst/ erst p. 30
just now /ˈdʒʌst naʊ/ gerade eben p. 126

K

(to) **keep** *(irr)* /kiːp/ halten; behalten; aufbewahren NHG 5
(to) keep *(irr)* /kiːp/ bleiben p. 100
kg (= kilogram) /ˈkɪləˌgræm/ Kilogramm p. 111, 12
(to) **kick** /kɪk/ treten NHG 5
kid /kɪd/ Kind NHG 5
kind /kaɪnd/ Art; Sorte NHG 5
all kinds of /ˌɔːl ˈkaɪndz‿əv/ alle möglichen p. 38, 7
king /kɪŋ/ König p. 19, 1
(to) kiss /kɪs/ küssen p. 78
kit /kɪt/ Ausrüstung p. 28
dragon-taming kit /ˈdrægənˌteɪmɪŋ kɪt/ *Drachenzähm-Ausrüstung* p. 100
kitchen /ˈkɪtʃən/ Küche NHG 5
knee /niː/ Knie p. 58, 5
knife (*pl* **knives**) /naɪf, naɪvz/ Messer NHG 5
(to) **knock** /nɒk/ klopfen p. 56, 1
(to) **know** *(irr)* /nəʊ/ wissen; kennen NHG 5
I don't know. /ˌaɪ ˌdəʊnt ˈnəʊ/ Ich weiß es nicht. NHG 5

L

lab (= laboratory) /læb, ləˈbɒrətri/ Labor p. 44, 3
(to) **label** /ˈleɪbl/ beschriften NHG 5
ladder /ˈlædə/ Leiter p. 52
lake /leɪk/ See NHG 5
lamp /læmp/ Lampe p. 111, 12
(to) land /lænd/ landen p. 53
language /ˈlæŋgwɪdʒ/ Sprache NHG 5
lantern /ˈlæntən/ Laterne p. 33, 1
large /lɑːdʒ/ groß p. 19, 1
last /lɑːst/ letzte(r, s) NHG 5
(to) **last** /lɑːst/ (an)dauern p. 33, 1
late /leɪt/ (zu) spät NHG 5
later /ˈleɪtə/ später NHG 5
(to) **laugh** /lɑːf/ lachen p. 92, 2
laughter /ˈlɑːftə/ Gelächter; Lachen p. 120, 12
lazy /ˈleɪzi/ faul p. 9, 2

lead /liːd/ Leine p. 66, 1
leader /ˈliːdə/ Leiter/in p. 117, 8
leaf (*pl* **leaves**) /liːf, liːvz/ Blatt p. 70, 7
(to) **learn** *(irr)* /lɜːn/ lernen p. 8, 1
(to) **leave** *(irr)* /liːv/ weggehen NHG 5; verlassen, abfahren p. 9, 2; (übrig) lassen; zurücklassen p. 46, 7; hinterlassen p. 80, 2
LED candle /ˌel‿iː ˌdiː ˈkændl/ LED-Kerze p. 39, 9
left /left/ links, nach links p. 22, 6
left /left/ übrig p. 129
on the left /ˌɒn ðə ˈleft/ links, auf der linken Seite NHG 5
on your left /ˌɒn jɔː ˈleft/ links, auf deiner linken Seite p. 128
leg /leg/ Bein p. 20, 2
lemon /ˈlemən/ Zitrone NHG 5
lemonade /ˌleməˈneɪd/ Limonade p. 50, 15
less /les/ weniger p. 23, 8
lesson /ˈlesn/ Stunde; Unterricht NHG 5
(to) **let** *(irr)* /let/ lassen NHG 5
let's (= let us) /lets, ˈlet‿əs/ lass(t) uns ... NHG 5
letter /ˈletə/ Buchstabe NHG 5; Brief p. 69, 6
silent letter /ˌsaɪlənt ˈletə/ stummer Laut p. 58, 5
level /ˈlevl/ Stufe; Level NHG 5
library /ˈlaɪbrəri/ Bücherei NHG 5
(to) lie down *(irr)* /ˌlaɪ ˈdaʊn/ sich hinlegen p. 53
life (*pl* **lives**) /laɪf, laɪvz/ Leben NHG 5
in his lifetime /ˌɪn hɪz ˈlaɪfˌtaɪm/ im Laufe seines Lebens p. 127
lift /lɪft/ Aufzug p. 19, 1
light /laɪt/ Licht NHG 5
(to) **light** *(irr)* /laɪt/ anzünden p. 33, 1
(to) light up *(irr)* /ˌlaɪt‿ˈʌp/ aufleuchten p. 90, 1
lighting /ˈlaɪtɪŋ/ Beleuchtung p. 115, 2
like /laɪk/ wie NHG 5
(to) **like** /laɪk/ mögen NHG 5
I would like ... (= I'd like ...) /aɪ ˌwʊd ˈlaɪk, aɪd ˈlaɪk/ Ich würde gern ... / Ich hätte gern ... NHG 5
What was that like? /ˌwɒt wɒz ðæt ˈlaɪk/ Wie war das? p. 12, 6
(to) **like best** /ˌlaɪk ˈbest/ am liebsten mögen NHG 5
(to) **like doing something** /laɪk ˈduːɪŋ ˌsʌmθɪŋ/ etwas gern tun p. 8, 1
like that /ˌlaɪk ˈðæt/ so p. 78
line /laɪn/ Linie; Zeile NHG 5
(to) change lines /ˌtʃeɪndʒ ˈlaɪnz/ umsteigen p. 162
linking word /ˈlɪŋkɪŋ wɜːd/ Verbindungswort p. 98, 12
list /lɪst/ Liste; auflisten NHG 5
(to) **listen** (to) /ˈlɪsn/ zuhören, anhören NHG 5
listening /ˈlɪsnɪŋ/ Hören p. 21, 4
little /ˈlɪtl/ klein NHG 5
a little /ə ˈlɪtl/ ein bisschen p. 46, 7
(to) **live** /lɪv/ leben; wohnen NHG 5
living room /ˈlɪvɪŋ ˌruːm/ Wohnzimmer NHG 5
'll (= will) /l, wɪl/ werden p. 80, 2
(to) **load** /ləʊd/ laden NHG 5
lonely /ˈləʊnli/ einsam p. 119, 11
long /lɒŋ/ lang NHG 5
no longer /ˌnəʊ ˈlɒŋgə/ nicht mehr p. 30
(to) **look** /lʊk/ aussehen NHG 5
(to) **have a look at** /ˌhæv‿ə ˈlʊk‿ət/ sich ansehen p. 43, 2
(to) take a (closer) look at /ˌteɪk‿ə ˌkləʊsə ˈlʊk‿ət/ sich (genauer) ansehen p. 146
(to) **look after** /ˌlʊk‿ˈɑːftə/ sich kümmern um; aufpassen auf NHG 5
(to) look around /ˌlʊk‿əˈraʊnd/ sich umsehen p. 76
(to) **look (at)** /ˈlʊk‿ət/ (an)sehen, (an)schauen NHG 5
(to) **look for** /ˈlʊk fə/ suchen nach NHG 5
(to) **look forward to** /ˌlʊk ˈfɔːwəd‿tʊ/ sich freuen auf p. 69, 6
(to) look out /ˌlʊk‿ˈaʊt/ hinausschauen p. 126
(to) look up /ˌlʊk‿ˈʌp/ nach oben sehen, aufschauen p. 48, 10; hochschauen p. 77
(to) be lost *(irr)* /ˌbi ˈlɒst/ verloren sein p. 102
(to) get lost *(irr)* /ˌget ˈlɒst/ sich verirren p. 14, 9
a lot /ə ˈlɒt/ viel, sehr NHG 5
thanks a lot /ˌθæŋks‿ə ˈlɒt/ vielen Dank NHG 5
a lot (of) /ə ˈlɒt/ viel(e), jede Menge NHG 5
lots /lɒts/ viel, jede Menge p. 52
lots of /ˈlɒts‿əv/ viel(e) NHG 5
loud /laʊd/ laut NHG 5
loudly /ˈlaʊdli/ laut p. 76
love /lʌv/ lieben, sehr mögen NHG 5; viele Grüße; alles Liebe *(in Briefen)* p. 45, 6
(to) **love doing something** /lʌv ˈduːɪŋ ˌsʌmθɪŋ/ etwas sehr gern tun NHG 5
lover /ˈlʌvə/ Liebhaber/in p. 146
lower /ˈləʊə/ niedriger p. 76
(good) luck /lʌk/ Glück p. 35, 4
Good luck! /ˌgʊd ˈlʌk/ Viel Glück! p. 28
lunch /lʌntʃ/ Mittagessen NHG 5
lunchtime /ˈlʌntʃtaɪm/ Mittagszeit; Mittagspause p. 56, 1

M

machine /məˈʃiːn/ Maschine; Apparat p. 96, 9
magical /ˈmædʒɪkl/ magisch p. 24, 9
magnifying glass /ˈmægnɪfaɪɪŋ glɑːs/ Lupe p. 127
main /meɪn/ Haupt- NHG 5
(to) **make** *(irr)* /meɪk/ machen NHG 5
(to) **make friends (with)** *(irr)* /ˌmeɪk ˈfrendz/ sich anfreunden (mit) p. 8, 1
(to) **make notes** *(irr)* /ˌmeɪk ˈnəʊts/ sich Notizen machen NHG 5
(to) **make sure** *(irr)* /ˌmeɪk ˈʃɔː/ darauf achten, dass ... p. 39, 9
(to) **make up** *(irr)* /ˌmeɪk‿ˈʌp/ erfinden, sich ausdenken p. 110, 11
man (*pl* **men**) /mæn, men/ Mann NHG 5
adverb of manner /ˌædvɜːb‿əv ˈmænə/ Adverb der Art und Weise p. 92
many /ˈmeni/ viele NHG 5
map /mæp/ Karte NHG 5

marble /ˈmɑːbl/ Murmel p. 100
March /mɑːtʃ/ März NHG 5
mark /mɑːk/ Note; Zensur p. 57, 1
market /ˈmɑːkɪt/ Markt NHG 5
(to) **be married** /ˌbiː ˈmærid/ verheiratet sein p. 82, 4
mashed potatoes *(pl)* /ˌmæʃt pəˈteɪtəʊz/ Kartoffelbrei p. 54
masterpiece /ˈmɑːstəˌpiːs/ Meisterwerk p. 111, 12
match /mætʃ/ Spiel NHG 5; passen zu p. 122, 15
(to) **match (with/to)** /mætʃ/ zuordnen NHG 5
mate *(informal)* /meɪt/ Kumpel p. 81, 2
maths *(informal)* /mæθ/ Mathe *(Schulfach)* NHG 5
may /meɪ/ können; dürfen p. 43, 2
May /meɪ/ Mai NHG 5
maybe /ˈmeɪbi/ vielleicht NHG 5
me, to me /miː/ mir; mich; ich NHG 5
meal /miːl/ Mahlzeit; Essen NHG 5
(to) **mean** *(irr)* /miːn/ meinen; bedeuten p. 38, 7
mechanic /mɪˈkænɪk/ Mechaniker/in p. 83, 6
mediation /ˌmiːdiˈeɪʃn/ Mediation; Sprachmittlung p. 15, 10
medical school /ˈmedɪkl skuːl/ medizinische Fakultät p. 127
medicine /ˈmedsn/ Medizin p. 127
(to) **meet** *(irr)* /miːt/ treffen; sich treffen NHG 5; kennenlernen p. 14, 9
Nice to meet you. /ˌnaɪs tə ˈmiːt jə/ Schön, dich / euch / Sie zu treffen. NHG 5
meeting /ˈmiːtɪŋ/ Versammlung; Treffen p. 62, 10
melody /ˈmelədi/ Melodie p. 15, 11
(to) melt /melt/ schmelzen p. 46, 7
member /ˈmembə/ Mitglied NHG 5
menu /ˈmenjuː/ Speisekarte; Menü NHG 5
message /ˈmesɪdʒ/ Nachricht; Botschaft NHG 5
message in a bottle /ˌmesɪdʒ‿ɪn‿ə ˈbɒtl/ Flaschenpost p. 30
method /ˈmeθəd/ Methode p. 127
metre /ˈmiːtə/ Meter p. 22, 5

microscope /ˈmaɪkrəˌskəʊp/ Mikroskop p. 104, 2
middle /ˈmɪdl/ Mitte NHG 5
midnight /ˈmɪdˌnaɪt/ Mitternacht p. 35, 4
might /maɪt/ könnte(st,n,t) p. 14, 9
mile /maɪl/ Meile p. 14, 9
milk /mɪlk/ Milch NHG 5
(to) milk /mɪlk/ melken p. 9, 2
milkshake /ˈmɪlkˌʃeɪk/ Milchshake p. 9, 2
(to) **change one's mind** /ˌtʃeɪndʒ wʌnz ˈmaɪnd/ seine Meinung ändern p. 9, 2
(to) **miss** /mɪs/ vermissen; verpassen NHG 5
missing /ˈmɪsɪŋ/ fehlend NHG 5
mission /ˈmɪʃn/ Einsatz p. 28
mistake /mɪˈsteɪk/ Fehler p. 147
(to) **mix** /mɪks/ sich (ver)mischen p. 36, 6
ml (= millilitre) /ˈmɪlɪˌliːtə/ Milliliter p. 46, 7
mobile (phone) /ˈməʊbaɪl/ Handy p. 22, 5
modal verb /ˈməʊdl vɜːb/ Modalverb p. 58
model /ˈmɒdl/ Modell p. 19, 1
Monday /ˈmʌndeɪ/ Montag NHG 5
(on) Mondays /ˈmʌndeɪz/ montags NHG 5
money /ˈmʌni/ Geld NHG 5
month /mʌnθ/ Monat NHG 5
mood /muːd/ Laune; Stimmung p. 122, 16
moon /muːn/ Mond NHG 5
more /mɔː/ mehr; weitere NHG 5
more interesting /ˌmɔːr‿ˈɪntrəstɪŋ/ interessanter p. 16, 13
morning /ˈmɔːnɪŋ/ Morgen NHG 5
mosque /mɒsk/ Moschee p. 33, 1
most /məʊst/ die / am meisten p. 77
mother /ˈmʌðə/ Mutter NHG 5
mountain /ˈmaʊntɪn/ Berg NHG 5
mountaintop /ˈmaʊntɪnˌtɒp/ Berggipfel p. 8, 1
mouse (*pl* mice) /maʊs, maɪs/ Maus p. 141
mouth /maʊθ/ Mund p. 100
move /muːv/ Bewegung NHG 5
(to) **move** /muːv/ umziehen p. 11, 5

(to) move /muːv/ (sich) bewegen p. 77
(to) move in /ˌmuːv‿ˈɪn/ einziehen p. 26, 13
(to) move out /ˌmuːv‿ˈaʊt/ ausziehen p. 117, 7
(to) move over /ˌmuːv‿ˈəʊvə/ aufrücken p. 53
(to) **move something** /ˈmuːv ˌsʌmθɪŋ/ etwas wegräumen, woanders hinstellen p. 11, 5
movement /ˈmuːvmənt/ Bewegung p. 76
moving /ˈmuːvɪŋ/ beweglich p. 19, 1
Mr /ˈmɪstə/ Herr *(Anrede)* NHG 5
Mrs /ˈmɪsɪz/ Frau *(Anrede)* NHG 5
much /mʌtʃ/ viel NHG 5
mum /mʌm/ Mama; Mutti NHG 5
mummy /ˈmʌmi/ Mumie p. 38, 7
music /ˈmjuːzɪk/ Musik NHG 5
musical /ˈmjuːzɪkl/ musikalisch p. 111, 12
musician /mjʊˈzɪʃn/ Musiker/in p. 24, 9
Muslim /ˈmʊzləm/ Muslim/in; muslimisch p. 33, 1
must /mʌst/ müssen p. 56, 1
must /mʌst/ Muss p. 24, 9
mustn't (= must not) /ˈmʌsnt, mʌst ˈnɒt/ nicht dürfen p. 56, 1
my /maɪ/ mein(e) NHG 5

N

nail /neɪl/ Nagel p. 70, 7
(to) **name** /neɪm/ (be)nennen NHG 5
national park /ˌnæʃnl ˈpɑːk/ Nationalpark p. 67, 1
the Natural History Museum /ðə ˌnætʃərəl ˈhɪstəri mjuːˌziːəm/ Naturkundemuseum p. 19, 1
nature /ˈneɪtʃə/ Natur NHG 5
near /nɪə/ nahe, in der Nähe von NHG 5
nearby /ˌnɪəˈbaɪ/ in der Nähe (gelegen) p. 125
necessary /ˈnesəsri/ notwendig, erforderlich NHG 5
(to) **need** /niːd/ brauchen NHG 5
(to) **need to** /ˈniːd‿tʊ/ müssen NHG 5

negative /ˈnegətɪv/ negativ p. 10, 3
neighbor *(AE)* (= neighbour *(BE)*) /ˈneɪbə/ Nachbar/in p. 54
neighbourhood /ˈneɪbəˌhʊd/ Viertel; Nachbarschaft NHG 5
nervous /ˈnɜːvəs/ nervös NHG 5
net /net/ Netz NHG 5
the Netherlands /ðə ˈneðələndz/ die Niederlande p. 30
never /ˈnevə/ nie, niemals NHG 5
new /njuː/ neu NHG 5
New Year /ˌnjuː ˈjɪə/ Neujahr p. 33, 1
New Year's Eve /ˌnjuː jɪəz‿ˈiːv/ Silvester p. 35, 4
New Zealand /ˌnju ˈziːlənd/ Neuseeland p. 28
news *(no pl)* /njuːz/ Neuigkeit; Nachrichten p. 126
newspaper /ˈnjuːzˌpeɪpə/ Zeitung p. 107, 6
next /nekst/ nächste(r, s) NHG 5; dann, als Nächstes p. 91, 1
next to /ˈnekst‿tə/ neben NHG 5
nice /naɪs/ schön; nett NHG 5
nice /naɪs/ *hier:* lecker p. 16, 12
Nice to meet you. /ˌnaɪs tə ˈmiːt jə/ Schön, dich / euch / Sie zu treffen. NHG 5
night /naɪt/ Nacht; Abend p. 33, 1
at night /æt ˈnaɪt/ nachts p. 144
no /nəʊ/ kein(e); nein NHG 5
no longer /ˌnəʊ ˈlɒŋgə/ nicht mehr p. 30
no more /ˌnəʊ ˈmɔː/ nicht mehr p. 95, 5
no one /ˈnəʊ wʌn/ keiner p. 117, 7
(to) nod /nɒd/ nicken p. 53
noise /nɔɪz/ Geräusch, Lärm p. 98, 13
noisy /ˈnɔɪzi/ laut p. 48, 11
Norman /ˈnɔːmən/ Normanne / Normannin p. 12, 6
North America /ˌnɔːθ‿əˈmerɪkə/ Nordamerika p. 129
North Island /ˈnɔːθ‿ˌaɪlənd/ Nordinsel p. 28
northern /ˈnɔːðən/ nördlich, Nord- p. 36, 6
Northern Ireland /ˌnɔːðən‿ˈaɪələnd/ Nordirland p. 146
nose /nəʊz/ Nase NHG 5
not /nɒt/ nicht NHG 5
not any /ˌnɒt‿ˈeni/ kein(e) NHG 5
not anymore /ˌnɒt‿ˌeni ˈmɔː/ nicht mehr p. 63, 11
not anything /ˌnɒt‿ˈeniˌθɪŋ/ nichts p. 34, 2
not anywhere /ˌnɒt‿ˈeniˌweə/ nirgendwo p. 9, 2
not yet /ˌnɒt ˈjet/ noch nicht p. 45, 6
note /nəʊt/ Nachricht; Notiz NHG 5; beachten, zur Kenntnis nehmen p. 66, 1
notepad /ˈnəʊtˌpæd/ Notizblock NHG 5
(to) **make notes** *(irr)* /ˌmeɪk ˈnəʊts/ sich Notizen machen NHG 5
nothing /ˈnʌθɪŋ/ nichts p. 67, 1
(to) **notice** /ˈnəʊtɪs/ bemerken; wahrnehmen p. 74, 13
noticeboard /ˈnəʊtɪsˌbɔːd/ Schwarzes Brett NHG 5
noun /naʊn/ Hauptwort; Substantiv; Nomen NHG 5
novel /ˈnɒvl/ Roman p. 127
November /nəʊˈvembə/ November NHG 5
now /naʊ/ jetzt NHG 5
number /ˈnʌmbə/ Zahl; Nummer; Anzahl NHG 5
phone number /ˈfəʊn ˌnʌmbə/ Telefonnummer NHG 5
nurse /nɜːs/ Krankenschwester; Krankenpfleger p. 83, 6
nut /nʌt/ Nuss p. 73, 10

O

o'clock /əˈklɒk/ Uhr *(bei Nennung einer Uhrzeit)* NHG 5
object /ˈɒbdʒekt/ Gegenstand, Objekt p. 94, 5
obviously /ˈɒbviəsli/ offensichtlich p. 95, 5
October /ɒkˈtəʊbə/ Oktober NHG 5
odd one out /ˌɒd wʌn‿ˈaʊt/ *Wort, das nicht zu den anderen passt* p. 88, 16
of /əv/ von; aus NHG 5
Of course! /əv ˈkɔːs/ Natürlich! NHG 5
off /ɒf/ von; hinunter, herunter p. 74, 12
(to) **offer** /ˈɒfə/ anbieten p. 36, 6
office /ˈɒfɪs/ Büro NHG 5
official /əˈfɪʃl/ offiziell p. 146
often /ˈɒfn/ oft; häufig NHG 5
oh dear *(informal)* /əʊ ˈdɪə/ oje p. 94, 5
old /əʊld/ alt NHG 5
on /ɒn/ auf; an; in NHG 5
on one's own /ˌɒn ˌwʌnz‿ˈəʊn/ allein NHG 5
on the left /ˌɒn ðə ˈleft/ links, auf der linken Seite NHG 5
on the right /ˌɒn ðə ˈraɪt/ rechts, auf der rechten Seite NHG 5
on time /ˌɒn ˈtaɪm/ pünktlich NHG 5
on your left /ˌɒn jɔː ˈleft/ links, auf deiner linken Seite p. 128
on your right /ˌɒn jɔː ˈraɪt/ rechts, auf deiner rechten Seite p. 128
one /wʌn/ ein(e); eins NHG 5
the other one /ði‿ˈʌðə wʌn/ der/die/das andere p. 39, 8
the ones /ðə ˈwʌnz/ diejenigen; diese p. 67, 2
the grey ones /ðə ˈgreɪ wʌnz/ die grauen p. 135
only /ˈəʊnli/ nur, bloß; erst; einzige(r, s) NHG 5
onto /ˈɒntə/ auf, in p. 22, 6
open /ˈəʊpən/ offen; geöffnet NHG 5
(to) **open** /ˈəʊpən/ öffnen; aufmachen NHG 5; sich öffnen, aufgehen p. 94, 5; eröffnen p. 112, 13
open-air /ˌəʊpən‿ˈeə/ im Freien p. 12, 6
opening /ˈəʊpnɪŋ/ Öffnung; Eröffnung p. 80, 1
opening times *(pl)* /ˈəʊpənɪŋ taɪmz/ Öffnungszeiten p. 24, 9
opinion /əˈpɪnjən/ Meinung; Ansicht p. 17, 14
in my opinion /ɪn ˈmaɪ‿əˌpɪnjən/ meiner Meinung nach p. 57, 2
opposite /ˈɒpəzɪt/ Gegenteil NHG 5
or /ɔː/ oder NHG 5
orange /ˈɒrɪndʒ/ Orange; Apfelsine; orange NHG 5
order /ˈɔːdə/ Reihenfolge, Ordnung p. 46, 7
(to) **organize (= organise)** /ˈɔːgənaɪz/ organisieren p. 17, 14
original /əˈrɪdʒnəl/ ursprünglich p. 127
other /ˈʌðə/ andere(r, s) NHG 5

the other one /ðiˌˈʌðə wʌn/ der/die/das andere p. 39, 8
our /aʊə/ unser(e) NHG 5
out /aʊt/ heraus, hinaus; aus NHG 5; draußen p. 43, 2
out and about /ˌaʊtˌənˌəˈbaʊt/ unterwegs p. 103
out of /ˈaʊtˌəv/ aus p. 38, 7
outdoor /ˌaʊtˈdɔː/ draußen; im Freien p. 8, 1
outside /ˌaʊtˈsaɪd/ außen; (nach) draußen NHG 5
outside /ˌaʊtˈsaɪd/ vor, außerhalb p. 100
over /ˈəʊvə/ über, hinüber; vorbei NHG 5
all over the world /ˌɔːlˌˌəʊvə ðə ˈwɜːld/ auf der ganzen Welt p. 33, 1
over there /ˌəʊvə ˈðeə/ dort (drüben) NHG 5
overnight /ˌəʊvəˈnaɪt/ über Nacht p. 74, 12
overstuffed /ˌəʊvəˈstʌft/ *zu prall ausgestopft* p. 108, 7
own /əʊn/ eigene(r, s) NHG 5
on one's own /ˌɒn ˌwʌnzˌˈəʊn/ allein NHG 5
owner /ˈəʊnə/ Besitzer/in p. 94, 5

P

p. (= page) /peɪdʒ/ Seite p. 8, 1
p (= penny, *pl* pence) /piː, ˈpeni, pens/ Penny *(brit. Währung)* NHG 5
(to) **pack** /pæk/ packen NHG 5
packed lunch /ˌpækt ˈlʌntʃ/ Lunchpaket p. 69, 6
packet /ˈpækɪt/ Packung NHG 5
page /peɪdʒ/ Seite NHG 5
(to) **paint** /peɪnt/ (an)malen NHG 5
painted /ˈpeɪntɪd/ bemalt, farbig p. 111, 12
painting /ˈpeɪntɪŋ/ Bild; Gemälde NHG 5
painting /ˈpeɪntɪŋ/ Anmalen p. 42, 1
pair /peə/ Paar p. 104, 2
(a pair of) trousers /ə ˌpeərˌəv ˈtraʊzəz/ Hose NHG 5
palace /ˈpæləs/ Palast p. 19, 1
paper /ˈpeɪpə/ Papier p. 94, 5
baking paper /ˈbeɪkɪŋ ˌpeɪpə/ Backpapier p. 46, 7
paragraph /ˈpærəˌgrɑːf/ Absatz; Abschnitt p. 95, 5
parents *(pl)* /ˈpeərənts/ Eltern NHG 5
parking /ˈpɑːkɪŋ/ Parken p. 66, 1
parliament /ˈpɑːləmənt/ Parlament p. 19, 1
part /pɑːt/ Teil NHG 5
(to) **pass** /pɑːs/ geben, herüberreichen NHG 5
past /pɑːst/ nach; Vergangenheit NHG 5; vorbei; vorüber p. 22, 6
past participle /ˌpɑːst ˈpɑːtɪsɪpl/ Partizip Perfekt p. 106
path /pɑːθ/ Weg; Pfad p. 66, 1
(to) **pay *(irr)*** /peɪ/ (be)zahlen NHG 5
(to) **pay attention (to) *(irr)*** /ˌpeɪˌəˈtenʃn tʊ/ aufpassen; achten auf p. 20, 3
payment /ˈpeɪmənt/ Bezahlung p. 69, 6
PE (= Physical Education) /ˌpiˌˈiː, ˌfɪzɪklˌedjʊˈkeɪʃn/ Sport *(Schulfach)* NHG 5
pen /pen/ Stift NHG 5
pencil /ˈpensl/ Bleistift NHG 5
pencil case /ˈpensl ˌkeɪs/ Federmäppchen NHG 5
pencil sharpener /ˈpensl ˌʃɑːpnə/ Bleistiftspitzer NHG 5
people /ˈpiːpl/ Leute; Menschen NHG 5
per /pɜː/ pro NHG 5
perfect /ˈpɜːfɪkt/ perfekt NHG 5
(to) **perform** /pəˈfɔːm/ aufführen; durchführen p. 114, 1
performance /pəˈfɔːməns/ Aufführung; Leistung p. 115, 2
perhaps /pəˈhæps/ vielleicht p. 30
permission /pəˈmɪʃn/ Erlaubnis; Genehmigung p. 69, 6
personal /ˈpɜːsnəl/ persönlich NHG 5
pet /pet/ Haustier NHG 5
phew *(informal)* /fjuː/ puh p. 43, 2
phone /fəʊn/ Telefon NHG 5
phone number /ˈfəʊn ˌnʌmbə/ Telefonnummer NHG 5
photo /ˈfəʊtəʊ/ Foto NHG 5
(to) **take a photo** /ˌteɪkˌə ˈfəʊtəʊ/ ein Foto machen NHG 5
photograph /ˈfəʊtəˌgrɑːf/ Fotografie; Foto p. 67, 1
photographer /fəˈtɒgrəfə/ Fotograf/in p. 85, 9
phrase /freɪz/ Satz; Ausdruck NHG 5
piano /piˈænəʊ/ Klavier NHG 5
(to) **pick up** /ˌpɪkˌˈʌp/ aufheben; abholen NHG 5
picnic /ˈpɪknɪk/ Picknick p. 11, 5
picture /ˈpɪktʃə/ Bild NHG 5
(to) **take a picture** /ˌteɪkˌə ˈpɪktʃə/ ein Foto machen NHG 5
piece /piːs/ Stück; Teil p. 39, 9
piece of art /ˌpiːsˌəvˌˈɑːt/ Kunstwerk p. 104, 2
pillow /ˈpɪləʊ/ Kissen p. 78
pipe /paɪp/ Pfeife p. 104, 2
place /pleɪs/ Ort; Platz; Haus, Zuhause; platzieren; stellen NHG 5
(to) **take place *(irr)*** /ˌteɪk ˈpleɪs/ stattfinden p. 33, 1
placemat /ˈpleɪsmæt/ Platzdeckchen *(Methode)* p. 51, 16
(to) **plan** /plæn/ planen NHG 5
plane /pleɪn/ Flugzeug p. 8, 1
plant /plɑːnt/ Pflanze p. 71, 7
plastic /ˈplæstɪk/ Plastik p. 87, 14
plate /pleɪt/ Teller NHG 5
platform /ˈplætˌfɔːm/ Bahnsteig; Plattform p. 22, 5
(to) **play** /pleɪ/ spielen NHG 5
play /pleɪ/ Spiel; (Theater)stück p. 103
(to) play a stage /ˌpleɪˌə ˈsteɪdʒ/ auf einer Bühne spielen p. 81, 2
(to) play a trick on somebody /ˌpleɪˌə ˈtrɪkˌɒn ˌsʌmbədi/ jemandem einen Streich spielen p. 38, 7
player /ˈpleɪə/ Spieler/in NHG 5
playground /ˈpleɪˌgraʊnd/ Spielplatz NHG 5
playing /ˈpleɪɪŋ/ Spielen NHG 5
playzone /ˈpleɪˌzəʊn/ *Spielbereich* p. 108, 7
please /pliːz/ bitte NHG 5
plot /plɒt/ Verschwörung p. 48, 10
pm (= post meridiem) /ˌpiːˈem, ˌpəʊst məˈrɪdiəm/ nachmittags; abends *(hinter Uhrzeit zw. 12 Uhr mittags und Mitternacht)* NHG 5
pocket /ˈpɒkɪt/ (Hosen)tasche p. 77
poem /ˈpəʊɪm/ Gedicht NHG 5

point /pɔɪnt/ Punkt NHG 5
(to) **point (at/to)** /pɔɪnt/ deuten (auf); zeigen (auf) NHG 5
information point /ˌɪnfəˈmeɪʃn pɔɪnt/ Informationsstelle p. 66, 1
Poland /ˈpəʊlənd/ Polen NHG 5
police officer /pəˈliːs‿ˌɒfɪsə/ Polizeibeamter / Polizeibeamtin p. 83, 6
polite /pəˈlaɪt/ höflich p. 17, 14
politely /pəˈlaɪtli/ höflich p. 90, 1
(to) pollinate /ˈpɒləneɪt/ bestäuben p. 71, 7
poor /pɔː/ arm p. 120, 12
popular /ˈpɒpjʊlə/ beliebt p. 19, 1
population /ˌpɒpjʊˈleɪʃn/ Bevölkerung p. 147
positive /ˈpɒzətɪv/ positiv p. 10, 3
possibility /ˌpɒsəˈbɪləti/ Möglichkeit p. 26, 12
possibly /ˈpɒsəbli/ möglicherweise; vielleicht p. 53
(to) **post** /pəʊst/ posten p. 14, 9
postcard /ˈpəʊstˌkɑːd/ Postkarte; Ansichtskarte NHG 5
pot /pɒt/ Topf p. 28
yoghurt pot /ˈjɒgət pɒt/ Joghurtbecher p. 73, 10
pound (= £) /paʊnd/ Pfund *(britische Währung)* NHG 5
practice /ˈpræktɪs/ Übung; Training p. 114, 1
(to) **practise** /ˈpræktɪs/ üben; trainieren NHG 5
prayer /preə/ Gebet p. 33, 1
prediction /prɪˈdɪkʃn/ Vorhersage; Prophezeiung p. 87, 13
(to) **prepare** /prɪˈpeə/ vorbereiten NHG 5
present /ˈpreznt/ Geschenk NHG 5; Gegenwart p. 24, 9
present perfect /ˌpreznt ˈpɜːfɪkt/ Perfekt p. 106
present progressive /ˌpreznt prəʊˈgresɪv/ Verlaufsform der Gegenwart p. 44
(to) **present (to)** /prɪˈzent/ präsentieren, vorstellen NHG 5
presentation /ˌpreznˈteɪʃn/ Präsentation; Vortrag NHG 5
(to) give a presentation /ˌgɪv‿ə ˌpreznˈteɪʃn/ eine Präsentation halten p. 147
(to) press /pres/ drücken p. 77
pretty /ˈprɪti/ ziemlich NHG 5
pro /prəʊ/ Vorteil; Pro p. 39, 7
probably /ˈprɒbəbli/ wahrscheinlich p. 36, 6
(to) **produce** /prəˈdjuːs/ herstellen p. 70, 7
product /ˈprɒdʌkt/ Produkt p. 147
professional /prəˈfeʃnəl/ beruflich; professionell p. 114, 1
profile /ˈprəʊfaɪl/ Profil; Porträt p. 146
programme /ˈprəʊgræm/ Programm p. 114, 1
project /ˈprɒdʒekt/ Projekt p. 71, 7
(to) **pronounce** /prəˈnaʊns/ aussprechen p. 122, 15
prop /prɒp/ Requisite p. 115, 2
(to) **protect** /prəˈtekt/ beschützen p. 70, 7
proud, proudly /praʊd, ˈpraʊdli/ stolz p. 90, 1
(to) be proud of /ˌbiː ˈpraʊd‿əv/ stolz sein auf p. 91, 1
public /ˈpʌblɪk/ öffentlich p. 80, 1
the public /ðə ˈpʌblɪk/ die Öffentlichkeit p. 19, 1
(to) **publish** /ˈpʌblɪʃ/ veröffentlichen; herausgeben p. 17, 14
(to) pull /pʊl/ ziehen p. 76
pumpkin /ˈpʌmpkɪn/ Kürbis p. 38, 7
pumpkin pie /ˈpʌmpkɪn paɪ/ Kürbiskuchen p. 54
puppet /ˈpʌpɪt/ Marionette; (Hand)puppe p. 54
purple /ˈpɜːpl/ violett; lila NHG 5
(to) **push** /pʊʃ/ schieben; stoßen p. 46, 7
(to) **put** *(irr)* /pʊt/ setzen; stellen; legen NHG 5
(to) **put on display** *(irr)* /ˌpʊt‿ɒn dɪˈspleɪ/ ausstellen p. 112, 13
(to) **put together** *(irr)* /ˌpʊt‿təˈgeðə/ zusammenstellen; zusammensetzen p. 99, 14
(to) **put up** *(irr)* /ˌpʊt‿ˈʌp/ aufhängen; aufstellen p. 41, 12
pyjamas *(pl)* /pəˈdʒɑːməz/ Pyjama; Schlafanzug p. 78

Q

quantifier /ˈkwɒntɪˌfaɪə/ *hier:* Mengenangabe p. 50, 14
quarter /ˈkwɔːtə/ Viertel NHG 5
queen /kwiːn/ Königin p. 19, 1
question /ˈkwestʃn/ Frage NHG 5
(to) queue /kjuː/ Schlange stehen p. 43, 2
quick /kwɪk/ schnell p. 29
quickly /ˈkwɪkli/ schnell p. 96, 8
quiet /ˈkwaɪət/ leise; ruhig NHG 5
in a quiet voice /ˌɪn‿ə ˌkwaɪət ˈvɔɪs/ mit leiser Stimme p. 76
quietly /ˈkwaɪətli/ leise; ruhig p. 77
quite /kwaɪt/ ziemlich p. 43, 2

R

rabbit /ˈræbɪt/ Kaninchen NHG 5
racing driver /ˈreɪsɪŋ ˌdraɪvə/ Rennfahrer/in p. 85, 9
(to) **rain** /reɪn/ regnen NHG 5
rain /reɪn/ Regen p. 105, 3
rainy /ˈreɪni/ regnerisch NHG 5
rather /ˈrɑːðə/ eher, lieber p. 94, 5
rather than /ˈrɑːðə ðæn/ anstatt p. 81, 2
(to) rattle /ˈrætl ˈreɪvn/ klappern; rasseln p. 120, 12
raven /ˈreɪvn/ Rabe Land und Leute 1
RE (= Religious Education) /ˌɑːr‿ˈiː, reˌlɪdʒəs‿edjʊˈkeɪʃn/ Religion *(Schulfach)* NHG 5
(to) reach /riːtʃ/ erreichen p. 100
(to) **react (to)** /riˈækt/ reagieren (auf) p. 121, 12
reaction /riˈækʃn/ Reaktion p. 48, 9
(to) **read** *(irr)* /riːd/ lesen NHG 5
(to) **read along** *(irr)* /ˌriːd‿əˈlɒŋ/ mitlesen NHG 5
(to) read something to somebody *(irr)* /ˈriːd ˌsʌmθɪŋ tʊ ˌsʌmbədi/ jemandem etwas vorlesen p. 90, 1
reading /ˈriːdɪŋ/ Lesen NHG 5
dramatic reading /drəˌmætɪk ˈriːdɪŋ/ szenische Lesung p. 121, 12
ready /ˈredi/ fertig, bereit NHG 5
(to) get ready *(irr)* /ˌget ˈredi/ sich fertig machen, sich vorbereiten auf p. 53

real /rɪəl/ wirklich; echt p. 17, 14
(to) **realize (= realise)** /ˈrɪəlaɪz/ sich bewusst sein, erkennen p. 93, 4
really /ˈrɪəli/ wirklich NHG 5
reason /ˈriːzn/ Grund p. 48, 10
(to) receive /rɪˈsiːv/ erhalten; empfangen p. 30
recipe /ˈresəpi/ Rezept p. 45, 6
(to) **recommend** /ˌrekəˈmend/ empfehlen p. 17, 14
(to) **record** /riˈkɔːd/ aufnehmen NHG 5
record /ˈrekɔːd/ *hier:* Platte p. 102
recording /riˈkɔːdɪŋ/ Aufnahme NHG 5
red /red/ rot NHG 5
registration /ˌredʒɪˈstreɪʃn/ *Überprüfung der Anwesenheit* NHG 5
regular /ˈregjʊlə/ üblich, normal p. 81, 2
relative /ˈrelətɪv/ Verwandte/r p. 8, 1
(to) **relax** /rɪˈlæks/ entspannen NHG 5
relaxed /rɪˈlækst/ entspannt p. 60, 7
religious /rəˈlɪdʒəs/ religiöse(r,s) p. 33, 1
(to) **remember** /rɪˈmembə/ sich erinnern an NHG 5
(to) **remove** /rɪˈmuːv/ entfernen p. 46, 7
(to) renovate /ˈrenəveɪt/ renovieren p. 11, 5
(to) rent /rent/ mieten p. 14, 9
(to) **repair** /rɪˈpeə/ reparieren p. 83, 6
repairs *(pl)* /rɪˈpeə/ Reparaturarbeiten p. 102
(to) **repeat** /riˈpiːt/ wiederholen NHG 5
(to) **reply** /rɪˈplaɪ/ antworten; erwidern p. 95, 5
reply /rɪˈplaɪ/ Antwort p. 30
(to) **report** /rɪˈpɔːt/ sich melden p. 56, 1
(to) **do research** /ˌduː rɪˈsɜːtʃ/ recherchieren NHG 5
(to) **respect** /rɪˈspekt/ respektieren p. 17, 14
respect /rɪˈspekt/ Respekt p. 56, 1

(to) **return** /rɪˈtɜːn/ zurückgeben p. 69, 6
rhyme /raɪm/ Reim p. 48, 10
rhyming pair /ˈraɪmɪŋ peə/ Reimpaar p. 88, 17
rhyming word /ˈraɪmɪŋ wɜːd/ Reimwort p. 78
rice /raɪs/ Reis NHG 5
(to) **ride** *(irr)* /raɪd/ fahren; reiten NHG 5
(to) **ride a bike** *(irr)* /ˌraɪd‿ə ˈbaɪk/ Fahrrad fahren NHG 5
(to) **ride a horse** *(irr)* /ˌraɪd‿ə ˈhɔːs/ reiten NHG 5
(to) **go riding** *(irr)* /ˌgəʊ ˈraɪdɪŋ/ reiten gehen p. 9, 2
right /raɪt/ richtig NHG 5; (nach) rechts p. 22, 6; genau; direkt p. 104, 2
(to) **be right** *(irr)* /ˌbiː ˈraɪt/ recht haben NHG 5
on the right /ˌɒn ðə ˈraɪt/ rechts, auf der rechten Seite NHG 5
on your right /ˌɒn jɔː ˈraɪt/ rechts, auf deiner rechten Seite p. 128
right now /ˌraɪt ˈnaʊ/ jetzt; im Moment p. 43, 2
ringing /ˈrɪŋɪŋ/ Klingeln p. 77
river /ˈrɪvə/ Fluss p. 19, 1
road /rəʊd/ Straße NHG 5
(to) roast /rəʊst/ rösten, braten p. 49, 12
robot /ˈrəʊbɒt/ Roboter p. 87, 14
role /rəʊl/ Rolle p. 42, 1
role play /ˈrəʊl pleɪ/ Rollenspiel p. 65, 15
Roman /ˈrəʊmən/ Römer/in; römisch p. 12, 6
Rome /rəʊm/ Rom p. 10, 3
room /ruːm/ Platz; Raum; Zimmer NHG 5
round /raʊnd/ rund NHG 5; (um ...) herum p. 24, 9
all year round /ˌɔːl ˈjɪə raʊnd/ das ganze Jahr lang p. 66, 1
roundhouse /ˈraʊndˌhaʊs/ Rundhaus p. 12, 6
royal /ˈrɔɪəl/ königlich p. 19, 1
rubbish /ˈrʌbɪʃ/ Müll NHG 5
rule /ruːl/ Regel NHG 5;
(to) **rule** /ruːl/ herrschen, regieren p. 36, 6

ruler /ˈruːlə/ Lineal NHG 5
(to) **run** *(irr)* /rʌn/ laufen; rennen p. 56, 1
(to) run away *(irr)* /ˌrʌn‿əˈweɪ/ weglaufen p. 100
runner /ˈrʌnə/ Läufer/in p. 66, 1

S

sad /sæd/ traurig p. 60, 7
safe /seɪf/ sicher; ungefährlich p. 66, 1
Be safe! /ˌbiː ˈseɪf/ Sei vorsichtig! p. 28
safely /ˈseɪfli/ sicher; ungefährlich p. 126
safety /ˈseɪfti/ Sicherheit p. 47, 8
saint /seɪnt/ Heilige/r p. 36, 6
salt /sɔːlt/ Salz NHG 5
the same /ðə ˈseɪm/ der/die/das Gleiche; derselbe/dieselbe/dasselbe NHG 5
Saturday /ˈsætədeɪ/ Samstag NHG 5
(on) Saturdays /ˈsætədeɪz/ samstags NHG 5
sausage /ˈsɒsɪdʒ/ Wurst; Würstchen p. 49, 12
(to) save /seɪv/ *hier:* zurücklegen lassen p. 115, 2; retten p. 126
(to) **say** *(irr)* /seɪ/ sagen NHG 5
(to) say goodbye *(irr)* (to somebody) /ˌseɪ gʊdˈbaɪ tə ˌsʌmbədi/ sich von jemandem verabschieden p. 126
(to) scare /skeə/ erschrecken p. 28
(to) scare away /ˌskeər‿əˈweɪ/ verscheuchen p. 36, 6
scared /skeəd/ verängstigt, ängstlich p. 60, 7
(to) **be scared (of)** /ˌbiː ˈskeəd‿əv/ Angst haben (vor) NHG 5
scarf (*pl* scarfs *or* scarves) /skɑːf, skɑːfs, skɑːvz/ Schal p. 124
scary /ˈskeəri/ Furcht erregend p. 36, 6
scene /siːn/ Szene NHG 5
school /skuːl/ Schule NHG 5
school grounds *(pl)* /ˈskuːl ˌgraʊndz/ Schulgelände p. 56, 1
school trip /ˈskuːl ˌtrɪp/ Schulausflug p. 105, 3

schoolbag /ˈskuːlˌbæg/ Schultasche NHG 5
schoolgirl /ˈskuːlˌgɜːl/ Schülerin p. 30
science /ˈsaɪəns/ Naturwissenschaft NHG 5
the Science Museum /ðə ˈsaɪəns juːˌziːəm/ Naturwissenschaftsmuseum p. 106, 5
(a pair of) scissors /ˈsɪzəz/ Schere NHG 5
Scotland /ˈskɒtlənd/ Schottland NHG 5
Scottish /ˈskɒtɪʃ/ schottisch p. 35, 4
(to) scream /skriːm/ schreien p. 52
screen /skriːn/ Bildschirm p. 110, 11
script /skrɪpt/ Drehbuch; Skript p. 119, 11
(to) sculpt /skʌlpt/ modellieren p. 111, 12
search /sɜːtʃ/ Suche; suchen NHG 5
(to) **search the Internet** /ˌsɜːtʃ ðiˍˈɪntənet/ im Internet suchen NHG 5
search engine /ˈsɜːtʃˍˌendʒɪn/ Suchmaschine p. 27, 14
seashell /ˈsiːˌʃel/ Muschel p. 8, 1
seaside /ˈsiːˌsaɪd/ (Meeres)küste; Meer p. 8, 1
second /ˈsekənd/ Sekunde; zweite(r, s) NHG 5
secretly /ˈsiːkrətli/ heimlich p. 126
section /ˈsekʃn/ Teil; Stück; Abschnitt p. 39, 9
(to) **see** *(irr)* /siː/ sehen NHG 5
We'll see about that! /wiːl ˌsiːˍəˌbaʊt ˈðæt/ Das werden wir sehen. p. 81, 2
See you (soon)! /ˌsiː juː ˈsuːn/ Bis bald! p. 11, 5
self (*pl* selves) /ˈself, selvz/ Selbst; Ich p. 102
(to) take a selfie *(irr)* /ˌteɪkˍə ˈselfi/ ein Selfie machen p. 24, 9
(to) **send** *(irr)* /send/ schicken NHG 5
sentence /ˈsentəns/ Satz NHG 5
September /sepˈtembə/ September NHG 5
series *(only plural)* /ˈsɪəriːz/ Serie p. 127
session /ˈseʃn/ Stunde; Session NHG 5

(to) **set the table** /ˌset ðə ˈteɪbl/ den Tisch decken NHG 5
(to) shake *(irr)* /ʃeɪk/ beben p. 101
(What a) shame /ˌwɒtˍə ˈʃeɪm/ (Wie) schade! p. 54
(to) **share** /ʃeə/ teilen NHG 5
she /ʃiː/ sie NHG 5
sheet /ʃiːt/ Blatt; Bogen p. 46, 7
shelf (*pl* shelves) /ʃelf, ʃelvz/ Regal NHG 5
shell /ʃel/ Schale p. 77
(to) shine *(irr)* /ʃaɪn/ scheinen p. 90, 1
shirt /ʃɜːt/ Hemd NHG 5
shoe /ʃuː/ Schuh p. 59, 6
shop /ʃɒp/ Geschäft; Laden NHG 5
shop assistant /ˈʃɒpˍəˌsɪstnt/ Verkäufer/in p. 84, 8
shopping /ˈʃɒpɪŋ/ Einkaufen; Einkaufs- NHG 5
(to) **do the shopping** /ˌduː ðə ˈʃɒpɪŋ/ einkaufen NHG 5
(to) **go shopping** /ˌgəʊ ˈʃɒpɪŋ/ einkaufen gehen p. 87, 13
shopping centre /ˈʃɒpɪŋ ˌsentə/ Einkaufszentrum NHG 5
short /ʃɔːt/ kurz NHG 5
short story /ˌʃɔːt ˈstɔːri/ Kurzgeschichte p. 127
shortly /ˈʃɔːtli/ kurz p. 54
should /ʃʊd/ sollte(st,n,t) p. 46, 7
(to) shout /ʃaʊt/ rufen; schreien p. 29
(to) **shout at somebody** /ˈʃaʊtˍət ˌsʌmbədi/ jemanden anschreien p. 57, 1
(to) **show** *(irr)* /ʃəʊ/ zeigen NHG 5
sick /sɪk/ krank p. 93, 4
side /saɪd/ Seite p. 62, 10
sight /saɪt/ Sehenswürdigkeit NHG 5
sign /saɪn/ Zeichen; Schild p. 61, 9
(to) sign up /ˌsaɪnˍˈʌp/ sich anmelden p. 117, 8
silent letter /ˌsaɪlənt ˈletə/ stummer Laut p. 58, 5
silently /ˈsaɪləntli/ lautlos, schweigend p. 94, 5
silly /ˈsɪli/ albern; dumm p. 61, 9
similar /ˈsɪmɪlə/ ähnlich p. 85, 9
simple past /ˌsɪmpl ˈpɑːst/ einfache Vergangenheit p. 10
simple present /ˌsɪmpl ˈpreznt/ einfache Gegenwart p. 34

simply /ˈsɪmpli/ einfach p. 94, 5
since /sɪns/ seit p. 111, 12
(to) **sing** *(irr)* /sɪŋ/ singen NHG 5
(to) **sing along** *(irr)* /ˌsɪŋˍəˈlɒŋ/ mitsingen NHG 5
singer /ˈsɪŋə/ Sänger/in p. 81, 2
singing /ˈsɪŋɪŋ/ Singen; Gesang p. 115, 2; Gesangs- p. 130
single /ˈsɪŋgl/ einzelne(r,s) p. 90, 1
sir/Sir /sɜː/ Sir; Herr (*Anrede vor Vornamen*) p. 105, 3
sister /ˈsɪstə/ Schwester NHG 5
(to) **sit down** *(irr)* /ˌsɪtˍˈdaʊn/ sich hinsetzen NHG 5
size /saɪz/ Größe NHG 5
skateboarding /ˈskeɪtbɔːdɪŋ/ Skateboardfahren NHG 5
skeleton /ˈskelɪtn/ Skelett p. 19, 1
skewer /ˈskjuːə/ Spieß p. 46, 7
skill /skɪl/ Fertigkeit; Kompetenz p. 8, 1
skirt /skɜːt/ Rock NHG 5
sky /skaɪ/ Himmel p. 53
skyscraper /ˈskaɪˌskreɪpə/ Wolkenkratzer p. 19, 1
(to) **sleep** *(irr)* /sliːp/ schlafen NHG 5
(to) go to sleep *(irr)* /ˌgəʊ tə ˈsliːp/ schlafen gehen p. 52
sleepy /ˈsliːpi/ schläfrig p. 120, 12
slide /slaɪd/ Rutsche p. 93, 4
slide off /ˈslaɪdˍɒf/ herunterrutschen p. 53
slip /slɪp/ Zettel p. 69, 6; ausrutschen p. 101
slow, slowly /sləʊ, ˈsləʊli/ langsam p. 91, 1
(to) slurp /slɜːp/ schlürfen p. 78
small /smɔːl/ klein NHG 5
smart /smɑːt/ schlau, clever p. 87, 13
smell *(irr)* /smel/ riechen p. 124
smelly /ˈsmeli/ übel riechend p. 105, 3
(to) **smile** /smaɪl/ lächeln p. 94, 5
smiley /ˈsmaɪli/ lächelnd p. 101
smoke /sməʊk/ Rauch p. 77
s'more *(AE)* /smɔː/ *Sandwich aus süßen Kräckern mit getoasteten Marshmallows und Schokolade* p. 45, 6
snail /sneɪl/ Schnecke p. 110, 11
snake /sneɪk/ Schlange p. 110, 11
(to) sniff /snɪf/ riechen (an) p. 124
snore /snɔː/ Schnarchen p. 77

snow /snəʊ/ Schnee p. 53
so /səʊ/ also; deshalb; daher NHG 5
so *(+ Verb)* /səʊ/ ... auch p. 104, 2
So am I. /ˌsəʊ‿æm‿ˈaɪ/ Ich auch. p. 130
so far /ˈsəʊ fɑː/ bisher p. 105, 3
so that /ˈsəʊ ðæt/ damit p. 95, 5
sock /sɒk/ Socke p. 12, 6
soft toy /ˌsɒft‿ˈtɔɪ/ Kuscheltier p. 112, 14
softly /ˈsɒftli/ leise; ruhig p. 76
solar-powered /ˈsəʊlə ˌpaʊəd/ solarbetrieben p. 87, 13
solution /səˈluːʃn/ Lösung p. 61, 8
(to) **solve** /sɒlv/ lösen p. 105, 3
some /sʌm/ einige, ein paar; etwas NHG 5
somebody /ˈsʌmbədi/ jemand; irgendwer p. 99, 14
someone /ˈsʌmwʌn/ jemand; irgendwer NHG 5
something /ˈsʌmθɪŋ/ etwas NHG 5
sometimes /ˈsʌmtaɪmz/ manchmal NHG 5
somewhere /ˈsʌmweə/ irgendwo p. 51, 16
son /sʌn/ Sohn NHG 5
song /sɒŋ/ Lied NHG 5
soon /suːn/ bald p. 30
See you (soon)! /ˌsiː juː ˈsuːn/ Bis bald! p. 11, 5
sorry /ˈsɒri/ es tut mir leid, Entschuldigung NHG 5
(to) **sort** /sɔːt/ sortieren NHG 5
sort /sɔːt/ Sorte; Art p. 119, 11
to) **sound** /saʊnd/ klingen, sich anhören NHG 5
sound /saʊnd/ Geräusch; Klang p. 18, 1
South Island /ˈsaʊθ‿ˌaɪlənd/ Südinsel p. 28
space /speɪs/ Raum; Platz p. 12, 6
space capsule /ˈspeɪs ˌkæpsjuːl/ Weltraumkapsel p. 108, 7
spacecraft /ˈspeɪsˌkrɑːft/ Raumfahrzeug p. 102
Spain /speɪn/ Spanien p. 35, 4
sparkler /ˈspɑːklə/ Wunderkerze p. 45, 6
(to) **speak** *(irr)* /spiːk/ sprechen; reden NHG 5
special /ˈspeʃl/ besondere(r, s); besonders NHG 5
speciality /ˌspeʃiˈæləti/ Spezialität p. 28
species (*pl* **species**) /ˈspiːʃiːz, ˈspiːsiːz/ Art; Spezies p. 19, 1
spectacular /spekˈtækjʊlə/ atemberaubend; spektakulär p. 8, 1
(to) **spell** *(irr)* /spel/ buchstabieren NHG 5
spelling /ˈspelɪŋ/ Buchstabieren; Rechtschreibung p. 20, 3
(to) **spend** *(irr)* /spend/ verbringen *(Zeit)*; ausgeben *(Geld)* p. 8, 1
spider /ˈspaɪdə/ Spinne p. 90, 1
spoon /spuːn/ Löffel NHG 5
sport /spɔːt/ Sport; Sportart NHG 5
(to) do sports *(irr)* /ˌduː ˈspɔːts/ Sport treiben p. 10, 3
sportspeople /ˈspɔːtsˌpiːpl/ Sportler/Sportlerinnen p. 146
spring /sprɪŋ/ Frühling p. 33, 1
squirrel /ˈskwɪrəl/ Eichhörnchen p. 66, 1
squirrelpox /ˈskwɪrəlpɒks/ *Eichhörnchenkrankheit* p. 129
stadium (*pl* stadiums *or* stadia) /ˈsteɪdiəm, ˈsteɪdiəmz, ˈsteɪdiə/ Stadion p. 26, 12
stage /steɪdʒ/ Bühne p. 83, 6
(to) play a stage /ˌpleɪ‿ə ˈsteɪdʒ/ auf einer Bühne spielen p. 81, 2
stair /steə/ Stufe p. 19, 1
stairs *(pl)* /steəz/ Treppe p. 90, 1
stalk /stɔːk/ Stängel; Stiel p. 46, 7
stall /stɔːl/ Stand p. 42, 1
(to) **stand** *(irr)* /stænd/ stehen p. 9, 2
(to) **stand for** *(irr)* /ˈstænd fɔː/ stehen für p. 33, 1
star /stɑː/ Stern NHG 5
(to) **start** /stɑːt/ anfangen; beginnen NHG 5
start /stɑːt/ Anfang; Beginn NHG 5
state /steɪt/ (Bundes)staat p. 148
statement /ˈsteɪtmənt/ Äußerung, Aussage NHG 5
station /ˈsteɪʃn/ U-Bahn-Station; Bahnhof NHG 5
(to) **stay** /steɪ/ bleiben; wohnen NHG 5
(to) stay out /ˌsteɪ‿ˈaʊt/ ausbleiben, wegbleiben p. 62, 10
(to) stay up (late) /ˌsteɪ‿ʌp ˈleɪt/ (lange) aufbleiben p. 64, 14
(to) **step** /step/ treten; steigen p. 104, 2
step /step/ Stufe; Schritt NHG 5
(to) stick to *(irr)* /ˈstɪk tʊ/ *hier:* sich halten an p. 63, 11
hockey stick /ˈhɒki stɪk/ Hockeyschläger p. 109, 9
still /stɪl/ (immer) noch NHG 5
(to) stomp /stɒmp/ stapfen, trampeln p. 100
stone /stəʊn/ Stein p. 102
(to) **stop** /stɒp/ stehen bleiben; anhalten NHG 5; aufhören p. 120, 12
stormy /ˈstɔːmi/ stürmisch p. 98, 13
story /ˈstɔːri/ Geschichte, Erzählung NHG 5
straight away /ˌstreɪt‿əˈweɪ/ sofort p. 126
straight on /ˌstreɪt‿ˈɒn/ geradeaus p. 22, 6
strange /streɪndʒ/ sonderbar; merkwürdig p. 16, 12
street /striːt/ Straße NHG 5
stress /stres/ Betonung p. 44, 5
strict /strɪkt/ streng p. 62, 10
string /strɪŋ/ Schnur; Kordel p. 73, 10
stripe /straɪp/ Streifen p. 111, 12
(to) stroke /strəʊk/ streicheln p. 124
student /ˈstjuːdnt/ Schüler/in NHG 5
(to) study /ˈstʌdi/ studieren p. 127
stuff *(informal)* /stʌf/ Zeug p. 9, 2
(to) stumble /ˈstʌmbl/ stolpern p. 120, 12
stupid /ˈstjuːpɪd/ dumm, blöd p. 38, 7
style /staɪl/ Stil p. 59, 6
writing style / ˈraɪtɪŋ staɪl/ Schreibstil p. 17, 14
subject /ˈsʌbdʒɪkt/ Schulfach NHG 5; Thema; Betreff *(in Emails)* p. 117, 8
such /sʌtʃ/ so; solch p. 102
sudden /ˈsʌdn/ plötzlich p. 76
suddenly /ˈsʌdnli/ plötzlich p. 67, 1
sugar /ˈʃʊgə/ Zucker p. 46, 7
(to) **suggest** /səˈdʒest/ vorschlagen p. 105, 3
suggestion /səˈdʒestʃn/ Vorschlag p. 48, 9
summarize (= summarise) /ˈsʌməraɪz/ zusammenfassen p. 30

summer /ˈsʌmə/ Sommer NHG 5
sun /sʌn/ Sonne NHG 5
sun cream /ˈsʌn kriːm/ Sonnenschutzcreme p. 66, 1
Sunday /ˈsʌndeɪ/ Sonntag NHG 5
(on) Sundays /ˈsʌndeɪz/ sonntags NHG 5
sunglasses *(pl)* /ˈsʌnˌglɑːsɪz/ Sonnenbrille p. 124
sunny /ˈsʌni/ sonnig NHG 5
sunset /ˈsʌnˌset/ Sonnenuntergang p. 33, 1
sunshine /ˈsʌnˌʃaɪn/ Sonnenschein NHG 5
superlative /sʊˈpɜːlətɪv/ Superlativ p. 20, 3
sure /ʃɔː/ sicher NHG 5
(to) **make sure** *(irr)* /ˌmeɪk ˈʃɔː/ darauf achten, dass ... p. 39, 9
surprised /səˈpraɪzd/ überrascht; erstaunt p. 93, 4
surprising /səˈpraɪzɪŋ/ überraschend p. 37, 6
surrounding /səˈraʊndɪŋ/ umgebend p. 144
sweet /swiːt/ süß NHG 5; Süßigkeit p. 36, 6
(to) **swim** *(irr)* /swɪm/ schwimmen NHG 5
swimming /ˈswɪmɪŋ/ Schwimmen NHG 5
(to) **go swimming** *(irr)* /ˌgəʊ ˈswɪmɪŋ/ schwimmen gehen p. 8, 1
swimming pool /ˈswɪmɪŋ puːl/ Schwimmbad NHG 5
(to) **switch on** /ˌswɪtʃ‿ˈɒn/ einschalten NHG 5
syllable /ˈsɪləbl/ Silbe p. 44, 5

T

table /ˈteɪbl/ Tisch NHG 5; Tabelle p. 87, 13
(to) **set the table** /ˌset ðə ˈteɪbl/ den Tisch decken NHG 5
table tennis /ˈteɪbl ˌtenɪs/ Tischtennis NHG 5
tail /teɪl/ Schwanz p. 77
(to) **take** *(irr)* /teɪk/ nehmen; bringen; benötigen; brauchen NHG 5; dauern p. 22, 5
(to) take a closer look at *(irr)* /ˌteɪk‿ə ˌkləʊsə ˈlʊk‿ət/ sich genauer ansehen p. 146
(to) **take a photo / picture** *(irr)* /ˌteɪk‿ə ˈfəʊtəʊ / ˈpɪktʃə/ ein Foto machen NHG 5
(to) take a ride *(irr)* /ˌteɪk‿ə ˈraɪd/ Karussell fahren p. 42, 1
(to) take a selfie *(irr)* /ˌteɪk‿ə ˈselfi/ ein Selfie machen p. 24, 9
(to) **take away** *(irr)* /ˌteɪk‿əˈweɪ/ wegnehmen; mitnehmen p. 67, 1
(to) **take care of** *(irr)* /ˌteɪk‿ˈkeər‿əv/ sich kümmern um p. 55
(to) **take notes (on)** *(irr)* /ˌteɪk ˈnəʊts/ sich Notizen machen (zu) NHG 5
(to) take off *(irr)* /ˌteɪk‿ˈɒf/ ausziehen *(Kleidung)* p. 124
(to) **take out** *(irr)* /ˌteɪk‿ˈaʊt/ hinausbringen NHG 5
(to) **take part in** *(irr)* /ˌteɪk ˈpɑːt‿ɪn/ teilnehmen an p. 65, 15
(to) **take place** *(irr)* /ˌteɪk ˈpleɪs/ stattfinden p. 33, 1
(to) **take turns** *(irr)* /ˌteɪk ˈtɜːnz/ sich abwechseln p. 116, 6
(to) **talk about** /ˈtɔːk‿əˌbaʊt/ sprechen über NHG 5
(to) **talk (to)** /tɔːk/ sprechen (mit); reden (mit) NHG 5
tall /tɔːl/ groß p. 19, 1
tame /teɪm/ gezähmt, zahm p. 77; zähmen p. 28
taming /ˈteɪmɪŋ/ Zähmen p. 28
tape /teɪp/ Klebeband p. 39, 9
target task /ˈtɑːgɪt ˌtɑːsk/ Zielaufgabe p. 17, 14
tart /tɑːt/ Törtchen p. 14, 9
task /tɑːsk/ Aufgabe NHG 5
(to) **taste** /teɪst/ schmecken p. 14, 9
tbsp (= tablespoon) /ˈteɪblspuːn/ EL (= Esslöffel) p. 46, 7
tea /tiː/ Tee NHG 5
(to) **teach** *(irr)* /tiːtʃ/ unterrichten NHG 5
teacher /ˈtiːtʃə/ Lehrer/in NHG 5
technology /tekˈnɒlədʒi/ Technologie; Technik p. 81, 2
(to) **brush one's teeth** /ˌbrʌʃ wʌnz ˈtiːθ/ sich die Zähne putzen NHG 5
telephone /ˈtelɪˌfəʊn/ Telefon p. 108, 7
telescope /ˈtelɪˌskəʊp/ Teleskop p. 108, 7
(to) **tell** *(irr)* /tel/ erzählen NHG 5
term /tɜːm/ Trimester; Begriff NHG 5
terrible /ˈterəbl/ schrecklich NHG 5
(to) test /test/ prüfen; testen p. 46, 7
(to) **text** /tekst/ eine Textnachricht schreiben NHG 5
text (message) /ˈtekst ˌmesɪdʒ/ Textnachricht NHG 5
Thames /temz/ Themse p. 19, 1
than /ðæn/ als *(bei Vergleich)* p. 19, 1
thank God /ˌθæŋk ˈgɒd/ Gott sei Dank p. 94, 5
thank goodness /ˌθæŋk ˈgʊdnəs/ Gott sei Dank p. 52
thank you /ˈθæŋk ju/ danke NHG 5
thanks /θæŋks/ danke NHG 5
thanks a lot /ˌθæŋks‿ə ˈlɒt/ vielen Dank NHG 5
I'm good, thanks. /aɪm ˈgʊd ˌθæŋks/ Es geht mir gut, danke. NHG 5
Thanksgiving /ˈθæŋksˌgɪvɪŋ/ Thanksgiving *(amerikanisches Erntedankfest)* p. 54
that /ðæt/ das; der/die/das (dort); dass NHG 5; so p. 43, 2
that's (= that is) /ðæts, ˈðæt‿ɪz/ *hier:* das kostet NHG 5
that's why /ˈðæts ˌwaɪ/ deshalb p. 125
the /ðə/ der/die/das NHG 5
theatre /ˈθɪətə/ Theater p. 104, 2
their /ðeə/ ihr(e) NHG 5
them /ðem/ sie; ihnen NHG 5
theme /θiːm/ Thema p. 27, 14
themselves /ðəmˈselvz/ sich; sie selbst p. 129
then /ðen/ dann NHG 5
there /ðeə/ dort; dahin NHG 5
there are /ðeər‿ˈɑː/ dort sind; es gibt NHG 5
there were /ðeə ˈwɜː/ dort waren; es gab p. 54
there's (= there is) /ðeəz, ðeər‿ˈɪz/ dort ist; es gibt NHG 5
these (*pl of* **this**) /ðiːz/ diese; das NHG 5
they /ðeɪ/ sie NHG 5
thing /θɪŋ/ Ding; Gegenstand NHG 5
(to) **think** *(irr)* /θɪŋk/ denken; glauben NHG 5

(to) **think about** *(irr)* /ˈθɪŋk‿əˌbaʊt/ denken an, nachdenken über NHG 5
(to) **think of** *(irr)* /ˈθɪŋk‿əv/ denken an, sich ausdenken NHG 5
third /θɜːd/ dritte(r, s) NHG 5
this /ðɪs/ diese(r, s) NHG 5
This way, please. /ˈðɪs weɪ ˌpliːz/ Hier entlang, bitte. p. 70, 7
those (*pl of* **that**) /ðəʊz/ diese, jene NHG 5
though (*nachgestellt*) /ðəʊ/ jedoch p. 54
thousand /ˈθaʊznd/ tausend p. 12, 6
through /θruː/ durch p. 14, 9
(to) **throw** *(irr)* /θrəʊ/ werfen NHG 5
(to) **throw away** *(irr)* /ˌθrəʊ‿əˈweɪ/ wegwerfen p. 114, 1
Thursday /ˈθɜːzdeɪ/ Donnerstag NHG 5
(on) Thursdays /ˈθɜːzdeɪz/ donnerstags NHG 5
tidy /ˈtaɪdi/ ordentlich; aufgeräumt NHG 5
(to) **tidy (up)** /ˈtaɪdi, ˌtaɪdi‿ˈʌp/ aufräumen NHG 5
tie /taɪ/ Krawatte NHG 5
till /tɪl/ bis NHG 5
time /taɪm/ Zeit; Mal NHG 5
all the time /ˌɔːl ðə ˈtaɪm/ die ganze Zeit p. 11, 5
at all times /æt‿ˌɔːl ˈtaɪmz/ jederzeit, immer p. 66, 1
at the time /ˌæt‿ðə ˈtaɪm/ damals; zu dem Zeitpunkt p. 30
for the first time /fə ðə ˈfɜːst‿taɪm/ zum ersten Mal p. 9, 2
on time /ˌɒn ˈtaɪm/ pünktlich NHG 5
What time is it? /wɒt‿ˈtaɪm‿ɪz‿ɪt/ Wie spät ist es? NHG 5
What's the time, please? /ˌwɒts ðə ˈtaɪm pliːz/ Wie spät ist es, bitte? NHG 5
time machine /ˈtaɪm‿məʃiːn/ Zeitmaschine Land und Leute 6
time travelling /ˈtaɪm ˌtrævlɪŋ/ Zeitreisen p. 24, 9
timeline /ˈtaɪmlaɪn/ Zeitachse p. 37, 6
timetable /ˈtaɪmteɪbl/ Stundenplan NHG 5; Fahrplan p. 22, 5
tip /tɪp/ Tipp p. 17, 14
tired /ˈtaɪəd/ müde p. 60, 7
title /ˈtaɪtl/ Titel; Überschrift p. 17, 14
to /tʊ/ (um) zu; in; nach; zu; an; bis; vor NHG 5
to /tʊ/ *hier:* für p. 25, 10
today /təˈdeɪ/ heute NHG 5; heutzutage p. 19, 1
toe /təʊ/ Zeh NHG 5
toffee apple /ˈtɒfi ˌæpl/ kandierter Apfel p. 43, 2
together /təˈgeðə/ zusammen NHG 5
toilet /ˈtɔɪlət/ Toilette NHG 5
toilet paper /ˈtɔɪlət ˌpeɪpə/ Toilettenpapier p. 38, 7
tomato (*pl* tomatoes) /təˈmɑːtəʊ, təˈmɑːtəʊz/ Tomate NHG 5
tomorrow /təˈmɒrəʊ/ morgen NHG 5
tonight /təˈnaɪt/ heute Abend p. 28
too /tuː/ auch; zu NHG 5
tooth (*pl* teeth) /tuːθ, tiːθ/ Zahn p. 52
top /tɒp/ beste(r, s) NHG 5; oberes Ende; Spitze p. 19, 1
at the top /ˌæt‿ðə ˈtɒp/ oben p. 52
the top /tɒp/ der/die/das oberste p. 39, 9
topic /ˈtɒpɪk/ Thema NHG 5
torch /tɔːtʃ/ Taschenlampe p. 90, 1
tortoise /ˈtɔːtəs/ Schildkröte p. 166
(to) **touch** /tʌtʃ/ berühren NHG 5
towards /təˈwɔːdz/ in Richtung, zu; gegenüber p. 22, 5
tower /ˈtaʊə/ Turm p. 19, 1
town /taʊn/ Stadt NHG 5
toy /tɔɪ/ Spielzeug NHG 5
soft toy /ˌsɒft‿ˈtɔɪ/ Kuscheltier p. 112, 14
traditional /trəˈdɪʃnəl/ traditionell p. 33, 1
train /treɪn/ Zug NHG 5
trainer /ˈtreɪnə/ Turnschuh p. 104, 2
transport /ˈtrænspɔːt/ Transport; Verkehrsmittel p. 95, 5
(to) **travel** /ˈtrævl/ reisen; fahren NHG 5
travel /ˈtrævl/ Reise p. 14, 9
day travelcard /ˈdeɪ ˌtrævlkɑːd/ Tageskarte p. 22, 5
travelling /ˈtrævlɪŋ/ Reisen p. 89, 18
treason /ˈtriːzn/ (Landes)verrat p. 48, 10
tree /triː/ Baum NHG 5
trick /trɪk/ Trick; Kunststück NHG 5
(to) play a trick on somebody /ˌpleɪ‿ə ˈtrɪk‿ɒn ˌsʌmbədi/ jemandem einen Streich spielen p. 38, 7
Trick or treat! /ˌtrɪk‿ɔː ˈtriːt/ *etwa:* Süßes oder es gibt Saures! p. 38, 7
trick-or-treating /ˌtrɪk‿ɔː ˈtriːtɪŋ/ *Spiel zu Halloween, bei dem die Kinder von Tür zu Tür gehen und entweder Süßigkeiten bekommen oder einen Streich spielen* p. 36, 6
trip /trɪp/ Ausflug; Fahrt p. 69, 6
trouble /ˈtrʌbl/ Ärger; Schwierigkeiten p. 57, 1
(a pair of) trousers /ə ˌpeər‿əv ˈtraʊzəz/ Hose NHG 5
true /truː/ wahr NHG 5
(to) trust /trʌst/ vertrauen p. 124
(to) **try** /traɪ/ (aus)probieren; versuchen NHG 5
the Tube /ðə ˈtjuːb/ (Londoner) U-Bahn p. 22, 5
Tuesday /ˈtjuːzdeɪ/ Dienstag NHG 5
(on) Tuesdays /ˈtjuːzdeɪz/ dienstags NHG 5
tune /tjuːn/ Melodie p. 111, 12
turkey /ˈtɜːki/ Truthahn p. 54
(to) **turn** /tɜːn/ abbiegen p. 22, 6
(to) **be one's turn** /ˌbiː wʌnz ˈtɜːn/ an der Reihe sein NHG 5
(to) **take turns** *(irr)* /ˌteɪk ˈtɜːnz/ sich abwechseln p. 116, 6
(to) turn on /ˌtɜːn‿ˈɒn/ einschalten p. 76
(to) turn to /ˈtɜːn tʊ/ (sich) wenden an p. 124
turtle /ˈtɜːtl/ Wasserschildkröte p. 166
TV (= television) /ˌtiː ˈviː, ˈtelɪˌvɪʒn/ Fernsehen; Fernseher p. 62, 10
(to) **watch TV** /ˌwɒtʃ tiː ˈviː/ Fernsehen gucken NHG 5
twin /twɪn/ Zwilling; Zwillings- NHG 5
type /taɪp/ Art p. 108, 7
typical /ˈtɪpɪkl/ typisch NHG 5

U

ugly /ˈʌgli/ hässlich p. 19, 1
the UK (= United Kingdom) /ðə ˌjuː ˈkeɪ, juːˌnaɪtɪd ˈkɪŋdəm/ Vereinigtes Königreich p. 19, 1

uncle /ˈʌŋkl/ Onkel NHG 5
under /ˈʌndə/ unter NHG 5
underground /ˈʌndəˌgraʊnd/ U-Bahn p. 24, 9
(to) underline /ˌʌndəˈlaɪn/ unterstreichen p. 34, 3
(to) **understand** *(irr)* /ˌʌndəˈstænd/ verstehen NHG 5
unfortunately /ʌnˈfɔːtʃnətli/ unglücklicherweise p. 16, 12
unit /ˈjuːnɪt/ Kapitel p. 128
university /ˌjuːnɪˈvɜːsəti/ Universität p. 102
unknown /ʌnˈnəʊn/ unbekannt p. 28
(to) unscramble /ʌnˈskræmbl/ in die richtige Reihenfolge bringen p. 26, 13
until /ənˈtɪl/ bis p. 19, 1
unusual /ʌnˈjuːʒuəl/ ungewöhnlich NHG 5
up /ʌp/ (nach) oben; hinauf NHG 5
upstairs /ˌʌpˈsteəz/ (nach) oben p. 78
us /ʌs/ uns NHG 5
(the) US (= United States) /ðə ˌjuː‿ˈes, juːˌnaɪtɪd ˈsteɪts/ US, Vereinigte Staaten (von Amerika); US- p. 54
the USA (= United States of America) /ðə ˌju‿es‿ˈeɪ, juːˌnaɪtɪd ˌsteɪts‿əv‿əˈmerɪkə/ USA; Vereinigte Staaten von Amerika p. 36, 6
(to) **use** /juːz/ benutzen NHG 5
used to + *infinitive* /ˈjuːst‿tuː/ früher + *Vergangenheitsform* p. 94, 5
useful /ˈjuːsfl/ nützlich NHG 5
usually /ˈjuːʒuəli/ gewöhnlich; normalerweise NHG 5

V

(to) **vacuum** /ˈvækjuəm/ staubsaugen NHG 5
vegetarian /ˌvedʒəˈteəriən/ Vegetarier/in; vegetarisch p. 88, 15
vehicle /ˈviːɪkl/ Fahrzeug p. 108, 7
verse /vɜːs/ Strophe; Vers p. 87, 14
version /ˈvɜːʃn/ Version, Fassung NHG 5
very /ˈveri/ sehr NHG 5
very much /ˌveri ˈmʌtʃ/ sehr p. 16, 12
vet /vet/ Tierarzt/-ärztin p. 83, 6
victory /ˈvɪktri/ Sieg p. 33, 1
view /vjuː/ (Aus)sicht p. 8, 1
viewing point /ˈvjuːɪŋ pɔɪnt/ Aussichtspunkt p. 19, 1
village /ˈvɪlɪdʒ/ Dorf p. 125
violin /ˌvaɪəˈlɪn/ Violine; Geige p. 104, 2
virtual /ˈvɜːtʃʊəl/ virtuell p. 95, 5
(to) **visit** /ˈvɪzɪt/ besuchen p. 8, 1
visit /ˈvɪzɪt/ Besuch NHG 5
(to) be worth a visit *(irr)* /ˌbiː ˌwɜːθ‿ə ˈvɪzɪt/ einen Besuch wert sein p. 24, 9
visitor /ˈvɪzɪtə/ Besucher/in p. 25, 10
voice /vɔɪs/ Stimme p. 120, 12
in a quiet voice /ˌɪn‿ə ˌkwaɪət ˈvɔɪs/ mit leiser Stimme p. 76
voice recording /ˈvɔɪs riˌkɔːdɪŋ/ Stimmaufnahme p. 102
volcano /vɒlˈkeɪnəʊ/ Vulkan p. 28
VR (= virtual reality) /ˌviː ˈɑː, ˌvɜːtʃʊəl riˈæləti/ virtuelle Realität p. 87, 13

W

(to) **wait** /weɪt/ (er)warten NHG 5
(to) **wake up** *(irr)* /ˌweɪk‿ˈʌp/ aufwachen p. 90, 1
(to) **walk** /wɔːk/ gehen NHG 5
walk /wɔːk/ Spaziergang NHG 5
(to) walk on /ˌwɔːk‿ˈɒn/ weiterlaufen p. 22, 6
(to) walk the dog /ˌwɔːk ðə ˈdɒg/ den Hund ausführen p. 30
walker /ˈwɔːkə/ Spaziergänger/in p. 66, 1
walkway /ˈwɔːkˌweɪ/ (Fuß)weg p. 25, 10
wall /wɔːl/ Wand p. 74, 12
walrus (*pl* walrus *or* walruses) /ˈwɔːlrəs, ˈwɔːlrəs, ˈwɔːlrəsɪz/ Walross p. 108, 7
(to) **want (to)** /wɒnt/ wollen NHG 5
wardrobe /ˈwɔːdrəʊb/ Schrank p. 78
(to) warn /wɔːn/ warnen p. 101
warning /ˈwɔːnɪŋ/ Warnung p. 76
(to) **wash** /wɒʃ/ waschen, sich waschen NHG 5
(to) wash up /ˌwɒʃ‿ˈʌp/ abwaschen p. 28
(to) **watch** /wɒtʃ/ beobachten; ansehen NHG 5
watch /wɒtʃ/ (Armband)uhr p. 90, 1
(to) watch out /ˌwɒtʃ‿ˈaʊt/ aufpassen p. 90, 1
(to) **watch TV** /ˌwɒtʃ tiː ˈviː/ Fernsehen gucken NHG 5
water /ˈwɔːtə/ Wasser NHG 5
(to) water /ˈwɔːtə/ gießen p. 78
wax model /ˈwæksˌmɒdl/ Wachsmodell p. 107, 6
wax statue /ˈwæksˌstætʃuː/ Wachsfigur p. 24, 9
way /weɪ/ Weg; Art NHG 5
This way, please. /ˈðɪs weɪ ˌpliːz/ Hier entlang, bitte. p. 70, 7
we /wiː/ wir NHG 5
We'll see about that. /wiːl ˌsiː‿əˌbaʊt ˈðæt/ Das werden wir sehen. p. 81, 2
(to) **wear** *(irr)* /weə/ tragen *(Kleidung)* NHG 5
weather /ˈweðə/ Wetter NHG 5
Wednesday /ˈwenzdeɪ/ Mittwoch NHG 5
(on) Wednesdays /ˈwenzdeɪz/ mittwochs NHG 5
week /wiːk/ Woche NHG 5
weekend /ˌwiːkˈend/ Wochenende NHG 5
(to) weigh /weɪ/ wiegen p. 111, 12
welcome (to) /ˈwelkəm tʊ/ willkommen (in) NHG 5
well /wel/ nun NHG 5; gut p. 90, 1
Well done! /ˌwel ˈdʌn/ Gut gemacht! p. 121, 12
Welsh /welʃ/ walisisch p. 12, 6
wet /wet/ nass p. 93, 4
whale /weɪl/ Wal p. 102
what /wɒt/ was; welche(r, s) NHG 5
What … would you like? /ˌwɒt … wəd jə ˈlaɪk/ Was für ein/e … hättest du/hättet ihr/hätten Sie gern? NHG 5
What about …? /ˌwɒt‿əˌbaʊt ˈ…/ Was ist mit …? / Wie wäre es mit …? NHG 5
What time is it? /wɒt‿ˈtaɪm‿ɪz‿ɪt/ Wie spät ist es? NHG 5
What was that like? /ˌwɒt wɒz ðæt ˈlaɪk/ Wie war das? p. 12, 6
What's on? *(informal)* /ˌwɒts‿ˈɒn/ Was ist los? p. 114, 1

What's the time, please? /ˌwɒts ðə ˈtaɪm pliːz/ Wie spät ist es, bitte? NHG 5
What's up? *(informal)* /ˌwɒts‿ˈʌp/ Was ist los? p. 54
whatever /wɒtˈevə/ was (auch immer) p. 80, 2
wheel /wiːl/ Rad p. 19, 1
when /wen/ wann; wenn; als NHG 5
whenever /wenˈevə/ wann auch immer p. 78
where /weə/ wo; wohin NHG 5
which /wɪtʃ/ welche(r, s); was NHG 5
while /waɪl/ während p. 62, 10
(to) whisper /ˈwɪspə/ flüstern; wispern p. 53
white /waɪt/ weiß NHG 5
who /huː/ wer; der/die/das NHG 5
whole /həʊl/ ganz, gesamt p. 26, 13
whose /huːz/ wessen NHG 5
why /waɪ/ warum NHG 5
wife (*pl* **wives**) /waɪf, aɪvz/ Ehefrau NHG 5
wildlife /ˈwaɪldˌlaɪf/ Flora und Fauna; Tier- und Pflanzenwelt p. 66, 1
will /wɪl/ werden p. 80, 1
win *(irr)* /wɪn/ gewinnen p. 131
window /ˈwɪndəʊ/ Fenster NHG 5
(to) wish /wɪʃ/ wünschen p. 52
with /wɪð/ mit; bei NHG 5
without /wɪðˈaʊt/ ohne NHG 5
woman (*pl* **women**) /ˈwʊmən, ˈwɪmɪn/ Frau NHG 5
won't /wəʊnt/ nicht werden p. 81, 2
(to) **wonder** /ˈwʌndə/ sich fragen p. 90, 1
wonderful /ˈwʌndəfl/ wunderbar, wundervoll p. 87, 14
wood /wʊd/ Holz p. 45, 6
wooden /ˈwʊdn/ Holz-, hölzern p. 46, 7
word /wɜːd/ Wort NHG 5
rhyming word /ˈraɪmɪŋ wɜːd/ Reimwort p. 78
word order /ˈwɜːd‿ɔːdə/ Satzstellung p. 68, 3
word web /ˈwɜːd web/ Wortnetz NHG 5
wordbank /ˈwɜːdbæŋk/ Wortsammlung NHG 5
(to) **work** /wɜːk/ arbeiten NHG 5; funktionieren p. 63, 11
work /wɜːk/ Arbeit; Werk NHG 5
workbook /ˈwɜːkbʊk/ Arbeitsheft p. 8, 1
world /wɜːld/ Welt NHG 5
all over the world /ˌɔːl‿ˌəʊvə ðə ˈwɜːld/ auf der ganzen Welt p. 33, 1
from all over the world /frəm‿ˌɔːl‿ˌəʊvə ðə ˈwɜːld/ aus der ganzen Welt NHG 5
around the world /əˌraʊnd ðə ˈwɜːld/ weltweit, überall auf der Welt p. 102
world-famous /ˌwɜːld ˈfeɪməs/ weltberühmt p. 127
worried /ˈwʌrid/ beunruhigt; besorgt p. 60, 7
(to) **worry** /ˈwʌri/ sich Sorgen machen NHG 5
worse /wɜːs/ schlechter, schlimmer p. 20
the worst /ðə ˈwɜːst/ der/die/das schlechteste, der/die/das schlimmste; am schlechtesten, am schlimmsten p. 20
(to) be worth a visit *(irr)* /ˌbiː ˌwɜːθ‿ə ˈvɪzɪt/ einen Besuch wert sein p. 24, 9
would /wʊd/ würde(st, n, t) NHG 5
I would like ... (= I'd like ...) /aɪ ˌwʊd ˈlaɪk, aɪd ˈlaɪk/ Ich würde gern ... / Ich hätte gern ... NHG 5
Would you like ...? /ˌwʊd juː ˈlaɪk/ Hättest du / Hättet ihr / Hätten Sie gern ...? NHG 5
(to) wrap /ræp/ einwickeln p. 38, 7
(to) **write** *(irr)* /raɪt/ schreiben NHG 5
(to) **write down** *(irr)* /ˌraɪt‿ˈdaʊn/ aufschreiben NHG 5
writing /ˈraɪtɪŋ/ Schreiben; Schreib- p. 15, 11
writing style /ˈraɪtɪŋ staɪl/ Schreibstil p. 17, 14
written /ˈrɪtn/ schriftlich p. 69, 6
wrong /rɒŋ/ falsch p. 110, 11

Y

year /jɪə/ Jahr NHG 5; Schuljahr; Klasse p. 69, 6
all year round /ˌɔːl ˈjɪə raʊnd/ das ganze Jahr lang p. 66, 1
yellow /ˈjeləʊ/ gelb NHG 5
yes /jes/ ja NHG 5
yesterday /ˈjestədeɪ/ gestern p. 9, 2
yoghurt pot /ˈjɒgət pɒt/ Joghurtbecher p. 73, 10
you /juː/ du; dich; dir; man; ihr; euch; Sie; Ihnen NHG 5
young /jʌŋ/ jung p. 20, 2
the young one /ðə ˈjʌŋ wʌn/ Junges p. 125
your /jɔː/ dein(e); euer/eure; Ihr(e) NHG 5
yours /jɔːz/ deine(r,s); eure(r,s); Ihre(r,s) p. 14, 9
yours sincerely /ˌjɔːz sɪnˈsɪəli/ mit freundlichen Grüßen *(am Ende eines formellen Briefes)* p. 69, 6
yourself /jɔːˈself/ dir, dich; sich NHG 5
youth club /ˈjuːθ ˌklʌb/ Jugendklub p. 114, 1
yummy *(informal)* /ˈjʌmi/ lecker p. 9, 2

Z

zoologist /zuˈɒlədʒɪst/ Zoologe / Zoologin p. 85, 9

Numbers

0	oh, zero, nil /əʊ, 'zɪərəʊ, nɪl/
1	one /wʌn/
2	two /tuː/
3	three /θriː/
4	four /fɔː/
5	five /faɪv/
6	six /sɪks/
7	seven /sevn/
8	eight /eɪt/
9	nine /naɪn/
10	ten /ten/
11	eleven /ɪ'levn/
12	twelve /twelv/
13	**thir**teen /ˌθɜː'tiːn/
14	fourteen /ˌfɔː'tiːn
15	**fif**teen /ˌfɪf'tiːn/
16	sixteen /ˌsɪks'tiːn/
17	seventeen /ˌsevn'tiːn/
18	**eigh**teen /ˌeɪ'tiːn/
19	nineteen /ˌnaɪn'tiːn/
20	**twen**ty /'twenti/
21	twenty-one /ˌtwenti'wʌn/
22	twenty-two /ˌtwenti'tuː/
30	**thir**ty /'θɜːti/
33	thirty-three /ˌθɜːti'θriː/
34	thirty-four /ˌθɜːti'fɔː/
40	**for**ty /'fɔːti/
45	forty-five /ˌfɔːti'faɪv/
50	**fif**ty /'fɪfti/
56	fifty-six /ˌfɪfti'sɪks/
60	sixty /'sɪksti/
67	sixty-seven /ˌsɪksti'sevn/
70	seventy /'sevnti/
78	seventy-eight /ˌsevnti'eɪt/
80	**eigh**ty /'eɪti/
89	eighty-nine /ˌeɪti'naɪn/
90	ninety /'naɪnti/
100	a/one hundred /ə/wʌn 'hʌndrəd/
101	one hundred and one /wʌn ˌhʌndrəd‿ən 'wʌn/
102	one hundred and two /wʌn ˌhʌndrəd‿ən 'tuː/
110	one hundred and ten /wʌn ˌhʌndrəd‿ən 'ten/
200	two hundred /tuː 'hʌndrəd/

1,000	one thousand /ə/wʌn 'θaʊznd/
2,000	two thousand /tuː 'θaʊznd/
1st	**first** /fɜːst/
2nd	**second** /'sekənd/
3rd	**third** /θɜːd/
4th	fourth /fɔːθ/
5th	**fif**th /fɪfθ/
6th	sixth /sɪksθ/
7th	seventh /sevnθ/
8th	**eigh**th /eɪtθ/
9th	**nin**th /naɪnθ/
10th	tenth /tenθ/
11th	eleventh /ɪ'levnθ/
12th	**twelf**th /twelfθ/
13th	thirteenth /ˌθɜː'tiːnθ/
14th	fourteenth /ˌfɔː'tiːnθ/
15th	fifteenth /ˌfɪf'tiːnθ/
16th	sixteenth /ˌsɪks'tiːnθ/
17th	seventeenth /ˌsevn'tiːnθ/
18th	eighteenth /ˌeɪ'tiːnθ/
19th	nineteenth /ˌnaɪn'tiːnθ/
20th	twent**ie**th /'twentiəθ/
21st	twenty-first /ˌtwenti'fɜːst/
22nd	twenty-second /ˌtwenti'sekənd/
23rd	twenty-third /ˌtwenti'θɜːd/
30th	thirt**ie**th /'θɜːtiəθ/
40th	fort**ie**th /'fɔːtiəθ/
50th	fift**ie**th /'fɪftiəθ/
60th	sixt**ie**th /'sɪkstiəθ/
70th	sevent**ie**th /'sevntiəθ/
80th	eight**ie**th /'eɪtiəθ/
90th	ninet**ie**th /'naɪntiəθ/
100th	hundredth /'hʌndrədθ/

$\frac{1}{2}$ a / one half /ə/wʌn 'hɑːf/

$\frac{1}{3}$ a / one third /ə/wʌn 'θɜːd/

$\frac{1}{4}$ a / one quarter /ə/wʌn 'kwɔːtə/

$\frac{1}{8}$ a / one eighth /ə/wʌn‿'eɪtθ/

$\frac{3}{4}$ three quarters /θriː 'kwɔːtəz/

> !
> Daten schreibst du entweder so:
> 1 August, 2 January, 5 November
> oder so:
> 1st August, 2nd January, 5th November

Names

First names

Adam *(m.)* /ˈædəm/
Ahmed *(m.)* /ˈɑːmed/
Albert *(m.)* /ˈælbət/
Anna *(f.)* /ˈænə/
Archie *(m.)* /ˈɑːtʃi/
Ari *(m.)* /ˈɑːri/
Arthur *(m.)* /ˈɑːθə/
Ava *(f.)* /ˈeɪvə/
Ben *(m.)* /ben/
Blaze *(m.)* /bleɪz/
Buzz *(m.)* /bʌz/
Christopher *(m.)* /ˈkrɪstəfə/
Conan *(m.)* /ˈkəʊnən/
Dan *(m.)* /dæn/
Daniel *(m.)* /ˈdænjəl/
David *(m.)* /ˈdeɪvɪd/
Edyta *(f.)* /əˈdiːtə/
Elizabeth *(f.)* /iˈlɪzəbəθ/
Ellen *(f.)* /ˈelən/
Eran *(f.)* /ˈerən/
Farida *(f.)* /fəˈriːdə/
George *(m.)* /dʒɔːdʒ/
Georgia *(f.)* /ˈdʒɔːdʒə/
Gina *(f.)* /ˈdʒiːnə/
Gus *(m.)* /gʌs/
Harry *(m.)* /ˈhæri/
Hiroto *(m.)* /ˌhɪrˈəʊtəʊ/
Israh *(m.)* /ˈɪzrə/
Jack *(m.)* /dʒæk/
Jacob *(m.)* /ˈdʒeɪkəb/
James *(m.)* /dʒeɪmz/
Jessica *(f.)* /ˈdʒesɪkə/
John *(m.)* /dʒɒn/
Jonathan *(m.)* /ˈdʒɒnəθən/
Joshua *(m.)* /ˈdʒɒʃjuə/
Jules *(m.)* /ʒyl/
Julie *(f.)* /ˈdʒuːli/
Kate *(f.)* /keɪt/
Katie *(f.)* /ˈkeɪti/
Katy *(f.)* /ˈkeɪti/
Kerem *(m.)* /ˈkerəm/
Kora *(f.)* /ˈkɔːrə/
Laura *(f.)* /ˈlɔːrə/
Lewis *(m.)* /ˈluːɪs/
Liam *(m.)* /ˈliːəm/
Lily *(f.)* /ˈlɪli/
Maria *(f.)* /məˈriːə/
Marty *(m.)* /ˈmɑːti/
Mehti *(m.)* /ˈmeɪti/
Melek *(f.)* /ˈmelɪk/
Melike *(f.)* /məˈlɪkə/
Mia *(f.)* /ˈmiːə/
Michael *(m.)* /ˈmaɪkl/
Mick *(m.)* /mɪk/
Nasaar *(f.)* /næˈsɑː/
Nick *(m.)* /nɪk/
Noah *(m.)* /ˈnəʊə/
Olivia *(f.)* /əˈlɪviə/
Ollie *(m.)* /ˈɒli/
Pablo *(m.)* /ˈpæbləʊ/
Paul *(m.)* /pɔːl/
Philipp *(m.)* /ˈfɪlɪp/
Piet *(m.)* /piːt/
Polly *(f.)* /ˈpɒli/
Poppy *(f.)* /ˈpɒpi/
Querx *(m.)* /kwɜːks/
Richard *(m.)* /ˈrɪtʃəd/
Robin *(m.)* /ˈrɒbɪn/
Roddy *(m.)* /ˈrɒdi/
Rosa *(f.)* /ˈrəʊzə/
Sami *(m., f.)* /ˈsæmi/
Sarah *(f.)* /ˈseərə/
Sharon *(f.)* /ˈʃærən/
Sherlock *(m.)* /ˈʃɜːlɒk/
Shirook *(f.)* /ʃɪˈrʊk/
Simon *(m.)* /ˈsaɪmən/
Steven *(m.)* /ˈstiːvən/
Tarek *(m.)* /ˈtærɪk/
Tim *(m.)* /tɪm/
Tom *(m.)* /tɒm/
Tony *(m., f.)* /ˈtəʊni/
Victoria *(f.)* /vɪkˈtɔːriə/
William *(m.)* /ˈwɪljəm/
Zoe *(f.)* /ˈzəʊi/

Families

Adil /əˈdiːl/
Bassett /ˈbæsɪt/
Bond /bɒnd/
Clarke /klɑːk/
de Canterville /də ˈkæntəvɪl/
Doyle /dɔɪəl/
Edwards /ˈedwədz/
Einstein /ˈaɪnstaɪn/
Holmes /həʊmz/
Kogan /ˈkəʊgən/
McFly /mækˈflaɪ/
Norris /ˈnɒrɪs/
Otis /ˈəʊtɪs/
Patel /pəˈtel/
Potter /ˈpɒtə/
Shakespeare /ˈʃeɪkspɪə/
Spielberg /ˈspilbɜːg/
Verne /vɜːn/
Watson /ˈwɒtsn/
Wells /welz/

Other names

Alexandra Palace /ˌælɪgˌzɑːndrə ˈpæləs/
All Hallows' Day /ˌɔːl ˈhæləʊz deɪ/
All Hallows' Eve /ˌɔːl ˌhæləʊz‿ˈiːv/
American football /əˌmerɪkən ˈfʊtˌbɔːl/
Apollo /əˈpɒləʊ/
apple bobbing /ˈæpl ˌbɒbɪŋ/
Arsenal /ˈɑːsnl/
Baker Street /ˈbeɪkə striːt/
Bakewell tart /ˌbeɪkwel ˈtɑːt/
basking shark /ˈbɑːskɪŋ ʃɑːk/
the Bassett's Farm Rocks /ðə ˌbæsɪts ˌfɑːm ˈrɒks/
the Beatles / ðə ˈbiːtlz/
Beefeater /ˈbiːfˌiːtə/
Big Ben /ˌbɪg ˈben/
Bond Street /ˈbɒnd striːt/
Bonfire Night /ˈbɒnˌfaɪə ˌnaɪt/
bottlenose dolphin /ˈbɒtlnəʊz ˌdɒlfɪn/
the British Museum /ðə ˌbrɪtɪʃ mjuːˈziːəm/
Buckingham Palace /ˌbʌkɪŋəm ˈpæləs/
Canterville /ˈkæntəvɪl/
Central Line /ˈsentrəl laɪn/
Circle Line /ˈsɜːkl laɪn/
Clan-Howlus /ˌklæn ˈhaʊləs/
Covent Garden /ˌkɒvənt ˈgɑːdn/
District Line /ˈdɪstrɪkt laɪn/
Diwali /dɪˈwɑːli/
Double /ˈdʌbl/
dreidel /ˈdreɪdl/
Eid /iːd/
Elizabeth Tower /iˌlɪzəbəθ ˈtaʊə/
Epping /ˈepɪŋ/
Fenchurch /ˈfentʃɜːtʃ/
Globe /gləʊb/
Green Farm /ˈgriːn ˌfɑːm/
the Gunpowder Plot /ðə ˈgʌnˌpaʊdə ˌplɒt/
Guy Fawkes /ˌgaɪ ˈfɔːks/
Halloween /ˌhæləʊˈiːn/
Hanukkah /ˈhɑːnəkə/
harbour porpoise /ˈhɑːbə ˌpɔːpəs/
Hogmanay /ˈhɒgmənеɪ/
Hogwarts /ˈhɒgwɔːts/
Holi /ˈhɒli/
Holland Park /ˌhɒlənd ˈpɑːk/
Horniman /ˈhɔːnɪmən/
the Houses of Parliament /ðə ˌhaʊzɪz‿əv ˈpɑːləmənt/
Hyde Park /ˌhaɪd ˈpɑːk/
i360 /ˌaɪ ˌθriː ˈsɪksti/
ISS (International Space Station) /ˌaɪ‿esˌ‿ˈes, ɪntəˌnæʃnəl ˈspeɪs‿ˌsteɪʃn/
Jesus Christ /ˌdʒiːzəs ˈkraɪst/
Jubilee /ˈdʒuːbɪliː/
King's Cross /ˌkɪŋz ˈkrɒs/
Lantern Festival /ˈlæntən ˌfestɪvl/
leatherback turtle /ˈleðəbæk ˌtɜːtl/
Loch Ness /ˌlɒk ˈnes/
the London Eye /ðə ˌlʌndən‿ˈaɪ/

the London Transport Museum /ðə ˌlʌndən ˈtrænspɔːt mjuːˌziːəm/
Madame Tussauds /ˌmædəm təˈsɔːdz/
menorah /məˈnɔːrə/
the Natural History Museum /ðə ˌnætʃərəl ˈhɪstəri mjuːˌziːəm/
Nordic walking /ˌnɔːdɪk ˈwɔːkɪŋ/
Notting Hill /ˌnɒtɪŋ ˈhɪl/
Notting Hill Gate /ˌnɒtɪŋ hɪl ˈɡeɪt/
Oglethorpe /ˈəʊɡlθɔːp/
pantomime /ˈpæntəˌmaɪm/
Polka /ˈpɒlkə/
Ramadan /ˌræməˈdɑːn/
s'more *(AE)* /smɔː/
the Science Museum /ðə ˈsaɪəns mjuːˌziːəm/
the Shard /ðə ˈʃɑːd/
the Sherlock Holmes Museum /ðə ˌʃɜːlɒk ˈhəʊmz mjuːˌziːəm/
Skkaddraa /ˌskæˈdrɑː/
Sky Garden /ˈskaɪ ˌɡɑːdn/
smart home /ˈsmɑːt ˌhəʊm/
squirrelpox /ˈskwɪrəlpɒks/
St Patrick's Day /sənt ˈpætrɪks deɪ/
Stonehenge /ˌstəʊnˈhendʒ/
T-Rex /ˌti ˈreks/
Thanksgiving /ˈθæŋksˌɡɪvɪŋ/
the Tower (of London) /ðə ˌtaʊər‿əv ˈlʌndən/
Tower Bridge /ˌtaʊə ˈbrɪdʒ/
Tower Hill /ˌtaʊə ˈhɪl/
Trafalgar Square /trəˌfælɡə ˈskweə/
trick-or-treating /ˌtrɪk‿ɔː ˈtriːtɪŋ/
Trouble /ˈtrʌbl/
the Unicorn /ðə ˈjuːnɪˌkɔːn/
V&A (= Victoria and Albert Museum) /ˌviː‿ən‿ˈeɪ, kˌtɔːriər‿ən‿ˈælbət mjuːˌziːəm/
Voyager /ˈvɔɪɪdʒə/
Watch-It 3000 /ˌwɒtʃɪt ˌθriː ˈθaʊznd/
the Welsh Folk Museum /ðə ˌwelʃ ˈfəʊk mjuːˌziːəm/
Wembley Stadium /ˌwembli ˈsteɪdiəm/
Westminster /ˈwestmɪnstə/
Westminster Abbey /ˌwestmɪnstər‿ˈæbi/
the Wimbledon Windmill Museum /ðə ˌwɪmbldən ˈwɪnˌmɪl mjuːˌziːəm/
Windsor Castle /ˌwɪnzə ˈkɑːsl/

Geographical names

Airlie Gardens /ˌeərli ˈɡɑːdnz/
Alaska /əˈlæskə/
Atlanta /ətˈlæntə/
Berlin /bɜːˈlɪn/
Boston /ˈbɒstən/
Brighton /ˈbraɪtn/
Bristol /ˈbrɪstl/
Britain /ˈbrɪtn/
Campden Hill /ˌkæmdən ˈhɪl/
Cardiff /ˈkɑːdɪf/
China /ˈtʃaɪnə/
Cumbria /ˈkʌmbriə/
Derby /ˈdɑːbi/
Derbyshire /ˈdɑːbiʃə/
East Yorkshire /ˌiːst ˈjɔːkʃə/
Edinburgh /ˈedɪnbərə/
Egypt /ˈiːdʒɪpt/
England /ˈɪŋɡlənd/
Europe /ˈjʊərəp/
Exeter /ˈeksɪtə/
France /frɑːns/
Germany /ˈdʒɜːməni/
Haldon /ˈhɔːldən/
Hamburg /ˈhæmbɜːɡ/
Hull /hʌl/
India /ˈɪndiə/
Ireland /ˈaɪələnd/
Italy /ˈɪtəli/
Kensington /ˈkenzɪŋtən/
London /ˈlʌndən/
Los Angeles /lɒs‿ˈændʒəliːz/
Manchester /ˈmæntʃɪstə/
Mars /mɑːz/
Moray Firth /ˈmʌri fɜːθ/
Mount Taranaki /ˌmaʊnt‿ˌtærəˈnæki/
Munich /ˈmjuːnɪk/
Nelson /ˈnelsən/
the Netherlands /ðə ˈneðələndz/
New York /ˌnjuː ˈjɔːk/
New Zealand /nju ˈziːlənd/
North America /ˌnɔːθ‿əˈmerɪkə/
Northern Ireland /ˌnɔːðən‿ˈaɪələnd/
Paris /ˈpærɪs/
Peak District /ˈpiːk ˌdɪstrɪkt/
Picton /ˈpɪktən/
Poland /ˈpəʊlənd/
Ravenglass /ˈreɪvnɡlɑːs/
the Rocky Mountains /ðə ˌrɒki ˈmaʊntɪnz/
Rome /rəʊm/
Rotterdam /ˈrɒtədæm/
San Francisco /ˌsæn frənˈsɪskəʊ/
Scotland /ˈskɒtlənd/
Southwold /ˈsaʊθwəʊld/
Spain /speɪn/
Stratford /ˈstrætfəd/
Thames /temz/
Trafalgar Square /trəˌfælɡə ˈskweə/
the UK (= United Kingdom) /ðə ˌjuː ˈkeɪ, juːˌnaɪtɪd ˈkɪŋdəm/
the US (= United States) /ðə ˌju‿ˈes, juːˌnaɪtɪd ˈsteɪts/
the USA (= United States of America) /ðə ˌju‿es‿ˈeɪ, juːˌnaɪtɪd ˌsteɪts‿əv‿əˈmerɪkə/
Wales /weɪlz/
Washington D.C. /ˌwɒʃɪŋtən diː ˈsiː/
Wellington /ˈwelɪŋtən/
Wimbledon /ˈwɪmbldən/

Irregular verbs

infinitive	simple past	past participle	German
(to) be /biː/	was/were /wɒz/wɜː/	been /biːn/	sein
(to) beat /biːt/	beat /biːt/	beaten /ˈbiːtn/	schlagen
(to) become /bɪˈkʌm/	became /bɪˈkeɪm/	become /bɪˈkʌm/	werden
(to) begin /bɪˈgɪn/	began /bɪˈgæn/	begun /bɪˈgʌn/	anfangen; beginnen
(to) break /breɪk/	broke /brəʊk/	broken /ˈbrəʊkən/	(zer)brechen; kaputt machen
(to) bring /brɪŋ/	brought /brɔːt/	brought /brɔːt/	mitbringen
(to) build /bɪld/	built /bɪlt/	built /bɪlt/	bauen
(to) buy /baɪ/	bought /bɔːt/	bought /bɔːt/	kaufen
(to) catch /kætʃ/	caught /kɔːt/	caught /kɔːt/	fangen
(to) choose /tʃuːz/	chose /tʃəʊz/	chosen /ˈtʃəʊzn/	wählen; sich entscheiden
(to) come /kʌm/	came /keɪm/	come /kʌm/	kommen
(to) cost /kɒst/	cost /kɒst/	cost /kɒst/	kosten
(to) cut /kʌt/	cut /kʌt/	cut /kʌt/	schneiden
(to) do /duː/	did /dɪd/	done /dʌn/	machen; tun
(to) draw /drɔː/	drew /druː/	drawn /drɔːn/	zeichnen
(to) drink /drɪŋk/	drank /dræŋk/	drunk /drʌŋk/	trinken
(to) drive /draɪv/	drove /drəʊv/	driven /ˈdrɪvn/	fahren
(to) eat /iːt/	ate /et/eɪt/	eaten /ˈiːtn/	essen
(to) fall /fɔːl/	fell /fel/	fallen /ˈfɔːlən/	fallen
(to) feed /fiːd/	fed /fed/	fed /fed/	füttern
(to) feel /fiːl/	felt /felt/	felt /felt/	(sich) fühlen
(to) fight /faɪt/	fought /fɔːt/	fought /fɔːt/	bekämpfen; ankämpfen gegen
(to) find /faɪnd/	found /faʊnd/	found /faʊnd/	finden
(to) fly /flaɪ/	flew /fluː/	flown /fləʊn/	fliegen
(to) forget /fəˈget/	forgot /fəˈgɒt/	forgotten /fəˈgɒtən/	vergessen
(to) get /get/	got /gɒt/	got /gɒt/	gelangen; kommen; werden; bekommen; holen; kaufen
(to) give /gɪv/	gave /geɪv/	given /ˈgɪvn/	geben; angeben, mitteilen
(to) go /gəʊ/	went /went/	gone /gɒn/	gehen; fahren
(to) grow /grəʊ/	grew /gru/	grown /grəʊn/	wachsen; anbauen
(to) hang (up) /ˌhæŋ‿ˈʌp/	hung (up) /ˌhʌŋ‿ˈʌp/	hung (up) /ˌhʌŋ‿ˈʌp/	hängen, aufhängen
(to) have /hæv/	had /hæd/	had /hæd/	haben; essen; trinken
(to) hear /hɪə/	heard /hɜːd/	heard /hɜːd/	hören
(to) hide /haɪd/	hid /hɪd/	hidden /ˈhɪdn/	(sich) verstecken
(to) hit /hɪt/	hit /hɪt/	hit /hɪt/	schlagen
(to) hold /həʊld/	held /held/	held /held/	(fest)halten
(to) keep /kiːp/	kept /kept/	kept /kept/	bleiben; aufbewahren; (be)halten
(to) know /nəʊ/	knew /njuː/	known /nəʊn/	kennen; wissen
(to) learn /lɜːn/	learnt/learned /lɜːnt/lɜːnd/	learnt/learned /lɜːnt/lɜːnd/	lernen

Irregular verbs

infinitive	simple past	past participle	German
(to) leave /liːv/	left /left/	left /left/	weggehen; (übrig) lassen; zurücklassen; hinterlassen; verlassen, abfahren
(to) let /let/	let /let/	let /let/	lassen
(to) lie down /ˌlaɪ ˈdaʊn/	lay down /ˌleɪ ˈdaʊn/	lain down /ˌleɪn ˈdaʊn/	sich hinlegen
(to) light /laɪt/	lit /lɪt/	lit /lɪt/	anzünden
(to) make /meɪk/	made /meɪd/	made /meɪd/	machen
(to) mean /miːn/	meant /ment/	meant /ment/	meinen; bedeuten
(to) meet /miːt/	met /met/	met /met/	kennenlernen; (sich) treffen
(to) pay /peɪ/	paid /peɪd/	paid /peɪd/	(be)zahlen
(to) put /pʊt/	put /pʊt/	put /pʊt/	legen; setzen; stellen
(to) read /riːd/	read /red/	read /red/	lesen
(to) ride /raɪd/	rode /rəʊd/	ridden /ˈrɪdn/	fahren; reiten
(to) run /rʌn/	ran /ræn/	run /rʌn/	laufen; rennen
(to) say /seɪ/	said /sed/	said /sed/	sagen
(to) see /siː/	saw /sɔː/	seen /siːn/	sehen
(to) send /send/	sent /sent/	sent /sent/	schicken
(to) shake /ʃeɪk/	shook /ʃʊk/	shaken /ˈʃeɪkən/	beben
(to) shine /ʃaɪn/	shone /ʃɒn/	shone /ʃɒn/	scheinen
(to) show /ʃəʊ/	showed /ʃəʊd/	shown /ʃəʊn/	zeigen
(to) sing /sɪŋ/	sang /sʌŋ/	sung /sʌŋ/	singen
(to) sit down /ˌsɪt‿ˈdaʊn/	sat down /ˌsæt‿ˈdaʊn/	sat down /ˌsæt‿ˈdaʊn/	sich hinsetzen
(to) sleep /sliːp/	slept /slept/	slept /slept/	schlafen
(to) smell /smel/	smelt/smelled /smelt/smeld/	smelt/smelled /smelt/smeld/	riechen
(to) speak /spiːk/	spoke /spəʊk/	spoken /ˈspəʊkən/	reden; sprechen
(to) spell /spel/	spelt/spelled /spelt/speld/	spelt/spelled /spelt/speld/	buchstabieren
(to) spend /spend/	spent /spent/	spent /spent/	ausgeben *(Geld)*; verbringen *(Zeit)*
(to) stand /stænd/	stood /stʊd/	stood /stʊd/	stehen
(to) stick to /ˈstɪk tʊ/	stuck to /ˈstʌk tʊ/	stuck to /ˈstʌk tʊ/	sich halten an
(to) swim /swɪm/	swam /swæm/	swum /swʌm/	schwimmen
(to) take /teɪk/	took /tʊk/	taken /ˈteɪkən/	nehmen; bringen; benötigen; brauchen; dauern
(to) teach /tiːtʃ/	taught /tɔːt/	taught /tɔːt/	unterrichten
(to) tell /tel/	told /təʊld/	told /təʊld/	erzählen
(to) think /θɪŋk/	thought /θɔːt/	thought /θɔːt/	denken; glauben
(to) throw /θrəʊ/	threw /θruː/	thrown /θrəʊn/	werfen
(to) understand /ˌʌndəˈstænd/	understood /ˌʌndəˈstʊd/	understood /ˌʌndəˈstʊd/	verstehen
(to) wake up /ˌweɪk‿ˈʌp/	woke up /ˌwəʊk‿ˈʌp/	woken up /ˌwəʊkən‿ˈʌp/	aufwachen
(to) wear /weə/	wore /wɔː/	worn /wɔːn/	tragen *(Kleidung)*
(to) win /wɪn/	won /wʌn/	won /wʌn/	gewinnen
(to) write /raɪt/	wrote /rəʊt/	written /ˈrɪtn/	schreiben

Tipp:

Einige Verben bilden das **simple past** und das **past participle** nach einem ähnlichen Muster. Wenn du sie dir in Gruppen sortierst, kannst du dir die Formen vielleicht besser merken.

bring	brought	brought	mitbringen
buy	bought	bought	kaufen
catch	c**au**ght	c**au**ght	fangen
fight	fought	fought	bekämpfen
think	thought	thought	denken; glauben

sing	sang	sung	singen
swim	swam	swum	schwimmen

draw	drew	dr**a**wn	zeichnen
fly	flew	flown	fliegen
grow	grew	grown	wachsen
know	knew	known	kennen; wissen
throw	threw	thrown	werfen

cost	cost	cost	kosten
cut	cut	cut	schneiden
hit	hit	hit	schlagen
let	let	let	lassen
put	put	put	legen, setzen, stellen

Seite Lern-phasen	Inhalte	Kompetenzen	Sprachliche Mittel
7	**Unit 1 – Holidays (Kompetenzschwerpunkt: Hören)**		
	PART A – Holiday fun		
8 Activate	Über Ferien lesen und sprechen	**Speaking:** über Bilder sprechen, die eigene Meinung äußern **Reading:** kurze Statements lesen, einen Gruppenchat lesen	**Wortschatz** *holidays, activities*
10 Practise	Strukturen bewusst machen und festigen	**Writing:** über Dinge, die man in den Ferien erlebt bzw. nicht erlebt hat, schreiben	**Strukturen** *simple past* **Aussprache** /t/, /d/, /ɪd/
11 Develop	Ferienerlebnisse Urlaub im Vereinigten Königreich	**Listening:** einem Videochat folgen, ein Telefongespräch verstehen **Reading:** Blogeinträge lesen **Viewing:** einen Videoclip verstehen **Mediation:** einen Videoclip sprachmitteln	**Wortschatz** *holidays* **Strukturen** *simple past*
16 Practise	Strukturen festigen, Vorbereitung auf die Target task	**Writing:** kurze Texte über Ferienerlebnisse vervollständigen, Adjektive verwenden	**Strukturen** *simple past* *adjectives*
17 Apply	**Target task** My holiday post **Check out** Selbsteinschätzung	**Writing:** einen *blog post* zum Thema Ferien verfassen und veröffentlichen	**Wortschatz** *holidays, activities* *good style*
	PART B – Sightseeing in London		
18 Activate	Einen Eindruck von London bekommen Erste Sehenswürdigkeiten in London kennenlernen	**Speaking:** Vorwissen zum Thema London mitteilen **Listening:** Bildern Geräusche zuordnen **Reading:** kurze Sachtexte lesen	**Wortschatz** *getting around*
20 Practise	Strukturen bewusst machen und festigen	**Writing:** Vergleiche anstellen	**Strukturen** *comparison of adjectives*
21 Develop	Mehr über London erfahren	**Speaking:** über eine Karte sprechen **Listening:** einen Dialog verstehen, Wegbeschreibungen folgen **Reading:** einen Fahrplan verstehen, kurze Texte aus einem Reiseführer lesen **Mediation:** Informationen aus einem Flyer sprachmitteln **Viewing:** einen Videoclip verstehen	**Strukturen** *comparison of adjectives* **Wortschatz** *holidays, getting around, places*
26 Practise	Strukturen festigen, Vorbereitung auf die Target task	**Writing:** Sehenswürdigkeiten und Orte beschreiben	**Wortschatz** *places, getting around* **Strukturen** *comparison of adjectives*
27 Apply	**Target task** A day out in London **Check out** Selbsteinschätzung	**Writing:** eine Seite für einen Reiseführer erstellen	**Wortschatz** *places, activities, getting around*
28 Story	Kora and the New Zealand dragons: A dragon-taming emergency	**Reading:** ein Kapitel der Fortsetzungsgeschichte lesen	
30 Challenge	Message in a bottle	**Reading:** einen Magazinartikel lesen	

Seite Lern-phasen	Inhalte	Kompetenzen	Sprachliche Mittel
31	**Unit 2 – Celebrations (Kompetenzschwerpunkt: Lesen)**		
	PART A – Festivals and traditions		
32 Activate	Feste aus verschiedenen Kulturen kennenlernen	**Speaking:** Bilder beschreiben, sagen, welche Feste man kennt **Reading:** beschreibenden Texten Informationen entnehmen	**Wortschatz** *celebrations*
34 Practise	Strukturen bewusst machen und festigen	**Writing:** wiederkehrende Ereignisse beschreiben	**Strukturen** *simple present (R)* **Wortschatz** *Strukturen erkennen*
35 Develop	Verschiedene Neujahrstraditionen kennenlernen Etwas über die historischen Hintergründe von Halloween erfahren Sich mit unterschiedlichen Sichtweisen auf Halloween auseinandersetzen	**Listening:** Radiointerviews verstehen **Speaking:** sich über die eigenen Neujahrstraditionen austauschen **Reading:** über die historischen Hintergründe von Halloween lesen, Meinungen zu Halloween verstehen **Writing:** einen Zeitstrahl erstellen, Notizen machen **Mediation:** eine Anleitung sprachmitteln	**Wortschatz** *celebrations*
40 Practise	Strukturen festigen, Vorbereitung auf die Target task	**Writing:** beschreibende Statements formulieren	**Strukturen** *simple present (R)* **Wortschatz** *Nomen kategorisieren*
41 Apply	**Target task** A festival poster **Check out** Selbsteinschätzung	**Writing:** eine Feier beschreiben und vorstellen	**Strukturen** *simple present (R)* **Wortschatz** *celebrations*
	PART B – Let's celebrate!		
42 Activate	Etwas über *Bonfire Night* erfahren	**Reading:** einen Flyer lesen **Listening:** einen Dialog verstehen **Speaking:** Vorlieben ausdrücken	**Wortschatz** *making plans*
44 Practise	Strukturen bewusst machen und festigen	**Writing:** über Pläne schreiben	**Strukturen** *present progressive (R)* **Aussprache** *stressed syllables*
45 Develop	Elemente einer *Bonfire Night* Party kennenlernen	**Reading:** einen Dialog lesen, ein Rezept verstehen und wiedergeben **Listening**: einem Telefongespräch folgen **Speaking:** einen Reim auswendig lernen, ein Bild beschreiben **Mediation:** Sicherheitstipps aus einem Videoclip sprachmitteln	**Strukturen** *present progressive (R)* **Wortschatz** *making plans, food, celebrations*
50 Practise	Strukturen festigen, Vorbereitung auf die Target task	**Writing:** Vorschläge formulieren	**Wortschatz** *making plans, celebrations*
51 Apply	**Target task** Our class party **Check out** Selbsteinschätzung	**Speaking:** Ideen vorstellen, Kompromisse und Lösungen finden	**Wortschatz** *making plans, discussions, food, celebrations*
52 Story	Kora and the New Zealand dragons: Looking for the dragon	**Reading:** ein Kapitel der Fortsetzungsgeschichte lesen	
54 Challenge	The Clarke family blog	**Reading:** Einen britisch-amerikanischen *family blog* lesen	

Seite Lern-phasen	Inhalte	Kompetenzen	Sprachliche Mittel
55	**Unit 3 – Living together (Kompetenzschwerpunkt: Sprachmittlung)**		
	PART A – Getting along		
56 Activate	Über Schulregeln sprechen	**Speaking:** über Regeln an der eigenen Schule sprechen **Reading:** Schulregeln verstehen	**Wortschatz** *rules*
58 Practise	Strukturen bewusst machen und festigen	**Writing:** Regeln und Verbote formulieren	**Strukturen** *modal verbs* **Aussprache** *silent letters*
59 Develop	Regeln in der Familie Konfliktpotentiale Kompromisse finden und andere unterstützen	**Listening:** einen Dialog verstehen, Bildern Dialoge zuordnen **Writing:** Dialoge zu Bildern schreiben **Reading:** einen Tagebucheintrag lesen **Mediation:** ein Hinweisschild sprachmitteln **Speaking:** über den Sinn von Regeln diskutieren	**Wortschatz** *rules, discussions* **Strukturen** *modal verbs*
64 Practise	Strukturen festigen, Vorbereitung auf die Target task	**Writing:** Fragen und Antworten zum Thema Regeln formulieren	**Strukturen** *word order* **Wortschatz** *rules*
65 Apply	Target task A family meeting Check out Selbsteinschätzung	**Writing:** Stichworte für ein kurzes Rollenspiel notieren **Speaking:** das Rollenspiel üben und präsentieren	**Wortschatz** *rules, discussions*
	PART B – Take care!		
66 Activate	Regeln für den achtsamen Umgang mit der eigenen Umwelt	**Reading:** Flyer lesen **Speaking:** über Umwelt-Erlebnisorte sprechen	**Wortschatz** *rules, wildlife*
68 Practise	Strukturen bewusst machen und festigen	**Writing:** Regeln formulieren	**Strukturen** *modal verbs* **Wortschatz** *rules, wildlife*
69 Develop	Respektvoller Umgang mit der Natur Tiere im Vereinigten Königreich	**Reading:** einen Brief verstehen, einem Gespräch zum Thema *wildlife in the UK* gezielt Informationen entnehmen **Writing:** Informationen notieren **Mediation:** eine Anleitung sprachmitteln **Listening:** ein Radiointerview verstehen **Viewing:** einer Slideshow folgen	**Strukturen** *modal verbs* **Wortschatz** *rules, wildlife*
74 Practise	Strukturen festigen, Vorbereitung auf die Target task	**Reading:** Anleitungen verstehen	**Strukturen** *imperatives* **Orthografie** Pluralformen
75 Apply	Target task Our environment brochure Check out Selbsteinschätzung	**Writing:** Anleitungen für *mini projects* erstellen	**Strukturen** *imperatives* **Wortschatz** *nature*
76 Story	Kora and the New Zealand dragons: In the dragon's cave	**Reading:** ein Kapitel der Fortsetzungsgeschichte lesen	
78 Challenge	Don't	**Reading:** ein Gedicht lesen	

Seite Lern-phasen	Inhalte	Kompetenzen	Sprachliche Mittel
79	**Unit 4 – The future (Kompetenzschwerpunkt: Schreiben)**		
	PART A – My dreams		
80 Activate	Zukunftspläne und -träume	**Reading:** einem Dialog folgen **Speaking:** die eigene Meinung äußern	**Wortschatz** *jobs, talking about the future*
82 Practise	Strukturen bewusst machen und festigen	**Writing:** über die Zukunft schreiben	**Strukturen** *will-future* **Aussprache** *v and w*
83 Develop	Zukunftsträume Berufsfelder	**Speaking:** über verschiedene Berufe sprechen **Mediation:** einen Podcast sprachmitteln **Writing:** ein Quiz erstellen, weitere Strophen zu einem Song schreiben **Viewing:** einen Videoclip verstehen **Reading:** einen Monolog über Zukunfstvorstellungen lesen	**Strukturen** *will-future* **Wortschatz** *jobs, talking about the future*
88 Practise	Strukturen festigen, Vorbereitung auf die Target task	**Writing:** Fragen zur Zukunft formulieren	**Strukturen** *will-future questions* **Wortschatz** *jobs, talking about the future*
89 Apply	Target task My ideas about the future Check out Selbsteinschätzung	**Writing:** eigene Ideen zum Thema Zukunft formulieren **Speaking:** etwas präsentieren	**Wortschatz** *talking about the future*
	PART B – Stories		
90 Activate	Kate and Jonathan's adventure part one Eine Geschichte verstehen	**Reading:** Anfang einer Geschichte als Bildergeschichte verstehen **Speaking:** zu einer Bildergeschichte spekulieren	**Wortschatz** *talking about the future*
92 Practise	Strukturen bewusst machen und festigen	**Writing:** über die Zukunft schreiben, Adverbien der Art und Weise verwenden	**Strukturen** *adverbs of manner* **Wortschatz** *the future*
93 Develop	Kate and Jonathan's adventure parts two and three Eine Geschichte verstehen	**Listening:** Fortführung der Geschichte als Hörbuch verstehen **Speaking:** über Gefühle der Protagonisten sprechen, die eigene Meinung äußern **Reading:** Hauptteil der Geschichte lesen, Absätzen Überschriften zuordnen **Writing:** Texte interessant gestalten	**Strukturen** *adverbs of manner* **Wortschatz** *describing people, good style*
98 Practise	Strukturen festigen, Vorbereitung auf die Target task	**Writing:** Adjektive, Adverbien und Konjunktionen verwenden	**Strukturen** *adverbs of manner*
99 Apply	Target task My story Check out Selbsteinschätzung	**Writing:** *creative writing* zum Thema Zukunft	**Strukturen** *Wortstellung* **Wortschatz** *describing people, good style*
100 Story	Kora and the New Zealand dragons: The Clan-Howlus dragon	**Reading:** ein Kapitel der Fortsetzungsgeschichte lesen	
102 Challenge	Time capsules	**Reading:** über Zeitkapseln lesen	

Seite Lern-phasen	Inhalte	Kompetenzen	Sprachliche Mittel
103	**Unit 5 – Out and about (Kompetenzschwerpunkt: Sprechen)**		
	PART A – A trip to the museum		
104 Activate	Sich über Museen austauschen	**Listening:** ein Gespräch verstehen **Speaking:** darüber sprechen, welche kulturellen Einrichtungen man selbst schon besucht hat	**Wortschatz** *places*
106 Practise	Strukturen bewusst machen und festigen	**Writing:** beschreiben, was jemand schon getan oder erlebt hat	**Strukturen** *present perfect* **Wortschatz** *places*
107 Develop	Ein Ausflug ins Sherlock Holmes Museum Museen in London	**Listening:** einem Dialog Informationen entnehmen, einem *audioguide* folgen, einen Song verstehen **Speaking:** einen Dialog präsentieren, über ungewöhnliche Gegenstände sprechen **Reading:** Informationstexte zu verschiedenen Museen und Ausstellungsstücken lesen **Mediation:** Eine Durchsage sprachmitteln	**Strukturen** *present perfect* **Wortschatz** *getting around*
112 Practise	Strukturen festigen, Vorbereitung auf die Target task	**Writing:** über schon Erledigtes schreiben, Dinge beschreiben	**Strukturen** *simple past (R)* **Wortschatz** *describing things*
113 Apply	**Target task** Our exhibition of everyday objects **Check out** Selbsteinschätzung	**Writing:** Texte für einen Ausstellungskatalog schreiben	**Wortschatz** *describing things*
	PART B – A play		
114 Activate	Pläne für die Ferien	**Reading:** ein Ferienprogramm verstehen **Listening:** ein Gespräch verstehen **Speaking:** über Ferienpläne sprechen	**Strukturen** *going to-future* **Wortschatz** *making plans, holiday activities*
116 Practise	Strukturen bewusst machen und festigen	**Writing:** Über Pläne berichten	**Strukturen** *going to-future*
117 Develop	Ein Theaterworkshop	**Listening:** ein Gespräch verstehen **Reading:** eine E-Mail lesen, ein Skript verstehen **Viewing:** eine Videonachricht verstehen **Mediation:** Informationen aus einer Broschüre sprachmitteln **Writing:** eine E-Mail schreiben	**Strukturen** *going to-future* **Wortschatz** *making plans*
122 Practise	Strukturen festigen, Vorbereitung auf die Target task	**Speaking:** Emotionen ausdrücken	**Wortschatz** *drama*
123 Apply	**Target task** Our play **Check out** Selbsteinschätzung	**Speaking:** *The Canterville Ghost* aufführen	**Wortschatz** *giving feedback*
124 Story	Kora and the New Zealand dragons: Taming the dragon / Saving the day	**Reading:** ein Kapitel der Fortsetzungsgeschichte lesen	
127 Challenge	Sherlock Holmes – a world-famous detective	**Reading:** einen Artikel über Sherlock Holmes lesen	
128	**Get together**		

Seite	Inhalt
146	**Projects**
146	Project 1: A country profile: the UK
148	Project 2: A country profile: the USA
150	**Skills**
150	Wortschatzarbeit
151	Hören
152	Mit anderen sprechen
153	Schreiben
154	Lesen
155	Sprachmittlung
156	Videoclips verstehen
157	Im Internet recherchieren
158	Präsentationen halten
159	Eine Szene vorspielen
160	**Wordbanks**
160	Holidays
162	Getting around
163	Celebrations
164	Rules
165	Talking about conflicts
166	Wildlife
167	Jobs
167	Talking about the future
168	Describing people
169	Good style
170	**Classroom phrases**
172	**Glossary**
174	**Grammar**
174	Die einfache Vergangenheit: bejahte Aussagen
175	Die einfache Vergangenheit: verneinte Aussagen
176	Die einfache Vergangenheit: Fragen
177	Die Steigerung von Adjektiven
178	Die einfache Gegenwart: Aussagen *(revision)*
179	Die einfache Gegenwart: Fragen *(revision)*
180	Die Verlaufsform der Gegenwart: Aussagen *(revision)*
181	Die Verlaufsform der Gegenwart: Fragen *(revision)*
182	Mengenangaben
183	Die Modalverben *must* und *mustn't*
184	Die Modalverben: *can, be allowed to* und *may*
185	Wortstellung im Aussagesatz *(revision)*
186	Das Futur mit *will*: Aussagen
187	Das Futur mit *will*: Fragen
188	Adverbien der Art und Weise
189	Verbindung von Sätzen mit *linking words*
190	Das Perfekt: Aussagen
191	Das Perfekt: Fragen
192	Das Futur mit *going to*: Aussagen
193	Das Futur mit *going to*: Fragen
194	**Words**
194	Erläuterung und richtige Aussprache
196	Bekannte Wörter
197	Wortlisten nach Units
221	*Dictionary*
244	*Numbers, Names*
247	*Irregular verbs*

Bildquellen

|Alamy Stock Photo, Abingdon/Oxfordshire: ACORN 1 14.4; Amikishiyev, Elnur 38.2; Bell, Graham 12.1; Bird, Joe 18.1; Britland, Kevin 38.1; Bronkhorst, Adam 83.5; Cracknell, Roger 47.1; Dewar, Gareth 12.3; GL Archive 36.2; Granger Historical Picture Archive 102.2; Greg Balfour Evans 118.1; Halley, Dave 66.2; imagebroker 112.2; Jani, Bhaven 32.3; Jozsef, Szasz-Fabian 14.5; Lawrence, Graham M. 32.1; Lloyd, Andrew 66.4; MacPherso, John 72.1; Mander, Tim 66.3; Marosy, Ann 39.3; Melling, Paul 32.4; milos luzanin 112.3; Novikov, Sergey 8.1; Ohlsen, Steve / Stockimo 102.1; PA Images 23.2; Peregrine 24.3; Petrychenko, Anton 112.1; Popov, Andriy 14.1; Radharc Images 36.1; Sira Anamwong 104.5; Smith, Alan 67.1; The Protected Art Archive 97.1; tony french 108.3; Vidler, Steve 25.1; Vinogradova, Lilyana 8.3; Vorobeva, Olga 39.2; Wayman, Richard 12.2, 147.1; Westend61 GmbH 14.2; Wordley, Samuel 14.3; Zeigler, Gavin 113.1. |Alamy Stock Photo (RMB), Abingdon/Oxfordshire: Athol Pictures 18.8; du Feu, Geoff 42.1; Granger Historical Picture Archive 127.2; Jon Arnold Images Ltd 104.1; Kellerman, John 127.3; LH Images 18.7; Mathews, Terry 66.1; Melting Spot 37.6; Robinson, Dominic 138.1, 141.1, 144.1; Scott Hortop Travel 24.1; Segre, Alex 108.4; Slusarczyk, Marek 108.2; Tulley, Steve 18.4; Visions from Earth 18.6; © IndiaPicture 37.9. |Amortegui, Miguel, Brighton: 15.1. |Ayres, Caitlin, Braunschweig: 37.1. |Bridgeman Images, Berlin: Sonia Halliday Photographs 36.3. |dreamstime.com, Brentwood: Kaphoto 37.7. |Ellert, Mario, Bremen: 21.1, 29.1, 48.1, 71.1, 73.1, 73.2, 78.1, 78.2, 78.3, 163.1, 164.1, 199.1, 201.1, 205.1, 206.1, 207.1, 211.1. |Fast, Lisa, Hannover: 39.1. |fotolia.com, New York: Delphimages 148.1; Dollars 37.3. |Fotostudio Henke, Paderborn: 130.1, 133.1, 136.1, 139.1, 142.1, 145.1. |Getty Images (RF), München: kali9 32.2; Merdan, Jasmin 32.5. |iStockphoto.com, Calgary: 1971yes 89.3; C007 Titel; fstop123 54.2; GummyBone 54.1; huronphoto 38.4; juicybits 37.13; LiubovTerletska 127.4; miriam-doerr 89.2; missaigong 18.5; Ridofranz 83.6; t_kimura 22.1; Wiese_Harald 148.3; ZambeziShark 18.3. |Koerner, Amy, Frankfurt am Main: 85.1. |mauritius images GmbH, Mittenwald: JOHN KELLERMAN/ Alamy 104.4. |PantherMedia GmbH (panthermedia.net), München: juergenfrese 113.3; kapu 154.1; rrrneumi 30.1. |Picture-Alliance GmbH, Frankfurt a.M.: dpa 18.2; dpa-Zentralbild / Schutt, Martin 102.3. |Ruthe, Oda, Braunschweig: 201.2. |Shutterstock.com, New York: a katz 38.5; astudio 37.5; Drop of Light 83.2; FrameStockFootages 83.3; IrinaK 8.2; Izzotti, Andrea 149.1; Kashevnik, Alexey 24.2; LightField Studios 89.1; pablofdezr 146.1; sirtravelalot 37.2; TFoxFoto 83.1; VGstockstudio 83.8. |stock.adobe.com, Dublin: Anney 158.2; Antonioguillem 129.1, 132.1, 135.1; Asier 38.3; babimu 113.2; donyanedomam 129.2, 132.2, 135.2; Hennigan, Carly 37.11; LIGHTFIELD STUDIOS 37.10; lukowski, andrys 83.4; Margaret 148.2; nateejindakum 37.12; NDABCREATIVITY 83.7; ovb64 8.4; Pixel-Shot 37.4; SAID OUAJDI 37.8; snaptitude 127.1; streptococcus 9.1, 9.2, 9.3, 9.4, 9.5, 9.6, 9.7, 23.1. |Victoria and Albert Museum, London: © Victoria and Albert Museum 104.2, 104.3. |Wefringhaus, Klaus, Braunschweig: 113.4, 158.1. |© Museum of London, London: 108.1.

Textquellen

78 „Don't" Richard Edwards/Simon & Schuster Education, Hampstead

120-121 „The Canterville Ghost" adaptiert von der Kurzgeschichte „The Canterville Ghost" von Oscar Wilde

Shetland Islands
Orkney Islands
Lewis
Outer Hebrides
Skye
Ben Nevis 1344 m
Balmoral
Aberdeen
Scotland
Glasgow
Edinburgh
Tweed
Atlantic Ocean
North Sea